# Forensic Evidence in Court

# Forensic Evidence in Court

## *A Case Study Approach*

Christine Beck Lissitzyn

CAROLINA ACADEMIC PRESS

Durham, North Carolina

Library of Congress Cataloging-in-Publication Data

Lissitzyn, Christine.
    Forensic evidence in court : a case study approach / by Christine Lissitzyn.
        p. cm.
    Includes bibliographical references and index.
    ISBN 978-1-59460-370-9    1-59460-370-7(alk. paper)
1.  Evidence, Expert--United States. 2.  Forensic sciences--United States. 3.
Evidence, Criminal--United States. 4.  Grant, Edward R., 1943?---Trials, litigation,
etc. 5.  Trials (Murder)--Connecticut--New Haven.  I. Title.

    KF9674.L55 2007
    363.25--dc22

                                                                          2007021368

Carolina Academic Press, LLC
700 Kent Street
Durham, North Carolina 27701
Telephone (919) 489-7486
Fax (919) 493-5668
www.cap-press.com

2016 Printing
Printed in the United States of America

# Contents

# Table of Cases

# List of Exhibits

# Acknowledgments

I have been a lawyer and now a teacher of law for all of my professional career. Yet my experience with criminal law is limited. I was, therefore, filled with little direct experience but a lot of enthusiasm when I decided to develop a course in The Law and Forensic Evidence at the University of Hartford in 2002. Fortunately, I met Brian Carlow, a public defender who had just lost a "cold case" in which two devastating pieces of forensic evidence had linked a 59-year old man to a 1973 murder in New Haven, Connecticut. With his help, I used the case to explore forensics and evidence with my class. Brian and Karen Goodrow, a friend and fellow teacher, now head the Connecticut Innocence Project and have also helped me with the chapter on DNA exonerations.

I thank Susan Marks, Tim Sugrue, and Maria Sheehan of the Connecticut Chief State Attorney's Appellate Division for assistance in researching the case study. I am indebted to many experts who have helped me research and develop this book. First, Ken Zercie and Chris Grice, of the Connecticut State Forensic Laboratory, have been generous with their time and have permitted me to watch forensic testing first-hand. Trooper Peter Valentin, of the Connecticut State Police, co-taught this course with me and helped me with police procedures. Leighton Hammond demonstrated the polygraph for me and shared his experience. Sargur Srihari of SUNY Buffalo showed me how he can identify handwriting using a computer system. Jason Gilder of Forensic Bioinformatic Services read my chapter on DNA and helped me correct many errors.

Patricia Sheeran offered helpful editing and proofreading. Linda Spagnola added much-appreciated pedagogical elements, and Cindy Stewart created graphics that I hope will help the reader better understand some of the concepts in the book.

Finally, I thank my three daughters for their patience and concern, and particularly my husband, Lawrence H. Lissitzyn, for helpful comments on drafts, proofreading and corrections and mostly, for moral support. I dedicate this book to them.

Christine Beck Lissitzyn

# Introduction

In criminal trials today, science has become the gold standard of evidence. In 1995, in the O.J. Simpson trial, a jury failed to convict Simpson of the murder of his wife, Nicole, and Ron Goldman, a waiter, and in the process rejected a mass of DNA and other scientific evidence pointing to his guilt. Today, three factors have coalesced to make scientific evidence virtually invincible to juries:

- Jurors have been steeped in a culture of media that makes it appear that science is both easy to obtain and test, and virtually invincible in its conclusions.

- Jurors are aware of defendants who have been exonerated based on subsequently tested DNA—they expect evidence at trial to ensure that they convict the right defendant.

- Jurors have come to expect the "dazzle" of the scientific presentation. Television shows and commentators have made many formerly esoteric technologies accessible to the public.

The public is fascinated with forensic evidence. It is the new medium in which murder mysteries are solved. But is all forensic evidence equal? Can some evidence impermissibly prejudice the jury? Have juries come to expect forensic evidence?

Is what you see on the television show CSI (Crime Scene Investigation) accurate? Is fingerprint matching done by a computer superimposing a picture of a fingerprint over a print taken from a crime scene? Do DNA results come back in twenty minutes (or even a day), identifying a specific person? Do forensic investigators go out to the crime scene and then try to track down the bad guys? Can all of this be done in one hour?

This book will examine several areas of forensic evidence in light of evolving standards in science, in the content and the application of the rules of evidence, and in the working of the judicial system. Most forensic evidence is admitted in criminal trials with the aid of an "expert," someone with scientific credentials who can explain the methodology to the jury. This expert frequently gives an "opinion" to the jury. For example, a fingerprint examiner may give his opinion that a fingerprint lifted from a crime scene identifies a particular suspect. A handwriting expert may show the jury similarities in writing between a ransom note and the suspect's normal handwriting and give his opinion that the suspect wrote the ransom note. These expert opinions are powerful evidence at trial, as they frequently carry great weight with the jury.

Not all experts are permitted to testify, however. First, they must be qualified based on training, education and experience. Second, they must be able to articulate the methodology used in their evaluation of the forensic evidence and convince the trial judge that the science itself is reliable. One test for reliability is whether the scientific community generally accepts the area of science. An example is DNA testing. The scientific community accepts the scientific hypothesis that one's DNA can conclusively identify a person to the exclusion of all others. They may not agree with a particular method of obtaining the DNA profile, but they all agree with the science and that proper profiling methods will yield a reliable DNA profile. A number of courts have decided that DNA profiling is "judicially accepted," which means that the party putting on the DNA evidence does not need to produce any evidence of the reliability of DNA testing.

This text examines in some depth six different areas of forensic evidence:

- Fingerprint identification
- DNA profiling
- Eyewitness identification
- Blood spatter analysis
- Handwriting analysis
- Polygraph

The first four types of evidence are routinely admitted in court. Fingerprint identification and DNA both rest upon accepted scientific principles. Blood spatter analysis is scientific at the level of measuring the size and shape of blood drops, but can become more hypothetical when analysts try to reconstruct a crime based on the blood patterns. Eyewitness identification has historically been viewed as the most important evidence in a criminal trial. Juries believe that a witness who identifies a suspect is one of the most important factors in a trial. Yet new science has shown that eyewitness identifications are subject to many possible errors and are not nearly as reliable as people once believed.

Handwriting analysis has been accepted in the courts for years, yet many examiners can give no particular method to their analysis or a specific number of handwriting characteristics that they must find in common to determine a match. Polygraph, by contrast, is extremely scientific in its measurement. No one disagrees that it accurately measures blood pressure, heart rate, and sweaty hands. But do those physiological measurements equate to evidence of deception or telling the truth? And even if they are accurate measures of deception, is the error rate—assumed to be about 20% at the most favorable—too high to allow it into court? As the jury is the one that is supposed to decide whether the defendant is telling the truth, doesn't polygraph take away an important jury responsibility?

Finally, both handwriting and polygraph are now developing new forms of science to measure the same phenomena but with more reliability. Computer programs have been developed to measure known handwriting characteristics. Scientists are experimenting with using a functional magnetic resource imaging technique to measure brain waves that they believe will automatically react to statements that can connect a suspect with a crime.

The court system is changing constantly in its approach to admitting new scientific evidence. At the same time, the science is changing as well.

How important is science in determining "truth" in the courtroom? Are today's juries overly impressed with science? Do they reject science if it sounds too complex or intimidating?

We will examine many of these questions in the context of case studies about actual criminal trials. The primary case study is *State v. Grant*, a cold case involving the stabbing death of a young woman in a New Haven, Connecticut garage in 1973. The case remained unsolved until 1997, when a fingerprint examiner at the Connecticut Forensic Science Laboratory found a match to an unidentified fingerprint taken from the crime scene by checking in an AFIS [Automated Fingerprint Identification System] database. The fingerprint belonged to Ed Grant, a garage mechanic who lived about a half hour away from the crime scene. The fingerprint led to a warrant for Grant's blood, which was matched by DNA to a small spot on a handkerchief that was found at the scene.

Based on these two powerful pieces of forensic evidence, Grant was arrested, tried and convicted in May of 2002. He was sentenced to 20 years in jail. Investigators were unable to link Grant with the victim or to show any motive for the crime. The eyewitnesses had given somewhat different descriptions of a man they saw running in the garage and one eyewitness actually identified Serra's boyfriend. The witness was wrong and the boyfriend was released based on his blood type and alibi. Investigators sought an arrest warrant for another man and were ready to begin his trial when blood results showed his DNA did not match the blood found at the scene and believed to be that of the murderer.

Yet, how could the jury ignore the fingerprint and the DNA on the handkerchief? As the prosecution commented, the defense offered no "innocent explanation" for their presence at the crime scene.

In the course of studying this case and other famous cases, we will also examine other issues such as:

- How does the way crime scene investigators handle evidence affect whether it can be admitted in court?

- What is circumstantial evidence? Is it as good as direct evidence? Why is forensic evidence circumstantial?

- Does a jury have to believe an expert witness?

- What causes eyewitnesses to remember a particular face, when subsequent events prove that is not the person they saw?

- How do the Rules of Evidence work to keep out statements such as the entries in Nicole Brown Simpson's diary that she was afraid O.J. would kill her?

- Why wasn't the jury allowed to hear that Grant's fingerprint was entered into the database as the result of a domestic dispute?

- Why does an appeals court allow an evidence ruling of a trial court to stand, even where the appeals court might have made a different decision if it were the trial court?

- How can a prisoner who believes he is innocent get access to the crime scene DNA for testing so that he can be exonerated?

- Is the judge better than the jury to evaluate whether scientific testimony is reliable? Why not just let all forensic evidence in and rely on opposing counsel to cross examine the experts?

- Do defendants have a Constitutional right to present certain forensic evidence, such as polygraph, in their defense?

- How can the court determine if evidence is based on a reliable science that has been reliably applied?

- Does the possible prejudice to the defendant of admitting the evidence justify excluding it?

- How does the fact that the examiner uses his judgment in evaluating the evidence affect its admissibility?

- Does the evidence require an expert to explain it to the jury, or can the jury understand it just by looking at it?

# Forensic Evidence in Court

# Chapter 1

# The Case Study: *State v. Grant*

## Overview

In the case of *State v. Grant*, Edward Grant was convicted in 2002 for the 1973 murder of Concetta "Penney" Serra in a New Haven, Connecticut garage. The case involved the collection and testing of fingerprints, blood, DNA, blood spatter patterns, and the creation of composite drawings of eyewitness identifications.

Investigators initially targeted a boyfriend of the victim, who was identified by a witness the day after the crime in a lineup. He was subsequently excluded based on the fact that his blood type differed from blood stains believed to be the perpetrator's and left at the scene. They then turned to two other men the victim had known, because they believed that the victim had known her attacker.

None of the fingerprints found at the scene could be matched to a possible perpetrator. Blood typing showed the victim's blood type—A—was found where Serra was killed, but type O blood, believed to be the attacker's, was present in a trail running through the garage. DNA testing was not available in 1973 to profile the DNA in the blood. Investigators took a fingerprint off a bloody tissue box found behind the driver's seat in the victim's car and compared it to the fingerprint cards on file in New Haven, but found no match.

Eventually a suspect was arrested and charged with the murder, but on the eve of trial, he was eliminated based on his DNA profile from the blood trail found in the garage, and the case was dropped.

In 1997, in a routine run of fingerprints from "cold cases" into a computerized Automated Fingerprint Identification System, or AFIS system, investigators found a match to the fingerprint—a print that had been entered into the system based on a domestic dispute. The fingerprint matched Ed Grant.

Investigators then got a warrant to take Grant's blood, which they subsequently matched to a small amount of genetic material, believed to be blood, on a handkerchief that had been found in the garage near Serra's discarded car keys. The DNA test of Grant's blood showed that he was the source of the genetic material on the handkerchief. However, none of the blood from the trail in the garage was testable. Serra's keys had been lost. Some of the witnesses had died.

Grant was tried in May of 2002 for Serra's murder. He did not take the stand. His defense was that he did not know Serra and did not commit the crime. The state was therefore required to prove each element of the crime of murder beyond a reasonable doubt.

The jury convicted Grant largely based on the two pieces of hard forensic evidence—his fingerprint on the tissue box and his genetic material on the handkerchief. His attorneys did not deny that the forensic tests were correct, but argued that there was no evidence to prove that the fingerprint was impressed on the tissue box at the time of trial. Nor was there any testimony that proved the handkerchief was Grant's or that it was dropped at the time of the crime. They also questioned how only one small spot of "blood" could have remained testable after years of moving the handkerchief from place to place under conditions that deteriorated the rest of the spots beyond testing.

Grant made pretrial motions to exclude the DNA testing based on his argument that the DNA testing method—Short Tandem Repeat—was too new. The court denied the motion. He also made a post-trial motion for a new trial on the grounds of prejudicial comments made by prosecutors and the failure to sanction the state for losing evidence. He lost that motion too. Grant was sentenced that August to 20 years in prison.

In August of 2006, Grant appealed his conviction. One of his main issues on appeal is that the affidavit used to get a warrant for his blood was defective because it did not disclose certain information about the fingerprint, including that the tissue box was moveable and therefore did not conclusively link him to the crime scene. The other is that a statement made by Grant after he was picked up by investigators in which he said "did you hear about the guy in Texas? They got him on a fingerprint too," violated his Constitutional rights and was inadmissible.

The State filed its reply brief in March of 2007. It responded that the affidavit for Grant's blood was not misleading and included all necessary information. It also responded that Grant's statement to investigators was made voluntarily and without any violation of law.

The appeal is unlikely to be resolved until 2008.

# Chapter Objectives

Based on this chapter, students will:

1.  Learn the basic facts of the case study in *State v. Grant*.

2.  Understand the investigators' theory of the case and how they proceeded to investigate possible suspects.

3.  Identify the forensic evidence tested at the time of the crime in 1973 and after the case was revived in 1997, as well as methods of forensic testing as they evolved from 1973 to 1997.

4.  Appreciate the length of time that forensic evidence can remain testable.

5.  Appreciate the potential prejudice to introducing evidence about a suspect's "character."

6.  Understand the various "motions" made by counsel, before, during, and after trial and their effect on the possible outcome of the case.

7.  Understand the appellate issues raised by Grant after his conviction and the response of the state to those issues.

*Penney Serra, trial exhibit 3.1*

*Latent print on tissue box,
trial exhibit 244*

*Car with tissue box in back (boxed),
trial exhibit 2.3*

*Latent print on tissue box with detective's
initials, bottom, trial exhibit 2.21*

*Tissue box with blood closeup,
trial exhibit 2.19*

*Handkerchief, trial exhibit 6.3*

## Crime Schematic
## Temple St. Parking Garage, New Haven, CT

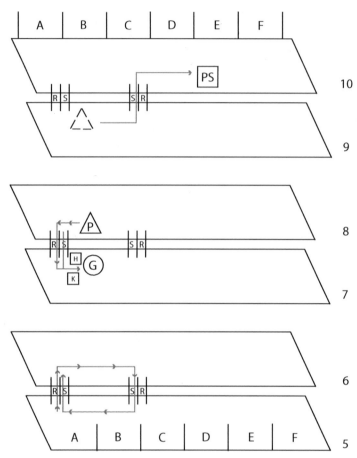

1. Serra's car is parked with Grant inside on level 9A; Serra runs out and up stairs to level 10, with Grant in pursuit; Serra is killed in stairwell from level 10 to roof.

2. Grant runs back to Serra's car on level 9A.

3. Grant drives Serra's car up to level 10 by mistake and then down to level 8A, looking for his own car. Grant exits Serra's car and proceeds on foot looking for his own car, leaving a blood trail as he walks.

4. Grant walks down to level 5 and then back up to level 7A, where he finds his car, leaving a trail of blood.

5. Grant enters his car, drops Serra's keys and his handkerchief and leaves the garage. Blood trail ends.

| | |
|---|---|
| PS | Penney Serra Body Found |
| P | Penney Serra Car Found |
| Serra | Serra Car Suspected Location Parked |
| H | Handkerchief |
| K | Keys |
| G | Grant Car Suspected Location Parked |
| R | Ramp |
| S | Stair |

*Crime schematic graphic*

# A Cold Case Is Reopened

The case of *State v. Grant* is a classic "cold case." Grant, the defendant, was convicted by a jury in 2002 of the 1973 murder of Concetta Serra, known as Penney to friends and family. His arrest and subsequent conviction were based largely on a "match" to a fingerprint on a box of tissues found in the victim's car. The fingerprint went unidentified until 1997. At that point, the fingerprint from the tissue box was submitted to see if there might be a match to an Automated Fingerprint Identification System (AFIS), which was done with unidentified fingerprints on a routine basis. The print was discovered to match a print of Edward Grant that had been entered into the database a few years earlier. This led to a warrant for his blood, which identified Grant's DNA profile on a small portion of a handkerchief that had been found near the crime site in 1973.

# The Crime and Investigation

The initial investigation disclosed the following facts:[1] On July 16, 1973, a worker in a New Haven garage discovered a dead woman in the stairwell leading to the 10th level. She was barefoot and dressed in a blue knit minidress with a large bloodstain on the bodice. Her body was curled in a fetal position. She had suffered a single stab wound to the left side of the chest which pierced the lower tip of the heart, causing death within a minute. Medical examination showed she had not been sexually molested. Her name was Concetta "Penney" Serra. She had apparently parked in the garage to shop in the attached mall.

## Theory of the Case

The police report filed on July 16, 1973 contained a theory of the crime. Serra was shoeless because she often took her shoes off to drive. She was driving a 1972 Buick. The police surmised that the assailant arrived at the Temple Street Garage in a separate vehicle about four minutes before Serra, based on the entry and exit times stamped on his garage ticket. Serra and her assailant entered from different entrance points at different ends of the garage.[2]

There was a bloody trail at the scene, which detectives believed to be that of her attacker. The blood was later determined as Type O. Serra was type A. Police then concluded that the blood was probably the assailant's. The police suspected the attacker to be someone Serra knew, because she had apparently let him into her car. Her purse and possessions were untouched.

By tracing the blood drops evidently left by the assailant and looking at the placement of Serra's car, police theorized that the assailant got into Serra's car and they rode

---

1. Some of the facts are taken from the initial police report filed July 16, 1973.
2. *State v. Grant*, CR6-481390, State's Exhibit (hereinafter "Exhibit") No. 241.

together to level 9 in her car. On level 9, Serra ran from the car and attempted to leave by the stairwell. She ran up the stairs from level 9 to level 10. A wig or "fall" attached to her hair was found on level 9, where it apparently landed during her flight.

Once on level 10, Serra tried to go to the top level, but found the stairwell was a dead end. Both Serra and her assailant were apparently wounded when she was attacked. The police found a blood trail back down the stairway to level #9, where the blood drops disappeared. Police theorized that the murderer ran back from level 10 to level 9 and got in Serra's car, searching for his own. They found Serra's car on level 8, where it was abandoned in an erratic position. On level 7, the police found Serra's car keys and a man's handkerchief containing bloodstains and traces of an "unidentified substance."

Police found a blood trail from level 8, where the assailant abandoned Serra's car, down to level 5 and back to level 7, when it once again disappeared.

## Semen

Experts concluded that there was evidence of semen on Serra's panties and slip. However, it was degraded and may have been residual after washing the garments.[3] In 1987, Dr. Henry Lee, the then director of the Connecticut Forensic Laboratory, was asked to reinvestigate the crime by John Kelly, the chief state's attorney for Connecticut.[4] He concluded in a book he wrote about the crime that it "meant that, in all probability, the sperm had been ejaculated outside the undergarments, the date of this deposit being impossible to determine."[5] Rape did not appear to be involved in the crime.

## Eyewitness Reports[6]

Two eyewitnesses on level 9 stated that they saw a man running toward the stairs with a "shiny object" and heard screaming. They also stated that the assailant later reappeared running, entered the victim's car and drove the length of level 9, apparently looking for the down ramp. He missed it, had to go up to level 10, where he was observed by a third witness who said the car was driving fast and erratically.

The eyewitness reports of the three witnesses inside the garage were somewhat conflicting. The assailant was variously described as "either white or Puerto Rican, 18–35 years of age," and was probably suffering from a cut on one hand or lower arm. One eyewitness created a composite sketch of the assailant and identified Phil DeLieto, Serra's former fiancé, at a lineup.

The parking attendant at the Frontage Road Exit stated that a man handed him a bloody ticket with his right hand in a "cross-body" motion. He did not see the driver, but said he spoke with a Hispanic accent and drove a blue car with little chrome, in the intermediate size range, with a possible Connecticut plate beginning "MR" followed by four digits.

---

3. Dr. Henry C. Lee with Thomas W. O'Neil, *Cracking More Cases,* Prometheus Books, 2004, at 39.
4. *Id.* at 36.
5. Lee and O'Neil, *supra* at 39.
6. Lee and O'Neil, *supra* at 23–24.

Medical examination showed the weapon was a knife at least three inches long, which was never recovered.

## Suspects

Three men connected with Serra were questioned, but were all eventually eliminated as suspects:

1.  Phil DeLieto, Serra's former fiancé.
2.  Anthony Golino, a High School classmate of Serra's.
3.  Selman Topciu, a patient at a dental practice where Serra had worked.

Serra and DeLieto had been in Rhode Island the weekend before she was murdered and had apparently quarreled the prior weekend. DeLieto was identified by an eyewitness in a lineup shortly after the crime, but was cleared based on both his blood type and an alibi.

Anthony Golino had been a classmate of Serra's at Wilbur Cross High School. Golino's wife, Melanie, told police in 1982 that her husband had threatened to kill her, saying essentially that "I will do to you what I did to Penney Serra."[7] Police questioned Golino, who had a one-inch scar on his left hand that he could not explain. They arrested him for the murder in 1984. In 1987, on the eve of trial, the state executed a search warrant for Golino's blood, which turned out to be Type A, the same as Serra's. This blood type excluded him as the source of the blood trail in the garage, which was Type O. The charges were dismissed.

Another suspect was Selman Topciu, a patient of the dental practice where Serra worked. Several invoices addressed to Topciu were found under the driver's side visor of Serra's car. Serra's father stated that they had not been there when his daughter had borrowed the car that morning. Topciu spoke with a foreign accent and had been seen at a diner when Penney was there. He also had a scar on his left wrist. His blood type was O, as was the blood found throughout the garage and in the car. Topciu's DQAlpha DNA marker, which was based on an early form of DNA testing, matched the blood lifted from the car.[8] At the time of the crime, Topciu drove a brown Buick with license plate HN5533.[9] Christopher Fagan, the parking lot attendant, described the suspect who handed him a bloody parking ticket as driving a green or blue Chrysler or GM car with MR or MH as the first two letters on the license plate.[10] New Haven detectives tried to obtain arrest warrants on two occasions after Topciu had moved out of Connecticut, but the court refused due to lack of evidence.[11]

In 1987, Lee began a reconstruction of the crime. At the same time, the CBS show *60 Minutes* ran a segment of the murder that focused attention on the possible murderer. The crime, before that a major cold case in New Haven, now had reached a nationwide audience.

---

7. Lee and O'Neil, *supra* at 33.

8. Memorandum of Law in Support of Appeal of Edward Grant, filed August 14, 2006 (hereinafter "Appellant Brief") at 16.

9. *Id.* at 15.

10. *State v. Grant*, CR6-481390, Trial Transcript, (hereinafter "Transcript") May 1, 2002 at 194.

11. Lee and O'Neil, *supra* at 35.

The murder remained unsolved for almost 30 years until May of 2002, when Edward Grant was convicted of the crime.

## The Forensic Evidence

> A latent print is invisible to the human eye, but can be lifted and preserved from a crime scene by dusting it with colored powder.

Three latent prints were lifted from the site—two within the car and one on a tissue box. Fingerprints were also lifted from envelopes under the visor of Serra's car.

The police did a visual search of all 70,000 fingerprints on file in New Haven. None matched. The police also recovered a handkerchief that appeared to have blood and perhaps red paint, or both, on it. DNA testing was not available at the time, but swatches were cut and showed that there was genetic material on the handkerchief.

## Cold Case Revived through a Fingerprint Match

> AFIS. Automated Fingerprint Identification System. The FBI and most state governments store fingerprints from individuals arrested for crimes in a database that can be searched for a match to a fingerprint taken from a crime scene.

Almost twenty-five years later, in 1997, Christopher Grice, a fingerprint analyst in the Connecticut Forensic Science Laboratory, fed the latent print into a automated fingerprint identification system (AFIS) computerized database, which reported a match to a print that had been entered into the system in 1994 as a result of a domestic dispute complaint against Grant.[12] That database did not exist at the time of the initial investigation. Grant's print did not come back as the closest match, but after Grice visually ruled out six other potential matches, he determined that Grant was the match. Grant was arrested in 1999 at the age of 59. The prosecutors got a warrant for a blood sample and found that Grant's DNA was consistent with genetic material on the handkerchief.[13]

Armed with the fingerprint and DNA match and some conflicting eyewitness identification, the prosecution secured a murder conviction against Grant in May of 2002. There was no evidence that Grant had ever known Serra and no evidence of any possible motive for the crime. There were no recoverable prints on the steering wheel of Serra's car, although the prosecution's theory posited that Grant drove it. There was no evidence as to when the fingerprint was placed on the tissue box or how Grant could have reached the box from the front seat. There was no explanation as to why all genetic material on the handkerchief had deteriorated beyond the point of testing, except for the one spot that identified Grant. The attendant recalled the bloody ticket and described the man driving the car as speaking with an Hispanic accent.[14] Grant is not Hispanic.

---

12. Exhibit 50.1.
13. Exhibit 76.
14. Exhibit 235.

The entire incident, based on the time-stamped entry of Serra's and the perpetrator's parking tickets to the time the perpetrator left, was between 6 and 10 minutes.[15]

# The Trial

## Fingerprint Testimony

The crime scene had yielded four sets of latent fingerprints that could not be identified, plus a bloody print on the parking ticket, which had been lost by the time of trial. None of the prints were ever identified, other than the one print on the tissue box. At trial, Christopher Grice of the New Haven police stated that the partial fingerprint on the tissue box matched Grant's.

> "I found that the same person who made the latent impression on the tissue box was the same person who left his left thumb print on an ink card ... the card was in the name of Edward Grant."[16]

Grice acknowledged under cross examination that there were other fingerprints in evidence that were not identifiable. He also said that it was impossible to establish when, how, or why the left thumbprint matching Edward Grant's got on the tissue box.[17]

The defense argued that the state had lifted several prints from Serra's car that had never been identified. There were no identifiable prints on the steering wheel or on the bloody parking ticket. The public defender planned to use Kenneth Moses, a fingerprint expert, to testify that the fingerprint was on the box before blood spattered on top of it.[18] However, Lee acknowledged this was true on cross examination, so it was unnecessary for the defense to call an additional witness.

## DNA

Carll Ladd, a DNA lab technician who worked for the Connecticut Forensic Lab, testified that the DNA on the handkerchief matched Grant's DNA. The significance of a match was stated as a statistical probability that someone other than the defendant could have contributed the specimen. The Connecticut State Forensic Laboratory at that time used the figure of 1 in 300 million, roughly the population then of the United States, even if the actual probability exceeded this ratio, as it did in the *Grant* case. In other words, if only 1 person in 300 million could have been the source of the DNA, and it matched Grant's DNA, theoretically there would be no one else in the entire country who would match that profile.

The Forensic Lab acknowledged that the handkerchief and tissue box had been moved from one location to another over the 30 years, and at one point were stored in a basement near a furnace.[19] Heat is known to degrade DNA.

---

15. Exhibit 241.
16. Christa Lee Rock, *No Motive Offered*, New Haven Register, May 15, 2002.
17. Lee and O'Neil, *supra* at 55.
18. Rock, *supra*.
19. Colleen Van Tassell, *Blood Never Lies. Does It?* New Haven Advocate, http://old.newhavenadvocate.com/articles/penney.html.

The defense did not contest the validity of the DNA match; however the state's expert agreed that there was no test that could tell when the blood was put on the handkerchief. The defense raised the inference that, as only one drop of blood had not degraded beyond the point of being tested, the drop of blood may have been planted by the Crime Lab, eager to close a long outstanding murder case. There was no question that the case had remained in the public view; Serra's father had made it his life mission to find his daughter's killer.[20] The prosecution's expert also agreed under cross examination that the fingerprint could have been placed on the tissue box in another location entirely.[21]

In addition to the genetic material found on the handkerchief, which could have been blood or saliva, Dr. Virginia Maxwell, a forensic chemist, testified that there were additional paint stains consistent with paint used at auto-body shops. Grant was employed at a body shop at the time of the killing.[22]

## Grant's Character

Grant did not take the stand, as was his right; his defense was that the prosecution had arrested the wrong man and had not proved his guilt beyond a reasonable doubt. The jury did not have an opportunity to assess his credibility as a witness. They were therefore free to form their own opinion of what kind of a man Grant was. One family witness testified Grant was a violent man. Another testified that he was a loving family man. Here is what Lee said in his book:

> In the summer of 1994, Edward R. Grant of Waterbury beat his then-fiancee so fiercely that she was hospitalized. This victim reported Grant's assault to the local police, and he was arrested. Subsequently, Edward Grant was fingerprinted. Grant was then fifty-one and had worked most of his adult life at his family's auto repair and towing business in Waterbury.

> In 1971, already married, Grant had been a member of the Connecticut National Guard and, while on his six months of active duty in South Carolina during the Vietnam War, has been injured in a Jeep accident. Depending on who is telling the tale, the intoxicated Grant was driving the Jeep or was simply a passenger when the vehicle rolled over. The injuries that Grant sustained resulted in a steel plate being placed in his head, and he was given an administrative discharge from the service. Grant returned to his home in Waterbury and went back to work for his family's successful business. The long-term effects of his injury were that he suffered from memory loss and severe mood swings.

> … The identification of [Grant's] print electrified those of us who had been waiting for years to catch a break in this case. Edward Grant's age, occupation, and track record for violence with women further galvanized investigators.[23]

In light of Lee's conclusions above, one can see why Grant would not want to take the stand and risk cross examination.

---

20. Paul Bass, *After 29 years, Phil DeLieto tells his side of the Serra case,* The New Haven Register, May 2003.
21. Transcript, May 21, 2002 at 139.
22. Transcript, May 9, 2002 at 139.
23. Lee and O'Neil, *supra* at 44.

## No Alibi Evidence

The defense originally planned to introduce evidence that Grant was at his cabin at the time of the murder, detained there due to local summer flooding from violent thunderstorms. However, the defense discovered evidence that the storms took place after the murder, and this evidence was not introduced.[24]

## Press Coverage of the Trial

The trial was covered daily, with much speculation about the evidence and guilt. The public learned background information the jury would not hear, either because the information was not admissible or because counsel chose not to bring it up. The evidence presented to the jury inside the courtroom did not reveal all the facts, which is always the case. Rules of court exclude evidence that is not relevant or may be prejudicial to the defendant. Also, if the defendant does not take the stand, the jury never hears him speak or gets to assess his credibility.

The press also covered the various "side stories," such as Golino's claims of having been unjustly accused and his assertion that Grant was innocent, as well as Serra's father's obsession with finding his daughter's killer, and interviews with friends and neighbors about Grant being a nice old guy who just liked to go fishing.

## The Lost Evidence

In the Serra case, certain evidence had been lost—the bloodstained parking ticket, the wig or "fall" Serra had been wearing, and a bloodstained key chain. Some pieces of evidence were altered, such as the handkerchief that had many holes chopped out of it, as police did testing over the years. The "chain of custody" of all these items was confused, as the evidence had been moved from one location to another and the numbering system had been changed. Some of the lost evidence then appeared, including some nasal hairs recovered from the handkerchief and a "negroid" hair in Serra's wig. The nasal hairs, according to a 1980 forensics report, still contained roots, which could have been tested for DNA.[25] However, although the defense requested that the hairs be tested, they did not have enough roots left for DNA testing, in part because they had been stored between glass slides.[26] Prosecution witness Dr. Kimberlyn Nelson, testified that she had conducted mitochodrial DNA tests on three nasal hairs but her results were "inconclusive."

## Written Statements Read at Trial

Courts generally exclude evidence of the statements made by witnesses who are unavailable. In other words, if a person cannot appear in person at trial, the court will not

---

24. Lee and O'Neil, *supra* at 49.

25. Christa Lee Rock *New twist in 28-year-old Serra Murder case*, New Haven Register, January 22, 2002.

26. Christa Lee Rock, *Hair test sought in Serra mystery*, New Haven Register, January 23, 2002.

allow a written statement, letter, or earlier sworn testimony to be read to the jury. But in this case, the trial judge allowed the jury to hear statements both by Serra's father and Chris Fagan, the parking lot attendant. Both had died before trial. Both men, according to defense attorneys, had given statements to police implicating Selman Topciu in the crime.[27] Serra's father had insisted that the bills addressed to Topciu, a patient at the dental office where Serra worked, had not been under the sun visor when he loaned Serra his Buick around 12:15 pm on the day of her murder.

In addition, Topciu had a long scar on his left hand. Police believe the killer was injured on his left side during the incident. Grant had no scar. Topciu also spoke with an Albanian accent, and Chris Fagan, the lot attendant, had testified the man who handed him the bloody ticket spoke with a Hispanic accent. The defense won its motion to allow the jury to hear that Topciu was initially investigated for the murder.

Although the jury did not hear the possibly prejudicial evidence that Grant's fingerprint was obtained from an arrest for domestic abuse in 1994, they also did not hear the possibly positive fact that he had never been convicted of a crime or committed any act of violence. Two ex-wives of Grant refused to testify about his alleged abusive past.[28] Grant had no criminal record and neighbors said he was quiet and loved fishing and fixing cars, but the jury never heard about it.

George Oliver, a friend of Grant's, stated out of court that Grant was in Groton, not New Haven, the day Serra was killed. However, he did not testify as an alibi witness for Grant.[29] This left the jury with no possible explanation of where Grant had been on the day of the murder.

## Lack of Motive

| Proof of motive is not required to convict for murder. |
| --- |

No evidence of motive was presented. Because proof of motive is not one of the legal elements required to find murder, the jury could find Grant guilty without evidence of why he might have killed the victim.

## How the Fingerprint Got on the Box

Dr. Lee testified as a blood pattern expert for the prosecution. Although Lee's testimony about how he believed the fingerprint was deposited on the box was somewhat disjointed at trial, he summarizes it as follows in his book:

> [following the stabbing of Serra] After running back to the lower level, the murderer got into the victim's car. He wanted to stanch the bleeding from a wound on his left hand, so he reached behind him as he started to drive the car through the garage. The tissue box must have been lying face down, so the

---

27. Christa Lee Rock, *Serra's grave won't speak*, New Haven Register, February 10, 2002.
28. Christa Lee Rock, *Portrait of a complex suspect*, New Haven Register, April 28, 2002.
29. *Id.*

murderer had to reach around the car's bucket seat to flip the box over in order to extract tissues to stop the bleeding.

In this dynamic flipping motion, the assailant had left behind three bloody finger marks, due to direct contact, none of which yielded any readable ridges for fingerprint comparison. But in gripping the upright portion of the tissue box, the killer left the one clear fingerprint, his left thumbprint. Subsequent to this, the assailant also transferred some blood from his wound up on top of this print.[30]

Lee did not give an opinion as to what happened to the bloody wad of tissues, or why the assailant would have either left the box on the backseat floor or deliberately put it in the backseat, given his obvious frantic activity in the aftermath of the crime. It is also unclear whether in the reenactment of the crime led by Lee in 1989, someone of the probable height and build of the assailant tried to reach a tissue box on the floor behind the driver's seat from the front of a 1971 Buick Electra.

# Pre-Trial and Post-Trial Motions

## Motion to Exclude DNA Results

In the Serra case, there were many motions (or requests made to the trial judge) to exclude particular pieces of evidence. The defense wanted the DNA evidence excluded on the ground that the form of DNA testing known as Short Tandem Repeat ("STR") testing was not yet proven reliable.

> A "motion" is a formal request by a party to the court to take some action, such as to rule that a witness cannot testify or to exclude certain evidence.

## Motion to Exclude Handkerchief Based on Chain of Custody

The defense also unsuccessfully attempted to exclude the DNA testing on the handkerchief on the ground that it had been moved from place to place since 1973 without a proper "chain of custody."

The DNA evidence identified Grant based on statistics cited by Dr. Carll Ladd that the chance of someone other than Grant being the source of the genetic material on the handkerchief was one out of 300 million. Public Defender Brian Carlow argued that the DNA profile was fatally flawed because it failed to detect certain "gene pairs" in blood on the handkerchief and

> Chain of Custody. The law requires that forensic evidence introduced at trial must be proved to be the same evidence as that collected at the crime scene by detailed notes and procedures accounting for everyone who has handled it.

because there was DNA from multiple sources on the sample. The court ruled against the defense and allowed the evidence following a detailed hearing in which it examined the Short Tandem Repeat form of DNA testing and found it to be reliable.

---

30. Lee and O'Neil, *supra* at 52.

## Motion to Exclude Statement Made by Grant to Police

Grant made the following comment to investigators at the police barracks:

"Did you read about the guy in Texas who killed all those people? They got him on a fingerprint, too."[31]

Prosecutors wanted the jury to hear the statement because it appeared that Grant acknowledged that Grant was guilty "too." Grant's lawyers argued Grant's statement was not a knowing and intelligent waiver of the defendant's privilege against self incrimination. The judge disagreed and admitted the statement. Grant has appealed on this issue.

Grant had also told investigators about his working in a family auto body shop in Waterbury in the 1970's and apparently stated that he had suffered frequent blackouts due to an Army injury and sometimes couldn't remember where he had been or what he had done.[32]

The defense won its motion to allow the jury to hear that the police had investigated both Philip DeLieto, Serra's ex-fiance, and Selman Topciu, a former restauranteur whose dental bills had been found in Serra's car. In support of its point, the defense argued that one of the eyewitnesses, Gary Hryb, had identified DeLieto out of a lineup within 12 hours of the murder.

## Motion during Trial for a "Mistrial"

Mistrial. A decision by the trial court to stop a trial before a verdict because of a substantial error, such as a prejudicial statement by one of the attorneys. A defendant can be re-tried after a mistrial is ruled.

When retired New Haven Police Detective Vincent Perricone testified that the fingerprint on the tissue box had been "fresh" and told the jury that there are factors you can use to approximate how long ago a suspect left his prints behind, the defense moved for a mistrial on the ground that the state was offering an expert opinion from Perricone without giving the defense notice of its expert, which it is required to do. The defense also argued that there was no scientific proof that a fingerprint could be dated. The court denied the motion.[33]

## Motion for New Trial

Following the verdict, Grant's attorneys moved for a new trial, citing such errors as the prosecution's offering a possible motive in their closing statement that Grant was trying to steal Serra's car, although no evidence to that effect had been introduced. The motion also argued that the prosecution had impermissibly stated that the jury would have to believe two investigators had lied to acquit. Finally, it asserted error because of the judge's failure to sanction the state for losing significant pieces of evidence.[34] The motion

---

31. Christa Lee Rock, *'Too' key word in slay case,* New Haven Register, January 12, 2002.
32. *Id.*
33. Christa Lee Rock, *Mistrial Denied,* New Haven Register, May 3, 2002.
34. Christa Lee Rock, *Citing misconduct, Grant's lawyers seek new trial,* New Haven Register, June 4, 2002.

was denied. On September 27, 2002, Grant was sentenced to 20 years to life for the murder of Serra. At the sentencing hearing after the jury's guilty verdict, the trial judge said:

> "No one can deny that someone killed Penney Serra and thrust a knife in her heart, … Someone left that beautiful young woman dead or dying in a dirty stairwell in a parking garage. No one can deny what the evidence shows beyond any doubt—that someone was you."[35]

Public Defender Brian Carlow, who represented Grant, in speaking about the case following Grant's conviction, maintained his client's innocence. He said: "Grant is the unluckiest man in the world."[36]

Carlow believed the jury would have acquitted if it had been presented with just the fingerprint or the blood spot. But the two together convinced the jury that Grant was guilty.

# Grant's Appeal

Grant filed his appeal brief on August 14, 2006—four years from his sentencing and imprisonment. As in his court trial, he is represented by the Public Defender's office. Grant properly filed his notice of appeal within the time period required by law; however, his appeal brief was not due until 60 days following the delivery of the last page of the trial transcript, which accounted for the delay.

The appeals court does not hear any testimony from witnesses. It must accept the written transcript of the trial as the only facts in the case. Appeals are based on legal arguments presented in appeal briefs with references to the testimony from the actual trial transcript of the witness testimony, exhibits and evidence admitted at trial.

> Appeal. A request by a party that a higher level court change or "reverse" an action that occurred at a lower court. A criminal defendant who is convicted may appeal if he has a legal reason for doing so, called "error."

## What Kind of Issues Can Be Appealed?

Grant's appeal asks the appellate court to grant a new trial based on certain errors of law he asserts were made at the trial level. He cannot appeal because he disagrees with what any of the witnesses said or thinks they were lying. He cannot appeal if he thinks the jury chose to believe or disbelieve any of the evidence. Issues of fact cannot be appealed. So, for example, the jury may have chosen to believe the eyewitnesses who placed Grant at the scene of the crime. Grant contended at trial that the eyewitnesses were inconsistent, impaired by drugs, and had on an earlier occasion identified a different person. Grant cannot appeal based on the fact that the jury apparently chose to believe the eyewitness testimony. That is an issue of fact.

The trial court has broad discretion in ruling on the admissibility of evidence. A reviewing court must make every reasonable presumption in favor of up-

---

35. Michelle Tuccitto, *Grant gets '20-to-life' in Serra murder*, New Haven Register, September 28, 2002.
36. Interview of Brian Carlow with the author, October 2004.

holding a trial court's evidentiary ruling and will overturn it only upon a clear and manifest abuse of discretion.... [T]he fact that evidence is susceptible of different explanations or would support various inferences does not affect its admissibility, although it obviously bears upon its weight.[37]

However, Grant can appeal if the judge made an error in admitting or refusing to admit the testimony, for example, of an expert witness who planned to testify that eyewitness identifications are subject to a high rate of error. Neither party tried to introduce such an eyewitness expert, but if they had, the decision to admit or exclude the testimony is an issue which can be appealed.

> Preserving an issue for appeal. Absent extraordinary circumstances, an objecting party must object during trial to have the right to present the issue to the appellate court.

Grant can appeal only issues to which his attorneys objected during the trial. Those objections "preserve" the legal issue for consideration on appeal. For example, during the closing argument made by the prosecution, the attorney referred to a possible motive for the murder as Grant wanting to steal Serra's car. No testimony or evidence had been presented at trial on this issue, so Grant's attorney objected that the prosecution referred to a fact that was "not in evidence." The judge did not agree. This now becomes another issue for appeal.

A defendant generally does not appeal on every issue to which he objects. For example, Grant did not appeal the issue of whether the PCR/STR method of DNA testing was reliable. The court ruled after a detailed hearing that it was reliable. Grant could have appealed this issue, but chose not to. Customarily, counsel will review the record and make a judgment as to which issues to appeal. The attorney should appeal all issues where there is a possibility for reversal or remand for a new trial, as the attorney cannot always predict which issue may be most persuasive to an appellate court. Some lawyers believe that even if raising a particular issue is not likely to be successful, the cumulative effect of a great many "close calls" may persuade the appellate court to rule in favor of the defendant. This is a tactical decision based on counsel's judgment and the facts of each case.

## Hurdles for a Defendant in Appealing a Conviction

### *Abuse of Discretion*

> Abuse of Discretion. An act taken by the court that is arbitrary, capricious, or beyond all reason.

There are two big hurdles that the appellant (the party taking the appeal from an unfavorable ruling or verdict in the lower court) faces on appeal. The first is that the appeals court will "defer to," or let stand, many decisions made by the trial judge during the course of the trial, so long as the trial court acted reasonably. The standard for appeal on such issues is whether the trial court "abused its discretion."

So, for example, in decisions on whether to admit the testimony of an expert witness, the appellate court may review the record and believe that the expert was not as qualified as it thinks he should be. But unless the trial court admitted the expert's opinion without

---

37. *State v. Grant*, Brief of State-Appellee (hereinafter Appellee Brief) at 46.

a showing of any qualifications at all, the appellate court will not challenge the decision. The ruling was, as the appellate courts say, "within the discretion of the trial court."

### *Harmless Error Rule*

The second big hurdle is that even if the appeals court finds that there was an error of law at the trial level, the appeals court will not reverse the conviction or grant a new trial if it decides that the error was "harmless error." For example, the appeals court may agree with Grant that the prosecutor should not have told the jury in closing that Grant may have been trying to steal Serra's car. But it may also decide that there was sufficient evidence without that comment for the jury

> Harmless Error. An error that would not have changed the outcome of the trial, given all the other evidence introduced, and is therefore too minor to reverse the verdict.

to find Grant guilty. In that case, the comment about motive would be harmless error and the conviction would stand. As of this writing, the appellate court has not yet ruled on Grant's appeal.

The fundamental remedy that Grant's appeal requests is a new trial. "This Court should declare that there was error below and order a new trial."[38] The prosecution can re-try him, if it wishes. But that decision is within its discretion. Of course, if the appeals court remands the case for a new trial, but the prosecution decides not to retry him, Grant would be a free man.

> Remand. Following decision on appeal, the appellate court sends the case back to a lower court for trial or other specified action.

As one of his grounds for appeal, Grant is asking that the DNA evidence be excluded because of the way it was obtained. If he wins that issue, the prosecution would have to decide whether it thought it could win a second conviction without introducing evidence of the DNA match to the handkerchief.

If he loses, and his conviction is affirmed on appeal, Grant can appeal to the state supreme court on the same grounds that he lost at the intermediate appellate court. The state supreme court can choose to accept the appeal or refuse to hear it. A defendant convicted in a state court can also appeal to the U.S. Supreme Court if he alleges his conviction violated a provision of the U.S. Constitution. Finally, after all appeals have been brought or appeals time periods have run, a prisoner can bring a *habeas corpus* petition in federal court asking to be released from prison due to a violation of the U.S. Constitution.

The same is true of appeals from convictions of federal crimes in the federal courts. If the defendant loses at the first level appellate court, he can petition the U.S. Supreme Court to hear a second appeal. This is called a petition for *certiorari*. However, the U.S. Supreme Court does not have to hear the appeal.

## The Grounds for Grant's Appeal

The legal grounds for Grant's appeal are described in chapter 14. The major legal issues are these:

---

38. Appellant Brief at 69.

- Did the warrant to take Grant's blood lack probable cause because certain facts were not included in the affidavit submitted to obtain the warrant?

- Should certain statements made by Grant have been kept from the jury because they violated his Miranda rights to be informed that any statement he made could be used against him in a court of law?

- Was there an improper "foundation" laid for testimony about blood without actual testing to show the substance was blood?

- Did the prosecution commit misconduct in the closing arguments by referring to a possible motive for the killing, when no evidence about motive had been submitted at trial?

## The State's Response

The State of Connecticut contended in its brief that there was no error.

- The State argued that none of the statements Grant argued should have been in the affidavit supporting probable cause were required. Statements such as the fact that other fingerprints were found in Serra's car or that other suspects had been investigated were not relevant at the time of the warrant, and even if they were, the result was harmless error. The state argued that the facts were not material to granting the warrant and were not omitted with any intent to mislead the judge who signed the warrant.

- Grant's appeal brief contended it was error to admit Grant's statement: "did you read about the guy in Texas that killed all those people? They got him on a fingerprint too." The state responded that Grant's statement was voluntary, not in response to a question from authorities, but that the trial court correctly concluded that "Grant wanted to talk and that the police allowed him to do so."[39] The state also claims that, even if the statement had violated Grant's Constitutional rights, it was "harmless error" because the properly admitted evidence showed beyond a reasonable doubt that Grant was guilty.

The state then summarized its view of the evidence that "overwhelmingly established guilt":

1. the defendant's admittedly unexplained bloody fingerprint on the tissue box.

2. the defendant's unique DNA profile on the handkerchief found near the terminus of the type O human blood trail;

3. type O human blood bearing the defendant's DQ Alpha genotype on a trim piece inside the Buick;

4. composite drawings of the killer that both bear remarkable similarities to the 1973 photo of the defendant; and

5. the traces of aftermarket automotive paint on the handkerchief.[40]

- Grant also appealed that certain testimony should have been excluded at trial, specifically any reference to "blood" unless there had been independent evidence

---

39. Appellee Brief at 37–38.
40. *Id.* at 44.

that the substance had in fact been tested to be blood. The State argued that the fact that evidence is susceptible of different explanations or would support various inferences does not affect its admissibility, although it obviously bears upon its weight. So long as the evidence may reasonably be construed in such a manner that it would be relevant, it is admissible.[41]

- Finally, as to Grant's argument that certain statements made by the prosecution were misconduct, the state responded that such statements did not result in an unfair trial and therefore were not error.

After Grant files a final reply brief, oral argument will be scheduled before the appellate court makes its decision. It is unlikely that the appeal will be heard and decided by the Connecticut appellate court before the year 2008.

# How Would You Decide?

Was Grant rightly convicted based on two irrefutable pieces of hard forensic science that conclusively placed him at the murder scene? What other possible explanation was there for the presence of two pieces of uncontested forensic evidence linking Grant to the scene of the crime? Or was a jury, eager to solve a cold case made famous over the years, unduly impressed by science to the exclusion of facts such as a lack of motive, an 8–10 minute time window for a horrendous crime, and the initial conclusion of both investigators and Dr. Lee that the victim must have known her killer? These are some of the questions we will examine as we look more closely at the process involved in gathering, processing, admitting, and challenging forensic evidence in court.

# Summary

The *Grant* case presents many of the aspects of the use of forensic evidence in court that we will discuss throughout this text. Issues involving fingerprint identification, DNA testing, blood spatter analysis, blood typing, and eyewitness identification were all crucial to the case. The case illustrates how forensic testing has changed since the time of the crime—1973—and the time of trial in 2002.

The case also illustrates issues in crime scene investigation, control and accounting for forensic evidence, the legal standards for admission of forensic evidence, and objections to certain types of testimony.

We will also examine the issue of pretrial and post-trial motions and the issues Grant raises on appeal, including Grant's claim that investigators were not entitled to get a warrant for his blood based solely on the fingerprint match they discovered in 1997.

---

41. *Id.* at 46.

# Discussion Questions

1. What facts led the investigators to suspect the murderer was someone Serra knew?

2. What type of testing on the blood at the scene was done in 1973? What did it show? How was it helpful in investigating suspects?

3. What type of testing was done in 1997? What genetic material was tested? What other facts would you want to know if you were trying to solve this crime?

4. In determining what happened to Serra, what do you think were the most important pieces of evidence?

5. What do you conclude from the fact that an eyewitness originally identified a suspect who was later cleared based on his blood type?

6. If you were a juror, what would you conclude based on Grant's failure to take the stand? What about his failure to offer any alibi evidence?

7. Why did the court deny Grant's motion to exclude the DNA test results?

8. Why did the court allow the jury to hear Grant's question to police "Did you read about the guy in Texas who killed all those people? They got him on a fingerprint, too."

9. Why wasn't the state required to prove that Grant had a motive to kill Serra?

10. What kind of issues can be appealed after a criminal conviction? What must the defendant do at trial in order to be permitted to appeal an issue?

11. What are Grant's primary legal arguments on appeal? What are the state's responses to those arguments? Who do you feel has the better arguments on which issues?

# Chapter 2

# What Is Forensic Evidence?

## Overview

How should the jury evaluate various types of forensic evidence? Is all forensic evidence "circumstantial?" What role does the law of probability play in forensic evidence? What types of "expert opinions" can forensic experts offer? When should the jury be able to look at the evidence and come to its own conclusions about the meaning of the evidence? Are some types of forensic evidence so powerful that they can unduly sway or "prejudice" a jury? We will examine these questions in detail.

Forensic evidence is any evidence based on science, technique, or expert evaluation entered into evidence at trial. It frequently requires an expert to explain the evidence to the jury. The expert's "opinion" is valuable to the party who presents the expert because it often links the evidence to an issue the jury must decide. The danger that the jury will be unduly impressed by the expert is called the "white coat" effect.

The jury must find all "elements" of a crime by a standard of beyond a reasonable doubt. For the crime of murder in Connecticut, there are three elements:

- the identity of the perpetrator,
- the intent to cause death, and
- that the defendant did cause the victim's death.

These three findings are the "ultimate issues" in a prosecution for murder. The level of certainty for *beyond a reasonable doubt* is not 100%. Proof beyond a reasonable doubt is proof that precludes every reasonable hypothesis except guilt and is inconsistent with any other rational conclusion.

Most forensic evidence is circumstantial evidence. It may tend to prove a fact from which the jury will need to infer or conclude another fact in order to reach a decision about guilt or innocence. The jury is not required to find that each circumstantial fact is true beyond a reasonable doubt, as long as the cumulative evidence proves guilt beyond a reasonable doubt.

Hearsay evidence is evidence of statements made by someone who is not in court to testify or be cross-examined about the statement. It is generally not admissible.

# Chapter Objectives

Based on this chapter, students will be able to:

1.  Define forensic evidence.

2.  Understand the difference between evidence that is common knowledge and evidence that requires expert testimony.

3.  Appreciate the jury's role as finder of fact.

4.  Understand court instructions that explain a jury is free to reject an expert opinion.

5.  Distinguish between direct and circumstantial evidence

6.  Describe the ultimate issues in a criminal trial and be able to identify their relationship to the legal elements of a crime

7.  Define the hearsay rule and the exception in the Crafts' case

8.  Identify the legal standard of proof for ultimate issues determined by one or more inferences from circumstantial evidence.

# What Is Forensic Evidence?

> Forensic evidence is any evidence based on science, technique or expert evaluation that can be used in a court of law as evidence of a fact in issue.

The term "forensic" does not mean "scientific." It means "of or used in legal proceedings or formal debate."[1] Forensic evidence is any evidence based on science, technique or expert evaluation that can be used in a court of law as evidence of a fact in issue. Although we think of forensic evidence as relating only to criminal trials, it also applies to civil matters, such as whether a particular drug causes injury. Forensic psychology is used to determine which parent would be best suited to have custody. Forensic accounting is used to determine the value of business assets.

We will examine forensic evidence in the context of a number of case studies involving crimes. Some of the crimes are famous—such as the murder trial of Sam Sheppard for killing his socialite wife, the JonBenet Ramsey murder, the "wood chipper" murder of Helle Crafts, and the O.J. Simpson case. We will also review in detail the murder conviction of Ed Grant for the murder of Penney Serra in New Haven, Connecticut in 1973.

Forensic evidence admitted in criminal trials includes: physical items discovered in the course of investigating a crime, such as a gun, knife, document, photograph, piece of clothing, etc. The evidence to be admitted must be "authenticated" by a witness who can identify it and explain its "chain of custody," which means how it got from the crime scene to the courthouse. It also includes the results of tests conducted by investigators, such as tests of DNA, fingerprints, fiber, hair or dental records. Finally, it may involve the results of experiments designed to reconstruct a crime or crime scene, involving the forensic science of ballistics or blood spatter.

---

1. The American Heritage Dictionary, 4th ed., Dell Publishing 2001.

The party seeking to introduce forensic evidence must establish a *chain of custody* of the evidence to prove that it has been controlled and accounted for from the time it was lifted from the crime scene. We will discuss chain of custody further in the next chapter.

# Forensic Evidence and Expert Testimony

Generally, a piece of forensic evidence requires an expert to explain its significance to the jury. The expert generally testifies to three things:

- What the forensic evidence consists of.

- The process the expert used to evaluate the forensic evidence.

- The expert's "opinion" as to the significance of the evidence to an issue at trial.

We will examine at length the various types of opinions the courts will allow. However, it is the ultimate opinion that is of primary value to the party presenting the evidence. That party hopes to convince the jury that if an expert comes to a certain opinion, then that opinion has more weight, and therefore is more likely to be true, than if the evidence were simply offered to the jury without an opinion. This is called the "white coat effect," the hope that the aura of respectability and superior knowledge of the expert will convince the jury to accept this opinion.

> Expert Opinion.
> An expert is a witness who because of his knowledge, skill, experience, training, or education, may testify to assist the trier of fact, usually the jury, to understand the evidence or to determine a fact in issue. An expert opinion is the testimony of an expert as to the significance of the evidence to a fact in issue.

> White coat effect. The tendency of an expert to impress the jury and make it more likely they will accept his opinion.

A jury is free to accept or reject an expert opinion. Here is how the judge in the *Grant* case instructed the jury on this issue:

> You have heard some testimony of witnesses who have testified as expert witnesses. Expert witnesses are witnesses who, because of their training, skill, education and experience, are permitted not only to testify about facts that they have personally observed, but to state their opinions.

> In making your decision whether to believe an expert's opinion, you should consider the expert's education, training and experience in the particular field, the information available to the expert, including the facts the expert had and the documents or other physical evidence available to the expert, the expert's opportunity and ability to examine those things, the completeness or incompleteness of the expert's report, the expert's ability to recollect the facts that form the basis for the opinion, and the expert's ability to tell you accurately about the basis for the opinion.

> You should ask yourselves about the methods employed by the expert and the reliability of the result. You should further consider whether the opinions stated by the expert have a rational and reasonable basis in the evidence.

"[T]he fact that a witness has qualified as an expert does not mean that you have to accept that witness's opinion. You could accept an expert witness's opinion or reject it in whole or in part."

Based on all of these things together with your general observation and assessment of the witness, it's up to you to decide whether or not to accept the opinion. You may believe all, some or none of the testimony of an expert witness. An expert's testimony is subject to your review like that of any other witness.[2]

# The Jury Is the "Finder of Fact"

The jury is free to believe or refuse to believe any witness. They are also free to disregard certain evidence if they find it is not credible, probative, or reliable. The *Simpson* jury apparently found that the government witnesses who testified about how they handled the blood evidence in the case were not credible. They could have found, as the defendant urged them to do, that the government mishandled blood evidence, contaminated it, and that certain investigators may have had a motive to build a case against O.J. Simpson because of his race.

After it has heard all the evidence, the judge will give the jury instructions. Here is the instruction the *Grant* jury was given about its role as a finder of fact:

> You are the sole judges of the facts. It's your duty to find the facts. You are to recollect and weigh the evidence and form your own conclusion as to what the facts are. You many not go outside the evidence presented in court to find the facts. You may not resort to guess work, conjecture, suspicion or speculation, and you must not be influenced by any personal likes or dislikes, prejudice or sympathy. You must carefully consider all of the evidence presented and the claims of each party.

> \* \* \*

> The evidence from which you are to decide what the facts are consists of the sworn testimony of witness, the exhibits that have been received into evidence as full exhibits and your observations at the view. [sic]

> The testimonial evidence includes both what was said on direct examination and what was said on cross-examination without regard to which party called the witness.[3]

The jury was also given the specific facts that it needed to find in order to convict the defendant.

> Let me now turn to the specific charge in the case. The State has filed an Information charging "that on July 16th, 1973 at a time between 12:36 p.m. and one o'clock p.m. at the Temple Street parking garage in New Haven, Edward Grant, with intent to cause the death of another person, caused the death of Concetta "Penney" Serra by stabbing her in the heart with a knife in violation of Section 53a of the Connecticut General Statutes.

> For you to find the defendant guilty of this charge, the State must prove each of three elements beyond a reasonable doubt:

---

2. Transcript, May 22, 2002 at 140–141.
3. Transcript, May 22, 2002 at 132–3.

- One, that it was the defendant and not some other person who was the perpetrator.

- Two, that the defendant intended to cause the death of another person.

- And three, that in accordance with that intent, the defendant caused the death of that person.[4]

Forensic evidence can be used to prove a number of critical issues. Typically, the evidence, by itself, will not prove guilt or innocence. The jury makes that decision and is not required to explain what other facts it decided were true or not. For example, a jury could reject the defendant's alibi evidence and still conclude that the prosecution had not proved its case beyond a reasonable doubt. Therefore, we do not know what facts a criminal jury has determined to be true in giving its verdict. "Ultimate issues" are issues which the jury must decide in order to determine its verdict. They are generally determined by the definition of the crime. The jury must find each of the ultimate issues stated above in order to find the defendant guilty

- Was *Grant* the person who killed Serra?

- Did he "intend" the results of his act?

- In accordance with that intent, did he kill Serra?

If the jury determined that the prosecution proved each of those three issues beyond a reasonable doubt, it was required to convict. In order to determine those issues, however, the jury must weigh testimony and evidence which would either prove or disprove a number of other facts that would be "probative," or likely to prove, those other facts.

> "Ultimate issues" are issues which the jury must decide in order to determine its verdict.

# The "Standard of Proof" for Crimes Is *Beyond a Reasonable Doubt*

In a criminal case, the jury must find the defendant is guilty by a standard of proof called *beyond a reasonable doubt.* This does not mean 100% certainty. It is certainly much more than the standard of proof in a civil trial, which is called a *preponderance of the evidence,* often referred to as 51% certainty or more. Here is how the judge instructed the jurors in *Grant* about the meaning of *beyond a reasonable doubt:*

> Proof beyond a reasonable doubt does not mean proof beyond all doubt. The law does not require absolute certainty on the part of a jury before it returns a verdict of guilty. The law requires that after hearing all of the evidence, if there is something in the evidence or lack of evidence that leaves in the minds of the jurors as reasonable men and women a reasonable doubt as to the guilt of the accused, then the accused must be given the benefit of that doubt and acquitted.

---

4. *Id.* at 145–6.

Proof beyond a reasonable doubt is proof that precludes every reasonable hypothesis except guilt and is inconsistent with any other rational conclusion. If you can in reason reconcile all of the facts proved with any reasonable theory consistent with the innocence of the accused, then you cannot find him guilty.[5]

The O.J. Simpson trials illustrate the difference between the standard of proof in a criminal trial and in a civil trial. In 1995 Simpson was tried and acquitted of the murder of his wife, Nicole Brown Simpson, and Ronald Goldman. The forensic evidence included blood stains matched to Simpson from the murder site, a blood stain matched to Nicole on one of Simpson's socks found in his home, a glove, shoeprints, and a variety of other pieces of evidence. Simpson did not take the stand. One of his defenses was that the Los Angeles police planted certain evidence and tampered with other evidence. Simpson's experts testified to evidence of tampering, for example, the fact that one of the blood stains from the crime site included a preservative used in taking a blood sample, raising the inference that the blood at the site had been planted from a vial of Simpson's blood.[6]

The jury acquitted O.J. Simpson. You can read comments by a number of jurors in chapter 15 in which they discuss the forensic evidence and why it did not convince them beyond a reasonable doubt that Simpson was guilty.

The following year, the families of Nicole and Ron Goldman sued O.J. Simpson for money damages for a civil claim called *wrongful death.* They presented much of the same forensic evidence. The ultimate issue was the same—did O.J. Simpson kill Nicole and Ron Goldman? The trial was held outside Los Angeles, the jury was composed of different people, and Simpson took the stand. The jury found Simpson liable for the claim and awarded substantial money damages to both families, including $12 million each in punitive damages, damages that are intended to punish the defendant.

Why did the same facts lead to Simpson winning his criminal trial and losing his civil trial? One of the reasons was the standard of proof. In the civil trial, the evidence convinced the jury by a preponderance of the evidence that Simpson did kill Nicole and Ron.

# Forensic Evidence Is Circumstantial Evidence

Circumstantial Evidence is evidence that proves a fact indirectly because it can prove one fact from which the finder of fact then can infer, or decide, another fact.

Direct Evidence is evidence that can be used to prove a disputed fact directly—eyewitness testimony, for example. When an eyewitness says "the man sitting at that table is the man I saw shoot the victim," that testimony is direct evidence of the act of homicide. Circumstantial Evidence is evidence that is probative of a fact indirectly in that it can prove one fact from which the finder of fact can conclude another fact is true.

---

5. Transcript, May 22, 2002 at 143–4.

6. William C. Thompson, *Proving the Case: The Science of DNA: DNA Evidence in the O.J. Simpson Trial,* 67 U. Colo. L. Rev. 827 (Fall 1996).

Let's say investigators recover a gun from the crime scene. The gun is forensic evidence. If investigators then introduce evidence that the defendant owns the gun found at the crime scene, this fact does not prove that the defendant was the person who fired the gun. However, the first fact is "probative," because based on

> Probative. A fact is probative if the jury would find it relevant to prove an issue in the case.

that fact, perhaps along with other facts, the jury may determine that the defendant fired the gun at the crime scene. A fact is "probative" if the jury would find it relevant in determining the truth or falsehood of some issue in a case. Forensic evidence is therefore generally circumstantial evidence because it requires the jury to *find another fact or facts based upon it* in order to conclude guilt or innocence.

From this example, you can see that most evidence is circumstantial evidence. Although defense attorneys often try to convince a jury that it is wrong to convict a defendant based on circumstantial evidence, because circumstantial evidence is somehow not good evidence, or of lesser value than direct evidence, it is the rare trial where a jury does not have to use circumstantial evidence to make a decision about guilt or innocence.

In the *Grant* case, for example, the presence of Type O blood at a crime scene may have convinced the jury to conclude that Grant was present in the garage and bled on the garage floor at the time of the murder. However, as the defense pointed out, there is no way to "date" when the blood was put there, and it is possible to "plant" blood, as the jurors in the *Simpson* case apparently concluded the police did. The jury, as finder of fact, was therefore free to conclude from the evidence that Type O blood was found in the garage that the blood came from Grant or that it did not. In that sense, the Type O blood was circumstantial evidence of the presence of Grant in the garage. It was also circumstantial evidence of *when* Grant was in the garage and of *how* his blood got there.

Circumstantial evidence therefore is proof of a fact from which the jury[7] can infer another fact. The trial judge in *Grant* gave the jury a standard instruction to explain what circumstantial evidence is. He said:

> You may consider both direct and circumstantial evidence. Direct evidence is testimony by a witness about what that witness personally saw or heard or did. Circumstantial evidence is evidence involving inferences reasonably and logically drawn from proven facts.

> Let me give you an example of what I mean by direct and circumstantial evidence. If you wake up in the morning and see water on the sidewalk, that is direct evidence that there is water on the sidewalk. It is also circumstantial evidence that it rained during the night. Of course, other evidence such as a turned on garden hose may explain the water on the sidewalk.[8]

# Linking Forensic Evidence to Ultimate Issues

Assuming a jury believes a fingerprint expert when he testifies that a print lifted from a crime scene "matches" or "identifies" the defendant, what does that mean? Does it

---

7. I will refer to the finder of fact as the "jury," although a judge in certain circumstances can also be a finder of fact.

8. Transcript, May 13, 2002 at 134–135.

mean that the defendant was at the crime scene? Absent an unusual circumstance, such as someone taking an imprint of the defendant's finger and deliberately planting it at the crime scene, yes, the testimony proves that the defendant left his print at the scene. But does it prove *when* the defendant left the print? No, it does not. Fingerprint experts agree that a fingerprint cannot be "dated." Does it prove that the defendant committed the crime, say, a burglary at the scene? For the fingerprint to be proof of the defendant's guilt, the jury must *infer* that the presence of the fingerprint at the crime scene convinces them that the defendant was there at the time of the crime and further, that he committed the crime.

Say the defendant has an alibi. He proves that he was in the hospital on the date of the burglary. Now what can the jury infer? It must infer that the fingerprint was placed at the scene on some other date and does NOT tend to prove the defendant was the burglar. Although the public tends to believe that forensic evidence "proves" guilt, this is rarely the case.

Even the presence of the defendant's semen in a rape victim does not "prove" the defendant raped the victim. The sex may have been consensual. The sex may have taken place hours before the rape, which can be proved by determining if the cells are still active or "motile," which can occur for up to 26 hours after ejaculation.[9] Perhaps the victim has semen from more than one source in her vagina. These were some of the defenses in the Kobe Bryant case. It was reported that DNA tests showed the victim was sexually active shortly after the time she reported the rape had occurred.[10] What seems "open and shut" can often be highly speculative.

Here are some examples of ultimate issues that a jury may infer from circumstantial forensic evidence. Each "therefore" below is an inference from the preceding fact:

- Is the defendant the person who did the act?

  The presence of blood matching the defendant's DNA profile can be used to conclude that the defendant was the source of the blood. Therefore the defendant was at the crime scene at the time of the crime. Therefore, the defendant was the perpetrator.

  The latent fingerprint lifted from the crime scene can be used to conclude that the defendant was the source of the fingerprint. Therefore, the defendant was at the crime scene at the time of the crime. Therefore, the defendant was the perpetrator.

  The defendant's handwriting appears on the ransom note. Therefore, the defendant wrote the note. Therefore the defendant was the kidnapper.

- What happened?

  The blood spatter pattern shows where the assailant was standing, the angle of the blows, the force of the blows, etc.

  The gunpowder residue shows how close the gun was to the target.

Each of these "what happened" facts must then be linked to the defendant if the jury is to find him guilty.

What alternative theories might prevent the jury from "jumping to conclusions" based on inferences from circumstantial evidence? For example, the *Simpson* jury could

---

9. Stuart H. James and Jon J. Nordby, *Forensic Science,* CRC Press, 2005 at 268.
10. Patrick A. Tuite, *Kobe case offered lessons in greed and sordidness,* Chicago Lawyer, April 2005.

well have found that the bloodstains at Nicole Simpson's home were O.J. Simpson's. That fact would be probative on the issue of whether he was the source of the blood. The jury could also have found that the blood was planted at the scene and did not result from O.J. Simpson having been actually present at the murder site. Likewise, they may have concluded that Nicole's blood was on Simpson's sock without necessarily concluding that the blood got on the sock during Simpson's murder of Nicole. Any of these conclusions would have prevented the fact of the presence of Simpson's blood from implicating him in the murder of Nicole Brown Simpson.

A fingerprint of a suspect identified from a weapon used at the crime scene may lead the jury to conclude the suspect handled the murder weapon; it may conclude that he handled the weapon at the time of the crime; it may also conclude that the suspect used the weapon to kill the victim. Each of these conclusions is an "inference" from a direct fact—the existence of the fingerprint. The inferences or series of inferences the jury must make to be convinced beyond a reasonable doubt that the suspect committed murder are what make the fingerprint "circumstantial" evidence. In other words, the fingerprint itself is simply a fact; the jury must consider all the circumstances of where and how the fingerprint was found, plus any other evidence about the fingerprint that the parties offer, to conclude that it proves an ultimate issue. This is why it is called circumstantial evidence.

# The Richard Crafts Case— A Challenge to Circumstantial Evidence

On November 19, 1986, a flight attendant named Helle Crafts was reported missing. A Connecticut jury later convicted her husband, Richard Crafts, of murdering his wife, putting her body in a freezer, renting a wood chipper, and chopping up her body in the chipper. The case was a major event because it was the first time in Connecticut that a jury was asked to convict someone of murder without a dead body.

A review of the facts introduced in evidence illustrates the difference between direct and circumstantial evidence.

Here is what the direct evidence showed:[11]

- On November 17, Crafts picked up a new freezer.
- Crafts told a witness that his old freezer had stopped working and he had taken it to the dump.
- On November 18 at 6 a.m., Crafts put his children in his car to go to his sister's house in Westport. It was snowing and the children were not dressed for the weather.
- Crafts later told witnesses he went to his sister's house because his house had no heat.
- Crafts house had kerosene heaters, fireplaces and a generator.
- Crafts told his children that his wife, Helle, had already gone to his sister's house.
- Helle was not at his sister's house and was never seen again.

---

11. *State v. Crafts*, 226 Conn. 237, 627 A.2d 877 (1993).

- On November 20, Crafts rented a truck and a wood chipper, as demonstrated by receipts.

- Between 3 and 4 a.m. on the night of November 21, witnesses saw a man in the vicinity of a steel bridge in Newtown, Connecticut, operating a wood chipper.

- At 4 a.m. on November 21, Crafts told a co-worker in the parking lot of the Town of Southbury offices that he rented the wood chipper to clean up limbs from the November 18 storm.

- There were no limbs down on Crafts' property after the November 18 storm.

- On November 21, Crafts returned the truck and wood chipper.

- The state began to investigate Helle's disappearance.

- Crafts made a number of conflicting statements as to where Helle was, such as at her sister's in Europe.

- When Crafts learned that state divers were looking for Helle's body, he told his brother "Let them dive. There's no body. It's gone."

- Investigators found the following evidence near the bridge: an envelope with Helle's name on it; blue fabric consistent with her uniform, pieces of bone and tissue, a human fingernail painted with fingernail polish consistent with that used by Helle, and crowns to some teeth.

- The crowns were identified as Helle's through dental records.

- Investigators found a chain saw in the water with blood, tissue, hair, and cotton fiber. The blood, tissue and hair were consistent with Helle's blood type and a hair found in her home.

- Helle had told several witnesses before she disappeared that if she suddenly disappeared, it would not be of her own free will.

Each of these pieces of evidence is direct evidence—statements made, items rented, tests on hair and fiber. But the jury needed to make inferences from each piece of evidence to determine whether Crafts killed his wife. Therefore the direct evidence was circumstantial evidence of another fact and *that* fact was circumstantial evidence of guilt of the crime.

Here are a few examples of the inferences the jury would need to draw from the evidence it heard to the issues required to determine guilt of murder.

1.  Rental of the wood chipper. The jury could infer that it was Crafts that witnesses saw at 3 a.m. on the hill, that Crafts was cutting up his wife, that he had killed his wife, and that he had premeditated the crime by renting the wood chipper in advance The rental of the wood chipper is circumstantial evidence of those facts.

2.  Purchase of new freezer and absence of old one. The jury could infer that Crafts put his wife's body in the old freezer, lied about it being broken, showing evidence of guilt, and bought a new one to falsely demonstrate the old one was broken.

3.  Presence of Helle's tooth crown on hill. The jury could infer that the tooth got there when her body was being cut up, that Crafts was the one operating the chipper and that Crafts killed her.

The cumulative power of all of the direct and circumstantial evidence was overpowering. On appeal, the court affirmed the conviction.[12] Crafts is still incarcerated.

---

12. *Crafts,* 226 Conn. 237.

## Were Helle's Statements Admissible under the Hearsay Rule?

The statements Helle made to friends about her fear of Crafts' killing her would normally not be admitted. Any statement made by a witness who is not in court, and therefore cannot be cross-examined, is not admissible to prove that the statement was true. Here is the definition of the hearsay rule under the Federal Rules of Evidence.[13]

> Hearsay. A statement, other than one made by the declarant while testifying at the trial or hearing, offered in evidence to prove the truth of the matter asserted.

The purpose of the hearsay rule is to guard against testimony that may not be true, where the opposing party has no opportunity to cross examine the person who made the statement in order to test whether or not it is true. As Helle was definitely not available to testify, her statement could not be admitted to prove that because she said she was afraid Crafts might kill her, it was likely that he did kill her. Nicole Brown Simpson's diary in which she stated her fear that her husband might kill her was kept out of evidence because of the hearsay rule.[14]

However, the court ruled that the statement could come in under one of the many exceptions to the Hearsay Rule. In general, statements that are hearsay can sometimes be admitted into court if their purpose is not to prove that the statement was true — for example, that Helle was afraid Crafts would kill her — but for a different purpose — in this case, to prove that Helle would not have left her home and children voluntarily. The court would probably still not have allowed the statement, as it was highly prejudicial to Crafts, but Crafts himself had argued before the court that Helle had left voluntarily. Therefore, Crafts "opened the door" to letting the prosecution introduce Helle's statements to counter or "impeach" Crafts' assertion that Helle left voluntarily.

Although the majority of the appellate court judges voted to affirm Crafts' conviction, two judges wrote a strong dissent opposing the admission of Helle's statements. They argued that her statement that if she suddenly disappeared, it would not be voluntary on her part, could just as easily be proof that she *did* run away in fear of Crafts. They would have excluded the statement.

> Dissent. An opinion written by one or more judges in an appeal in which they disagree with the decision of the majority opinion.

## Fingernail, Hair, Fiber, Tooth and Tissue

The fingernail, hair, fiber, tooth crown, and tissue were all forensic evidence. If the jury chose to believe the forensic experts, they could conclude that all this forensic evidence came from Helle. But that is all the forensic experts could say. They could give no opinion about how the items came to be there or whether Crafts was guilty of murder. Some of the evidence, such as the strand of hair, were consistent with Helle's

---

13. Federal Rule of Evidence 801.
14. *Note: The Problem of Using Hearsay in Domestic Violence Cases; Is a New Exception the Answer?*, 49 Duke L.J. 1041, 1067 (February 2000).

hair, but not unique. It was up to the jury to draw inferences from the forensic evidence. If body parts of Helle's were found near a bridge where a man was seen with a wood chipper at night, what could they infer? They could infer that Helle was dead; they could infer that she was chipped into small pieces, and they could infer that Crafts did it. All the forensic evidence was circumstantial evidence for these three important conclusions.

## Standard of Proof Where One Inference Depends on Another

Crafts' first trial resulted in a hung jury. At his second trial, he was convicted and sentenced to fifty years in prison. He appealed, arguing that the jury was required to find *each fact* necessary to build upon another fact by the standard of "beyond a reasonable doubt." The Connecticut Supreme Court heard this appeal in 1993 and denied Crafts' claim. Even though Crafts' conviction rested almost exclusively on circumstantial evidence, the court held that the jury had used the correct legal instructions and upheld the conviction. Here is part of the opinion:

### *State v. Crafts*, 226 Conn. 237, 627 A.2d 877 (1993)[15]

The principal issue in this criminal appeal is the sufficiency of largely circumstantial evidence to support a conviction for the crime of murder. The state charged the defendant, Richard B. Crafts, with having committed the crime of murder in violation of General Statutes §53a-54a, by killing his wife, Helle Crafts.

After an earlier trial resulted in a mistrial because of the jury's inability to arrive at a verdict, the state retried the defendant and a jury found him guilty of murder. The trial court then rendered a judgment sentencing the defendant to a term of fifty years' imprisonment. The defendant appeals his conviction to this court pursuant to General Statutes §51-199(b)(3). We affirm.

At the trial, the state's theory of the offense was that the defendant had intentionally killed the victim as a result of the deterioration of their marriage. To conceal detection of the crime, the defendant had allegedly devised and executed an elaborate plan to destroy the victim's body. In support of this proposition, the state presented extensive, but primarily circumstantial, evidence describing the couple's marital troubles as well as the defendant's actions during the fall and winter of 1986–1987 to establish that the defendant, with the requisite intent, had murdered the victim. The defendant maintained, to the contrary, that he had not killed his wife, but that he nonetheless did not know her present whereabouts.

The jury could reasonably have found the following facts. Because of the defendant's continued extramarital affairs, the victim contacted an attorney and began divorce proceedings against him. She hired a private detective, who carried out surveillance of the defendant. The detective confirmed that the defendant was involved with another woman, and presented the victim with photographs of the

---

15. Throughout this text, I have edited cases by omitting certain sections, deleting citations and footnotes, and altering paragraphing in order to improve clarity in reading. I have included some footnotes that appeared in the original court opinions, marked without the original footnote numbers, but indicated as [footnote].

defendant's activities. Not only was the defendant himself aware of the victim's intention to divorce him, but she also had told a number of people of her plans.

The victim's marital troubles would not, however, have led to her voluntary departure from her home and family. The victim was extremely devoted to her children, was planning to seek their custody in the divorce proceedings, and would not under any circumstances have left them voluntarily. Furthermore, the victim warned several people that, if anything unusual were to happen to her, they should not believe that such an event was of her own making.

The victim was last seen or heard from on November 18, 1986, as she was dropped off at her home by a coworker. On the morning of November 19, 1986, the defendant ushered the children and the family's live-in au pair helper from the home at 6 a.m. to leave for his sister's house in Westport purportedly, according to what the defendant told the au pair helper at the time, because of the lack of heat due to a power failure during a snowstorm the night before.

The defendant's home, however, had alternative sources of heat, including kerosene heaters, a fireplace and a generator. The victim was not present, and at that time the defendant explained that she had left earlier, probably to go to his sister's house. In his rush to leave the house, the defendant made no attempt to dress the children for the severe weather and drove through difficult conditions to leave the children with his sister in Westport.

Although the victim was not at the sister's house, the defendant neither mentioned her absence nor inquired regarding her whereabouts. The jury could reasonably have inferred that, in light of all of the evidence, the defendant had already killed the victim during the night and was proceeding with the execution of his plan to conceal the crime.

Thereafter, the defendant offered to different parties various stories regarding his wife's whereabouts, all of which were demonstrated to be incorrect. In addition to the explanation for the victim's absence on the morning of November 19 offered as he brought his children to his sister's house, he initially told several of the victim's friends that in fact she had gone to Denmark to be with her ill mother. He later began to tell acquaintances that the victim might be visiting her friends overseas. In an interview with the police on December 4, 1986, the defendant indicated that he had last seen the victim on November 19, 1986, but that, at the time of the interview, she might be visiting a friend in the Canary Islands.

Besides numerous inaccurate and contradictory statements regarding the victim's whereabouts, the defendant also made several incriminating remarks to acquaintances regarding the police investigation, which the jury could reasonably have found to indicate further a consciousness of guilt. For instance, when advised by his brother-in-law of the state police diving efforts, the defendant replied, "Let them dive. There's no body. It's gone."

Relying on this evidentiary showing, the jury hearing the defendant's case found him guilty of murder as charged. The defendant's appeal challenges his conviction on five grounds. He claims that the trial court improperly:

(1) denied his motion for acquittal because his conviction, resting primarily on circumstantial evidence, was the result of impermissible inferences that

were not supported by proof beyond a reasonable doubt, thereby denying his right to due process;

(2) instructed the jury that it might infer specific intent to commit murder from the mere fact of the death of the victim, thus denying his right to due process;

(3) refused to instruct the jury on three lesser included homicides not requiring a finding of intent to kill;

(4) admitted into evidence out-of-court statements made by the victim to others; and

(5) denied him a fair trial because of extensive pretrial publicity implicating, again, his right to due process.

We are unpersuaded.

\* \* \*

In light of the state's presentation of extensive circumstantial evidence, the principal issue raised by this claim is whether special procedural rules govern the validity of the jury's ultimate findings regarding each element of the crime of murder if, in making these findings, the jury presumably relied upon sets of multiple inferences, in other words, inferences derived from previous inferences.

The defendant maintains that recourse to multiple inferences potentially leads to speculative ultimate findings. From this premise, he contends that due process requires that a verdict of guilty depending on such inferences cannot be sustained unless each successive inference is itself established beyond a reasonable doubt. We reject this contention.

Due process requires that the state prove each element of an offense beyond a reasonable doubt. It follows that insufficiency of the evidence to support a jury's ultimate findings on each of these elements requires acquittal.

\* \* \*

> "Due process does not, however, require that each subordinate conclusion established by or inferred from evidence, or even from other inferences, be proved beyond a reasonable doubt." *State v. Crafts*

Due process does not, however, require that each subordinate conclusion established by or inferred from evidence, or even from other inferences, be proved beyond a reasonable doubt. We have regularly held that a jury's factual inferences that support a guilty verdict need only be reasonable. Equally well established is our holding that a jury may draw factual inferences on the basis of already inferred facts.

\* \* \*

The defendant's argument that a special standard of proof is required to guard against attenuated probabilities associated with inferences based on inferences is, however, an argument the basis of which we have previously considered and rejected. More than seventy years ago, we concluded, in *Sliwowski v. New York*, that "there is, in fact, no rule of law that forbids the resting of one inference upon facts whose determination is the result of other inferences...."

It is but a rule of caution; its true function is to guide the court in the exercise of its judgment in determining whether or not evidence offered is too remote ... or, in making its final decision, in deciding whether the plaintiff has established a reasonable probability."

We have adhered to that position, noting that "it is not one fact, but the cumulative impact of a multitude of facts which establishes guilt in a case involving substantial circumstantial evidence."

... As we explained, however, in *State v. McDonough*, "Where a group of facts are relied upon for proof of an element of the crime, it is their cumulative impact that is to be weighed in deciding whether the standard of proof beyond a reasonable doubt has been met and each individual fact need not be proved in accordance with that standard. It is only where a single fact is essential to proof of an element ... such as identification by means of fingerprint evidence, that such evidence must support the inference of that fact beyond a reasonable doubt."

\* \* \*

### [The hearsay objection]

The defendant claims that the trial court incorrectly allowed the state to introduce into evidence certain statements made by the victim tending to show the victim's belief that, if something should "happen" to her, it would not be the result of her own actions. He claims that the statements were inadmissible because they were hearsay, irrelevant and prejudicial. We find no reason to overturn the trial court's rulings.

Over the defendant's objections, the state presented the testimony of five witnesses who offered statements made by the victim during the fall of 1986. Diane Andersen, the victim's attorney handling the divorce proceeding, testified that the victim had told her that "if something should happen to her I should not assume that it was an accident." Lee Ficheroulle, a coworker and friend, testified that the victim had told her that "her husband would find her wherever she went ... [and that] he would have an alibi and a well thought out plan."

\* \* \*

Our review of claims of alleged error in evidentiary rulings is limited. The issue before us is whether the trial court's admission of this testimony was an abuse of its discretion.

The defendant initially claims that these out-of-court statements were hearsay. An out-of-court statement is hearsay, however, only if it is offered to prove the truth of the matter asserted in the statement. A statement that is offered to establish circumstantially the state of mind of the declarant is not offered for the truth of the statement. As the trial court correctly observed, because the state offered the evidence to establish only the victim's state of mind, the statements were not hearsay.

\* \* \*

In the present case, similarly, the victim's state of mind became relevant when the defendant questioned whether the victim was in fact dead, or was merely missing or in hiding. Although not overtly adopted as a "theory of defense" at trial and although disavowed on appeal, the defendant's assertion that he was not guilty because the "victim" had voluntarily left the country or had otherwise disappeared without leaving a trace appears repeatedly in the trial record.

Additionally, the defendant at trial challenged not only the state's assertion that the human fragments in evidence at trial proved that a person had died, but also its claim that the human fragments were those of an identifiable victim, his wife. This evidence of the victim's state of mind, therefore, was probative of whether she was likely to leave. From this evidence the jury could have concluded that, despite the victim's concern for her safety, she intended to remain with her family.

* * *

> "The defendant claims that the testimony regarding the five statements by the victim referring to the defendant was unduly prejudicial because the jury may have focused on the alleged accusatory aspect of the statements ..."
> *State v. Crafts*

The defendant claims that the testimony regarding the five statements by the victim referring to the defendant was unduly prejudicial because the jury may have focused on the alleged accusatory aspect of the statements and, despite the court's curative instructions, may have impermissibly considered them as probative of the defendant's conduct rather than as evidentiary of the victim's state of mind.

We recognize the risk of prejudice in allowing surrogates to speak for the victim "pointing back from the grave." We conclude, nonetheless, that the defendant has not established that the trial court, which carefully evaluated the statements, noted the absence of any direct accusations of the defendant and determined that in this case the statements were not unduly prejudicial, abused its discretion by admitting them into evidence.

The judgment is affirmed.

DISSENT:

Berdon, J., dissenting....

I would reverse on the ground that the trial court abused its discretion by admitting into evidence the hearsay statements of the alleged victim, Helle Crafts. Helle Crafts' lawyer and friends were permitted to testify, over the defendant's objection, that Helle had stated that if anything happened to her they should not believe it was an accident and that the defendant would have a well planned alibi. The majority justifies the admission of these statements on the ground that they were not offered to prove the truth of the matter asserted, but merely to show Helle Crafts' state of mind. But how is her state of mind relevant in this case? The majority concludes that her state of mind is relevant to disprove the "theory" of the defendant's defense—that is, Helle Crafts is still alive.

To me, the victim's fear of the defendant, if relevant at all, would tend to support the opposite conclusion—that she ran off out of fear. The logic of the state's argument, that Helle's fear and apprehension show that she would not have left voluntarily—eludes me. How could one logically conclude that, because she feared the defendant and was apprehensive about him, she was dead. In *State v. Duntz*, dealing with the precise issue of whether the deceased's hearsay statements of fear may be admitted into evidence, we held the admission of such evidence to be reversible error. "The victim's alleged fear of the defendant was not relevant, and therefore ... the testimony was not admissible under the state of mind exception to the hearsay rule. Evidence is relevant only if it has some tendency 'to establish the existence of a material fact.'"

\* \* \*

Furthermore, the claim that Helle Crafts was still alive was not the "theory of defense" in the defendant's second trial. The defendant did not testify at the second trial; rather, the state introduced the defendant's testimony from the first trial, thereby raising this issue. Similarly, defense counsel did not argue this theory to the jury in closing argument. The majority merely passes this off by stating that although it was "not overtly adopted," it was in the record. It was in the record, but only because the state put it there.

\* \* \*

To admit into evidence these hearsay statements, which tend to prove the crime for which the defendant was charged, violates the defendant's constitutional rights "to be confronted by the witnesses against him" and to due process of law.

# Circumstantial Evidence in the *Grant* Case

The vast majority of the evidence in the *Grant* case was circumstantial evidence. Although several eyewitnesses gave statements about a man they saw running in the Temple Street garage, and the garage attendant also made a statement about the man who handed him a bloody ticket when exiting the garage on the day of the murder, the accounts differed a good deal. Two of the eyewitnesses had been smoking marijuana, and one of them picked out Phil DeLieto from a lineup as the man he saw. DeLieto was cleared from the investigation and the prosecution admitted at trial that the eyewitness was wrong. These statements were all circumstantial, as no one saw the murder occur. However, they could be used by the jury to infer that Grant had been present in the garage at the time of the murder.

The two major pieces of forensic evidence were both circumstantial. The fingerprint on the tissue box, identified as belonging to Grant, proved only that Grant had touched the tissue box sometime before the crime was committed. In order to use this "fact" to convict Grant, the jury needed to draw the following inferences:

- Grant was present at some point in Serra's car;
- Grant reached for and touched the tissue box at some point when he was in the car;
- Grant subsequently touched the same part of the tissue box and smeared his blood on it;
- Grant then placed the tissue box on the floor behind the driver's seat of Serra's car;
- Grant had a reason for picking up the box, presumably to get a tissue or tissues;
- Grant used the tissue or tissues and then removed them from Serra's car and took them with him when he left the garage;
- Grant was bleeding as a result of a fight with Serra, presumably as a result of a cut with the same knife that was used to kill Serra, which was never found;
- Grant used the knife to kill Serra in the stairwell of the garage.

## The Handkerchief

The second piece of forensic evidence was the handkerchief, which Lee concluded in 1989 was not connected with the crime.[16] He later revised his opinion when he had learned that a DNA test of genetic material on the handkerchief had identified Grant. In order to conclude that the DNA test proved Grant murdered Serra, the jury would have to make the following circumstantial conclusions:

- The handkerchief belonged to Grant.
- The blood spot on the handkerchief that identified Grant was placed on the handkerchief in the garage at the time of the murder.
- The blood spot resulted from a fight between Grant and Serra in which Grant was cut with a knife that he used in the murder
- Grant dropped the handkerchief on the 7th floor of the garage after driving Serra's car around looking for his own car, leaving her car on level 8, proceeding on foot until he found his car on level 7, and then throwing out both Serra's car keys and his own handkerchief before fleeing.
- One blood spot on the handkerchief survived 23 years of being moved around for testing and being subjected to heat and other conditions likely to degrade the DNA.
- The presence of Grant's bloodstained handkerchief in the garage proved that he was in a fight with Serra that resulted in his bleeding on the handkerchief at the time of the crime, and therefore he murdered Serra.

The jury doubtless did not move step-by-step through this logic. Absent any strong alternative explanations, they concluded that the forensic evidence put Grant at the crime scene and so Grant committed the crime. The defense argued that Grant may have touched the tissue box at the Pathmark before it was purchased. They also argued that it was incredible that one blood spot on the handkerchief could survive degradation over time. The jury was apparently not impressed with either argument.

# Jury Instruction on Circumstantial Evidence

In the case of *State v. Grant*, the court told the jury how to consider circumstantial evidence:

> You may consider both direct and circumstantial evidence. Direct evidence is testimony by a witness about what that witness personally saw or heard or did. Circumstantial evidence is evidence involving inferences reasonably and logically drawn from proven facts.[17]

By contrast, the instruction given on circumstantial evidence in the trial of Sam Sheppard, convicted in 1955 for the murder of his wife, under Ohio law was as follows:

> It is for you to determine how much of circumstantial evidence adduced in this case is credible and what fair inferences are to be drawn from it. You are in-

---

16. Transcript, May 9, 2002 at 36.
17. Transcript, May 22, 2002 at 134.

structed that any inference drawn must in every instance be drawn from a proven or established fact. In other words, you are not to draw a second or further inference upon an inference but that is not to say that you are confined to drawing only one inference from one fact.

There is no limit to the number of independent inferences that may be drawn from a fact. The rule is simply that every inference must be drawn from, and based on, a fact and that once having drawn an inference one may not draw a second inference from the first.

It is necessary that you keep in mind, and you are so instructed, that where circumstantial evidence is adduced it, together with all other evidence, must convince you on the issue involved beyond a reasonable doubt and that where circumstantial evidence alone is relied upon in the proof of any element essential to a finding of guilt such evidence, together with any and all other evidence in the case, and with all the facts and circumstances of the case as found by you must be such as to convince you beyond a reasonable doubt and be consistent only with the theory of guilt and inconsistent with any theory of innocence. If evidence is equally consistent with the theory of innocence as it is with the theory of guilt it is to be resolved in favor of the theory of innocence.[18]

The jury in the *Sheppard* case was told that they were not permitted to draw one inference based on another inference. Yet, as you can see from the list of inferences presented above for the *Crafts* case, the jury needed to make multiple inferences from certain facts in order to conclude that Crafts murdered his wife.

# Summary

Forensic evidence is any evidence based on science, technique, or expert evaluation entered into evidence at trial. It frequently requires an expert to explain the evidence to the jury. The expert's "opinion" is valuable to the party who presents the expert because it often links the evidence to an issue the jury must decide. The danger that the jury will be unduly impressed by the expert is called the "white coat" effect.

Most forensic evidence is circumstantial evidence. It may tend to prove a fact from which the jury will need to infer or conclude another fact in order to reach a decision about guilt or innocence. The jury must find all "elements" of a crime by a standard of beyond a reasonable doubt. This standard is more than a *preponderance of the evidence,* but it does not require 100% certainty.

The jury must find guilt beyond a reasonable doubt, but this does not mean the jury must find each circumstantial "fact" to be true beyond a reasonable doubt. In the Crafts case, these elements were whether Crafts was the perpetrator, whether he intended the act, and whether that act resulted in Helle's death. In *State v. Crafts*, the Connecticut Supreme Court held that the jury can find individual facts based on circumstantial evidence by a standard of a "preponderance of the evidence." It rejected Crafts' argument that each circumstantial inference must be proved by a standard of beyond a reasonable doubt.

---

18. *Ohio v. Sheppard*, 165 Ohio St. 293, 300–301, 135 N.E. 2d 340, 345–346 (Ohio 1956).

# Discussion Questions

1. What does the term "forensic" mean? Before you began this course, what did you think it meant?

2. Why does forensic evidence generally require an expert at trial to introduce and explain it?

3. What is the white coat effect? Do you believe juries today are influenced by it?

4. What does it mean for the jury to be a finder of fact?

5. What is the difference between circumstantial and direct evidence?

6. What is the standard of proof the court used in the *Crafts* case for the proof of issues based on multiple inferences from circumstantial evidence?

7. What is the difference between *beyond a reasonable doubt* and *a preponderance of the evidence*? Which standard was used in which of the cases involving O.J. Simpson and why?

8. Why do the rules of evidence prohibit hearsay evidence? What exception was used to admit statements made by Helle Crafts? Do you believe the court decided Crafts' objection to this testimony rightly or wrongly? Why?

# Chapter 3

# From Collecting Forensic Evidence to the Trial

## Overview

Locard's principle says that every person who comes in contact with an object or person will make a cross transfer of evidence that will identify him. This principle is why crime scene investigators examine a crime scene in detail. Forensic evidence must be collected carefully and follow all laws in order to be admitted in trial. The process requires investigators to carefully document all evidence and to remain objective.

One of their objectives is to link forensic evidence to suspects. Forensic evidence may demonstrate either class characteristics or individual characteristics. Class characteristics are those that will "include" the suspect, such as the same shoeprint, but individual characteristics are those that can conclusively identify a suspect, such as DNA. Both investigators and juries need to be aware of the difference.

Chain of custody requires that evidence be properly controlled and accounted for in order to be admissible at trial.

The nature of the forensic expert's opinion will differ, depending on the type of evidence. For forensic evidence that proves only a class characteristic, the expert can say only that it "includes" the defendant. Fingerprint analysts can say a fingerprint identifies a defendant to the exclusion of all others. DNA experts frequently give an opinion in terms of probabilities, for example, that the profile is "consistent' with the defendant and the chances of someone else having the same sample is 1 in 300 million.

Counsel must carefully select and prepare the forensic expert in order to persuade a jury that the expert's opinion is correct. Some believe that the criminal justice system favors the prosecution in the area of expert testimony, as states have forensic laboratories and technicians to test and testify, whereas defendants must hire expensive experts to evaluate or contest the state's evidence.

The amount of evidence and many other factors will determine whether the defendant testifies at trial.

Both the prosecution and the defense must have a "theory of the case" that they expect to prove. Often, the full theory of the case will not be apparent until the close of evidence, when each side will summarize the testimony and what they want the jury to conclude. The defendant has the right not to testify and he does not need to present any alternative view of the facts. He can simply force the state to try to prove his guilt beyond a reasonable doubt. This, however, leaves the jury with only one "story," which can sometimes be dangerous for the defendant.

# Chapter Objectives

Based on this chapter, students will be able to:

1.  Define Locard's "Exchange Principle" and how it affects the processing of crime scenes.
2.  Explain basic steps involved in securing and investigating a crime scene.
3.  Describe why investigators should get a warrant to search a crime scene.
4.  Distinguish the difference between class and individual characteristics in evidence.
5.  Explain the importance of maintaining a chain of custody.
6.  Describe the challenges in the *Grant* case to chain of custody.
7.  Evaluate the importance at trial of the expert's opinion, and identify differences in expert opinions based on the type of forensic evidence involved.
8.  Tell how to find and prepare an expert witness.
9.  Understand how parties to a case develop and prove their "theory of the case."

# How Forensic Evidence Is Processed

Forensic evidence cannot be admitted in court unless the court is assured that it is genuine. It must also be introduced through the testimony of a witness who can personally identify it or who is in charge of a record-keeping process and can explain how the evidence was handled and safeguarded. Generally, this means that someone with custody or control over the evidence must show that the evidence was collected properly and that the "chain of custody" remains unbroken. Otherwise, the evidence could have been tampered with, replaced, destroyed or substituted. From the moment the forensic evidence is removed from the scene until it is presented in court, it must be accounted for. Generally, this requires that anyone who removes or handles the evidence must sign the evidence log with the time and date the evidence was removed and replaced.

## Who Handles Forensic Evidence?

Forensic evidence is generally collected from the crime scene by investigators working for law enforcement. Therefore, it is critical that the original crime scene investigators do their job properly. Although the actors on CSI make investigating look simple and dramatic, it is not. The actors often wade into a crime scene before it has been blocked off and secured. They almost never get a warrant before searching. They pick up and hand around pieces of evidence. And then they go back to the lab and process the evidence themselves—all in one hour!

Forensic processing involves two important groups of people. The crime scene investigators on the scene are typically local police officers or members of a major crime unit of law enforcement officers who are trained to collect evidence and investigate crimes. In Connecticut, for example, the state maintains four major crime units that respond to all crimes involving police officers and any other crime scene if asked for help by local law enforcement. A number of the larger cities maintain their own crime scene units, but smaller towns do not. In the event that local law enforcement arrives on the scene and contaminates it in any way, this may impede the ability of the crime scene unit to process the scene. This was one of the claims made in the murder investigation of Jon-Benet Ramsey, which today is a cold case. This case is discussed in the chapter on handwriting.

The second group is composed of laboratory technicians. These technicians typically do not travel to crime scenes to gather evidence, but instead test evidence in the laboratory. Some technicians began as law enforcement officers. Christopher Grice, for example, the fingerprint expert who identified Grant's fingerprint and testified to the match at trial, began as a detective in New Haven and is now a fingerprint expert at the Connecticut State Forensics Laboratory. Today, many forensic laboratories hire only graduates of forensic training programs, or individuals with degrees in the hard sciences.

## Crime Scene Processing

Whether conducted by local law enforcement or a highly specialized team of forensic scientists, the objectives of crime scene investigation are to recognize, preserve, collect, safeguard, interpret and reconstruct all relevant physical evidence at a crime scene.[1]

> The purpose of crime scene investigation is to: Recognize, preserve, collect, safeguard, interpret and reconstruct all relevant physical evidence.

## Locard's Exchange Principle

This principle states that whenever two objects come into contact, there will be a mutual exchange of matter. This means that the suspect will leave something of himself at the crime scene and will take something of the scene away with him. Of course, these items may be microscopic, but the investigator's job is to find them. The investigator seeks to link the victim and the crime scene to a suspect and/or objects identified with the suspect.

> Locard's Exchange Principle. At every crime scene, a person who comes in contact with an object or person will make a cross transfer of evidence to and from the scene.

## On-Site Investigation

The steps in on-site crime scene investigation must be done in order:

1. Ensure that the victim is not present or in need of help.

---

1. James and Nordby, *supra* at 169.

2.  Ensure that the scene is safe and no suspects are present.

3.  Block off the scene.

4.  Detain all witnesses. Establish a security log to document all people who come in and out.

5.  Observe and take notes.

6.  Determine if the scene is the primary or a secondary crime scene.

7.  Photograph the scene; videotape the scene.

8.  Draw a sketch of the scene and add to notes.

9.  Collect evidence, bag it and seal it for transport to the lab.

When the crime scene is on private property, detectives should obtain a warrant rather than relying on the consent of the owner for the search. Consent can be revoked. A warrant ensures legal validity of the search. Although police can search legally without a warrant in emergencies or to prevent the immediate loss or destruction of evidence, the Supreme Court has reversed some convictions based on searches that took place without a warrant. In one such case, an undercover policeman entered the defendant's apartment during a drug raid and was killed. Police thereafter searched the apartment without a warrant over the next four days, and found bullets, drugs and other items entered in evidence at trial against the defendant. The court reversed the conviction, stating:

> Search Warrant. A search warrant is issued by a court based on a finding of probable cause, and ensures that a search of a scene is legal and the evidence can be introduced against the defendant.

There was no indication that evidence would be lost, destroyed or removed during the time required to obtain a search warrant. Indeed, the police guard at the apartment minimized that possibility. And there is no suggestion that a search warrant could not easily and conveniently have been obtained. We decline to hold that the seriousness of the offense under investigation itself creates exigent circumstances of the kind that under the Fourth Amendment justify a warrantless search.[2]

> The crime sketch puts the pieces of evidence into visual perspective.

A sketch of the crime scene is essential to the process. The sketch indicates the scale of the crime scene, so that photographs then relate to their actual location and size. Photographs of small items are taken with a ruled scale in the photograph to indicate actual size. You can see an example on the tissue box exhibit in Chapter 1. Videotape is an important tool because it can capture three dimensional views that otherwise cannot be seen later.

Investigators will review the scene to determine if it is the primary crime scene or a secondary crime scene. The primary scene is where the crime took place, whereas a secondary scene may be where evidence has been moved, or where a victim may have been taken. For example, if a murder victim is placed in an unnatural position, investigators will look for the original site of the murder. If there is no evidence of bloodstain or blood spatter, investigators may conclude the victim was murdered elsewhere.

---

2. *Mincey v. Arizona*, 437 U.S. 385, 394 (1978).

Evidence such as blood-stained items must be bagged in paper rather than plastic. Plastic will cause wet items to decay and bacteria to grow. Wrapping paper, manila envelopes or paper bags allow the items to breathe. However, charred debris from a suspected arson must be stored in an airtight container to avoid evaporation of a possible accelerant. Each item must be packaged separately to avoid contamination, breakage, evaporation, scratching or bending.

Investigators search the entire scene systematically. They may use a grid approach, dividing the scene into small squares and searching each one. Other patterns include the link, line or strip, zone, wheel or ray, and spiral.[3] Investigators mark, but do not touch, items until they are documented. Here are the types of information that can be learned from the crime scene:

- Information about the victim, placement of the body, whether the body was moved after death, the apparent cause of death, based on physical appearance, and time of death, based on morbidity and lividity.[4]

- Information about possible modus operandi of the crime can be obtained by checking method of entry, whether cash or valuables appear missing, any damage to the scene, etc.

- Linkage of people and objects to the scene.

- Credibility of initial witness statements.

- Identification of possible suspects.

- Identification of unknown substances, such as fluids, drugs, and fingerprints.

- Reconstruction of the crime can be determined by examining blood spatter patterns, possible weapons and other details.

The investigator will generally write a formal police report, sometimes with the aid of or at the request of local law enforcement.

## Laboratory Testing

After the evidence has been collected, it goes to the crime laboratory for testing. The lab will need control samples for some of its testing. This is not necessary for gun shot residue or evidence of drugs. However, fingerprints cannot be matched without "rolled" prints taken from suspects; likewise DNA cannot be matched without a DNA sample from the suspect. The same holds true for examination of hair or fiber.

Laboratory testing can be time-consuming. DNA testing may take from three weeks to longer. The process is laborious and expensive.

Blood spatter analysis is incredibly tedious, in particular if investigators attempt to reconstruct the trajectory of the blood. It may involve stringing multiple strings from the spatter marks back to a common point of origin. Trace evidence, such as hair and fiber, is difficult to collect, and each hair or fiber must be separated onto different slides for microscopic examination.

---

3. James and Nordby, *supra* at 177.
4. Morbidity is the extent of rigor mortis; lividity is the coloring caused by pooling of blood post mortem.

Fingerprints, particularly latent prints, which are not visible, must be lifted, transferred, preserved and then either visually compared to hard copy fingerprint cards or scanned into a computer for comparison with an AFIS database. If the technician is sure what finger he or she is looking for, this shortens the time the database must search. A full ten finger search can take up to an hour before a written report of possible matches prints out.[5] In addition, fingerprint identification must generally wait behind a long line of prints waiting to be evaluated.

# Determining Class versus Individual Characteristics in Evidence

> Individual characteristics are those characteristics of evidence which can belong only to the suspect and therefore will conclusively identify him.

Some forensic evidence can identify a suspect because of its individual characteristics. An example is DNA. If a DNA sample from the site matches a DNA sample taken from a suspect, even defense lawyers will typically admit that the crime scene sample came from the defendant. In the *Grant* case, the defense did not contest that the blood drop on the handkerchief contained Grant's DNA. A fingerprint match is also conclusive, as no two people have the same fingerprint. If the print lifted from the crime scene is of sufficient size and quality, most people would agree that it identifies the suspect.

> Class Characteristic. Characteristics of a piece of evidence that can be associated with a group, but not with a specific individual.

Other forensic evidence, however, can do no more than "include" the suspect in a class of people who share that type of evidence. This is called a "class characteristic." Hair is an example. Even if a hair from the crime scene under magnification looks exactly like the suspect's, there is no scientific basis for concluding that the hair from the crime scene actually came from the defendant, unless the hair is tested for DNA. In other words, 30% of the population may have the exact same color and quality of hair. In the *Crafts* case, the hair found on the hillside where witnesses saw the wood chipper looked under a microscope to be identical to a hair belonging to Helle Craft that had been found in her bedroom. However, science does not support the conclusion that each person's hair is unique. Therefore, the most an expert could say is that the hair from the site was "consistent" with the hair of Helle Crafts.

In the trial of Mark Reid for sexual assault and kidnapping, an expert testified that he compared a hair recovered from the victim's clothes to a sample from the defendant and found "that the characteristics of the known hairs from the defendant were similar to the characteristics of those recovered from the victim's clothing."[6] This was an opinion about a class characteristic. You will see in the chapter on DNA that Reid on appeal was able to show that the hair was not his, based on mitochondrial DNA testing.

---

5. Based on an interview with Christopher Grice, Connecticut Forensic laboratory, July 2005.

6. *State v. Reid*, 254 Conn. 540, 757 A.2d 482 (2000), *pet. for new trial granted*, CV020818851 2003 Conn. Super. LEXIS 1496 (Conn. Sup. 2003).

The same is true for shoeprints. The suspect may own a pair of shoes that creates an identical print to that found at the crime scene; however, so may 100,000 other people. In order to "identify" the defendant, the prosecution would have to prove that the defendant's shoes were one of a kind, or that some mark on them, such as a tack stuck in the sole in a particular location, made such a rare mark that it could only be defendant's.

This does not mean that footprint evidence is inadmissible. However, an expert cannot testify that it absolutely identifies the defendant.

### *United States v. Mahone*, 328 F. Supp. 2d 77 (D. Maine 2004)

While footwear impression evidence may appear to the Defendant a simple matching process not requiring any specialized skill, and Ms. Homer's testimony will "provide undeserved weight to a comparison which the jury as fact finder is equally qualified to make," it is apparent the process requires a critically trained eye to ensure accurate results.

The Defendant's contention that any lay person can perform the comparisons presumes any lay person will know what to look for and how to apply the information—the significant versus insignificant markings and the weight to ascribe each. In this way, the examiner functions like a radiologist, directing attention to the relevant aspects of the impression or medical image. That the conclusion is readily apparent after the professional explains the image more likely speaks to the effectiveness of the professional, not the simplicity of the science.

Further, even if the Court accepts the Defendant's contention that a lay person could arrive at the conclusion for herself, Ms. Homer's testimony is admissible under Rule 702 because it will undoubtedly assist the trier of fact in determining whether the impressions from the crime scene match those from the shoes.

# Chain of Custody

Forensic evidence cannot be introduced at trial by the attorney for either the prosecution or the defense. There must be a witness on the stand who can identify the evidence and assure the court that it is reliable. How do we know that the firearm introduced into evidence is in fact the firearm taken from the crime scene many weeks, months, or sometimes years ago? And even if the crime scene investigator were on the stand, what are the chances he or she could look at the firearm and absolutely identify it as the one found in connection with this particular crime?

The process of authenticating forensic evidence involves proving a formal "chain of custody," starting with the crime scene investigator and ending with the location where the evidence has been stored immediately before being introduced. This involves keeping the evidence in a sealed container of some type and requiring any person who removes it to sign, stating the dates and times of removal and replacement.

## The Chain of Custody in the *Grant* Case

The defense contended that various items of evidence should not be introduced into trial because some items had been lost, such as Serra's keys and the parking ticket, and because evidence had been moved from place to place and stored under improper conditions.

Here is the decision of the court on the Chain of Custody motion to exclude evidence:

**State v. Grant, 2002 Conn. Super. LEXIS 1127**

\* \* \*

The principal question presented by the motions now before the court is whether forensic DNA evidence obtained by a technique involving amplification of loci containing Short Tandem Repeats (the "STR" technique) is admissible. For the reasons set forth below, the answer to this question is in the affirmative.

### I. FINDINGS

The factual backdrop of these motions has been discussed in a number of prior decisions. On July 16, 1973, the body of Concetta ("Penney") Serra was found in a stairway of the Temple Street parking garage in New Haven. The medical examiner determined that she died as the result of a stab wound to the heart. No one was apprehended at the scene. There was, however, a substantial amount of blood at the scene, and some of this blood is thought to be that of the killer.

(Serra's blood was Type A; the blood thought to be that of the perpetrator is Type O.) Edward Grant, the defendant herein, was arrested for Serra's murder in 1999, largely on the basis of the State's allegation that the blood found at the scene is consistent with a DNA profile of Grant's blood.

\* \* \*

Grant, who is about to be tried, understandably wishes to exclude the DNA evidence that the State seeks to introduce. On January 4, 2002, he filed a motion to preclude evidence because of an assertedly insufficient chain of custody. On February 4, 2002, he filed a separate motion to preclude all evidence relating to STR testing. (No. 74.) The motions were the subject of evidentiary hearings held over the course of several days in January and February 2002.

Numerous witnesses testified at the chain of custody hearing. The sole witness at the STR hearing was Dr. Carll Ladd, the supervisor of the forensic biology unit of the State Forensic Science Laboratory ("Laboratory"). The motions were argued on April 5, 2002.

Although the chain of custody motion facially seeks exclusion of numerous items of evidence, Grant has narrowed its scope considerably in his post-hearing briefs. He presently seeks to exclude only

- "Item 6" (a handkerchief found at the crime scene) and
- "Item 12" (blood on tape lifts taken from inside an automobile

belonging to John Serra, also found at the crime scene).

The evidentiary importance of these items is primarily related to scientific testing that has been performed on them.

Grant has not complained, at least for purposes of these motions, of the scientific testing performed on "Item 12" (some of which has been actually favorable to him in that it has potentially implicated a third-party suspect). In this context, it is difficult to know what to make of his chain of custody attack on that item. Given the fact that the evidentiary importance of "Item 12" consists of the traces of blood that it preserves, the test is whether "there is a 'reasonable probability' that the substance has not been changed in important respects."

After a full consideration of all of the evidence surrounding "Item 12's" preservation and custody and the lack of any likelihood of tampering with that item by intermeddlers, the court determines that the State has met its burden of showing an appropriate chain of custody with respect to that item.

The State has met its burden of showing an appropriate chain of custody with respect to "Item 6" as well. The evidence shows appropriate preservation and custody of that item, and there is no possibility that intermeddlers somehow tampered with that item to contaminate it with material containing Grant's DNA.

The only real question with respect to "Item 6" is whether the handling of that item by a variety of testers over the years has compromised the DNA material remaining on that item to the point where the State's DNA testing can no longer be considered reliable. After a full consideration of all of the evidence, the court is convinced that the answer to this question is no. Grant's factual assertions involving contamination and degradation of the DNA material on "Item 6" go to the weight rather than the admissibility of the evidence....

> "there is no possibility that intermeddlers somehow tampered with that item to contaminate it with material containing Grant's DNA"
> *State v. Grant*

The court denied Grant's motions to preclude evidence.

# Linking the Forensic Evidence to Witness Statements

Many investigators develop ideas about possible theories of the crime after the initial crime scene has been processed. Even before laboratory work begins or is finished, they have located potential witnesses and begun to question them. All suspects should be treated initially as witnesses, even though investigators are often influenced by what they know about patterns of crimes. For example, they know most burglaries are committed by someone who knows the house—a workman, friend of a family member, or other regular guest. Most murders take place between people who know each other. Initial witness lists consist of such people. However, the investigator must always remain objective, and question witnesses with a view to ruling them out as a suspect, rather than to "solve the crime."

Investigators seek to tie the forensic evidence to a witness, who may become a suspect and ultimately a perpetrator. Crime scene officers are trained in questioning strategy. They also can frequently tell if a witness is hiding something. For example,[7] if an innocent person is accused of something he did not do, he will usually be angry at being falsely accused and will remain angry throughout an interview. A guilty person, by contrast, will initially act angry, because he thinks that is what he should do, but will even-

---

7. Interview with Trooper Peter Valentin, of the Connecticut 4th district Major Crime Unit, October 2006.

tually forget or be unable to continue the "act." This same theory is used by the polygrapher in dealing with witnesses who try to use "countermeasures" in an attempt to influence the results of the polygraph. Most witnesses cannot consistently apply their attempted countermeasure over time.

Some detectives ask each witness to recount every moment of the day. An innocent person can sometimes be excluded based on the written statement. Frequently, he will divide the day into equal parts—for example, before lunch, lunch until mid-afternoon, and so forth, whereas the guilty person will often skip over the timeframe when the crime occurred, resulting in an unnatural break in the timeline.[8]

# Types of Forensic Opinions

As discussed above, the prosecution hopes that the expert testimony will convince the jury of guilt; the defense hopes to either discredit the forensic evidence or limit its force by raising other possible "inferences" the jury can draw.

When the issue of forensic testimony is whether an evidence sample connects the crime site to the defendant, the expert will generally offer a different opinion, depending upon whether the linkage is a class characteristic or an individual characteristic. Even in situations where the forensic evidence indicates an individual is the source, the opinions may vary.

However, more important than his role in teaching the jury about the forensic evidence process is the expert's "opinion." In the area of criminal forensics, the language used for expert opinions varies depending upon the type of evidence, whether it is individual or only class evidence, and the strength of the examiner's opinion. Here are some examples:

### Hair examination:
- The hair I examined from the crime scene is consistent with that of the defendant.
- The hair I examined excludes the defendant as a contributor.

### Fingerprint examination:
- The latent fingerprint I examined identifies the defendant.
- The latent fingerprint I examined excludes the defendant.
- The results of my examination of the latent fingerprint were inconclusive.

### DNA testing:
- The DNA sample I tested is consistent with the DNA profile of the defendant. The chance of someone other than the defendant being the source of the DNA sample is 1 in 300 million.
- The DNA sample I tested identifies the defendant. [This opinion has recently been accepted by some courts.]
- The DNA sample I tested excludes the defendant.
- The DNA sample I tested was inconclusive. [Why? Because it was degraded, too small too test, contaminated, etc.]

---

8. *Id.*

**Handwriting:**

- The defendant is the author of the questioned document.

- I could not rule the defendant out as the author of the questioned document.

- The defendant is not the author of the questioned document.

The first opinion about hair involves a class characteristic. Just because the hair is consistent or similar to the defendant's does not mean that it came from the defendant. Class characteristics can absolutely exclude the defendant, but they cannot absolutely identify the defendant.

The remaining opinions—about fingerprints, DNA, and handwriting—are all opinions on types of evidence with individual characteristics. In other words, based on the scientific hypothesis that DNA, fingerprints, and handwriting are unique to each individual, an expert can compare the evidence to the defendant's sample and conclude that it definitely identifies the defendant.

A fingerprint expert, such as Chris Grice in the *Grant* trial, gave his opinion at trial that the "the person who made the latent impression … was Edward Grant."[9] A "conclusive" fingerprint match equals an opinion that the fingerprint identifies the defendant. However, a DNA expert generally does not testify that examination of a DNA sample left at the scene of a crime identifies a particular defendant. A DNA "match" does not mean conclusive identity. The expert will testify instead that the DNA sample is "consistent with" the defendant and that, for example, the "likelihood of a random individual having the same DNA profile is 1 in 300 million."[10]

So, why is it that fingerprint experts can identify a defendant and DNA experts cannot? The answer depends in part on history. Fingerprint opinions have been used in court since 1911, when the first opinion was given in *People v. Jennings*.[11] The court accepted the opinion based on the common knowledge that fingerprints are unique and permanent. At that time, no scientific study had corroborated this hypothesis.

In the case of DNA, by contrast, long term scientific studies preceded the use of DNA typing for courtroom identification. Once scientists had mapped the human genome, they knew there were approximately 2,000 locations on a human chromosome that could differ from person to person, but the purpose of the gene is unknown. These are called "junk DNA." The decision was made to focus on measuring about 15 junk DNA locations. Scientists first determined what proportion of the population had which variation of the gene at each location. Once a particular location was measured, the probability of that length occurring at that location, times the probability of the next length occurring at the next location, were multiplied, resulting in a statistic such as 1 in 4 trillion for a random match.[12] As a practical matter, this equates to absolute identification, but scientists have been reluctant to give this opinion.

Also, the fingerprint expert can generally see the entire fingerprint. He therefore can exclude based on any dissimilarity between two fingerprints that he can see. This

---

9. Transcript, May 17, 2002 at 154–5.

10. The statistical probability will vary depending upon the analysis of matching alleles, which will be discussed in a later chapter.

11. 252 Ill. 534, 96 N.E. 1077 (1911).

12. A random match is someone other than the suspect sharing the exact same DNA at those 15 locations.

assumes the examiner has a good quality print that is of adequate size. The DNA expert, by contrast, does not know what the markers at all of the other DNA locations might be.

Could the same scientific studies as were done with DNA be made for fingerprints? The National Institute of Justice issued a call for research proposals in March of 2000 for Forensic Friction Ridge (Fingerprint) Examination Validation Studies.[13] This was a call for scientific research that would prove the underlying hypotheses of using a small number of ridge characteristics to conclude identity.

If scientific studies were conducted to show the relative distribution of different fingerprint characteristics, it is possible to develop a statistical probability of another person having the same 20, 30, or 40 characteristics in the same location on his print as another person. This would allow a fingerprint examiner to give an opinion as to the likelihood of a random match. However, fingerprint examiners are not likely to agree to give a less certain opinion than they have given in the past:

> The judgment whether a match exists or not and whether the latent and the known share a common origin or not have not evolved beyond subjective appraisal. Finally, while the practical and realistic goal of fingerprint identification would be to make probability statements about the likelihood that a latent print which appears to match a suspect's rolled print actually came from someone *other than* the suspect (that is, the probability of a coincidental match), the fingerprinting field eschews probability statements as an "ethical" offense, and demands that its members offer only opinions of an absolute and certain nature or give no opinion.[14]

As DNA becomes more common in the courtroom, DNA experts have begun to testify to conclusive identification, rather than probability statistics. In 2006, one court recognized this:

> When the random match probability is sufficiently minuscule, the DNA profile may be deemed unique. In such circumstances, testimony of a match is admissible without accompanying contextual statistics. In place of the statistics, the expert may inform the jury of the meaning of the match by identifying the person whose profile matched the profile of the DNA evidence as the source of that evidence; i.e. the expert may testify that in the absence of identical twins, it can be concluded to a reasonable scientific certainty that the evidence sample and the defendant sample came from the same person.[15]

# Finding and Preparing the Expert Witness

As we will see later, for any expert to offer an opinion, he or she must be qualified by education, training or experience. This requires a satisfactory experience and education, adequate review of the forensic evidence and a scientific basis for the conclusion that meets the standards for "real science."

---

13. David L. Faigman, David H. Kaye, Michael J. Saks and Joseph Sanders, *Science in the Law, Forensic Science Issues*, West Group, 2002 at 62.

14. Faigman et al., *supra* at 63.

15. *People v. Johnson*, 139 Cal. App. 4th 1135, 1146 (Cal. App. 5th dist 2006).

The purpose of an expert witness is to educate the jury and help the jury understand evidence. A number of courts have refused to allow experts to testify if the area of testimony is "common knowledge" or where the jury can just as easily evaluate the evidence.

However, at least one court has cautioned that experts may have an important role in clarifying an area where jurors have some knowledge already.

*New York v. Legrand*, 747 NYS 2d 733, 741 (2002)

＊ ＊ ＊

The third requirement under the Frye test involves an inquiry into whether the proffered expert testimony is beyond the ken of the jury. "The guiding principle is that expert opinion is proper when it would help to clarify an issue calling for professional or technical knowledge, possessed by the expert and beyond the ken of the typical juror". As a result, expert testimony may be admissible "where the conclusions to be drawn from the facts 'depend upon professional or scientific knowledge or skill not within the range of ordinary training or intelligence'" of a jury.

Thus, the trial judge must determine "'when jurors are able to draw conclusions from the evidence based on their day-to-day experience, their common observation and their knowledge, and when they would be benefitted by the specialized knowledge of an expert witness.'" However, "even if the proposed testimony was not beyond the jury's ken, [the Court of Appeals] has repeatedly upheld the admission of expert testimony for the purpose of clarifying an area of which the jurors have a general awareness". Therefore, trial judges are to be wary "not to exclude such testimony merely because, to some degree, it invades the jury's province".

## Expert Qualifications

All forensic witnesses are not created equal. Obviously, a party wants to find an expert who is well-qualified in his or her field, someone who has published in scientific journals, and is an authority in an area of science. The expert should also be someone willing to review the evidence and become thoroughly familiar with the case. A big name may impress the jury, but an expert who is not prepared will alienate them more.

Scientists tend to speak a different language, so the attorney may have to spend time helping the expert to speak in terms the jury can understand. The jury in the O.J. Simpson case, for example, were annoyed that the DNA expert talked down to them as if they were children.[16] Scientists also tend to want to answer the question they think the examining attorney *should be* asking, not the one the attorney is actually asking. In other words, the scientist wants to educate everyone, including the opponent. Getting an expert to listen carefully to the question and not volunteer any information on cross examination can be extremely difficult.

Most experts are paid to prepare and to testify. Generally, the only experts who are not paid are those who work for the state. In the *Grant* trial, Chris Grice, the fingerprint expert, was not paid to testify, as he worked for the forensic lab. Dr. Henry Lee, by contrast, was an outside expert at that point and was paid. A good attorney will always ask

---

16. *Talk or Teach?*, American Lawyer Media, L.P., The Recorder, May 19, 1995.

his expert on direct examination if he is being paid and how much. This gets the issue right out in front of the jury and avoids embarrassment on cross examination. Does being paid create potential bias? Of course it does. But as the experts on both sides are generally both being paid, the bias tends to cancel itself out.

Experienced attorneys know that it helps to find an expert who has testified before and read the transcript of the earlier testimony. An expert can be severely discredited on cross examination if the opposing attorney can point to a prior inconsistent opinion. This is called "impeaching" a witness. Experts who become rattled or arrogant on cross examination are a poor choice, as even the expert who is absolutely right will not be believed by a jury if he is unlikeable. In the *Grant* case, the defense attorney referred in closing arguments to a joke that expert Henry Lee made during his testimony.[17] This prompted an unpleasant exchange between attorneys and the judge, alternately attacking and defending Lee. The expert should never become a personality rather than a source of expert testimony.

In criminal cases, the experts for the prosecution tend to be criminalists and forensic scientists who work for the state. The defendant generally must locate and pay for his own experts. Particularly for poor defendants, this can create an unfair system. There have been a number of appeals based on defendants arguing that inadequate resources were used to prepare for their defense. These appeals generally fail, unless the defendant can prove that his counsel's performance was so deficient that it prejudiced the defense. For example, the decision of an attorney not to pursue psychological testing for his client was not prejudicial because the appeals court held that there was overwhelming evidence of guilt and the defendant failed to show there was a reasonable probability that, but for the challenged errors, he would have been acquitted.[18]

Slowly, courts are coming to the realization that a defendant is prejudiced by the inability to obtain and independently test forensic evidence. For example, many states now provide that prisoners may petition for DNA evidence on a claim of actual innocence. If the defendant cannot pay for the testing, the state will do so.[19]

# Trial Strategy and Theory of the Case

Both the prosecution and the defense must develop a "theory of the case" that will make sense to the jury. The prosecution must present sufficient evidence to convince the jury that the defendant is guilty "beyond a reasonable doubt." As the trial judge instructed the *Grant* jury "this is not beyond *any* doubt, but a reasonable doubt." The prosecution in a murder case does not need to show motive. Although the prosecution does not need to prove motive, it is one fact that the jury can consider in deciding guilt beyond a reasonable doubt. There was no evidence of motive presented in the *Grant* trial, although the prosecution brought up the idea in his closing argument that maybe Grant wanted to steal Serra's car. This did not make too much sense, as its theory of the case was that Grant abandoned Serra's car and drove off in his own. This theory was not

17. Transcript, May 22, 2002 at 105.
18. *Link v. Luebbers*, 469 F.3d 1197 (8th Cir. 2006).
19. See, e.g., Conn Gen. Stat. §54-102kk (2006).

supported by any trial testimony, and Grant's attorney moved for a mistrial based on the comment, which was denied, and then appealed on this ground as well.

## Should the Defendant Testify?

Grant did not take the stand, as is every defendant's Constitutional right. The decision not to put a defendant on the stand is a difficult one, because even though the jury is instructed that the defendant has this right and they must draw no inference (conclusion) from this fact, on some level, any juror is going to think that the defendant did not take the stand because he had something to hide.

Sometimes the defendant has a prior criminal record that his counsel fears will be admitted. Sometimes the defendant simply is not a very likeable person and his counsel fears the jury may decide he is guilty simply because he is cold or unpersuasive.

The defense may need to put the defendant on the stand in the following situations:

- The defendant has an alibi that only he can prove.
- The defendant has a defense, such as self defense.
- The defendant has an explanation for some fact introduced by the prosecution (for example, how did the victim's blood get on his clothes?).

Most defense counsel will decide that if there is nothing to be gained by having the defendant testify, it is better not to expose the defendant to cross examination or to other witnesses who might question his veracity, or ability to tell the truth. This was a problem in the Richard Crafts case, in which Crafts' defense was that his wife had left and moved abroad. This "opened the door" to testimony about statements that Helle Crafts had made to the effect that if she disappeared, Crafts would have murdered her. This testimony was damning to him.

In the *Grant* case, the defense chose not to put Grant on the stand. The defense was essentially that the prosecution had the wrong man—Grant was not involved in the murder. They attempted to show that there was reasonable doubt about much of the state's evidence. For example, the defense argued that the following created reasonable doubt:

1. The police first thought the murderer was two different men, both of whom had a connection with Serra.
2. There was no evidence of motive.
3. An eyewitness identified the wrong man.
4. Dr. Lee originally said the handkerchief was not connected to the crime.
5. No weapon was recovered.
6. The fingerprint on the tissue box was beneath the blood and could have been deposited before the crime.

## Missing Evidence

The *Grant* team was unsuccessful is dismissing the case because of the missing keys and parking ticket. Clearly, if two pieces of evidence had been lost, they could potentially have exonerated Grant or at least pointed to another possible defendant. Unfortunately, the Connecticut Forensics Laboratory is one of the finest in the nation. Claims of deliberate destruction or planting of evidence fell flat in face of the obviously dedicated and professional members of the laboratory who testified at trial.

## No Experts for the Defense

The Grant defense did not call any expert witnesses. They cross examined Christopher Grice, who said that the fingerprint he identified as Grant's from the tissue box could have been placed on the box prior to the time of the crime. They also cross examined Carll Ladd, the DNA expert, on various technical issues about the DNA alleles from the handkerchief. He also agreed that he could not say when the genetic material was placed on the handkerchief.

Finally, the defense cross examined Dr. Lee in an effort to discredit him by showing that in 1989, he had concluded that the handkerchief was not a part of the crime scene. Dr. Lee succeeded in stating both that he changed his mind once he knew that Grant's DNA was on the handkerchief *and* that he made his decision about the handkerchief being connected to the crime without resort to anything other than the crime scene itself.[20]

Therefore, the jury did not need to decide which of two opposing experts to believe.

## Prosecution's Theory of the Case

The major evidence in the prosecution's case was the DNA evidence on this handkerchief and the fingerprint on the tissue box. These two pieces of forensic evidence tied Grant to the crime scene. With two such damning pieces of evidence, the prosecution did not have to explain various inconsistencies in the case to gain a conviction. However, as both pieces of evidence were circumstantial, the prosecution explained to the jury in its closing argument what inferences the jury could draw from those pieces of evidence. Here are portions of the Closing Argument, with those inferences highlighted:

* * *

[L]ook at what happened between 12:37, when the killer entered the garage, and 1:01, when he handed the bloody ticket across his body to Christopher Fagan and drove out. And some of that, what happen in that period of time, you're never going to know. Some things only Penney Serra knew and the killer knows.

So, while it would be extremely interesting to know everything that happened in that garage on July 16, 1973, it's unlikely that you will. But if it's not part of those three elements, we don't have to prove it.

And I submit that the evidence you have is sufficient for you to make your determination without knowing everything that happened in that garage. And any suggestions that you do know what happened, for instance, between the time that the parking ticket was checked in at the entrance, where you all stood the other day, and the car was seen in approximately that location by Mr. Petzold and Mr. Woodstock, is pure speculation.

---

20. Transcript, May 9, 2002 at 36.

You know the car got—you know Penney Serra's car got up there, **you know by inference that the defendant's—I'm sorry, that the killer's car got to level eight, seven somewhere, where he eventually gets into it from the blood trail**, but you don't know anything in-between there and you don't have to. But to suggest that you do know what is in-between, unless it's a reasonable inference from evidence that is in this case, is pure speculation and not permitted; and that's part of the reasonable doubt instruction and something you all knew in *voir dire*. Speculation is not appropriate and not something that you could do or draw conclusions from.

> Voir dire is the process of examining potential jurors to uncover bias, conflicts, or any other reason why they should not serve.

We know that the blue Buick stops there and that Mr. Woodstock, who is a car guy, says that it was pulled over as if someone slammed on the brakes and cut the wheel. And you know that it was not parked in a parking space, but in the travel lane. And it's been placed there kind of between the two spots that are drawn on the model by the two witnesses. You know that from the direction of that car.

**And I think here you could infer coming out that the killer is chasing Penney Serra, he lunges after her.** Mr. Woodstock's statement, which you have in evidence, says, it looked liked he grabbed her hair. And you know that her wig, her fall is on the ground in approximately that location when it's picked up by Arthur Acker, whose testimony you have, but who is not alive to come and talk to you personally.

You could imagine that she is terrified at this point, probably real scared when she is starting to run, terrified now because he almost has got her. And Mr. Woodstock said she screamed. She runs up the stairs and around the corner and **we don't know the mechanics of how this happened, but we know that he catches her and stabs her to death and she gets a defensive wound on her right hand. It's shown in other photographs, but you could also see it right there.**

And Dr. Lee described to you his reconstruction of what occurred after she is stabbed. She is crawling up the stairs where she dies and then rolls to this position when she can no longer support herself. And then a short time later, I think there were various estimates, and you could check what they are or remember what they are, a minute or less, back comes the killer. **And Mr. Petzold and Mr. Woodstock see him again coming back towards the car carrying something shiny in his hand, and they don't conclude what that is, but it's pretty clear that you could infer what that shiny thing in his hand about six inches long is.**

And you also know something else, that although Penney Sera is lying there dying, she gave this killer something in return, whether it was up on that floor or whether it was while they were still near the car, we don't know exactly, there are some things from which you could infer that I'll talk about later, but she left him with a cut. And I think that you will find from the evidence the cut—the evidence shows that the cut was left handed because all the blood essentially is on the left side of the car and everywhere else it is. He is bleeding. Her type is A, her type of blood is found only on her own clothing, nowhere else at the scene; and there is O type blood all over this garage.

We don't know exactly how it happened and we don't know exactly what the murder weapon is and we don't have to prove that. **But you do know that there** was a knife in her car from a week earlier, that that knife was never returned to the Hurleys. In fact, you have an exhibit which is an exact copy from the same set of that same knife. Is that the weapon she was killed with? You will probably never know, but we don't have to prove that. **And certainly it's an inference that you could draw, that that is not only the knife that killed her, but the knife that injured him.**

He comes back to the car, and this you do know, the car is seen by Jane Merold driving here. Jane Merold is coming down the stairs; Gary Hyrb is standing next to her when this car goes by and going really fast. And what does Jane Merold see? A car going by really fast. She can't see the driver; she is on the passenger's side. And she sees the car come up here and that's when she stops seeing it. When she goes into Malley's, you don't know what happens after that, but you know that the car eventually ends up down here; that's the next thing you know about that car from this evidence.

Can you draw some inferences about how these ramps work, and how it all goes down the center to get out, and this car is angled that way? **Can you draw inference that he came down the ramp and turned the wrong way and realized that it was going up next and maybe he'd better get out of that car and not go by the people that he already saw above?** We don't know whether he saw these people, but he knows that he looked directly into Woodstock's eyes. Whatever the reason, he abandons it; it's not parked very well.

Again, that's the stairway where Jane Merold is standing. And this is where you see the car parked like that in that location.

You could imagine how panicked he is now. He is hurting, he knows he has killed somebody or at least—he knows he killed somebody. You know when you are panicked, when you are panicked, when you are excited, when you are scared, your heart beats fast. On a hot day, which is what this was described as, you are sweating. You know there are various items in this car that have blood on them. You know it's all O type blood. **Does he grab the tissue box when the car is back there or when the car is here? I don't know, but you know he grabs it.**

And Henry Lee shows you a logical common sense and reconstruction expert's opinion as to how that box was picked up by this killer and how the print got on it and how the blood stains on it are consistent with the way that it was picked up and put on that. He can't pick it up from under the car so it was probably turned the other way to get these fingerprints on it. But these fingerprints, he told you, were from below and the blood on the top here and here and here comes from a regrab, that's completely consistent with where that fingerprint is. Even though the blood hadn't flowed down to the finger tip onto the thumb yet, we know that it was on here.

But if the cut isn't right there on the thumb, the blood can come essentially simultaneously thereafter, within seconds, within half a second, or within six weeks. But what makes sense, and what did Henry Lee tell you was his best opinion as to what happened was yes, the blood came after the fingerprint, but it came right then. He also leaves blood on this tissue, O type blood. He also leaves blood here … This is from the photographs that you have. And I think you would agree that that looks like the largest single quantity of blood in any one location.

**And you know that when he leaves the garage that he is bleeding because he is handing this over, and you know that his left hand is the most likely one to have been damaged because the left hand — all the blood is on the left-hand side and he doesn't use his left hand when he leaves passing Mr. Fagan.** Was he just hanging it down there? Is that why there is more blood on this location than, say, this one tiny little spot here? It's common sense. It makes sense. **You could draw the inference if you think that it makes sense, that's your job.**

So, he leaves the car here, he gets out of the car, and you know that he leaves a blood trail that starts at the door where there is plenty of blood and you have other photographs of blood on the door handles.

And he follows that route that you all walked the other day, behind the car, down the stairs, down the ramp, and now he is a level below this on six, walks down to the stairs on six, goes down yet another side — another level. **He is lost. The inference is that he is wandering around the garage because he can't remember where his car is, possibly because it's kind of a confusing place,** therefore, causing him to go the wrong way. Does it matter where he is wandering around? No, not for those elements. But you could, again, draw reasonable inferences that that is what he was doing, he is lost.

He eventually comes back up the stairway, he comes across to here. The keys, two places marked here, but you got pictures, you could figure out exactly where they were in that parking space, and everybody agrees on which parking space it was. You could figure out exactly where the handkerchief was on this parking space. **And by counting spaces at the time, the blood trail ends within a few feet of where that handkerchief is and within six to eight feet of where those keys are.** By memory, it's one space further on, but in either case, it passes by both those bloody items, both of which have O blood on them. And there they are.

You have testimony from both of the people who seized the evidence that those are the car keys and that's the handkerchief. There are four different photographs of these things. And any suggestion that they weren't important, I think you could find, you will find is belied by four photographs. Keys and handkerchief, the lines are there. You could place them both in your memory from when you were there and on this model, which you know is a scale model.

**And Dr. Lee told you that the reason that there are all these blood drops together in one place where the blood trail ends is that the guy is getting into his own car and he is driving away.**

And one of the interesting things you may find is that here are the car keys down here. When he has abandoned this car, he doesn't need them. He doesn't need those car keys, but it's a reflection of some people, and you may find it's a reflection of you, you get out of the car and take the car keys. When he gets to his car, he realizes they are in his hand and drops them and drops the other thing in his hand too, which is the handkerchief he is carrying with blood on it, with O blood on it.

Now, one thing you don't have any direct evidence of in this case is the motive for this crime. And one of the things that the Judge is going to tell you is that is not an element. You know, you might not like it. You might even find that the lack of motive is something that is really important to you. You might find that it raised reasonable doubt. But you've got to look at the issue of motive, was there a lack of motive completely in this case? Was there a motive that you could infer? And even if there isn't, the Judge will tell you that if you find the case proved otherwise beyond a reasonable doubt, then that's okay because it isn't an element of the crime.

**But you know this about motive; you know that that killer had some reason to kill Penney Serra. You may not ever know what the motive was. But he stabbed her in the heart, most likely after she cut him, and you know that or you could conclude that from the evidence** because you got blood on the left-hand side coming down here, and you have those two blood spots on the back of her dress completely consistent with a lunge to grab her, the location of where her fall would have been because there are two O blood spots, that's the only non-A blood on her dress. And the cuttings are there, they are the only holes in the back of that dress and they are right there where your hand would be if you grabbed for that wig and contacted the dress. Whether it was at the car or as he stabbed her, it's not an element of the crime. You could make your own decisions. Like many of the other things that you can't know the details, that you can't know motive may be one of them.

But you know this, that every important piece of evidence in this case points to Edward Grant as being at the scene and it points to no one else.[21]

## Defense Theory of the Case

Grant's defense was that the prosecution had the wrong man. His attorneys presented evidence to show that Grant had no ties to New Haven and that he was not a violent man. In essence, Grant had no theory of the case except that someone else murdered Serra. His defense relied upon the concept of "reasonable doubt." Unfortunately, this gave the jury only one "story" to consider.

The defense had no alibi, which is understandable given that the crime was twenty-five years old. Primarily, however, the defense relied on attempts to discredit the prosecution's case.

The eyewitness testimony was contradictory. Grant did not have a scar, which would be expected given such a quantity of blood at the crime scene. The timeframe of the crime—eight minutes—indicated that the murderer probably knew Serra. The state presented no motive for the killing. In essence, the jury would have to conclude that Grant was a sociopath or a homicidal maniac, which did not fit the picture of the 76-year old defendant before them.

But working against Grant were two powerful forces. The first factor was the fact that this was a "cold case." The jury knew that the crime had happened in 1973. Now over twenty-five years later, science identifies a murderer. The photos of a young girl covered in blood curled up in a concrete stairwell were chilling. In fact, one juror later stated that seeing the little blue dress covered in blood was a turning point for her in deciding that Grant was guilty. In its summation, here is how the defense tried to defuse the cold case idea:

Cold cases, we hear about those on the television and we read about those in newspapers all the time. And when we hear about those things, we think of

---

21. Transcript, May 22, 2002 at 19–30.

these cases that are sometimes years or decades old where new discoveries in science are used to answer questions that couldn't be answered before those discoveries came into existence. But in those cases, the new discoveries in science are to supplement, to add on to other evidence that has already been there, connections between people, people that knew each other. Identifications, motive, the new technologies could be used to supplement, to add on to that, but that is not the case here.

* * *

I mean, you look at those photographs of Penney Serra with her father and her sister. And you have heard her sister testify, there is no way to categorize that. There is no way to sort of label that other than an absolute tragedy. A tragedy that has gone on for years. It's not the kind of thing that ends. It's the kind of thing her father had to live with and it's the kind of thing that her sister lives with to this day. And we talked about that during jury selection, that that can raise feelings of sympathy or feelings of empathy, and it's perfectly appropriate. And I don't know how many of us in this room watching that didn't feel that. But that is not what you're here to decide.

You are here to decide whether or not the State's evidence convinces you beyond any reasonable doubt that it was Grant that killed Penney Serra.

Another factor comes in when you are talking about a case that is as old as this, 30 years old, almost 30 years old, I guess 29 this summer, and that's an issue of closure. The issue of, it would be wonderful to be able to kind of put this to rest, to kind of put this behind everyone, allow Rosemary Serra to put it behind, to have the mystery finally solved. But we talked about this also; **your job here is not to solve this 30 year old homicide, not to solve this case that law enforcement and scientists have been working on for years. Your job isn't to solve the mystery.**

Your job is to assess the evidence and decide whether or not you are convinced beyond any reasonable doubt that Edward Grant, not anybody else, but Edward Grant is the one on July 16th who caused Penney Serra's death.[22]

The second powerful factor against Grant was the forensic evidence. Although the defense successfully showed that neither the fingerprint nor the genetic material on the handkerchief could be "dated" to connect to the time of the crime, the combination of two pieces of undisputed forensic evidence was overwhelming. The defense did not contend that the fingerprint was not Grant's or that the handkerchief did not contain his DNA. The defense argued that the handkerchief was not properly stored. It argued that the fingerprint was beneath the blood, not above it, supported by the testimony of Dr. Lee, the state's expert. But the defense could not convince the jury that somehow two unrelated items—a tissue box and a handkerchief—both connected to the defendant, were coincidences.

At the end of its closing argument, the defense summarized the state's "theory of the case" in an attempt to convince the jury that Grant did not kill Serra: "There are more holes in this, the State's case, than there are holes in the handkerchief."

In order for you to believe that Grant did this, here is what you have to believe: That Grant, a married man with two children three years old and 18 months old, living in the city of Waterbury, goes to work in the City of Waterbury at a family business, that he has to drive, he drives his vehicle to work every day, an

---

22. Transcript, May 22, 2002 at 34–35.

orange or gold colored Jeep Wagoneer, goes to work in his work clothes every day, dark blue pants, light blue shirt with the logo on it.

You have to believe that at some point in time he drives to a city that he usually doesn't work in and he drives in a vehicle that he doesn't drive, a blue car with an MR license plate on it. And at some point he has to change his clothes and then get into some kind of a Polo shirt and dress shoes, and at some point he has to pick out the Temple Street garage for some unknown reason to arrive there, and then he has to meet a complete stranger virtually.

And then at some point Grant has to chase her for some unknown reason and kill her for some unknown reason. And then he has to get back into her car and he has to put on his Phil DeLieto mask because that's how he is described after that. And then he has to park that car, get back into this foreign car, assume a foreign accent, real remarkable for someone who has received this substantial wound on his left arm, side, hand or wrist and drive off. And in the meantime, look like he is a dark-skinned Hispanic male.

That's what has to happen. And he has to go back to Waterbury. After 26 years, nothing comes up. He raises his kids. You heard he was at the Christening for his grandchildren in December of 2000 or 1999. Every time he is approached by the police, he is at work. The last time when he was arrested, he is working on a car in the driveway of his house. That's the set of facts that have to happen for him to be the killer in this case. It's totally preposterous.[23]

# Summary

Forensic evidence must be collected carefully and follow all laws in order to be admitted in trial. The process required investigators to carefully document all evidence and to remain objective. One of their objectives is to link forensic evidence to suspects. Forensic evidence may demonstrate either class characteristics or individual characteristics. The nature of the forensic expert's opinion will differ, depending on the type of evidence. Counsel must carefully select and prepare the forensic expert in order to persuade a jury that the expert's opinion is correct.

The evidence also will help determine the prosecution and defense theory of the case. The prosecution must prove the three elements of murder beyond a reasonable doubt. Although the defendant can choose not to testify, there are risks that the jury may conclude he has something to hide. In the *Grant* case, as the defense did not present an alternate theory about how Serra might have been killed, the prosecution had an advantage in linking together the circumstantial evidence in the case to build its theory.

# Discussion Questions

1. Why is it important to secure the crime scene and to collect evidence as quickly as possible?

---

23. *Id.* at 85–86.

2. Name the steps to investigating a crime scene. Why is it important to do the steps in the order given? What would happen if the investigators left out or varied one of the steps?

3. How does what the crime scene investigator does or does not do affect the admissibility of evidence at trial?

4. Watch an episode of CSI and explain anything you saw the actors do that a real crime scene investigator would not do.

5. Why is a sketch of the scene better than photographs or video alone?

6. What procedures ensure that the prosecution can establish a "chain of custody" of forensic evidence at trial?

7. Why did Grant lose his chain of custody challenge? Do you agree?

8. What is the difference between evidence that contains class versus individual characteristics? Give an example of each.

9. What would an expert need to say in order to convince a jury that a shoeprint left at a crime scene positively identified a suspect?

10. What are the ways that an expert witness can show his qualifications to testify?

11. What kinds of evidence are within the jurors' common knowledge so that an expert is not required?

12. Do you think an expert is required to help a jury understand comparisons of hair, shoeprints, lip prints, fibers, all of which the jury can see?

13. Find the following website: truthsleuth.com. What does this tell you about how investigators use witness statements?

14. What is the difference between the expert's "testimony" and the expert's "opinion?"

15. What are some types of opinions an expert can give regarding fingerprint evidence?

16. What is the difference between a primary crime scene and a secondary crime scene? How does this apply to the Grant case?

17. How can an expert satisfy the burden of proving his or her qualifications?

# Chapter 4

# The Rules of Evidence

## Overview

Forensic evidence cannot be admitted in front of a jury unless all applicable rules of evidence are met. These rules are contained in the Federal Rules of Evidence for cases in federal court and in similar laws adopted by each state for trials held in those states. We will discuss the Federal Rules of Evidence, as they apply in federal courts in all states. These require that:

- the evidence be relevant to an issue in the trial,

- it not be unduly prejudicial to the defendant,

- a proper chain of custody be established for the evidence,

- the expert be qualified by knowledge, skill, experience, training, or education, and the expert disclose the facts or data upon which he relied in giving his opinion.

Most crimes have a required set of legal issues that must be proved and that appear in the state or federal laws. The judge will give the jury instructions on how to apply the law to the facts. In Connecticut, for example, the three elements of murder are legal tests to which the jury must apply the facts. "Intent" requires the specific intent that the defendant intended to cause the death of the victim. Motive is not an element of the crime. A finding of motive may help establish guilt beyond a reasonable doubt, but it is not required.

The rules of evidence are designed to safeguard trials against unreliable or prejudicial evidence. Evidence must be relevant to the legal issue. If prejudice results to the defendant from introducing the evidence, the court may exclude the evidence. Evidence of prior crimes or bad acts of a defendant is generally not admissible to show that because the defendant already did one bad thing, he probably did the one charged at trial.

The rules of evidence contain separate rules for admitting testimony by experts. These rules govern forensic testimony and provide that testimony by a qualified expert is admissible if it will assist the jury to understand the evidence or determine a fact in issue.

Judicial notice means that a trial court may accept a fact as having been proved without either party putting on evidence. The reliability of the science of DNA has been the subject of judicial notice. The jury may still refuse to accept a fact that is judicially noticed.

# Chapter Objectives

Based on this chapter, students will be able to:

1. Explain the difference between state and federal courts.
2. Describe the difference between trial and appellate courts.
3. Understand the concept of double jeopardy.
4. Identify the legal elements of the crime of murder in the *Grant* case.
5. Understand the concept of relevance in Federal Rules of Evidence 401 and 402.
6. Describe Federal Rule of Evidence 403 and the balancing test used to keep prejudicial evidence out of the courtroom.
7. Evaluate the federal rules relating to evidence of prior crimes or bad acts in terms of possible prejudice to a defendant.
8. Identify the federal rules relating to qualification and admission of expert testimony.
9. Explain the concept of judicial notice and how it applies to forensic evidence.
10. Describe how the court analyzed whether to take judicial notice of DNA testing in the case of *Crawford v. Virginia.*

# Admission of Evidence Depends on Rules of Evidence

To answer what types of forensic evidence a jury may hear, we must evaluate two inter-connected issues:

- the rules that govern admission of evidence in court, and
- the role the court plays in "pre-qualifying" experts before they testify before a jury.

## State and Federal Courts Have Different Rules

The country has a dual system of courts: each state has its own court system and the federal government also has an entirely separate court system. Crimes that violate state law are heard in state trial courts. Crimes that violate federal law are heard in federal courts. Both sets of trial courts have written rules of evidence that govern what types of evidence are admissible. The defendant has a right to a trial before a jury. But the defendant may waive that right, and have his or her case tried by a judge without a jury.

The first question to ask when determining whether certain evidence will be admissible is whether the matter is being heard in state or federal court, although many of the

## State and Federal System of Trial and Appellate Courts
### Example: State of Connecticut
### Criminal Trials

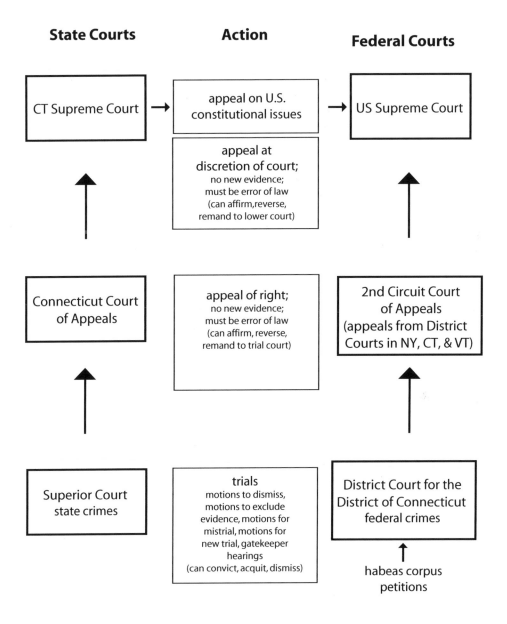

**State Courts**  **Action**  **Federal Courts**

CT Supreme Court → appeal on U.S. constitutional issues → US Supreme Court

appeal at discretion of court; no new evidence; must be error of law (can affirm, reverse, remand to lower court)

Connecticut Court of Appeals

appeal of right; no new evidence; must be error of law (can affirm, reverse, remand to trial court)

2nd Circuit Court of Appeals (appeals from District Courts in NY, CT, & VT)

Superior Court state crimes

trials
motions to dismiss, motions to exclude evidence, motions for mistrial, motions for new trial, gatekeeper hearings (can convict, acquit, dismiss)

District Court for the District of Connecticut federal crimes

habeas corpus petitions

rules are similar. Let's assume that a prosecution takes place in Connecticut state court, as did the *Grant* case. The prosecution goes first. It must introduce evidence to prove all of the elements of the alleged crime and establish the defendant's guilt beyond a reasonable doubt. The defendant does not need to present a defense, testify, or otherwise refute the prosecution's case. He is not required to offer an alibi or an alternate theory of how the crime occurred.

# The Role of the Courts in Admitting Forensic Evidence

The courts affect the admission of forensic evidence at two levels: the trial court and the appellate courts.

## Trial Courts

The trial court is where the jury hears evidence, finds facts, and decides ultimate questions, such as whether a defendant is liable for a plaintiff's injuries in a civil trial or whether defendant is guilty in a criminal trial. In the federal system, the trial court is called a "District Court." In Connecticut, the trial court is called the District of Connecticut. The state trial court in Connecticut is called the Superior Court. Trial courts do not publish opinions of the jury's verdict: this is generally a one-line statement. Sometimes juries are asked a series of questions by the court, which they answer. This is also generally not published.

Trial courts frequently decide "motions" during the course of a trial, and they may write opinions or they may rule "from the bench." These motions ask the trial court to take some action based on the law. One example is a motion to exclude evidence on the theory that it was obtained without a warrant. In Chapter 1, we reviewed a number of the motions made by Grant's attorneys during his trial. When forensic experts are involved, if an opposing party challenges the introduction of expert testimony on a scientific issue, the courts are required to hold a hearing outside the presence of the jury before the trial begins to determine whether the subject of the expert's testimony is reliable and is good science. Frequently, these rulings are accompanied by an opinion. If the court rules against the moving party, he can appeal the issue.

## Appellate Courts

> Actions an Appellate Court may take: affirm, reverse, reverse and remand for further action.

In the federal system, the first level appellate court is called a Circuit Court. In Connecticut, it is called the Second Circuit Court of Appeals, which hears appeals from District Courts in New York and Vermont as well as Connecticut. In the Connecticut state court system, it is called the Connecticut Court of Appeals. If the appellate court disagrees with a ruling or action of the trial court, it can reverse and remand the case. In the example above, the case would go back to the trial court with instructions that it must hold a new trial and exclude the piece of evidence. If the appellate court agrees with the ruling or action of the trial court, it will "affirm" the judgement.

The losing party can then petition for a second appeal to the highest level appellate court. This is the U.S. Supreme Court or the Connecticut Supreme Court, depending on federal or state system. However, this appeal is discretionary with the final appellate court. It can take the appeal if it wishes, but it is not required to do so. For example, at

the federal court level, there were 54,697 appeals filed in the year 2000 at the Circuit Court level. The Circuit Courts were required to dispose of all of them. There were 5,633 petitions for appeal to the U.S. Supreme Court, called petitions for a *writ of certiorari,* of which the Supreme Court granted only 99,[1]
less than 2% of those filed.

At the appellate court level, the court does not hear any new evidence or take any testimony. It is "bound" by the record of proceedings in the trial court. A defendant cannot appeal simply because he does not like the jury's verdict. Therefore, if the jury rejects the conclusion of a forensic expert, this is not a ground for appeal. Appeals must present a "question of law" to the appellate court.

> Question of Law. An appealing party (appellant) can appeal only an error in applying the law made by the trial court. This is called a question of law.

In the example above, say the prosecutor wanted to introduce a weapon the police found in the defendant's home, which they searched without a warrant. The appellate court cannot decide that the police did not search the home without a warrant [a fact] but it can decide that the search was unconstitutional [a question of law.]

## The Effect of a Not Guilty Verdict

If the jury acquits a defendant, this means the defendant has been found "not guilty." It does not mean that the defendant is "innocent." A not guilty verdict is not the same as a finding of innocence. This is why the family of Sam Sheppard sued to have a determination of actual innocence after his conviction was reversed based on pretrial publicity. [*See* Chapter 13.] A finding of innocence was required in order for them to sue the state for unlawful imprisonment. Also, a defendant cannot use a verdict of "not guilty" to prove his innocence in a later civil trial, as the standards of proof are different.

## More than One Trial Can Result from the Same Set of Facts

As discussed earlier, in the *Simpson* case, Simpson was acquitted of murder. The families of Nicole Brown and Ron Goldman later sued Simpson in civil court to recover damages for the "wrongful death" of the victims and won. Simpson was found liable in that case. A defendant can be both convicted of a crime and then sued in civil court for damages based on the same acts.

A defendant can also be convicted of both state and federal crimes resulting from the same set of facts. Mayor Philip Giordano of Waterbury, Connecticut, was being investigated by wiretap for corruption when federal officials discovered that his phone conversations included making arrangements with a woman to have sex with her young nieces. He was convicted in federal court of depriving the two children of their due process liberty right to be free from sexual abuse and of conspiracy to use a facility of interstate commerce for the purpose of enticing a person under the age of sixteen to engage in sex.[2] Following sentencing, he was then tried by the State of Connecticut for sexual as-

---

1. Frank A. Schubert, *Introduction to Law and the Legal System,* 8th ed., Houghton Mifflin, at 152.
2. *United States v. Giordano,* 172 Fed. Appx. 340 (2d Cir. 2006).

sault in the first degree, risk of injury to a minor and conspiracy to commit sexual assault.[3] Giordano was convicted of the second crime as well.

## Double Jeopardy

> Double Jeopardy. The defendant may not be tried twice for the same crime.

Why wasn't the second *Giordano* case "double jeopardy?" Double jeopardy prohibits being tried again for the same crime if the defendant is found not guilty. There is never a double jeopardy issue with a later civil trial in a case, just as the *Simpson* case, because the second trial was not a trial for a "crime." Also, the standard of proof in a civil trial is different. Instead of beyond a reasonable doubt, the jury needs to find by a preponderance of the evidence that the defendant committed the act, in this case homicide. A preponderance of the evidence is anything over 50%.

In the *Giordano* cases, the defendant was tried for two different crimes, so the second criminal trial is not double jeopardy. A defendant can also be re-tried for the same crime if his first case results in a mistrial, or if the appellate court reverses his conviction due to an error at the trial court level. In the *Grant* appeal, Grant is asking the Connecticut Court of Appeals to reverse his conviction and grant a new trial for a number of legal errors, including his claim that the warrant for his blood lacked probable cause. If he were to win this issue, the appellate court would reverse his conviction and order a new trial to be held without including the blood evidence. In such a case, an appellate court will sometimes order that the state must retry the defendant promptly or release him.

## The Legal "Elements" of the Crime of Murder

> Jury Instructions. Instructions given by the trial judge to the jury after all evidence and testimony has concluded that tells the jury what legal rules to use in its deliberation.

The legal "elements" to a crime are found in the statute books of laws enacted by the state or federal legislature. These elements contain words such as "intent," which have specific legal meanings. The jury will hear the evidence and determine certain facts. The judge will explain to the jury in the "jury instructions" how to use those facts to apply to the legal elements, such as intent.

As noted above, in the *Grant* case, the jury was instructed that it had to find three facts to convict Grant of murder:

1. the defendant was the perpetrator;
2. the defendant intended to cause the death of another [Serra]; and
3. that with the intent to cause the death of [Serra], the defendant caused her death.

These three facts comprise the "elements" of the crime of murder in Connecticut.

---

3. *State v. Giordano*, CR403319736, 2004 Conn. Super. LEXIS 1538 (2004).

# Intent

The word "intent" does not mean that the defendant hated the victim or even that the defendant wanted the victim to die. It means only that the defendant acted in such a way that the jury could infer that he intended the act to cause the death of the victim. But how can a

> Intent. The jury must find that the defendant intended to cause the death of the victim.

jury find intent when Grant did not testify and no one saw the crime? Basically, the jury can conclude the defendant intended to commit murder if the jury finds that the defendant purposefully committed the act that caused the death.

However, at least one court has cautioned that a jury must *not* conclude intent merely from the result that the victim has died from a homicide:

> An instruction on intent that, instead of focusing on inferences to be drawn from the defendant's conduct permits inferences to be drawn from the *result of that conduct* is problematic because intent cannot be inferred directly from results. The fact that a victim was struck by a bullet would not, in itself, support the inference that the perpetrator intended to kill the victim, because the perpetrator might have acted with a variety of mental states. In this case, similarly, the jury could not properly have inferred an intent to commit murder from the mere fact of the death of the victim, even from her death at the hands of the defendant.[4]

Murder is a "specific intent" crime. Under the Connecticut statute, for example, the intent required is the "intent to cause the death of another person."[5] One court addressed a claim of error in the following jury instruction on intent:

> Intentional conduct is purposeful conduct rather than conduct which is accidental or inadvertent. As defined by our statute, a person acts intentionally with respect to a result or to conduct when his conscious objective is to cause such result or to engage in such conduct. Now, what a person's purpose, intention or knowledge has been is usually a matter to be determined by inference.

> No person is able to come into court and testify that he looked into another's mind and saw therein a certain intent, a certain purpose or intention to do harm to another or a certain knowledge regarding conduct of a particular circumstance. The only way in which the jury can ordinarily determine what a person's purpose or intention or knowledge was at any given time, aside from the person's own statements or testimony, is by determining what a person's conduct was and what the circumstances were surrounding that conduct and from that infer what his purpose or intention or knowledge was ... Intent to kill someone or inflict physical injury or to do any act can be formed instantaneously or it can be formed over time.[6]

The defendant had objected to the instruction because it included the concept of "general intent" along with the intent required for murder, which is intent to cause the death of another person. The court held that the instruction was not in error because it included the specific intent language within the broader instruction.[7]

---

4. *Crafts*, 225 Conn. at 248.
5. Conn. Gen. Stat. § 53a-54a.
6. *State v. Brown*, 97 Conn. App. 837, 849 (2006).
7. *Id.*

## Motive

The prosecution does not need to show motive. The jury is instructed that if it finds the defendant had a motive, it may use that fact in determining guilt beyond a reasonable doubt. But the jury is not required to find motive in order to convict. [*See* Jury Instructions, Chapter 14.]

# Safeguards against "Unfair" Evidence

The rules of evidence require that admissible evidence must be relevant and not unduly prejudicial to the defendant. Obviously, all evidence which the prosecution offers is prejudicial to the accused in that it tends to show that the defendant committed the crime alleged. But "unduly" prejudicial means that certain evidence may tend to inflame the jury more than it tends to prove an element of the crime.

The prosecution and the defendant exchange witness lists and proposed conclusions of the witnesses before trial. If a party objects to the introduction of certain evidence, that objection is made to the judge before the trial begins or if during trial, outside the hearing of the jury. The trial judge rules on such "motions to exclude." If a party disagrees with the ruling, that party may later appeal on that issue.

In the next several paragraphs, we will review the Federal Rules of Evidence. Each state has its own rules of evidence, although many state rules are similar to the federal rules. We will look at the federal rules because they apply in the federal courts in every state.

### Relevance. To be admissible, evidence must first be relevant.

### Federal Rule 401. Definition of "Relevant Evidence."

Relevant evidence means evidence having any tendency to make the existence of any fact that is of consequence to the determination of the action more probable or less probable than it would be without the evidence.

### Federal Rule 402. Relevant Evidence Generally Admissible; Irrelevant Evidence Inadmissible.

All relevant evidence is admissible, except as otherwise provided by the Constitution of the United States, by Act of Congress, by these rules, or by other rules prescribed by the Supreme Court pursuant to statutory authority. Evidence which is not relevant is not admissible.

The test for relevance is fairly broad. "Any tendency" to prove a fact gives wide discretion to the party offering the testimony and to the judge deciding its admissibility. In the *Grant* case, evidence of what kind of car Grant drove was relevant, because Christopher Fagan described the car as a dark blue or brown GM or Chrysler. However, where Grant bought his car or how he financed it is irrelevant. Those facts cannot possibly help a jury decide whether Grant's car was at the scene of the crime.

Although courts sometimes state that evidence must be "relevant, probative, and material," the words are very closely related and the Federal Rules do not use the terms "probative" and "material." "Probative" means tending to prove or disprove an issue. "Material" means evidence that has more than a minor relationship to an issue in dispute. The definition of "Relevant" in the Federal Rules incorporates these concepts. It requires that the evidence have a tendency to make the existence of any fact that is of consequence to the determination of the action more probable or less probable than it would be without the evidence. The phrase "any fact that is of consequence" includes the concept of "material." The phrase "more probable or less probable" includes the concept of "probative."

### Federal Rule 403. Exclusion of Relevant Evidence on Grounds of Prejudice, Confusion, or Waste of Time.

Although relevant, evidence may be excluded if its probative value is substantially outweighed by the danger of unfair prejudice, confusion of the issues, or misleading the jury, or by considerations of undue delay, waste of time, or needless presentation of cumulative evidence.

Rule 403 is designed to balance the jury's need for all relevant evidence with the defendant's fear that the jury may be unduly swayed against the defendant by certain evidence. For example, Grant was arrested because a routine submission of an unmatched fingerprint from the tissue box into an Automated Fingerprint Identification System [AFIS] by the Connecticut Forensic Laboratory turned up a match to a fingerprint of Grant's that had been entered into the database as a result of an earlier domestic dispute. If the jury heard that Grant had been involved in a domestic dispute, what would it conclude? Would it think that a defendant who was involved in a domestic dispute would be more likely to have been a murderer? One juror stated after the trial that once she knew this fact, it convinced her that her verdict had been right.[8] So this was a very significant piece of evidence, but it was excluded because it was also prejudicial.

Some experts argue that giving the trial judge the right to exclude certain expert testimony from the jury deprives the jury of its right to be a "finder of fact." This argument was made in a recent polygraph case, which we will review in detail in that chapter. Certainly, jurors are rightly upset when they learn of evidence that they did not hear in court. The jurors in the *Simpson* case made this very clear:

> Like everyone else, I've heard a lot of things that we didn't get to hear during sequestration.... What I hate is that a lot of that information I did not receive I think would have been important information to me. I'm not saying that the same reasonable doubt issues may not have come up, but I think I would have weighed them a little bit differently.... [Amanda Cooley]

> The ten thousand dollars, the passport, the fake beard, the fibers from the Bronco, Nicole's words from her diary, all those things I believe should have been presented to the jury ... I have a problem with the judicial system presenting itself—presenting the truth, the whole truth, and nothing but the truth. The whole truth was not an issue. And to put those people in that posi-

---

8. *See* Chapter 15.

tion to say make a decision based on the evidence and only giving them a part of the evidence was very unfair to the jury. [Jeanette Harris][9]

## Is DNA Testimony Prejudicial?

In 1997, a defendant appealed his conviction for murder based on the admission of DNA testing. The expert, Vick, testified that the chances of someone other than the defendant matching the bands from the swab on three probes was 1 in 500,000. The defendant claimed the testimony should be excluded because it was prejudicial:

### State v. Fleming, 1997 Me. 158, 698 A.2d 503 (1997)

Vick's testimony regarding the significance of the DNA match produced by RFLP testing was relevant. Once the jury heard testimony that Fleming's known sample matched the tested portion of the crime scene DNA, it was necessary for the jury to know the degree to which such a match suggested Fleming produced the semen found at the scene. The statistical data admitted reflected the rarity of finding two people who shared the same genetic patterns at several sites on their DNA strands. The evidence on the subject was relevant, therefore, to a determination of Fleming's guilt.

\* \* \*

The process has been reviewed, debated, and discussed in scholarly articles (both formal peer review and otherwise). There is no definitive proof that statistical results derived by applying genetic principles to DNA database figures have a known or potential risk of error. Finally, it appears that the relevant scientific community has generally accepted the application of the product rule in calculating the statistical component of DNA match evidence

Having determined that the statistical portion of the DNA profiling evidence was both relevant and reliable, we must also consider whether the evidence is inadmissible because its probative value was substantially outweighed by the danger of unfair prejudice. As we have stated, "prejudice, in this context, means more than simply damage to the opponent's case. A party's case is always damaged by evidence that the facts are contrary to his contention; but that cannot be ground for exclusion. What is meant here is an undue tendency to move the tribunal to decide on an improper basis ..."

\* \* \*

| Prejudice. "What is meant here is an undue tendency to move the tribunal to decide on an improper basis ..." *State v. Fleming* | Although the DNA statistics could be considered prejudicial, they are not unfairly so, and in no event did unfair prejudice substantially outweigh the probative value of this evidence. The DNA statistical evidence was relevant and reliable, and the court committed no error in admitting the evidence against Fleming. |

---

9. Amanda Cooley, Carrie Bess, and Marsha Rubin-Jackson, *Madam Foreman—A Rush to Judgment?* Dove Books, 1995, at 196–7.

# Evidence of Prior Crimes Is Generally Not Admissible

Evidence of prior crimes or "bad acts" is generally not admissible to prove that a person is more likely to have acted in the same way. For example, evidence that a defendant committed a prior burglary is generally not admissible to show that it is likely he committed the burglary charged in the current trial.

### Rule 404 (b). Other Crimes, Wrongs, or Acts.

> Evidence of other crimes, wrongs, or acts is not admissible to prove the character of a person in order to show action in conformity therewith.
>
> It may, however, be admissible for other purposes, such as proof of motive, opportunity, intent, preparation, plan, knowledge, identity, or absence of mistake or accident, provided that upon request of the accused, the prosecution in a criminal case shall provide reasonable notice in advance of trial, or during trial if the court excuses pretrial notice on good cause shown, of the general nature of any such evidence it intends to introduce at trial.

All of the exceptions to Rule 404(b) in the second paragraph above indicate the balancing of relevance with prejudice. If the prosecution can find an exception and the evidence comes in, the jury will be instructed that it can use the evidence only for the purpose in the exception. As you can imagine, however, most people cannot follow such an instruction. This is human nature, and no amount of cautionary instructions can "unring a bell that has rung."

In the same case we examined above, in which David Fleming was convicted of rape and murder based in part on DNA testing, Fleming also appealed based on evidence introduced of prior DNA testing of his blood. He argued that the jury would assume the prior testing involved an earlier crime and that this was prejudicial to him as evidence of a prior "bad act." The court rejected this claim:

> Fleming contends that testimony relating to prior DNA testing of his blood was improperly admitted as evidence of a prior bad act. Although he did not object to the admission of this evidence, he argues that, by its admission, the jurors were forced to conclude that he had raped or murdered another person. When the defense fails to object or otherwise preserve an error, we review for obvious error affecting substantial rights. Obvious error is error that is so highly prejudicial and so taints the proceedings as to virtually deprive the defendant of a fair trial.

> At the trial Fleming vigorously cross-examined all the expert witnesses on their labelling of the evidentiary samples. At a sidebar conference that occurred during the cross examination of Vick, the State warned defense counsel that he was opening the door for the State to dispel any confusion about the mislabelling of the samples. After Fleming's counsel replied, "well, go ahead and do it," the court told the State that it was entitled to clear up opposing counsel's "improper spin" on redirect.

> During the ensuing redirect examination of Vick, the State elicited testimony that a sample of Fleming's blood had been submitted to him "earlier on a prior occasion," that he had already run the sample through the DNA testing proce-

dure, and that he would be able to lay the test results produced on that occasion over the test results produced in this case to establish that there was no inconsistency between Fleming's known sample and the other samples he had received. Defendant offered no objection.

The State then requested a sidebar conference and obtained the court's permission to have Vick compare the test results. The State then asked Vick to compare one of Fleming's test results in this case with a comparable test result obtained on a "separate occasion," and he subsequently testified that the band patterns lined up perfectly. The State then offered the other test result into evidence without objection.

The jury only heard testimony that Vick had obtained Fleming's whole blood sample on a "separate occasion." Fleming's contention that the jury was then forced to conclude that he had raped or murdered another person is without merit. There was no evidence that a whole blood sample is only obtained by the FBI in rape and murder cases. The jury was free to conclude that the FBI obtained two whole blood samples from Fleming solely as a result of this case. Contrary to Fleming's assertion, the court did not commit obvious error.[10]

Some would argue that the prior domestic dispute is not relevant to whether Grant killed Serra, who as far as anyone knows he had never met. Others would argue that the domestic incident shows that Grant is violent toward woman and therefore would be more likely to commit a crime of violence against a woman. But regardless of whether the evidence is relevant, it is clearly prejudicial. This shows that the court must balance the desire of the prosecution to present all relevant evidence with the desire of the defendant to receive a fair trial free of undue prejudice.

There is always *some* prejudice in every trial. For example, even though Grant had a Constitutional right not to testify and the judge so directed the jury, many jurors conclude that a defendant does not take the stand because he is hiding something.

# Evidence Rules and Expert Forensic Testimony

Three additional Federal Rules of Evidence affect the admissibility of forensic evidence. They are Rules 702, 703 and 705. Rule 702 says:

### Rule 702. Testimony by Experts.

If scientific, technical, or other specialized knowledge will assist the trier of fact to understand the evidence or to determine a fact in issue, a witness qualified as an expert by knowledge, skill, experience, training, or education, may testify thereto in the form of an opinion or otherwise.

As we will see, Federal Rule of Evidence 702 was the subject of an important United States Supreme Court case, *Daubert v. Merrell Dow*, in 1993. In this case, the U.S. Supreme Court required that the trial court hold a hearing before trial and outside the

10. *Id.* at 508–9.

presence of the jury to determine if expert forensic testimony was valid "science." The case listed criteria the trial court should use in making that decision. It also decided that Rule 702 superseded an earlier federal court case that set down a different rule for accepting expert testimony. This case is discussed in detail in chapter 5.

In order for an expert to testify, he must disclose the facts or data upon which he relies:

### Rule 703. Bases of Opinion Testimony by Experts.

> The facts or data in the particular case upon which an expert bases an opinion or inference may be those perceived by or made known to the expert at or before the hearing. If of a type reasonably relied upon by experts in the particular field in forming opinions or inferences upon the subject, the facts or data need not be admissible in evidence.

### Rule 705. Disclosure of Facts or Data Underlying Expert Opinions.

> The expert may testify in terms of opinion or inference and give reasons therefore without first testifying to the underlying facts or data, unless the court requires otherwise. The expert may in any event be required to disclose the underlying facts or data on cross-examination.

There is no federal rule that requires that experts have any specific training or experience in order to testify. However, the attorney offering the expert will ask about the expert's qualifications in the presence of the jury, and would be foolish to offer a witness without qualifications, because opposing counsel would destroy the expert's credibility on cross examination. Experts frequently rely on textbooks or other "learned articles" in their area of expertise. Where the expert has not done any independent research but relies only on the expertise of others, some courts have held the expert is not qualified. Generally, the expert must establish independent knowledge in the area of testimony. The expert generally must also have personally examined the evidence to give an opinion.

An expert cannot give an opinion as to who committed the crime, but only an opinion as to the forensic facts. For example, in the *Grant* case, Chris Grice, the fingerprint expert, testified that in his expert opinion, the latent fingerprint lifted from the tissue box found in Penney Serra's car was Grant's. However, he could not testify as to when the fingerprint was placed on the tissue box. He could not testify that in his opinion, Grant had been in Penney Serra's car. After all, the print could have been deposited before the box got in the car. He also could not testify that in his opinion, Grant murdered Serra. The jury could infer that Grant was in the car; the jury could further infer that he was in the car on the day of the murder and that he was therefore the murderer. The forensic evidence, however, does not prove those facts.

Finally, to the extent that a forensic expert testifies about a piece of concrete evidence (for example, a gun or a piece of clothing), counsel must offer evidence establishing a chain of custody of the item. For example, in the *Grant* case, the jury heard testimony about a latent fingerprint lifted from a tissue box that was found in the back seat of Penney Serra's car. In order for the fingerprint expert to testify, counsel must establish that the box was taken by law enforcement officers at the scene and logged in under proper procedures. Moreover, the article must have been stored properly, and it must have been logged in and logged out by anyone who handled the evidence. In general, its presence, and the conditions of its storage, must be accounted for from the time it was found to its presentation at trial. The prosecution must be able to establish the entire "chain of custody" by testimonial or documentary evidence. In fact, as we saw in Chapter 1, the defense objected to the chain of custody because the Serra evidence had been kept in a basement for years where it was said to have deteriorated. The court disagreed and admitted the evidence.

# Judicial Notice

Judicial Notice. A decision by the trial court to accept a fact as proved without presentation of evidence by the parties. The jury is free to accept or reject such fact.

Once a court has determined that an area of science is valid and reliable, the court can take "judicial notice" of this as a fact. The effect of judicial notice simply means that the parties do not need to "prove" the area of science is valid. Judicial notice is not actually a form of evidence, but serves to save time by avoiding the need to prove an accepted fact over and over in trials. For example, the defense in the Grant case challenged the validity of the "STR" method of DNA testing. The trial judge held a hearing, heard from the experts outside the presence of the jury, and ruled that the area of science was valid and reliable. Therefore, the parties did not need to put on any further proof of this issue at the trial. Once a trial court accepts a fact as judicially noticed, parties in later cases before the court do not need to prove the fact.

### Rule 201. Judicial Notice of Adjudicative Facts.

(a) Scope of rule. This rule governs only judicial notice of adjudicative facts.

(b) Kinds of facts. A judicially noticed fact must be one not subject to reasonable dispute in that it is either (1) generally known within the territorial jurisdiction of the trial court or (2) capable of accurate and ready determination by resort to sources whose accuracy cannot reasonably be questioned.

(c) When discretionary. A court may take judicial notice, whether requested or not.

(d) When mandatory. A court shall take judicial notice if requested by a party and supplied with the necessary information.

(e) Opportunity to be heard. A party is entitled upon timely request to an opportunity to be heard as to the propriety of taking judicial notice and the tenor of the matter noticed. In the absence of prior notification, the request may be made after judicial notice has been taken....

(f) Instructing jury.... In a criminal case, the court shall instruct the jury that it may, but is not required to, accept as conclusive any fact judicially noticed.

The Modern Federal Jury Instructions for Criminal Cases contains a sample or "Pattern" Jury Instruction concerning judicial notice as follows:

**Pattern Instruction 2.04. Judicial Notice (Fed. R. Evid. 201).**

> Even though no evidence has been introduced about it, I have decided to accept as proved the fact that [insert fact noticed.] I believe this fact [is of such common knowledge] [can be so accurately and readily determined from (name accurate source)] that it cannot reasonable be disputed. You may therefore treat this fact as proved, even though no evidence was brought out on the point. As with any fact, however, the final decision whether or not to accept it is for you to make and you are not required to agree with me.

A recent Connecticut case stated that the court will take judicial notice of a scientific principle only if it is "considered so reliable within the relevant [medical] community that there is little or no real debate as to its validity."[11] For example, the courts have taken judicial notice of the fact that the Horizontal Gaze Nystagmus test is reliable in determining alcohol consumption for driving under the influence limits and that blood tests can accurately disprove paternity.[12]

Courts have taken judicial notice of the "science of DNA testing."[13] For example, one court concluded:

> At the motion *in limine* and at the trial, [the defendant] failed to challenge the general theory and techniques of DNA profiling. The state now asks us to take judicial notice of the reliability of RFLP testing. We may properly take judicial notice on appeal. "A judicially noticed fact must be one not subject to reasonable dispute in that it is either (1) generally known within the territorial jurisdiction of the trial court or (2) capable of accurate and ready determination by resort to sources whose accuracy cannot be reasonable questioned.[14]

> *In limine.* A hearing *in limine* is held outside the hearing of the jury regarding proper evidence prior to the start of trial.

On the other hand, a Virginia appeals court held that it was error for the trial court to instruct the jury in a rape case that DNA testing is deemed a reliable scientific technique because the specific wording of the instruction unduly emphasized the DNA results over other evidence presented in the case tending to establish the assailant's identity. This decision was subsequently vacated on procedural grounds, but it is instructive on the issue of the prejudice to a defendant from a positive DNA match:

***Crawford v. Commonwealth,* 33 Va. App. 431, 534 S.E.2d 332 (Va. App. 2000)**[15]

Jeffery Andrew Crawford was convicted in a jury trial of armed statutory burglary, rape, robbery, and abduction. The sole issue on appeal is whether the trial court erred by instructing the jury "that DNA testing is deemed to be a reliable scientific technique under the laws of Virginia when admitted to prove the person's identity." We hold that the jury instruction was improper and that the trial court abused its discretion. Accordingly, we reverse and remand.

11. *Maher v. Quest Diagnostics,* 269 Conn. 154, 847 A.2d 978 (2004).
12. *Id.* at 171.
13. In *United States v. Shea,* 957 F. Supp. 331, 345, the court stated: "The theory and techniques used in PCR are sufficiently established that a court may take judicial notice of their general reliability."
14. *State v. Fleming,* 1997 Me. 158, 698 A.2d 503,506 (1997).
15. *Vacated* 546 S.E.2d 207 (Va. Ct. App. 2001).

In November 1995, Crawford unlawfully entered Colleen Caton's home, put a knife to her throat, covered her eyes with his hand, and demanded money. Caton stated that she did not have any money in the house. Crawford then tied Caton's hands and raped her. After the assault, Crawford tied Caton's ankles together, searched for money, and left. Caton freed herself, immediately reported the incident, and gave the police a physical description of her assailant. A seminal fluid sample was recovered from Caton's clothing.

Two years later, Crawford was apprehended in Washington, D.C. At trial, Nathaniel Lockley, who had been incarcerated with Crawford in August 1997, testified that while in jail, Crawford confessed to him to having raped a woman two years earlier in Gloucester County and having fled to Maryland after the incident.

A forensic scientist performed a polymerase chain reaction (PCR) analysis of the DNA recovered from the victim's clothing and Crawford's DNA. The forensic scientist testified that she typed the DNA in six different systems and that Crawford's DNA was consistent with the DNA from the seminal fluid recovered from the crime scene in all six tests. The expert testified that the possibility of randomly selecting an African-American male whose DNA was consistent with the DNA in the seminal fluid sample in all six systems was one in 970. Had the DNA not matched in any one of the six systems, the test would conclusively have excluded Crawford as the person who deposited the seminal fluid at the crime scene.

The trial judge, over defense counsel's objection, gave the following jury instruction:

> DNA testing is deemed to be a reliable scientific technique under the laws of Virginia when admitted to prove the person's identity. In deciding what weight, if any, to give the DNA evidence, you may consider any evidence offered bearing upon the accuracy and reliability of the procedures employed in the collection and analysis of a particular DNA sample. Regardless of the results of any DNA analysis, you may consider any other evidence offered to prove the identity of the defendant.

Crawford was convicted of each offense and was sentenced to a total term of life plus sixty years imprisonment.

* * *

Crawford contends the trial judge erred in giving the DNA jury instruction. He argues that by instructing the jury that "DNA testing is deemed to be a reliable scientific technique," the court impermissibly told the jury that the Commonwealth's DNA evidence compelled a particular finding that the DNA test conducted here was reliable in identifying him as the rapist. He also argues that the instruction constituted an improper comment upon a specific piece of evidence and gave undue prominence to the DNA evidence.

"A reviewing court's responsibility in reviewing jury instructions is 'to see that the law has been clearly stated and that the instructions cover all issues which the evidence fairly raises.'"

When a trial judge instructs the jury in the law, he or she may not "single out for emphasis a part of the evidence tending to establish a particular fact." The danger of such emphasis is that it gives undue prominence by the trial judge to the highlighted evidence and may mislead the jury.

However, in admitting scientific evidence, "the court must make a threshold finding of fact with respect to the reliability of the scientific method offered." "If the court determines that there is a sufficient foundation to warrant admission of the evidence, the court may, in its discretion, admit the evidence with appropriate instructions to the jury to consider the disputed reliability of the evidence in determining its credibility and weight."

Code § 19.2-270.5, enacted by the General Assembly in 1990, provides, in part, that "in any criminal proceeding, DNA ... testing shall be deemed to be a reliable scientific technique and the evidence of a DNA profile comparison may be admitted to prove or disprove the identity of any person."

By enacting Code § 19.2-270.5, the General Assembly has declared that DNA testing and profile comparisons are recognized in the scientific community as reliable procedures for purposes of admitting the results into evidence in Virginia courts to prove or disprove a person's identity....

Here, the instruction, based on Code § 19.2-270.5, not only informed the jury that DNA testing is recognized in Virginia as a valid scientific procedure in identifying a person as the source of DNA material, but also told the jury, in effect, that the DNA technique used in this case, which identified Crawford as the person who most probably deposited the DNA at the crime scene, was reliable—subject to "any evidence offered bearing upon the accuracy and reliability of the procedure employed in the collection and analysis of a particular DNA sample."

By informing the jury that DNA testing was reliable, in the absence of an evidentiary challenge to the accuracy and reliability of the collection and analysis procedure for the particular sample, the court gave credence to the specific test results even though the Commonwealth offered no proof that the collecting and testing procedure for this sample was reliable.

Although the instruction did not tell the jury that they were to give any particular weight to the test results or that they were bound to find Crawford guilty based on the test results, the instruction unduly emphasized the DNA results over other evidence presented in the case tending to establish the assailant's identity.

Thus, the court's instruction did more than inform the jury that DNA testing is a competent and reliable scientific procedure and that the methodology is sound; it "singled out" the DNA test results and stated that DNA test results were reliable in establishing Crawford's identity as the perpetrator. Code § 19.2-270.5 permits trial courts to admit DNA test results without having to prove the scientific reliability of DNA testing; it does not, however, authorize trial courts to comment upon the reliability of particular DNA test results or techniques in a case.

Accordingly, the trial court erred by granting the DNA instruction based on Code § 19.2-270.5. We, therefore, reverse and remand the case for further proceedings.

The decision reported above of the Court of Appeals for Virginia was not unanimous, and the Commonwealth of Virginia made a motion for a rehearing by the entire panel of judges on the appeals court. This is called a rehearing *en banc*. The judges in the second hearing

> "the court's instruction ... 'singled out' the DNA test results and stated that DNA test results were reliable in establishing Crawford's identity as the perpetrator." *Crawford v. Commonwealth*

did not agree with the majority in the first hearing and held that the instruction was proper. Therefore, the conviction was affirmed. However, the legal reasoning for affirming the conviction was not based on the wording of the DNA instruction and its possible prejudice, but rather on the fact that the defendant had not objected to the instruction at trial and therefore had not "preserved the objection" in order to raise it on appeal:

> [The defendant] did not proffer an alternative instruction, did not offer any alternative language, and did not specify his objection. On appeal, the appellant argues the instruction was improper because it unduly emphasized the DNA evidence, contained permissive language, and required the jury to make a distinction they were unqualified to make. Accordingly, the opinion previously rendered by a panel of this Court on September 19, 2000 is withdrawn and the mandate entered on that date is vacated.[16]

This is a "procedural ruling." If the appealing party has not followed proper procedures, the appeal will not be heard and the result of the prior court will stand.

Many people believed that the jury in the *Simpson* case refused to accept the DNA test results because they rejected DNA testing as valid. As the rules of judicial notice make clear, the jury had the right to reject the science of DNA testing. However, some jurors protested that they did not reject DNA testing. They concluded that the testing gave correct results, but the DNA samples had been planted or contaminated. Therefore they concluded that the presence of DNA in the locations where it was found was not related to the crime. In effect, they accepted the technique as reliable, but concluded that it had not been reliably conducted.[17]

# Summary

Forensic evidence cannot be admitted in front of a jury unless all applicable rules of evidence are met. These require that:

- the evidence be relevant to an issue in the trial,
- it not be unduly prejudicial to the defendant,
- a proper chain of custody be established for the evidence,
- the expert be qualified by knowledge, skill, experience, training, or education, and the expert disclose the facts or data upon which he relied in giving his opinion.

The judge will give the jury instructions on how to apply the law to the facts. In Connecticut, the three elements of murder are legal tests to which the jury must apply the facts. "Intent" requires the specific intent that the defendant intended to cause the death of the victim. Motive is not an element of the crime. A finding of motive may help establish guilt beyond a reasonable doubt, but it is not required.

Judicial notice means that a trial court may accept a fact as having been proved without either party putting on evidence. The reliability of the science of DNA has been the

---

16. *Crawford v. Virginia*, 546 S.E.2d 207 (Ct. App. Va. 2001).
17. *See* Chapter 15 for juror comments.

subject of judicial notice. The jury may still refuse to accept a fact that is judicially noticed.

# Discussion Questions

1. What is the purpose of having rules of evidence?

2. What Rules of Evidence affect the admission of forensic evidence at trial?

3. What is the relationship between Federal Rule of Evidence 702 and 703?

4. What is the difference between relevant and material evidence?

5. What is the relationship between the federal rules of evidence and state rules of evidence?

6. How can the same facts be used to convict a defendant of a crime in state and federal court? Why doesn't this violate the rule against double jeopardy?

7. What is the definition of murder in Connecticut? What does the prosecution need to show to demonstrate "intent" to commit murder?

8. What does Federal Rule of Evidence 403 say? Why did the court in the *Fleming* case decide that admission of DNA evidence did not violate this rule?

9. What other kinds of evidence would be so prejudicial to the defendant that they should be excluded, even though they might be relevant to a jury?

10. Define the concept of judicial notice. Is a jury required to accept the truth of a fact that is subject to judicial notice?

11. Why did the court in *Crawford v. Commonwealth* decide that DNA testing should be subject to judicial notice? Does this mean that a jury must accept that a DNA test conclusively identifies the defendant?

# Chapter 5

# The General Acceptance Rule and the *Daubert* Case

## Overview

The admissibility of forensic evidence based on science was governed in the federal courts by the General Acceptance Rule first stated in the case of *Frye v. United States,* decided in 1923. Shortly after Congress passed the Federal Rule of Evidence 702, governing admissibility of expert opinions, the Supreme Court ruled in 1993 that Rule 702 had superseded the *Frye* test. In this case, *Daubert v. Merrrell Dow,* the Court held that scientific testimony should be admissible if it meets alternate tests of reliability, such as a scientific hypothesis, publication and peer review, and error rate. It retained general acceptance as simply one test for admissibility. This ruling governs the admissibility of expert opinions about forensic evidence in all federal courts.

The *Daubert* test *was* soon adopted in some state courts, but not in all. Some states retain the *Frye* test, and some use other tests. The *Daubert* test requires the trial court to act as a gatekeeper and decide outside the hearing of the jury whether the forensic expert testimony is admissible or not.

The *Kuhmo* case decided that the *Daubert* test should apply to experts testifying about a technique—such as examination of a tire to determine any defect—as well as science. The *General Electric* case held that an appeals court must defer to the trial court's gatekeeper decision, unless the trial court abused its discretion. After *Daubert,* courts have expanded the gatekeeper questions to include such issues as whether the science was developed specifically for litigation.

## Chapter Objectives

Based on this chapter, students will be able to:

1. Explain the General Acceptance Test from the *Frye* case.
2. Describe how the case of *Daubert v. Merrell Dow* changed the *Frye* test.
3. Identify the elements of the *Daubert* tests.

4. Explain what happened to the plaintiffs' case in *Daubert* after the case was remanded back to the trial court.

5. Detail the role of the court in conducting gatekeeper hearings.

6. Explain the facts of the case of *Kuhmo Tire* and how it expanded the *Daubert* rule.

7. Understand whether state courts are required to follow *Daubert.*

8. Describe the Connecticut state case of *State v. Porter* and its relationship to the *Daubert* case.

9. Identify the standard of appellate review of gatekeeper hearings in federal court under the *General Electric v. Joiner* case.

10. Identify issues courts have confronted in applying *Daubert*, including science generated for use in the courtroom.

# The General Acceptance Test

In 1923, Congress had not yet adopted the rules about expert witnesses referred to in the prior chapter. The question of what standard to use in admitting forensic evidence was left to each individual court to decide. The Court of Appeals for the District of Columbia, a federal appeals court, made an important ruling in the case of *Frye v. United States.*[1] In this case, the court adopted a standard to be applied by all federal trial courts in the District of Columbia in determining whether an expert could testify. This standard was called the "general acceptance test." In effect, the court was guarding against letting juries hear "junk science" by requiring that any scientific expert could testify only about a scientific theory that was "generally accepted" by all scientists in the same field. The *Frye* case involved whether the jury could hear an expert opinion about a test similar to a polygraph. The court refused, on the ground that the science had not been proven. Here is part of its reasoning:

*Frye v. United States,* 293 F. 1013 (Ct. App. D.C. 1923)

\* \* \*

A single assignment of error is presented for our consideration. In the course of the trial, counsel for defendant offered an expert witness to testify to the result of a deception test made upon defendant. The test is described as the systolic blood pressure deception test. It is asserted that blood pressure is influenced by change in the emotions of the witness, and that the systolic blood pressure rises are brought about by nervous impulses sent to the sympathetic branch of the autonomic nervous system.

Scientific experiments, it is claimed, have demonstrated that fear, rage, and pain always produce a rise of systolic blood pressure, and that conscious deception or falsehood, concealment of facts, or guilt of crime, accompanied by fear of detection when the person is under examination, raises the systolic blood pressure in a curve, which corresponds exactly to the struggle going on in the subject's mind,

---

1. 293 F. 1013 (Ct. App. D.C., 1923).

between fear and attempted control of that fear, as the examination touches the vital points in respect of which he is attempting to deceive the examiner.

In other words, the theory seems to be that truth is spontaneous, and comes without conscious effort, while the utterance of a falsehood requires a conscious effort, which is reflected in the blood pressure. The rise thus produced is easily detected and distinguished from the rise produced by mere fear of the examination itself. In the former instance, the pressure rises higher than in the latter, and is more pronounced as the examination proceeds, while in the latter case, if the subject is telling the truth, the pressure registers highest at the beginning of the examination, and gradually diminishes as the examination proceeds.

Prior to the trial defendant was subjected to this deception test, and counsel offered the scientist who conducted the test as an expert to testify to the results obtained. The offer was objected to by counsel for the government, and the court sustained the objection. Counsel for defendant then offered to have the proffered witness conduct a test in the presence of the jury. This also was denied.

Counsel for defendant, in their able presentation of the novel question involved, correctly state in their brief that no cases directly in point have been found. The broad ground, however, upon which they plant their case, is succinctly stated in their brief as follows:

> "The rule is that the opinions of experts or skilled witnesses are admissible in evidence in those cases in which the matter of inquiry is such that inexperienced persons are unlikely to prove capable of forming a correct judgment upon it, for the reason that the subject-matter so far partakes of a science, art, or trade as to require a previous habit or experience or study in it, in order to acquire a knowledge of it. When the question involved does not lie within the range of common experience or common knowledge, but requires special experience or special knowledge, then the opinions of witnesses skilled in that particular science, art, or trade to which the question relates are admissible in evidence."

Numerous cases are cited in support of this rule. Just when a scientific principle or discovery crosses the line between the experimental and demonstrable stages is difficult to define. Somewhere in this twilight zone the evidential force of the principle must be recognized, and while courts will go a long way in admitting expert testimony deduced from a well-recognized scientific principle or discovery, the thing from which the deduction is made must be sufficiently established to have gained general acceptance in the particular field in which it belongs.

We think the systolic blood pressure deception test has not yet gained such standing and scientific recognition among physiological and psychological authorities as would justify the courts in admitting expert testimony deduced from the discovery, development, and experiments thus far made.

The judgment is affirmed.

---

The General Acceptance Test: "the thing from which the deduction is made must be sufficiently established to have gained general acceptance in the particular field in which it belongs." *Frye v. United States*

The *Frye* case was subsequently referred to as the source of the General Acceptance Test. Following the *Frye* case, many courts—both state courts and federal courts in other appellate circuits—adopted the general acceptance test for scientific experts. When Congress enacted Federal Rule of Evidence 702, however, it was not clear whether Congress intended it to change the general acceptance test. The United States Supreme Court answered this question in 1993, in the case of *Daubert v. Merrell Dow*.

# The *Daubert* Rule

In 1993, the Supreme Court issued a landmark decision in the case of *Daubert v. Merrell Dow*. This case was not a criminal case. It was a civil liability case for damages. Although many students think of forensic evidence only in the criminal context, this is not the case. In fact, the three major U.S. Supreme Court cases about forensic evidence, which are discussed in this chapter, were all civil liability cases.

In *Daubert*, the issue was whether Bendectin, a drug manufactured by Merrell Dow, caused birth defects. The plaintiff's expert was prepared to testify that it did, based on test-tube and live-animal studies and pharmacological studies, as well as a reanalysis of previously published studies. The defendant objected on the ground that no published epidemiological (human statistical) study had demonstrated a statistically significant association between Bendectin and birth defects. In effect, the defendant argued that there was no "general acceptance" in the medical community that Bendectin caused birth defects.

The plaintiff was relying in large part on a re-analysis of data that had previously concluded that Bendectin did not cause birth defects. This was called a meta-data test.

A meta-analysis is defined as follows:

> The term "meta-analysis" refers to "the process or technique of synthesizing research results by using various statistical methods to retrieve, select, and combine results from previous separate but related studies" ..."With the help of a relatively new procedure, the meta-analysis, we are now in a position to statistically compare the results of a large number of experiments."[2]

The trial court refused to accept the plaintiffs' expert testimony, finding that its conclusions were not "generally accepted" in the scientific community. The U.S. Supreme Court determined that Rule 702 had superseded the *Frye* case. As a result, it stated that the test to admit scientific expert testimony had changed to include more factors than just "general acceptance." It remanded the case back to the appellate court, with instructions to apply a new test about the admissibility of the expert testimony. The new rule required a more liberal test for admissibility than the general acceptance standard set forth in *Frye*. The Court acknowledged that general acceptance was one test for admissibility, but it added others that could be used even if general acceptance was not met. These included:

- whether the science had been tested,
- whether it had a known error rate, and
- whether it had been subject to peer review and publication.

---

2. *New York v. Legrand*, 747 NYS 2d 733 (2002).

The court's reasoning was that juries should be able to hear cutting edge science, even if the general scientific community had not yet accepted it, as long as the evidence followed the scientific method and had other signs of reliability, such as being published and critiqued by other scientists. Here is an excerpt of the *Daubert* opinion:

### *Daubert v. Merrell Dow Pharmaceuticals,* 509 U.S. 579 (1993)[3]

In this case we are called upon to determine the standard for admitting expert scientific testimony in a federal trial.

Petitioners Jason *Daubert* and Eric Schuller are minor children born with serious birth defects. They and their parents sued respondent in California state court, alleging that the birth defects had been caused by the mothers' ingestion of Bendectin, a prescription anti-nausea drug marketed by respondent. Respondent removed the suits to federal court on diversity grounds.

After extensive discovery, respondent moved for summary judgment, contending that Bendectin does not cause birth defects in humans and that petitioners would be unable to come forward with any admissible evidence that it does. In support of its motion, respondent submitted an affidavit of Steven H. Lamm, physician and epidemiologist, who is a well-credentialed expert on the risks from exposure to various chemical substances. Doctor Lamm stated that he had reviewed all the literature on Bendectin and human birth defects—more than 30 published studies involving over 130,000 patients. No study had found Bendectin to be a human teratogen (i.e., a substance capable of causing malformations in fetuses).

On the basis of this review, Doctor Lamm concluded that maternal use of Bendectin during the first trimester of pregnancy has not been shown to be a risk factor for human birth defects.

Petitioners did not (and do not) contest this characterization of the published record regarding Bendectin. Instead, they responded to respondent's motion with the testimony of eight experts of their own, each of whom also possessed impressive credentials. These experts had concluded that Bendectin can cause birth defects. Their conclusions were based upon "in vitro" (test tube) and "in vivo" (live) animal studies that found a link between Bendectin and malformations; pharmacological studies of the chemical structure of Bendectin that purported to show similarities between the structure of the drug and that of other substances known to cause birth defects; and the "reanalysis" of previously published epidemiological (human statistical) studies.

* * *

In the 70 years since its formulation in the *Frye* case, the "general acceptance" test has been the dominant standard for determining the admissibility of novel scientific evidence at trial. Although under increasing attack of late, the rule continues to be followed by a majority of courts, including the Ninth Circuit.

[The court then explained the holding of the *Frye* case.] The merits of the *Frye* test have been much debated, and scholarship on its proper scope and application is legion. Petitioners' primary attack, however, is not on the content

---

3. Affirmed on remand by *Daubert v. Merrell Dow,* 43 F.3d 1311 (9th Cir. 1995).

but on the continuing authority of the rule. They contend that the *Frye* test was superseded by the adoption of the Federal Rules of Evidence. We agree.

We interpret the legislatively enacted Federal Rules of Evidence as we would any statute.... Rule 402 provides the baseline:

"All relevant evidence is admissible, except as otherwise provided by the Constitution of the United States, by Act of Congress, by these rules, or by other rules prescribed by the Supreme Court pursuant to statutory authority. Evidence which is not relevant is not admissible."

\* \* \*

Nothing in the text of this Rule establishes "general acceptance" as an absolute prerequisite to admissibility. Nor does respondent present any clear indication that Rule 702 or the Rules as a whole were intended to incorporate a "general acceptance" standard. The drafting history makes no mention of *Frye*, and a rigid "general acceptance" requirement would be at odds with the "liberal thrust" of the Federal Rules and their "general approach of relaxing the traditional barriers to 'opinion' testimony."

\* \* \*

Rule 702 further requires that the evidence or testimony" assist the trier of fact to understand the evidence or to determine a fact in issue." This condition goes primarily to relevance. "Expert testimony which does not relate to any issue in the case is not relevant and, ergo, non-helpful.".... The study of the phases of the moon, for example, may provide valid scientific "knowledge" about whether a certain night was dark, and if darkness is a fact in issue, the knowledge will assist the trier of fact. However (absent creditable grounds supporting such a link), evidence that the moon was full on a certain night will not assist the trier of fact in determining whether an individual was unusually likely to have behaved irrationally on that night. Rule 702's "helpfulness" standard requires a valid scientific connection to the pertinent inquiry as a precondition to admissibility.

\* \* \*

Ordinarily, a key question to be answered in determining whether a theory or technique is scientific knowledge that will assist the trier of fact will be whether it can be (and has been) tested.

> "Scientific methodology today is based on generating hypotheses and testing them to see if they can be falsified; indeed, this methodology is what distinguishes science from other fields of human inquiry."

\* \* \*

Another pertinent consideration is whether the theory or technique has been subjected to peer review and publication. Publication (which is but one element of peer review) is not a sine qua non of admissibility; it does not necessarily correlate with reliability, and in some instances well-grounded but innovative theories will not have been published. Some propositions, moreover, are too particular, too new, or of too limited interest to be published. But submission to the scrutiny of the scientific community is a component of "good science," in part because it increases the likelihood that substantive flaws in methodology will be detected.

\* \* \*

Additionally, in the case of a particular scientific technique, the court ordinarily should consider the known or potential rate of error, and the existence and maintenance of standards controlling the technique's operation. Finally, "general acceptance" can yet have a bearing on the inquiry. A "reliability assessment does not require, although it does permit, explicit identification of a relevant scientific community and an express determination of a particular degree of acceptance within that community." Widespread acceptance can be an important factor in ruling particular evidence admissible, and "a known technique which has been able to attract only minimal support within the community."

The inquiries of the District Court and the Court of Appeals focused almost exclusively on "general acceptance," as gauged by publication and the decisions of other courts.

> The Daubert Tests.
> In deciding whether to admit scientific testimony under FRE 702, the trial judge should ask:
>
> a. Is it based on a scientific methodology?
>
> b. Is the methodology published and peer reviewed?
>
> c. Does it have a known or potential error rate?
>
> d. Is it generally accepted in the scientific community?

Accordingly, the judgment of the Court of Appeals is vacated, and the case is remanded for further proceedings consistent with this opinion.

## Remand of the *Daubert* Case

The case was remanded back to the 9th Circuit Court of Appeal. That court declined to send the case back to the trial court for a gatekeeper hearing, but instead reviewed the expert testimony from the trial record under the new standard set out by the Supreme Court. It decided that the testimony failed to qualify under *Daubert* and therefore affirmed the trial court's original grant of summary judgment.[4]

It is largely because the opinions proffered by plaintiffs' experts run counter to the substantial consensus in the scientific community that we affirmed the district court's grant of summary judgment the last time the case appeared before us. The standard for admissibility of expert testimony in this circuit at the time was the so-called *Frye* test: Scientific evidence was admissible if it was based on a scientific technique generally accepted as reliable within the scientific community. We found that the district court properly applied this standard, and affirmed. The Supreme Court reversed, holding that *Frye* was superceded by Federal Rule of Evidence 702, and remanded for us to consider the admissibility of plaintiffs' expert testimony under this new standard.

First, however, we address plaintiffs' argument that we should simply remand the case so the district court can make the initial determination of admissibility under the new standard announced by the Supreme Court. There is certainly something to be said for this position, as the district court is charged with making the initial determination whether to admit evidence. In the peculiar

---

4. *Daubert v. Merrell Dow*, 43 F.3d 1311 (9th Cir. 1995).

circumstances of this case, however, we have determined that the interests of justice and judicial economy will best be served by deciding those issues that are properly before us and, in the process, offering guidance on the application of the *Daubert* standard in this circuit.

> **Summary Judgment.**
> A ruling by a trial court, generally to dismiss a claim, on the ground that there is no genuine issue as to any material fact and the moving party is entitled to judgment as matter of law.

The district court already made a determination as to admissibility, albeit under a different standard than we apply on remand, and granted summary judgment based on its exclusion of plaintiffs' expert testimony. A grant of summary judgment may be sustained on any basis supported by the record, so we shall consider whether the district court's grant of summary judgment can be sustained under the new standard announced by the Supreme Court.

Our review here is, of course, very narrow: We will affirm the summary judgment only if, as a matter of law, the proffered evidence would have to be excluded at trial. The district court's power is far broader; were we to conclude that the expert testimony is not *per se* inadmissible, the district court on remand would nevertheless have discretion to reject it under Rule 403 or 702. Such a ruling would be reviewed under the deferential abuse of discretion standard.

\* \* \*

[T]he question is whether plaintiffs adduced enough admissible evidence to create a genuine issue of material fact as to whether Bendectin caused their injuries. It is to that question we now turn.

Plaintiffs have made no such showing. As noted above, plaintiffs rely entirely on the experts' unadorned assertions that the methodology they employed comports with standard scientific procedures. In support of these assertions, plaintiffs offer only the trial and deposition testimony of these experts in other cases. While these materials indicate that plaintiffs' experts have relied on animal studies, chemical structure analyses and epidemiological data, they neither explain the methodology the experts followed to reach their conclusions nor point to any external source to validate that methodology. We've been presented with only the experts' qualifications, their conclusions and their assurances of reliability. Under *Daubert,* that's not enough.

As the district court properly found below, "the strongest inference to be drawn for plaintiffs based on the epidemiological evidence is that Bendectin could *possibly* have caused plaintiffs' injuries." The same is true of the other testimony derived from animal studies and chemical structure analyses—these experts "testify to a possibility rather than a probability." Plaintiffs do not quantify this possibility, or otherwise indicate how their conclusions about causation should be weighted, even though the substantive legal standard has always required proof of causation by a preponderance of the evidence.

Unlike these experts' explanation of their methodology, this is not a shortcoming that could be corrected on remand ... Plaintiffs' experts must, therefore, stand by the conclusions they originally proffered, rendering their testimony inadmissible under the second prong of Fed. R. Evid. 702.

# *Daubert* Requires Gatekeeper Hearings

*Daubert* was viewed as a "landmark" decision for two reasons:

- It rejected the old "general acceptance" test as the only test for admissibility and proposed some new tests that would make it easier to admit scientific testimony about a science which might not have reached general acceptance.

- It established the trial judge as a "gatekeeper" to evaluate a list of factors in order to decide whether the expert could testify at all.

The role of the trial court in evaluating the reliability of the scientific testimony before it is presented to the jury has been called the "gatekeeper" role. The trial court may open or close the gate to allow the testimony to reach the jury. The Ninth Circuit court explained that *Daubert* requires a trial court to engage in a two-part analysis:

> First, we must determine nothing less than whether the experts' testimony reflects "scientific knowledge," whether their findings are "derived by the scientific method," and whether their work product amounts to "good science."

Gatekeeper. The role of the trial court in determining if scientific or technical evidence is admissible under Federal Rule of Evidence 702 or a similar state rule.

> Second, we must ensure that the proposed expert testimony is "relevant to the task as hand," i.e., that it logically advances a material aspect of the proposing party's case. The Supreme Court referred to this second prong of the analysis as the "fit" requirement.[5]

Congress amended Rule 702 on December 1, 2000 to reflect the Supreme Court's holding.

### Rule 702.

If scientific, technical, or other specialized knowledge will assist the trier of fact to understand the evidence or to determine a fact in issue, a witness qualified as an expert by knowledge, skill, experience, training, or education, may testify thereto in the form of an opinion or otherwise, if (1) the testimony is based upon sufficient facts or data, (2) the testimony is the product of reliable principles and methods, and (3) the witness has applied the principles and methods reliably to the facts of the case.

Note that the revised Rule 702 does not specifically refer to a "gatekeeping" function by the trial judge, who must decide whether the witness is qualified to testify in the first instance. However, by stating specific criteria for when a witness is "qualified as an expert," and requiring that the testimony be based on "sufficient facts or data" which is the product of "reliable principles and methods," the rule in effect requires the trial judge to evaluate the science behind the expert's proposed testimony.

Federal Rule of Evidence 702 does not incorporate any of the specific *Daubert* tests, such as publication and peer review, error rate, etc. In part, this is because the Supreme

---

5. 43 F.3d 1311 at 1315.

Court's list of *Daubert* tests were meant to be nonexclusive guidelines. Congress chose to keep Rule 702 more general, thus giving more discretion to the trial judge.

But exactly how is the trial court to ensure that scientific testimony is reliable? As the Ninth Circuit stated after the remand of *Daubert*:

> The Court held.... that federal judges perform a "gatekeeping role; to do so they must satisfy themselves that scientific evidence meets a certain standard of reliability before it is admitted. This means that the expert's bald assurance of validity is not enough. Rather, the party presenting the expert must show that the expert's findings are based on sound science, and this will require some objective, independent validation of the expert's methodology.[6]

The judge is generally in a better position to evaluate evidence and determine questions of admissibility. Judges make such rulings every day and therefore are familiar with the rules of evidence. The *Daubert* hearing allows the judge to become educated on an issue before ruling on admissibility. As certain areas of testimony in criminal cases will occur repeatedly, such as DNA, fingerprints, handwriting, eyewitness identification and blood stain analysis, judges will build up expertise which can be applied to subsequent hearings. Although each expert will present different issues, a trial judge will know the questions to consider, such as whether the expert has omitted certain variables from his scientific hypothesis or whether internal inconsistencies appear in his testimony.

> Judges must know enough about a subject to identify indicia of reliability and to apply them competently. Beyond this threshold level of knowledge, the judiciary's expertise is in deconstructing an argument: assessing the logic of the argument, the validity of its premises, the rigor with which the witness applied the technique, the faithfulness of the witness's application of the methodology to her description of it, the magnitude of the inference drawn by the witness in forming her opinion and the sufficiency of the facts to support the inference. Parties' identification of contested issues and potential weaknesses in a proffered expert's methodology or reasoning should assist judges in this endeavor.[7]

# The Gatekeeper Process

So how exactly is the trial court to act as a gatekeeper? Must it hear testimony outside the hearing of the jury? Must it hold a hearing if neither party objects to the expert witness? The trial judge has broad latitude in holding pretrial hearings, and an appeals court will generally not reverse unless the trial judge has clearly abused its discretion. This makes a high hurdle for parties who try to challenge the court's decision at a Daubert hearing.

The trial court need not hold a full pretrial hearing in every case. This was shown by the trial court's decision to affirm summary judgment on the remand of the *Daubert* case without holding a gatekeeper hearing. Some courts have held *Daubert* hearings by reviewing the trial transcript of the *Daubert* hearing held in another, similar case.[8] The courts

---

6. *Id.* at 1316.

7. Note: *Reliable Evaluation of Expert Testimony*, 116 Harvard Law Review 2142, 2150 (May 2003).

8. *See United States v. Plaza*, 179 F. Supp.2d 492 (E.D. Pa. 2002); *vacated*, 188 F. Supp.2d 549 (E.D. Pa. 2002).

have also stated that a party waives the right to argue on appeal that expert testimony should not have been admitted if he does not request a *Daubert* hearing at trial. In one case where a defendant failed to object to testimony that a mark found in a photograph of a corpse was the defendant's tooth pattern, the appellate court denied a new trial because the defendant had not objected to the testimony at trial. However, defendant was successful on a habeas corpus petition that his counsel's failure to raise the issue was a denial of his right to counsel.[9] Trial courts frequently bend over backwards to avoid being reversed on appeal. For this reason, if a party requests a *Daubert* hearing, most trials will grant the motion.

The Reference Manual on Scientific Evidence[10] made a number of predictions of the outcome of *Daubert* on criminal trials:

> [C]hallenges to reliability have been raised with regard to numerous techniques of forensic identification, such as fingerprinting, handwriting analysis, ballistics, and bite-mark analysis. DNA typing may well be the only area of forensic identification in which research has been conducted in accordance with conventional scientific standards. In other areas, experts have in large measure relied on their experience to arrive at subjective conclusions that either have not been validated or are not objectively verifiable.

> The post-*Daubert* challenges to forensic identification have been largely unsuccessful if looked at solely in terms of rulings on admissibility. Courts have by and large refused to exclude prosecution experts.... That courts continued to allow forensic identification experts to testify is not, however, the whole story. It is clear that in the aftermath of *Daubert*, empirical research has begun to examine the foundation of some forensic sciences.[11]

In the *Grant* case, the defendants requested a *Daubert* hearing on whether the DNA testimony was reliable. The trial court took extensive testimony and wrote a separate opinion after the hearing, stating specific findings for a reviewing court to consider if the holding was appealed. This issue is not included in Grant's appeal.

The trial judge has flexibility in what standards to apply in a gatekeeper hearing: "In sum, Rule 702 grants the district judge the discretionary authority, reviewable for its abuse, to determine reliability in light of the particular facts and circumstances of the particular case."[12] Trial judges also have discretion to use court-appointed experts, special masters, and specially trained law clerks, and to narrow the issues in dispute at pretrial hearing and conferences.

The Supreme Court of Nebraska[13] described the gatekeeper process as follows:

> Under our recent *Daubert/Schafersman* jurisprudence, the trial court acts as a gatekeeper to ensure the evidentiary relevance and reliability of an expert's opinion. Most recently, we described a trial court's evaluation of the admissibility of expert testimony as essentially a four-step process.

---

9. *Ege v. Yukins*, 380 F. Supp. 2d 852 (E.D. Mich. 2006).
10. Reference Manual on Scientific Evidence, Federal Judicial Center, 2000, available at http://www.fjc.gov.
11. Margaret A. Berger, *Supreme Court's Trilogy on Admissibility of Expert Testimony*, at 31, Reference Manual on Scientific Evidence, *supra*.
12. *Id.* at 158.
13. *Epp v. Lauby*, 715 N.W.2d 501 (Sup. Neb. 2006).

First, the court must determine whether the witness is qualified to testify as an expert.

If the expert is and it is necessary for the court to conduct a Daubert analysis, the court must next determine whether the reasoning or methodology underlying the expert testimony is scientifically valid and reliable.

Once the reasoning or methodology has been found to be reliable, the court must next determine whether the methodology was properly applied to the facts in issue.

Finally, the court determines whether the evidence and opinions related thereto are more probative than prejudicial, as required under Neb. Evid. R. 403.[14]

# How State Courts Reacted to *Daubert*

Following the *Daubert* decision, many states decided to adopt the *Daubert* approach. This was not required by the *Daubert* decision, as it applied only to the federal courts. Each state is free to make its own rules, so long as they do not violate the U.S. Constitution. To date some states still retain the *Frye* approach, some have adopted the *Daubert* approach and others have different rules altogether.[15] Connecticut, for example, adopted the *Daubert* rule in a case called *State v. Porter,* discussed below. The Connecticut rule of evidence governing expert testimony is numbered Rule 7-2 and appears below:

> A witness qualified as an expert by knowledge, skill, experience, training, education or otherwise may testify in the form of an opinion or otherwise concerning scientific, technical or other specialized knowledge, if the testimony will assist the trier of fact in understanding the evidence or in determining a fact in issue.

In *State v. Porter,*[16] Connecticut reviewed its long-standing application of *Frye* and adopted the *Daubert* standard. In *Porter,* the defendant appealed the judgment of the Appellate Court affirming his conviction for first degree arson. Prior to trial, Porter underwent a polygraph examination and, in the opinion of the expert polygrapher, was truthful when he answered "no" to a series of questions relating to his guilty knowledge of any participation in the burning of his home. When Porter moved to have the trial court admit the results of the polygraph test, his motion was denied and Porter was convicted of first degree arson.

The *Porter* Test. Connecticut adopted the Daubert test in *State v. Porter,* so its test is called the *Porter* test.

On appeal, Porter claimed that the trial court erred when it refused to admit the results of his polygraph test. In affirming the decision of the trial court, the Appellate Court addressed only the issue of Connecticut's *per se* rule that polygraph evidence is inadmissible at trial. In granting Porter's petition for certification to appeal, the Connecticut Supreme Court limited its review to whether Connecticut should adopt *Daubert* as the standard for admissibility of scientific evidence and whether Connecticut

14. *Id.* at 508.
15. *The Demise of Daubert in State Courts,* Mealey's Daubert Report, June 2005, at 3.
16. 241 Conn. 57, 698 A.2d 739 (1997).

should abandon its per se rule that polygraph evidence is inadmissible at trial. In its decision, the court held that "*Daubert* provides the proper threshold standard for the admissibility of scientific evidence in Connecticut."[17]

# The Standard of Appellate Review Is "Abuse of Discretion"

Shortly after *Daubert*, the Supreme Court heard another case called *General Electric Co. v. Joiner*.[18] The issue was whether the plaintiff, who had small-cell lung cancer, could sue for exposure to polycholorinated biphenyls (PCBs) on the theory that it had promoted his cancer. This case was important because it established that the appellate court must affirm the trial court's gatekeeping decision unless it was an "abuse of discretion," a very high standard of proof to meet. In effect it meant that the appellate courts will defer to the trial court, which had the opportunity to see the expert and hear the testimony about the various *Daubert* tests.

One court defined abuse of discretion this way:

> An abuse of discretion can occur where the district court applies the wrong law, follows the wrong procedure, bases its decision on clearly erroneous facts, or commits a clear error in judgment.[19]

# *Kuhmo* Extends *Daubert* to "Technical" Testimony

In *Kuhmo Tire Co. v. Carmichael*,[20] the plaintiffs sued Kuhmo Tire Company for injuries sustained when the tire on their van blew out. Kuhmo contended that the blowout was caused by the plaintiff's putting too little air in the rear tires. This resulted in overdeflection, which consists of underinflating the tire so that it carries too much weight and generates heat that can cause it to unravel. The plaintiff's expert, Carlson, contended that the tire was defective and that the blowout was caused by a manufacturing or design defect. He based his testimony on his visual inspection of the tire and his experience as a tire inspector for Michelin.

The Supreme Court did not doubt the expert's qualifications. However, it said that the *Daubert* factors would apply to this technical testimony, although not necessarily all of the factors would be relevant. In affirming the trial court's decision to exclude plaintiffs' expert, the Court decided that the methodology used by the expert in analyzing certain data obtained by his visual inspection, such as the wear on the

---

17. The Court also held that Connecticut should not abandon its *per se* rule that polygraph evidence is admissible at trial, thereby affirming the lower court's conviction of Porter.

18. 522 U.S. 136 (1997).

19. *United States v. Brown*, 415 F.3d 1257, 1266 (11th Cir. 2005), *cert. den.*, 126 S.Ct. 1570 (2006).

20. 526 U.S. 137 (1999).

tire treads, was unreliable and "fell outside the range where experts might reasonably differ."[21]

> ... [T]he specific issue before the court was not the reasonableness *in general* of a tire expert's use of a visual and tactile inspection to determine whether overdeflection had caused the tire's tread to separate from its steel-belted carcass. Rather, it was the reasonableness of using such an approach, along with Carlson's particular method of analyzing the data thereby obtained, to draw a conclusion regarding *the particular matter to which the expert testimony was directly relevant.*

The trial court had found that none of the *Daubert* factors, including general acceptance, were satisfied by Carlson's testimony and therefore excluded it as unreliable. The appellate court reversed. On appeal to The Supreme Court, it found that the decision by the trial court was not an "abuse of discretion" and therefore plaintiff's expert was properly excluded. Finally, the Court stated that the *Daubert* factors apply to both scientific and technical testimony, but that the factors must be "flexible" and that not all factors will apply in all cases:

### *Kuhmo Tire Co. v. Carmichael*, 526 U.S. 137, 155–158 (1999)

\* \* \*

Carlson testified precisely that in the absence of at least two of four signs of abuse (proportionately greater tread wear on the shoulder; signs of grooves caused by the beads; discolored sidewalls; marks on the rim flange) he concludes that a defect caused the separation. And his analysis depended upon acceptance of a further implicit proposition, namely, that his visual and tactile inspection could determine that the tire before him had not been abused despite some evidence of the presence of the very signs for which he looked (and two punctures).

\* \* \*

[T]he transcripts of Carlson's depositions support both the trial court's initial uncertainty and its final conclusion. Those transcripts cast considerable doubt upon the reliability of both the explicit theory (about the need for two signs of abuse) and the implicit proposition (about the significance of visual inspection in this case). Among other things, the expert could not say whether the tire had traveled more than 10, or 20, or 30, or 40, or 50 thousand miles, adding that 6,000 miles was "about how far" he could "say with any certainty." The court could reasonably have wondered about the reliability of a method of visual and tactile inspection sufficiently precise to ascertain with some certainty the abuse-related significance of minute shoulder/center relative tread wear differences, but insufficiently precise to tell "with any certainty" from the tread wear whether a tire had traveled less than 10,000 or more than 50,000 miles.

\* \* \*

The particular issue in this case concerned the use of Carlson's two-factor test and his related use of visual/tactile inspection to draw conclusions on the basis of what seemed small observational differences. We have found no indication in the record that other experts in the industry use Carlson's two-factor test or that tire experts such as Carlson normally make the very fine distinctions about, say, the symmetry of comparatively greater shoulder tread wear that were necessary, on Carlson's own theory, to support his conclusions. Nor, de-

---

21. *Id.* at 153.

spite the prevalence of tire testing, does anyone refer to any articles or papers that validate Carlson's approach.

* * *

[T]he court ultimately based its decision upon Carlson's failure to satisfy either Daubert's factors or any other set of reasonable reliability criteria. In light of the record as developed by the parties, that conclusion was within the District Court's lawful discretion.

> The *Daubert* test applies to technical as well as scientific testimony.

In the year 2000, the Supreme Court again addressed a procedural question: if the appellate court found that the expert testimony had been admitted against the defendant in violation of *Daubert,* could the court simply enter judgment in favor of the defendant or did it have to send the case back to the trial court to let plaintiff try the case again without the expert testimony? In *Weisgram v. Marley,*[22] the Supreme Court reversed a jury verdict in a wrongful death action based on plaintiff's claim that a heater manufactured by the defendant had been defective and caused a fire that resulted in the death of his mother. The circuit appellate court held that the plaintiffs' expert opinions were speculative and not scientifically sound. The Supreme Court recognized that an appellate court has the discretion to remand the case for a new trial, but stated that it is not required to do so where it decides that the remaining evidence that had been properly introduced at trial was legally insufficient to support the verdict.

One of the requirements of the Daubert test is to show peer review and publication within the scientific community. Yet, as personal injury claims continue to expand into new areas of possible dangers—mold, electromagnetic force fields, breast implants, etc., plaintiffs' lawyers have begun to commission their own "scientific" studies for use in court.

# Post-*Daubert* Issues

## "Science" Developed Specifically for Litigation— Is It Suspect?

As courts have tried to perform their gatekeeping function, they have developed several other tests to determine if purported expert forensic testimony should be admitted. One of these is whether the evidence was developed for a purpose other than litigation. The theory is that the evidence will be more objective and reliable if the researchers did not undertake the research hoping for a favorable outcome in litigation.

When this test is applied to many standard forms of forensic science, such as fingerprints, handwriting analysis, ballistics, blood spatter, footprint, tire print or fiber analysis, the proposing party cannot argue that any of these forensic methods were developed for a purpose other than investigating crime and for use in the criminal justice system. In this context, it would seem that the test of whether the science was developed for an independent use seems pointless.

---

22. 528 U.S. 440 (2000).

Additional *Daubert* questions: Was the "science" developed specifically for litigation? Does the expert use the science for any purpose outside the courtroom?

However, this inquiry is worthwhile when applied to the many personal injury civil lawsuits that depend upon an expert opinion establishing the element of causation. A court will justifiably inquire whether the studies that show that the crucial element of causation was developed independently by researchers in medicine, or whether they were commissioned especially for litigation. Given the multi-million dollar verdicts that tantalize personal injury lawyers—think of the $3.2 billion verdict against Dow for what was believed to be causation of failure of the autoimmune systems of women who had breast implants—such lawyers might choose to arrange studies with a friendly "expert" specifically to use in litigation.

The *Daubert* case itself was an example of litigation-generated testimony.[23] There, the plaintiffs' counsel commissioned an expert to "review" the studies previously performed by Merrell Dow, which did not show a tetragenic effect, i.e., the existing tests had disproved causation. The plaintiffs' experts performed a "meta analysis" and concluded that the data actually did show a link between Bendectin and birth defects. "After the Supreme Court remanded the case, ... the Ninth Circuit discussed the difference in reliability between independent research and litigation research. But the circuit court did not automatically exclude the plaintiffs' study."[24] However, the circuit court said that additional evidence must be offered to show that the test was based on valid scientific principles, specifically peer review and publication through the process of normal scientific research. Here are just a few of the plaintiff-generated studies that have been reported:[25]

- A study that linked the MMR vaccine and autism, published by a researcher who had received $90,000 from the plaintiffs' law firm to investigate the link.

- A link between insecticide and birth defects, published by an expert witness for plaintiffs for over twenty years in all of the similar cases. The expert had not published her protocols, reasoning or methodology. This deficiency meant it was impossible to replicate her work, which is an important element in determining the validity of the "science" and, thus, its admissibility.

- A study that showed asbestos in schools caused a variety of illnesses.

Although the Supreme Court in *Daubert* did not make this point, the circuit court on remand stated that one important factor is whether the science involved in expert testimony was developed for a purpose other than litigation. Such studies create concerns about bias and undue influence by a particular sponsor.

Courts should be particularly wary of studies of the effect of substances on animals when the dosage is much higher than that to which any human would likely be exposed. Other examples of biased scientific research include using in vivo (animal) or in vitro (laboratory cell tests) to propose a link between a substance and a human disease. Furthermore, experts that try to use studies of one substance to establish a point by arguing that another chemical has a similar composition are likewise regarded as suspect.

---

23. Anderson and Parsons, *The Growing Role of Litigation-Generated Science,* Vol 10 Mealey's *Daubert* Report January 2006, issue no. 1.

24. *Id.*

25. *Id.*

The temptation to achieve the hoped-for result may prove irresistible. Scientists see large dollars and lucrative contracts on the horizon. In 2005, a South Korean researcher named Dr. Hwang Woo Suk was discredited after being caught forging evidence of human stem cell cloning, which many believe was a result of pressure to gain publicity and fame.[26]

## Is General Acceptance Alone Sufficient for Admissibility?

The cases after *Daubert* have shown that courts still routinely admit certain types of expert testimony without requiring a *Daubert* analysis. For example, handwriting experts testify, although there have never been any scientific tests cited in court to establish what characteristics will absolutely identify a person's handwriting or what error rates occur in identifying handwriting. Prior to the *Kuhmo* decision that said *Daubert* applied to "technical" as well as scientific testimony, one court stated that handwriting analysis would definitely not pass the *Daubert* test, but because it was technical and not scientific, it could be admitted. After the *Kuhmo* court stated that *Daubert* applied to technical as well as scientific testimony, the courts have continued to admit handwriting testimony, but now on the theory that it is "generally accepted." But there is a difference between "generally admitted" and "generally accepted." A long history of admitting certain evidence does not mean that it is scientifically sound.

Another area of testimony that is admitted as "generally accepted" is fingerprint analysis. Experts agree that fingerprints are unique and that matching "ridge characteristics" of fingerprints will yield a very high rate of accuracy, at least if a sufficient number of ridge characteristics are found in common. However, no studies have been completed to show exactly what number of points in common are required to make a "match." One trial court refused to admit a fingerprint examiner's testimony about a fingerprint match after a full *Daubert* hearing; however, the court later retracted its opinion on less than satisfactory grounds. We will examine this case in detail in the chapter on fingerprints.

It is unlikely that the Supreme Court meant for courts to admit expert testimony simply because it had always been admitted in the past. In effect, by using the phrase "generally accepted," courts can sidestep a genuine examination of whether the science or technique is based on a reliable scientific hypothesis that has been subjected to review, critique, and duplication by other scientists.

Although *Daubert* used general acceptance as one of the tests for admitting expert testimony, it seems unlikely that the court meant that science that is generally accepted but does *not* meet the other criteria stated in the test should be admitted. As the Ninth Circuit stated on the second *Daubert* appeal:

> Under *Frye,* the party proffering scientific evidence had to show it was based on the method generally accepted in the scientific community. The focus under *Daubert* is on the reliability of the methodology, and in addressing that question the court and the parties are not limited to what is generally accepted; methods accepted by a minority in the scientific community may well be sufficient.

---

26. Nicholas Wade, *University Panel Faults Cloning Co-Auther*, The New York Times, February 11, 2006.

However, the party proffering the evidence must explain the expert's methodology and demonstrate in some objectively verifiable way that the expert has both chosen a reliable scientific method and followed it faithfully. Of course, the fact that one party's experts use a methodology accepted by only a minority of scientists would be a proper basis for impeachment at trial.[27]

## How Well Do Trial Judges Understand Science?

*Daubert* hearings can be lengthy and complex. Experts for each side come prepared with scientific theories and experiments. The consequences for the litigating parties of refusing to allow expert testimony can be devastating. Yet, most judges are not trained in science. How can they possibly evaluate the competing theories?

In 2000, the Federal Judicial Center published an extensive Reference Manual on Scientific Evidence[28] for federal judges, explaining the science behind many types of forensic testimony. Here is the assessment by one scientist of the relationship of the *Daubert* decision to the process of scientific research:

> The presentation of scientific evidence in a court of law is a kind of shot gun marriage between the two disciplines. Both are forced to some extent to yield to the central imperatives of the other's way of doing business, and it is likely that neither will be shown in its best light. The *Daubert* decision is an attempt (not the first, of course) to regulate that encounter. Judges are asked to decide the "evidential reliability" of the intended testimony, based not on the conclusions to be offered, but on the methods used to reach those conclusions. In particular, the methods should be judged by the following four criteria:
>
> • The theoretical underpinnings of the methods must yield testable predictions by means of which the theory could be falsified.
>
> • The methods should preferably be published in a peer-reviewed journal.
>
> • There should be a known rate of error that can be used in evaluating the results.
>
> • The methods should be generally accepted within the relevant scientific community.
>
> The doctrine of falsification is supplemented by a bow to the institution of peer review, an acknowledgment of the scientific meaning of error, and a paradigm check (really, an inclusion of the earlier *Frye* standard).
>
> All in all, I would score the decision a pretty good performance. The justices ventured into the treacherous crosscurrents of the philosophy of science—where even most scientists fear to tread—and emerged with at least their dignity intact. Falsifiability may not be a good way of doing science, but it's not the worst *a posteriori* way to judge science, and that's all that's required here.[29]

---

27. 43 F.3d 1311, n. 11.
28. Reference Manual on Scientific Evidence, *supra.*
29. David Goodstein, *How Science Works,* Reference Manual on Scientific Evidence, *supra* at 81–82.

# Summary

The admissibility of forensic evidence based on science was governed in the federal courts by the General Acceptance Test from the case of *Frye v. United States*, decided in 1923. Shortly after Congress passed the Federal Rule of Evidence 702, governing admissibility of expert opinions, the Supreme Court ruled in 1993 that Rule 702 had superseded the *Frye* test. In this case, *Daubert v. Merrrell Dow*, the Court held that scientific testimony should be admissible if it meets alternate tests of reliability, such as a scientific hypothesis, publication and peer review, and error rate.

The *Daubert Test was* soon adopted in some state courts, but not in all. Some states retain the *Frye* test. The *Daubert* test requires the trial court to act as a gatekeeper and decide outside the hearing of the jury whether the forensic expert testimony is admissible or not. However, the court will conduct a gatekeeper hearing only if a party objects to the admission of expert testimony. It has no independent obligation to hold such a hearing. If the opposing party does not challenge the testimony, he generally cannot raise the issue on appeal.

The *Kuhmo* case decided that the *Daubert* test should apply to experts testifying about a technique—such as examination of a tire to determine any defect—as well as science. The *General Electric* case held that an appeals court must defer to the trial court's gatekeeper decision, unless the trial court abused its discretion. After *Daubert*, courts have expanded the gatekeeper questions to include such issues as whether the science was developed specifically for litigation.

# Discussion Questions

1. How does the *Frye* test differ from the *Daubert* test? Give an example of evidence that might be excluded under the Frye test but included under the Daubert test?

2. What happened to the plaintiffs' case in *Daubert* after the Supreme Court vacated the Court of Appeals judgment and remanded the case back to the Court of Appeals? Did the trial court hold a *Daubert* hearing? Why or why not?

3. Was the *Daubert* case likely to result in the admissibility of more scientific evidence or less? Why?

4. What would have to happen for a court to conclude that bite-mark identification is admissible under Frye? Under Daubert?

5. Were all state courts required to change to the *Daubert* test after the case was decided? Why or why not?

6. What are three questions a trial court should ask in conducting a Daubert hearing?

7. What is your state's test for the admissibility of scientific testimony?

8. What was the effect of the changes Congress made to FRE 702 after the *Daubert* decision? Does FRE 702 specifically require a gatekeeping hearing?

9. How did the court extend the *Daubert* decision in the case of *Kuhmo Tire v. Carmichael*?

10. How did the opinion in *General Electric v. Joiner* affect gatekeeper hearings? Did this decision make it harder or easier for the losing party to get the appellate court to overturn the trial court's *Daubert* ruling on admissibility of forensic testimony?

11. What is the definition of "abuse of discretion?" What do you think a trial court would have to do in a gatekeeper hearing to be an abuse of discretion?

12. Do you believe that the *Daubert* decision means a trial court should refuse to admit forensic testimony *solely* because it has been generally accepted by the scientific community? What if the testimony otherwise would fail to meet the other tests in *Daubert*?

# Chapter 6

# The Scientific Method and Forensic Evidence

## Overview

The first requirement of the *Daubert* test is that scientific testimony must be based on a valid hypothesis and methodology. This requires that the court distinguish between "true science" and theories called "junk science," either because they are based on an hypothesis that has not been tested or proved or because they are simply part of the "folk wisdom." For example, does consuming sugar make children hyper? Will you get stomach cramps if you go swimming right after lunch?

Many of the areas that have been called "junk science" have either been disproved or have turned into real science as they have been tested and refined.

The area of junk science that is most difficult to prove by the scientific method are hypotheses that exposure to certain chemicals or forces causes a specific disease. The reason is because in order to prove causation, the scientist must rule out all other possible causes. Isolating one particular agent to the exclusion of all others is a daunting scientific task. It is ironic that *Daubert* involved just such an hypothesis, namely, that ingesting Bendectin caused birth defects.

There have been two issues regarding causation that engendered much research and litigation: the question of whether electro-magnetic force fields cause cancer and the question of whether silicone breast implants cause autoimmune disease. Although broad-based studies have shown neither hypothesis can be proved, many people continue to dispute the research and insist on the causal link.

In the area of forensics in criminal law, some techniques have not been proven under the scientific method to be reliable as a form of individual identification. These include bite-mark identification, lip print identification, and bullet identification through lead composition. Handwriting analysis has been questioned because the process does not have one standard protocol, but rather relies on the judgment and experience of the examiner. Polygraph has been rejected by most courts due to its high error rate and the likelihood that it may prejudice the jury into substituting the polygraph for an independent finding of guilt or innocence.

# Chapter Objectives

Based on this chapter, students will be able to:

1. Explain the scientific method.
2. Identify the scientific hypotheses underlying fingerprints, DNA testing and eyewitness identification.
3. Understand the concept of "error rate" in science.
4. Describe the concept of junk science.
5. Identify the reason various types of junk science fail to meet the scientific method.
6. Appreciate the difference in proving causation in a personal injury civil case and proving identity in a criminal case.
7. Read and explain the results of a gatekeeper hearing, including identifying the test the court is using (*Daubert*, *Frye*, or something else), the scientific hypothesis, the issue of proof for which the expert testimony is being offered, the standard of review, and the result of the challenge.

# The Scientific Method

Science. The observation, identification, description, experimental investigation, and theoretical explanation of phenomena.

As we saw in the previous chapter, the *Daubert* test and Rule 702 are designed to ensure that scientific and technical forensic testimony is based on reliable science. The dictionary definition of "science" is "the observation, identification, description, experimental investigation, and theoretical explanation of phenomena."[1] In essence, a scientific "theory" results from the observation of phenomena, the creation of a hypothesis and the testing of that hypothesis to support or disprove the phenomena in question. A scientist and his or her colleagues create tests or experiments to try to test the validity of the hypothesis.

In an effort to help federal judges assess scientific evidence, the Federal Judicial Center published an extensive Reference Manual on Scientific Evidence.[2] David Goodstein, in his article "What is Science," which appears in the Manual, says:

If one asks a scientist the question, What is science?, the answer will almost surely be that science is a process, a way of examining the natural world and discovering important truths about it. In short, the essence of science is the scientific method.

Another author of the Manual defined "good science" as follows:

Good science is usually described as dependent upon qualities such as falsifiable hypotheses, replication, verification, peer-review and publication, general acceptance, consensus, communalism, universalism, organized skepticism, neu-

---

1. American Heritage Dictionary.
2. Reference Manual on Scientific Evidence, *supra*.

trality, experiment/empiricism, objectivity, dispassionate observation, natural-istic explanation, and use of the scientific method."[3]

# Proving a Theory Wrong

A theory can never be proved right by observation until every conceivable alternate explanation has been discounted. However, it can be proved wrong. Thus evolved the scientists' quest to prove theories were wrong.

> The scientific process as set forth by Karl Popper and well-described in Peter Huber's book *Judging Science*, requires repeated research, revision of hypotheses, yet more testing, until ultimately there has been enough pounding on the post that it feels secure enough to build something on. This process takes place through replication in multiple studies, repeated conference presentations, and lots of back and forth in the scientific community.[4]

The process that can prove hypotheses that originally seem like "junk science" are true involves testing under controlled circumstances and ruling out alternative explanations for results.

The word "error" in law means that a court has made a mistake—something no court being reviewed on appeal wants to hear. The word "error" in science is not a problem as it is in law. In science, error is intrinsic to any process of measurement. Scientists expect error and, indeed, search for it. In fact, one of the hallmarks of science is that an "error rate" can be ascribed to the results of testing. That is why you hear plus or minus x% as an error rate. Error can result from two causes: mistakes that occur in the testing process as a random event and human error.

Certain "ideal standards of conduct" should govern scientific inquiry in order to legitimize it. The scientist should be unbiased, self-critical and open-minded. Edmond and Mercer, in "Trashing Junk Science" put it this way:[5]

> There have been a number of attempts to formulate the ideal standards of conduct (norms) and institutional imperatives of science. Robert Merton provided the most famous formulation of these imperatives, categorizing them under the four headings of communalism, universalism, disinterestedness, and organized skepticism."[6]

Some commentators reject the notion that there is one all-purpose scientific method. For example, Edmond and Mercer say:

> The notion that there is a simple, identifiable, universal scientific method used in some kind of standard way by scientists to distinguish science from non-science is difficult to support on any kind of empirical basis. One of the factors which illustrate the implausibility of this contention is the sheer diversity of activities which can be placed beneath the umbrella of modern science. Given such diversity, various branches of scientific knowledge rely, to different degrees, upon observational practices, experimental tests, mathematical proofs, and so on.

---

3. *Id.* at 13.
4. William L. Anderson and Barry M. Parsons, *The Growing Role of Litigation-Generated Science,* 10-1 Mealey's *Daubert* Rep. 25 (2006).
5. Edmond and Mercer, *Trashing Junk Science,* 1998 Stan. Tech. L. Rev. 3, 29.
6. *Id.* at 25.

For instance, in some branches of industrial chemistry, test situations can be established where there are strong linkages between theory, practice and phenomena. In contrast, other areas of science rely upon situations intrinsically difficult to test. These situations, then, may rely on statistical methods, new, sensitive measuring devices, and phenomena not easily modeled in the laboratory. The latter is true in many areas of atmospheric physics, ecology, and epidemiology."[7]

Science does not proceed smoothly in properly sequential "baby steps." To the contrary, it appears to advance is large "jumps." Whereas science may have been a "gentlemen's calling" in the 1800's, characterized by collecting and cataloging butterflies and rocks, today it involves peer review and publication, government grants, prestige and money in the form of prizes, such as the Nobel Prize.[8] It may also result in discoveries of enormous economic value such as patents for stem cells and new drugs.

To summarize, the scientific method requires these steps:

1. **An hypothesis**
2. **Observation and/or experimentation to prove the hypothesis false**
3. **Sufficient sample size to draw valid conclusions**
4. **Elimination of any alternative hypothesis for the results**
5. **Explanation for any contradictions of the evidence**

# The Science Underlying Forensic Identification

Four of the types of forensic science that we will examine in detail are all different methods of determining identification: fingerprint identification, DNA typing, eyewitness identification, and handwriting analysis are used to identify a person based on comparison of a sample or samples. In order to be accepted by the trial court, each type of science must demonstrate that it is reliable and has been reliably applied. The trial court must first determine if there is a valid scientific hypothesis and whether the test results have accounted for all alternate explanations.

There is one basic scientific hypothesis that underlies all four identification forensics we will review, which is the concept that the item being tested is unique between individuals:

- Each person's fingerprints are unique, so a fingerprint match will identify a person to the exclusion of all others.

- Each person's DNA is unique, so a DNA profile will identify a person to the exclusion of all others (except an identical twin).

- No two people look exactly alike, so an eyewitness identification is reliable in identifying a suspect.

- No two people write exactly alike, so an examination of samples of handwriting will reveal if a person has written another document.

---

7. Edmund and Mercer, *supra* at 29.

8. The scandal in Korea over falsified data and the subsequent resignation of its chief scientist shows the pressure to publish results is international in scope. *See* Nicholas Wade, *University Panel Faults Cloning Co-Author*, The New York Times, February 11, 2006.

What follows is a brief overview of the science and challenges to these four areas of forensic identification, each of which will be discussed in detail in a subsequent chapter.

# Fingerprints

The validity of a fingerprint identification rests on two hypotheses: first, that fingerprints are unique and second, that the methodology of identification is sufficient to distinguish one print from another. How do we *know* that each person's fingerprints are unique? We obviously cannot take fingerprints from everyone in the world and compare them. So scientists examine a sample of people to see if the fingerprints in that sample are unique. This presents the first obstacle to evaluating scientific accuracy. How many fingerprints are enough to prove the hypothesis? You would agree that looking at the prints of ten people would not be useful. Even if they were all unique, there might be other people who shared the same fingerprints. Scientists must therefore combine a representative sample with sufficient sample size, using the laws of statistics to generalize to the general population. Depending on the size of the sample, scientists may give a level of confidence to their conclusion that is less than 100%.

For example, if scientists looked at the fingerprints only of white males, someone might question if the sample were representative. What if white females had a different pattern in their fingerprints? What if race made a difference? The job of the scientists is to think up as many explanations as possible for why the theory might be wrong and then test those theories.

As a result of fingerprint testing and the use of databases in which the three basic patterns of all prints—arch, loop, and whorl—have been entered, scientists concluded that approximately 65% of all people have a loop pattern, 30% have a whorl and 5% have an arch.[9] Based on this statistic, there would be no way to identify a person based on a whorl pattern alone, as someone with a whorl print would have the same pattern—and therefore be indistinguishable from—30% of the population.

The next step was for scientists to look at smaller patterns within the patterns. They identified approximately ten "ridge characteristics," smaller patterns such as a ridge ending, an island or a crossover line. As each fingerprint has up to 200 of these characteristics, the statistical chances of someone else having the exact same characteristics in the same specific locations on his or her fingerprint is astronomically small.

> The statistical chances of someone else having the exact same "ridge characteristics" in the same specific locations on his or her fingerprint is astronomically small.

But *how* small? Scientists do not know. No one has yet studied a random population to determine how many ridge endings, islands, or crossovers occur. Of the 200 characteristics, do 80% of people have crossovers, but only 20% have islands? We do not know. In addition, are the characteristics spread over a fingerprint randomly, or do islands appear in the upper left quadrant of 90% of the population? We don't know that either.

---

9. Moenssens, Starrs, Henderson and Inbau, *Scientific Evidence in Civil and Criminal Cases,* 4th ed., Foundation Press, at 506.

The "science" behind fingerprint matching is not perfect. Scientists do not match prints by overlaying a photograph of one perfect fingerprint over another on a computer screen that then displays the word MATCH! This is a scene made to entertain television audiences in show such as Crime Scene Investigation. Examiners do most of their work looking under magnification at small, blurred and splotchy lines, trying to determine if there are any dissimilarities. They work first to exclude, and then to include.

Fingerprint examiners in some states are permitted to declare that a partial fingerprint lifted from a crime site absolutely identifies a suspect if the expert finds only 10 ridge characteristics in common.[10] Is this adequate to absolutely identify someone? The FBI has no minimum number of points required to declare a match. Law enforcement points to the fact that there are almost no errors reported; hence, the system must be valid. But this is not a scientific proof.

The lack of scientific validity between the number of ridge characteristics matched and the lack of data about the distribution of ridge characteristics in the population led one court to reject fingerprint analysis as being unreliable.[11] The court agreed with the hypothesis that no two fingerprints are alike, but disagreed that the methodology of identification had controlling standards, peer review, and other evidence of reliability discussed in *Daubert*.

# DNA

> A DNA profile includes fewer than 20 of more than 2,000 possible genetic markers. A match results from using probability statistics.

Because DNA typing was developed after scientists had mapped the entire human genome, they created a database showing the proportion of genetic variations at each site tested in a DNA profile. As pointed out earlier, DNA profiles do *not* display a person's total DNA profile. In fact, as with fingerprints, DNA profiling generally looks at 13[12] of a possible 2,000 places where DNA variations occur with no known association with a genetic trait. But because scientists know the relative proportions of variations at those 13 locations, they can create statistical probabilities of the likelihood of a "random match." The science underlying DNA typing is well accepted. Some defendants have challenged specific methods of DNA typing, as did Grant, but the courts routinely reject such motions. We will review this in more detail in the DNA chapter.

# Eyewitness Identification

> Prisoners have been exonerated by DNA, even though the victim still believes that his or her visual identification was correct.

The scientific proposition that a suspect of a violent crime will be able to categorically identify the perpetrator even when the crime takes place for only a few minutes and under extraordinary stress, has been seriously undermined by testing and research. Many prisoners have been convicted on the strength of a positive iden-

---

10. *United States v. Plaza*, 179 F. Supp. 2d (E.D. Pa. 2002), vacated, 1888 F. Supp. 2d 549 (2002).
11. *Id.*
12. The two most common test kits contain 15 markers, but 2 overlap. See p. 186.

tification by a victim. Some of these prisoners have been exonerated by DNA, even though the victim still believes that his or her visual identification was correct! Besides the fact that many people *do* look alike, there are other factors that may show visual identifications are particularly "unscientific." Most of the eyewitnesses experiments actually disprove the hypothesis of valid visual identification. We will examine these in the chapter on eyewitness identification.

These examples show that proof of a scientific hypothesis rests on many subsidiary scientific hypotheses and testing of those hypotheses to establish validity. And that is the job of the trial judge following the *Daubert* decision.

## Handwriting

The scientific hypothesis underlying handwriting comparisons is that each person's handwriting is unique and consistent from one piece of writing to the next. However, this hypothesis has a number of caveats. First, analysts agree that each writer will exhibit small variations within his own writing. In addition, handwriting is known to change based on age, stress, mental impairment, and other factors.

Albert S. Osborn wrote an extensive manual on handwriting analysis in the 1930s called Questioned Documents, and he testified as an expert about the authorship of the ransom note in the Lindbergh baby kidnapping. Nevertheless, neither Osborn nor any subsequent expert can point to any protocol for what specific similarities to look for or in what order, nor how many similarities are required to determine common authorship. Experts commonly state that their opinion is based on their experience and training. This factor has led some courts to conclude that there is no reliable science to handwriting analysis.

Yet as we will see in the chapter on handwriting, expert opinions are commonly admitted in court on the ground that handwriting analysis is generally accepted.

## Junk Science

The term junk science was coined in the late 1980s and early 1990s. Peter Huber, of the Manhattan Institute, promoted the term in a number of publications, including one called "Gallileo's Revenge: Junk Science in the Courtroom."[13] He argued that scientific theories are promoted by special interest groups, entrepreneurial scientists, and the press—eager to "explain" various phenomena to the public.

Some critics argue that the courtroom, with its emphasis on an adversarial system and use of cross examination of experts to impeach their credibility, their credentials, and method of experiment, actually promotes junk science. Scientists who might otherwise be willing to admit error rates or other problems with experimen-

> Junk science is a conclusion presented as a scientific "truth" that has been derived without using the scientific method as its source.

---

13. Peter W. Huber, *Galileo's Revenge: Junk Science in the Courtroom*, New York: Basic Books, Harper Collins, 1991.

tal results are forced to overstate certainty as a result of the process. Others argue that the court system is the best possible place to test scientific conclusions because it is an adversarial system.

## Junk Science Is Not New

In the opinion of many historians, President George Washington died in 1799 as a result of his doctors "bleeding" him after he was injured in a horse fall. Doctors withdrew almost 4 pounds of blood.[14] At the time, it was an accepted scientific "truth" that a person who was ill would recover if part of his diseased blood were removed from his body. This led to the use of leeches to suck blood from the patient, or cutting open of a vein in order to speed the outflow of blood. Bloodletting, now referred to in medicine as phlebotomy, was used from the time of the Egyptians. Blood was considered one of the four "humors" along with phlegm, black bile and yellow bile. The concept of bloodletting was based on the assumption that reduction in the amount of blood would help balance the humors.[15]

We now know that lack of blood can actually lead to death by exsanguination. In 1628, William Harvey disproved the basis of bloodletting and Pierre Louis showed it was ineffective in the treatment of pneumonia and various fevers in the 1800s.[16]

However, bloodletting remained popular, in part because the key to curing disease was slow in developing and doctors preferred to prescribe some treatment rather than nothing at all. Until the late 1800s, the only medicines available were mercury, quinine, digitalis, amyl nitrate and colchicum.[17]

Why is bloodletting an example of "junk science?" First, what was the scientific hypothesis? An ill person will recover if some of his blood is removed in order to balance his humors. The observation of the effects of blood-letting seemed to confirm the hypothesis. That is, it must have appeared that more people recovered than died as a result of bloodletting. But do those ideas prove that the bloodletting caused the recovery? That is where the scientific method fell apart.

> A controlled experiment involves two groups of subjects, who are the same in every way possible, but only one of which is given the treatment being studied.

The scientists who supported bloodletting failed to use a controlled experiment to test their hypothesis. What would such an analysis have entailed? First, the scientists would need two people suffering from the same disease. Then one would have blood removed and the other would not. The results would tend to show whether the bloodletting helped. Of course, just two patients would not be a sufficiently large sample to even suggest any measure of accuracy. How many people would need to be a part of the experiment to be satisfied that it was valid? Two, two hundred or 2 million?

---

14. Vibal V. Vadakon, M.D., *The Asphyxiating and Exsanguination Death of President George Washington,* http://xnet.kp.org/.

15. Gilbert R. Seigworth, M.D., *Bloodletting Over the Centuries,* http://www.pbs.org/wnet/red-gold/basics/bloodlettinghistory.html.

16. Edmund and Mercer, *supra.*

17. *Id.*

Next is the problem of alternative theories. Assume that in the test performed above, all the patients recovered at the same rate. Did that mean that the bloodletting helped or had no effect? Now assume further that the patients who underwent the bloodletting recovered and those without bloodletting did not. What other variable might have resulted in the bloodletting patients' recovery? Perhaps each of the patients was not as ill to begin with, perhaps they had a stronger blood count to begin with, perhaps they were in rooms with open windows and other patients were housed next to people with another infectious disease. You can see that there are as many variables as there is imagination. Of course, our knowledge today about disease and how it is transmitted is very helpful in seeing why bloodletting was junk science.

Bloodletting is an example of a scientific hypothesis involving causation. Causation is particularly difficult to prove, because the scientist must use carefully controlled experiments and must account for all other explanations. This can often prove almost impossible. Today, the public is constantly bombarded with the latest test results that show causation of disease or injury. For example, in 2004, two scientific publications reported that taking high levels of folate and vitamin B6 reduced the risk of heart attack by one half.[18] In 2007, an article in The Journal of the American Medical Association reported that a study of 68 large trials with more than 232,000 adults showed that large amounts of vitamins A, E and beta carotene were associated with a slightly increased risk of death resulting from heart problems.[19] Were the vitamins identical? Were the doses identical? And were the groups of subjects identical? Are vitamins a wonderful preventive or a cause of injury?

As soon as the 2007 study was released, scientists cautioned that many other factors may have caused this apparent result.[20] A representative of a trade group for the vitamin industry stated "most of these patients already had disease, so the conclusions simply aren't relevant to a healthy population." The authors of the new study shot back: "Previous studies have included a select group of trials, risking cherry-picking, either good or bad. Our systematic review is based on more trials and more participants, and hence is more powerful."[21] Other scientists cautioned that a randomized clinical trial, the "gold standard for medical research, may not be the best way to evaluate vitamin supplements."[22]

Although bloodletting is now discredited as a method of healing, the lowly leech has recently been shown to have healing properties. Surgeons performing microsurgery have discovered that leeches can help heal tiny veins that must connect correctly in hand surgery. Applying a leech to the site results in the leech injecting a natural anti-coagulant into the wound, which creates an artificial circulation. This gives the finger a chance to grow new vein attachments and the wound to heal.[23] This is an example of how true science can grow out of junk science.

The following are some examples of scientific conclusions that are currently viewed as "junk science:"

---

18. Chris Gupta, *Share the Wealth*, http://www.mewmediaexplorer.org/chris/2004/11/02/vitamins_prevent_heart_disease.htm.

19. Michael Mason, *Another Supplement under the Microscope*, The New York Times, March 13, 2007.

20. *Id.*

21. *Id.*

22. *Id.*

23. Gerry Rising, *Leeches have a healing role in modern surgery,*" Buffalo News, August 28, 2005.

## Can Anthropometry Conclusively Identify a Person?

Anthropometry was the practice of measuring detailed body parts, developed in 1879 by Alphonse Bertillon, a Parisian law enforcement officer.[24] His scientific hypothesis was that each person's body is unique, so that a series of specific bodily measurements would absolutely identify an individual. One purpose was to identify a person who had been recently arrested and compare it to records made at an earlier arrest to establish the existence of a prior record. This would avoid the use of false identities to conceal one's true identity.

Bertillon used calipers to measure the hands, head, limbs, torso and face of an individual. Here are some examples of the detailed measurements contained with Anthropometry:

1. length and width of the head
2. left middle finger, left foot and left forearm
3. height, span of arms, trunk, right ear
4. profile of head
5. ear
6. front view of face
7. ridge and base of nose and nose dimensions
8. left eye
9. eye pigmentation

In his book, Signaletic Instructions Including the Theory and Practice of Antropometrical Identification, published in 1896,[25] Bertillon presented detailed measurements of all parts of the ear. Although Anthropometry was not the result of the scientific method, perhaps the presence of particular "instruments" for measurement, combined with a detailed set of measurements and chart of results, led people to believe it was science simply because it "looked like science." Again, keep this idea in mind as we review some more recent junk science.

> The Bertillon system of anthropometric measurements … was abandoned worldwide because it failed to provide reliable and unique measurements and was too cumbersome to administer in a uniform manner, never relied on a single measurement of any part of the body for identifying a specific individual.[26]

Ironically, anthomopometry is still used for certain purposes today. For example, NASA uses anthropometry in designing space capsules to fit human proportions.[27] Cranofacial Anthropometry—mesurements of the skull and face—can help diagnose plagiocephaly, a condition in infants that may require surgery.[28] Anthromopometry evolved into the science of measuring just one body part—the fingerprint—in order to distinguish individuals. This hypothesis has been tested, and today no one seriously disputes that fingerprints can absolutely identify an individual.

---

24. http://www.onin.com/fp/fphistory.html.
25. *See* http://www.forensic-evidence.com/site/ID/ID_bertillion.html.
26. *Id.*
27. National Aeronautics and Space Administration, 3 Anthropometry and Biomechanics, http://msis.jsc.nasa.gov/sections/section03.htm.
28. www.plagiocephaly.org/headshape/anthropometry.htm.

# Do Electromagnetic Fields Cause Breast Cancer?

An example of how scientific hypotheses can become engrained in the public's view of "truth" is the possible association between electromagnetic fields and breast cancer. Beginning in the 1990s, breast cancer researchers noticed that women who lived near the magnetic fields generated by power lines on Long Island, New York, exhibited a higher incidence of breast cancer than the national average. This led to the hypothesis that something about the electromagnetic field (EMF) generated by the electrical wires was a carcinogen.

In 1993, Public Law 103-43 was enacted to direct the National Cancer Institute to conduct a study of "potential environmental and other risks contributing to the incidence of breast cancer" in Nassau, Suffolk and Schoharic counties, New York, and Tolland County, Connecticut. The study on Long Island was to include the use of a geographic system to evaluate the current and past exposure of individuals, including direct monitoring and cumulative estimates of a number of environmental factors, including pesticides, hazardous and municipal waste, and electromagnetic fields.[29]

In 1996, the Harvard Center for Cancer Prevention issued a report entitled "Harvard Report on Cancer Prevention, Volume 1: Causes of Human Cancer." Its section on Electromagnetic fields stated "Based on current research, a cause and effect relationship between EMF and cancer, or any other disease, has not been established but cannot be definitively ruled out."[30] The report added:

> In spite of the fact that a number of scientific review groups have failed to establish a hazardous EMF level or even a definitive EMF-disease link, the issue continues to capture the public interest.[31]

The National Cancer Institute and the National Institute of Environmental Health Sciences then began a study of Long Island women. Their hypothesis was the following:

> Exposure to extremely low frequency magnetic fields may increase breast cancer risk by affecting melatonin production.

Melatonin is a hormone produced by the pineal gland, which is located at the base of the brain. Melatonin levels were initially believed to be inversely related to estrogen levels in that when melatonin levels are low, estrogen levels rise. Since increased levels of estrogen are hypothesized to increase the risk of breast cancer, a suppression of melatonin rates would increase estrogen and therefore possibly increase the risk of breast cancer. This hypothesis was based on the observation that exposure to light-at-night (for example, as in night shift work) suppresses a normal rise at nighttime in melatonin production. More specically, the hypothesis was that electromagnetic fields might work similarly to light-at-night in suppressing melatonin.

The study consisted of over 1,000 women. Of that number, 576 women had been newly diagnosed with breast cancer between August 1, 1996 and June 20, 1997 and 585 women, the control group, did not have the disease. All of the women were under 75 years of age and all had lived in their current homes for at least 15 years before the time of diagnosis of breast cancer or the time they were identified in the control group.

---

29. National Cancer Institute, "Questions and Answers about the Electromagnetic Fields and Breast Cancer on Long Island Study," at http://cancer.gov/newscenter/doc.aspx?.

30. Harvard Center for Cancer Prevention, Harvard Report on Cancer Prevention, at http://www.hsph.harvard.edu/cancer/ublications/reports/vol1_full_text/vol1_emfields.html.

31. *Id.*

The study included a comprehensive home assessment through personal interviews and taking a variety of EMF measurements within and around the outside of the home. Included were 24-hour measurements in the bedroom and the most frequently used room, aside from the bedroom and kitchen, coupled with spot measurements in other locations of the home, ground-current magnetic field measurements, and an analysis of the wire coding in the home. A questionnaire was used to gather data on residential history, housing construction history, occupational exposures, electric appliance use, and exposure to light-at-night shift work.

The study found no association between residential exposure to EMFs and breast cancer. The levels of EMFs between the breast cancer group (those who developed breast cancer) and the control group did not differ. Further, there were no differences in risk between the two groups when the data were analyzed, controlling for age, family history of breast cancer, personal history of benign breast disease, number or children, or education.

The results of the study were reported in June of 2003.[32] It did not, however, settle the controversy, and various groups still contend that EMFs are responsible for breast cancer. This report was greeted with disbelief and anger by many who had already formed their own opinion on the issue. The public was sure the study was rigged by industry sympathetic to the EMF industry. Or perhaps, it was conducted in a sloppy manner. When they heard the results of the study, the utility companies breathed a sigh of relief that they would not be subject to multi-million dollar lawsuits.

Assuming that the study is a sufficient sample and was conducted based on scientific protocol, it would appear that the increase in breast cancer on Long Island (in fact there is an increase all along the Northeast corridor over nationwide rates) must be caused by another factor.[33]

Cancer research, in general, is very difficult because scientists believe that no one carcinogen (cancer causing agent) "causes" cancer and that even known carcinogens, such as nicotine, may lead to lung cancer in one patient and leave another cancer-free.

> Research studies have not stopped litigation. Plaintiffs continue to sue alleging damage from electromagnetic fields.

The research studies have not stopped litigation. Plaintiffs continue to sue alleging damage from electromagnetic fields. In a case in Indiana state court, the court rejected plaintiffs' expert because he had not examined the plaintiffs or ruled out any other possible cause of their alleged injuries. The court also commented that one of the experts was questionable because he held no medical degree.[34]

## Do Silicone Breast Implants Cause Autoimmune Disease?

Another example of junk science is whether silicone breast implants cause disease. In the 1990s, women began to suspect that silicone implants caused various autoimmune diseases. A class action was filed against Dow Corning, the largest manufacturer of sili-

---

32. *Id.*
33. Lisa Diedrich and Emily Boyce, *'Breast Cancer on Long Island': The Emergence of a New Object through Mapping Practices,* http://journals.cambridge.org/action/displayAbstract:jsessionid=1032936#.
34. *Indiana Michigan Power v. Runge,* No. 50A05-9811-CV 529 (Ind. App. 1999).

cone implants. Dow settled the case in 1994 for $3.2 billion dollars. In November of 1998, Dow filed for bankruptcy.[35]

Shortly thereafter, in June of 1999, the Institute of Medicine released a 400-page report prepared by 13 scientists independent of Dow. The report concluded that although silicone breast implants may be responsible for localized problems, such as hardening or scarring, they do not cause any major disease such as lupus or rheumatoid arthritis. This report did not put the controversy to rest, in part because the Committee formed its opinion by reviewing past data rather than conducting any original research.[36]

In 1992, the F.D.A. had asked manufacturers to voluntarily take silicone breast implants off the market. By the year 2000, manufacturers began applying to the FDA for approval to market silicone implants. In November of 2006, the F.D.A. granted permission to two manufacturers to begin selling silicone breast implants again. Doctors stated that the silicone implants were far preferable in feel to saline, which was the product of choice once silicone implants were removed from the market.[37] Unfortunately, this ruling came too late for Dow Corning Company. It had gone bankrupt.

Although the thousands of claims against Dow Chemical for injury allegedly caused by silicone implants were foiled by the company's bankruptcy, and a federal study showed no link between the implants and any type of systemic disease, plaintiffs continue to sue other manufacturers on similar claims. In 2004, a Florida district court refused to allow testimony by Dr. Douglas Radford Shanklin, who was prepared to testify that silicone implants caused rheumatologic disease, connective-tissue disease and autoimmune disease. His theory was that silicone degrades and that one can detect silica in breast tissue. The court ruled that such a claim did not withstand evidence submitted by the defendant that showed substantial evidence of the "lack of general acceptance of the methodologies and principles underlying Plaintiff's proposed testimony."[38]

Furthermore, the court held that the use of polarizing microscopy was not reliable as a means of detecting crystalline silica. Even if such silica were present, the court found that there was no credible evidence that silicone antibodies were linked with immune system dysfunction.

Breast implant experts have also been denied in Texas,[39] and in federal court in New York.[40] In another breast implant case, the plaintiff's expert was excluded because he was not qualified and failed to demonstrate that his opinion was reliable.[41] These cases illustrate the difficulty of proving causation by scientific testimony, particularly when long-term government studies have been published refuting the argument.

The breast implant controversy illustrates that unless controlled studies with large sample sizes are conducted, the public will not accept "official" reports. Skepticism remains high, particularly in areas where the public believes that corporate manufacturers may have a motive to withhold the truth.

---

35. http://www.pbs.org/wgbh/pages/frontline/implants/cron.html.

36. *Id.*

37. Stephanie Saul, *FDA Will Allow Breast Implants Made of Silicone; Decision ends 14-year Ban,* The New York Times, November 6, 2006.

38. *Clegg v. Medical Engineering Corp.,* No. 97-004438-CA, (Fla. Cir. 2004) reported in 8-3 Mealey's Daubert Rep. 12 (2004).

39. *Polston v. McGhan,* No. 96-1443, 2000 Tex. App. LEXIS (Tex. Ct. App., May 22, 2000).

40. *Pozefsky v. Baxter Healthcare Corp.,* No. 92-CV-0314, 2001 U.S. Dist. LEXIS 11813 (N.D.N.Y. 2001).

41. *Schrott v. Bristol-Myers,* No. 03 C 1522, 2003 U.S. Dist. LEXIS 18890 (N.D. Ill. 2003).

## What Causes Fibromyalgia?

Consider the disease called "fibromyalgia." This condition, sometimes called a syndrome, is characterized by chronic fatigue, insomnia, and general pain. A syndrome is a set of symptoms that appear to occur together without a clear cause. There is no blood test, x-ray, or biopsy than can diagnose fibromyalgia. In fact, the common way doctors presently diagnose this disease is by first observing the symptoms, and second, by eliminating every other disease which might account for those symptoms.

In *Black v. Food Lion, Inc.* the Fifth Circuit said that because neither the expert nor medical science knows the exact process that triggers fibromyalgia, the expert's use of a general methodology cannot support a causation conclusion for which there is no underlying medical support:

**Black v. Food Lion, Inc., 171 F.3d 308 (5th Cir. 1999)**

\* \* \*

First, Dr. Reyna's theory has not, according to the evidence at trial, been verified by testing and, thus, has not been peer-reviewed. In fact, Dr. Reyna acknowledged that fibromyalgia has no known etiology (i.e., medical science does not know if the cause of the condition is muscle, nerve, or hormone damage).

If medical science does not know the cause, then Dr. Reyna's "theory" of causation, to the extent it is a theory, is isolated and unsubstantiated. Even Dr. Reyna recognized the limits of her opinion. When asked if she had been able to identify the cause of Black's fibromyalgia, she stated, "I didn't find the cause. I found an event that contributed to the development of the symptom. I did not find the cause." On its own terms, Dr. Reyna's opinion includes conjecture, not deduction from scientifically-validated information.

It also follows from the scientific literature that Dr. Reyna's theory has failed to gain acceptance within the medical profession. Experts in the field conclude that the ultimate cause of fibromyalgia cannot be known, and only an educated guess can be made based on the patient's history. Mere conjecture does not satisfy the standard for general acceptance, except to demonstrate general acceptance of a proposition contrary to Dr. Reyna's. Finally, Dr. Reyna's theory of causation, which has not been verified or generally accepted, also has no known potential rate of error.

The magistrate judge either substituted his own standards of reliability for those in *Daubert*, or he confused the *Daubert* analysis by adopting an excessive level of generality in his gatekeeping inquiry. Thus, the magistrate judge read the Vancouver Report to approve "an accepted protocol in rendering an opinion in terms of reasonable medical probability." He then found that Dr. Reyna followed this protocol by (a) taking a medical history from Black, (b) ruling out prior or subsequent "causes" of fibromyalgia, (c) performing or reviewing physical tests [which all turned up negative], and (d) deducing that the Food Lion fall was the only possible remaining cause of fibromyalgia that appeared nine months later.

\* \* \*

The underlying predicates of any cause-and-effect medical testimony are that medical science understands the physiological process by which a particular disease or syndrome develops and knows what factors cause the process to occur. Based on such predicate knowledge, it may then be possible to fasten legal liability for a person's disease or injury.

* * *

In this case, neither Dr. Reyna nor medical science knows the exact process that results in fibromyalgia or the factors that trigger the process. Absent these critical scientific predicates, for which there is no proof in the record, no scientifically reliable conclusion on causation can be drawn. Dr. Reyna's use of a general methodology cannot vindicate a conclusion for which there is no underlying medical support.

A Washington court also rejected an expert who proposed to testify that trauma caused fibromyalgia. The appellate court concluded that science is still unclear as to how fibromyalgia is triggered. The plaintiffs had argued that the *Frye* test was inapplicable because the theory was not new or novel. "Here, given the clear disagreement in the relevant scientific community as to the cause of fibromyalgia, which conflict has also been recognized in other jurisdictions," the court held the expert was properly disqualified.[42]

However, the supreme court of Nebraska held that the fact that there is controversy in the scientific community as to whether trauma causes fibromyalgia is no reason to exclude expert testimony that rests on a sound theory:

**Epp v. Lauby, 271 Neb. 640, 715 N.W.2d 501 (2006)**

* * *

Handke concluded that Epp's fibromyalgia was caused by the physical trauma of the accident after conducting a differential diagnosis.

In Carlson v. Okerstrom, we addressed the reliability of a differential diagnosis. We stated that differential diagnosis is a technique which generally has widespread acceptance in the medical community, has been subjected to peer review, and does not frequently lead to incorrect results.

We emphasized, however, that an expert's opinion is not admissible simply because he or she conducted a differential diagnosis. To the contrary, in order for an expert's opinion to be reliable, the court must determine whether the expert conducted a reliable differential diagnosis.

In Carlson, we set forth a two-step process for determining whether an expert conducted a reliable differential diagnosis.

The first step in conducting a reliable differential diagnosis is to "compile a comprehensive list of hypotheses that might explain the set of salient clinical findings under consideration." ... If the expert "rules in" a potential cause that is not capable of causing the patient's symptoms, the expert's opinion is of questionable reliability.... Similarly, if the expert completely fails to consider a cause that could explain the patient's symptoms, the differential diagnosis is not reliable....

Once the expert has ruled in all plausible causes for the patient's condition, the next step is to "engage in a process of elimination, eliminating hypotheses on the basis of a continuing examination of the evidence so as to reach a conclusion as to the most likely cause of the findings in that particular case.... In analyzing the second step of a differential diagnosis under the *Daubert/Schafersman* framework, the question is whether the expert had a reasonable basis for con-

---

42. *Grant v. Boccia*, 133 Wn. App. 176, 137 P.3d 20 (2006).

cluding that one of the plausible causative agents was the most likely culprit for the patient's symptoms. In other words, the expert must be able to show good grounds for eliminating other potential hypotheses.

\* \* \*

After reviewing the evidence and applying the *Daubert/Schafersman* standards, the trial court found that the theory of a causal link between physical trauma and fibromyalgia has not been verified by sufficient testing, has not been subject to peer review, and does not enjoy general acceptance within the medical community. Consequently, the court excluded Handke's testimony on the cause of Epp's fibromyalgia. Upon our review, we determine that the court abused its discretion by excluding Handke's testimony.

\* \* \*

Although important, general acceptance of the causal link between physical trauma and fibromyalgia is not determinative of the admissibility of expert testimony under *Daubert/Schafersman* standards. So long as the expert's opinion is based on reliable methodology, his or her opinion is admissible, whether or not the court agrees with the expert's conclusion.

In the instant case, Handke arrived at the conclusion that Epp's fibromyalgia was caused by physical trauma after conducting a reliable differential diagnosis, as we will determine later in this opinion. Handke's conclusion is supported by medical literature in evidence which supports the theory that fibromyalgia may be caused by physical trauma.

\* \* \*

Although the issue is disputed, there is support in the medical literature for the theory that physical trauma can cause fibromyalgia. That support, while controverted, is the result of peer-reviewed research conducted pursuant to appropriate methods of scientific inquiry. While there is not a sufficient scientific consensus to say that the theory is generally accepted, nor has a rate of error been established, the theory that trauma can cause fibromyalgia has been the subject of empirical research, the results of which have been subjected to peer review and publication.

We cannot conclude that Handke and Bennett's reliance on this research, instead of literature to the contrary, was methodologically unreliable. If proffered scientific evidence rests on sound scientific reasoning or methodology and properly can be applied to the facts in issue, it meets the *Daubert* requirements for admissibility, even if the conclusion is novel or controversial. Despite the existence of "spirited dissent," the lack of a scientific consensus on the link between trauma and fibromyalgia was not sufficient to render reliance upon that literature methodologically unreliable.

We, therefore, conclude that the evidence was sufficient to support the theory of a causal relationship between physical trauma and fibromyalgia and that the trial court abused its discretion in concluding otherwise.

## Toxins

Expert testimony about the effects of toxins have met with similar results. Numerous cases have been filed alleging respiratory and other injury caused by mold in the school or workplace.[43] In a *Daubert* hearing in federal court in Illinois, the magistrate refused an expert for railroad employees who alleged they had been injured by mold in the workplace. The magistrate wrote: "there are two fundamental problems: a lack of precision in the data and facts upon which the opinions are based, and a lack of reliability in the methodology and the application of the methodology to the facts. "The major thrust of the expert testimony was to show reports of high colonies of spores and molds coincided with the time when plaintiffs' experienced symptoms. The court stated that the testimony lacked precision and did not present a controlled experiment to "eliminate alternative explanation."[44]

However, a Delaware court recently allowed testimony by a mold expert,[45] holding that any dispute as to the validity of the mold data, which involved a differential diagnosis, went to the weight of the testimony. The testimony of plaintiff's four experts was doubtless more precise than that in the prior case; nonetheless, the court did not rule that mold causation was generally accepted in the scientific community, merely that the jury could hear the evidence and weigh its reliability for itself. A Michigan court also allowed mold testimony in a case by a plaintiff who purchased a newly constructed condominium and claimed illness after moving in.[46] The plaintiff's expert, a certified industrial hygienist, conducted an air quality assessment of the residence. Because the expert did not attempt to argue a direct effect between mold and adverse health effects, the court affirmed a trial court ruling that the defendant could not dismiss the case by a directed verdict.

In a recent lawsuit in which plaintiffs contended that their use of hormone replacement therapy caused cancer, the plaintiffs filed a motion with a federal judge in Arkansas to allow their experts' opinions based on 15 published epidemiological studies that showed hormone therapy is associated with breast cancer to the extent of doubling the risk.[47] It remains to be seen if the appellate court will allow such testimony in a case based on causation of cancer, which most experts agree has no one specific cause.

In another cancer case, a New York court refused to grant the city's request to dismiss a case against it in which plaintiffs argued that they contracted lymphoid leukemia or Hodgkin's Disease, a form of cancer, by contamination of their neighborhood by various toxins. The court held that the experts laid a proper foundation for their opinions, "followed generally accepted methods for collection and analysis of evidence and applied proper techniques to reach their conclusions."[48]

In summary, the area of scientific testimony about causation of injury presents the trial court with unique challenges. Even if the scientific hypothesis that a particular agent causes a certain injury is clear, opponents can challenge the scientific studies by arguing one of the following:

> Expert testimony on causation of injury is subject to challenge based on conflicting studies, study methodology, and failure to account for alternative causes.

- the sample studied was too small

---

43. Lisa Siegel, *Mold's Dangers Gain New Respect,* The Connecticut Law Tribune, January 15, 2007.

44. *Denton v. Northeast Ill. Reg. Commuter Railroad,* No. 02-2220, 2006 LEXIS 57900 (N.D. Ill, August 17, 2006).

45. *Brandt v. Rokeby Realty,* No. 97C-10-132, 2006 Del. Super. LEXIS 280 (Super. Del. 2006).

46. *Groom v. Knoll Construction,* No. 254797, 2005 LEXIS 2283 (Mich. App. 2005).

47. *In re Prempro Products Liability Litigation,* MDL No. 1507 (E.D. Ark. 2006).

48. *Nonnon v. New York,* 32 A.D.3d 91 (N.Y. Sup. 2006).

- the sample was not representative
- there are other conflicting studies that come to the opposite conclusion
- the studies did not account for alternative explanations for the injury

## Psychological Expert Testimony

Other, more creative views of science involving psychological evidence have generally been rejected by the courts in which motions under state rules of evidence similar to *Daubert* or *Frye* have been upheld on appeal. This may be partly due to the fact that such testimony is designed to prove or disprove guilt in criminal trials, where the stakes are higher. For example, a teenaged defendant in a murder trial sought to introduce an expert to testify about false confessions and their alleged presence among juveniles. In an extended *Daubert* hearing, the court held that although the expert was qualified in the study of false confessions, he could not point to any test to determine whether a false confession had occurred.[49]

Psychological testimony was also rejected in a New Jersey case. There the court refused to permit a witness in a criminal trial whose recollection was "hypnotically refreshed," because such testimony was suspect. The court pointed out that guidelines for conducting witness hypnosis to ensure that the results are reliable no longer outweigh the potential harm of the testimony.[50]

Similarly, Connecticut rejected testimony by a psychologist that a teenage defendant had limited ability to understand his *Miranda* rights to refuse to speak without an attorney. An expert proposed to testify that the defendant was unable to understand his rights, based on an evaluation, an interview, IQ testing, personality testing and general achievement testing. The Connecticut Supreme Court agreed with the trial court that this test was an innovative scientific technique that should be subject to a *Daubert* analysis. The only articles the expert submitted in support of the scientific validity of the "Grisso test" were published by Grisso himself, which the court held to be self-promotion and not peer evaluation.[51]

> Psychological testimony introduced to explain a person's actions or reactions is frequently rejected by the court.

On the other hand, psychological testimony about whether a sex offender who had a history of assaulting young girls was highly motivated to reoffend was admitted. In that case, the Pennsylvania court decided that as the expert was applying a "statutory formula" designed to determine whether the offender must register as a sex offender under "Megan's Law," the science was not novel and did not require a *Frye* hearing.[52]

## Who Is the "Relevant Scientific Community?"

One important issue is identifying the relevant "scientific community." For example, in evaluating polygraph reliability, should a court look at the studies conducted by the

49. *Edmonds v. Mississippi*, No. 2004-KA-02081, 2006 LEXIS 88 (Miss App. 2006).
50. *State v. Moore*, 188 N.J. 182, 902 A.2d 1212 (2006).
51. *State v. Griffin*, 273 Conn. 266, 869 A.2d 640 (2004).
52. *State v. Dengler*, 586 Pa. 54, 890 A.2d 372 (2005).

American Polygraph Association? If it did, the reliability statistics would approach 80%.[53] On the other hand, if the court looked at the myriad of websites that claim they can teach someone how to fool a polygraph in ten hours,[54] it might come to the opposite conclusion. Should the court allow both arguments and let the jury decide if the testimony is reliable?

## Admit the Testimony and Let the Jury Decide Its Reliability

Some courts have admitted challenged expert testimony on the theory that the jury should decide what weight to give it. A Georgia court allowed an expert to testify about the level of carbon monoxide in the blood of a victim, who died in the cab of his Freightliner truck.[55] The victim's wife (estate) argued that the carbon monoxide had leaked into the cab. She won her claim for negligence against the owner. The defendants had moved before trial to exclude the blood tests because they did not eliminate the interference caused by methemoglobin, a substance produced by decomposition in the blood of the dead driver. Methemoglobin, the defendant argued, could have increased the level of carbon monoxide found in the deceased body during autopsy.

The Eleventh Circuit Court of Appeals affirmed the $4 million verdict for the plaintiff. However, it disagreed with the trial court that the test had been peer reviewed or that it was reliable. In particular, it said that approval by the agencies did not constitute peer review. However, the court stated that because the defendants had agreed that the underlying test procedure was reliable, they could not contend otherwise on appeal. The defendants had argued simply that the chemical used in the postmortem testing process skewed the results and diminished their accuracy. That argument, the appellate court stated, was an issue relating to the weight of the evidence, not the validity of the underlying testing process.

> Because the defendants had agreed that the underlying test procedure was reliable at the trial court, they could not contend otherwise on appeal.

# *Daubert* Hearings Involving Criminal Forensic Evidence

Cases that involve expert testimony used in criminal trials generally do not involve the same issues as the science involving causation. Some general areas of testimony, such as DNA testing, are subject to judicial notice. Therefore, the court requires no proof of validity of the science. However, gatekeeping hearings about other types of forensic testimony require that they be reliable, generally accepted, or both. The following are some of the issues courts have discussed in gatekeeper hearings about criminal

---

53. http://www.polygraph.org.
54. http://www.wikihow.com/Cheat-a-Polygraph-Test (Lie-Detector).
55. *Nelson v. Freightliner*, 154 Fed. Appx 98 (September 29, 2005).

forensic testimony. For some of these areas, we will discuss the legal issues in detail in a separate chapter.

## Shoeprints

"Matching" shoeprints are generally at best a "class characteristic," meaning that they can exclude a defendant if they do not match, but they cannot conclusively identify a defendant, unless the shoeprint is so unique or rare that the likelihood of anyone else having the identical shoeprint is virtually impossible. Britain is currently launching a database of thousands of shoes and shoe types, similar to the DNA databases, in order to help identify criminals. Dr. Romelle Piercy, of the Forensic Science Service in London, says "footwear marks at the scene are the second biggest evidence type behind blood and DNA."[56] The archive will include shoe type, color, branding and marks as well as demographic information. It already contains over 1,000 distinguishing marks on Nike training shoes alone.[57]

> Shoeprints are not an individual characteristic unless they are so unique that no other person could have the same print.

However, where a criminologist with the state crime lab used a side-by-side comparison of shoeprints found in powder at a laundry with the defendant's shoes, the court said the testimony was not "scientific,"[58] and did not require a *Daubert* hearing. The appellate court said that a hearing held by the trial court in which the expert described her methods satisfied the requirements of *Daubert* anyway. Even where the expert had limited training and experience, a trial court accepted shoeprint testimony.

> Effect of failure to request a gatekeeper hearing at trial: the defendant cannot raise the issue on appeal.

In a Texas case, the expert was primarily a fingerprint expert, but was allowed to testify. The appellate court said that the defendant had been instructed to request a Rule 702 [*Daubert*] hearing during trial, but failed to do so. He simply challenged the expert's qualifications, which challenge was denied. His appeal was denied. This shows what happens if a party fails to request a *Daubert* hearing. It is not the trial court's job to hold a *Daubert* hearing; the party who opposes the testimony is required to request the hearing. If he does not, he generally cannot argue the issue on appeal.

## Novel Identification Theories

The scientific community agrees that fingerprints, DNA, and dental records can conclusively identify a person. This theory extends to palm prints and footprints.[59] However, a number of new identification methods have been tried but not yet proved to conclusively identify anyone. Are lip prints unique? One website states there are five basic types of lip prints that can be used for identification, but admits

56. Patricia Reaney, *Shoe Database to help forensic investigators,* Reuters, January 29, 2007.
57. *Id.*
58. *Ratliff v. Alaska,* 110 P.3d 982 (Alas. Ct. App. 2005).
59. Interview with Christopher Grice, January 2007.

the credibility of lip prints has not been firmly established.[60] What about ear prints? One commentator says it currently has "non-status as an identification science."[61] A Florida court rejected a crime technician's opinion that a particular knife definitely caused a wound and reversed defendant's conviction. Using the *Frye* test, it said there was no evidence to show that a specific knife can be identified by the marks made on cartilage.[62]

A defendant convicted of murder contested the introduction of a computer-enhanced image that matched his teeth to the bite mark on the victim's breast. He contended that the evidence required an expert. His attorney stated "This is nascent technology. It's brand-new. It was imperative that the defendant had an opportunity to explore how it works."[63] The Connecticut Supreme Court disagreed, holding that the defendant had an opportunity to cross examine and that even if there were error, it was harmless.[64]

## Forensic Evidence Offered to Prove "What Happened"

### Post Mortem Hair Banding

In a New York rape and murder trial, the defendants tried to introduce an expert who would testify that a hair of the victim had been planted in their van. The testimony involved post-mortem "hair banding" and the amount of time it would take for this to occur. The court held that the theory of post-mortem hair banding is generally accepted under *Frye*. Defense experts testified that it generally takes two days for post-mortem hair banding to occur. Because the state argued that the defendants disposed of the body shortly after placing it in their van, defendant's theory of hair banding would support their argument that someone planted the hair belonging to the victim in their van. The court held that the theory of microscopic analysis of hair shafts is grounded in science.[65]

### Ballistics and Gun Shot Residue

Experts have testified for years that a bullet fired from a particular weapon will bear striation marks associated with only that weapon. Although this level of general acceptance may be true for striation analysis, on the theory that bullets with the exact same striation must have been fired from the same gun, identification based on lead composition of different bullets has been rejected. In a decision by the Kentucky Supreme Court, testimony by a forensic scientist that the metallurgical composition of a bullet that killed the victim was identical to bullets found in the defendant's rifle was ruled inadmissible. The appellate court said that the trial court should have rejected the testimony because FBI studies showed that bullets manufactured at different times and different places may have the same lead composition.[66]

Similarly, an expert was not permitted to testify that a defendant had recently fired a gun, handled a gun or been near a gun when it was fired, because the standard for the

---

60. http://www.geocities.com/Athens/Atrium/5924/lipprintsbackground.htm.

61. http://www.forensic-evidence.com/site/ID/ID_bertillion.html.

62. *Ramirez v. Florida,* 810 So.2d 836 (Fla. Sup. 2002).

63. Lynne Tuohy, *Murder Appeal Centers on Technology,* The Hartford Courant.

64. *State v. Swinton,* 268 Conn. 781 (2004).

65. *State v. Kogut,* 806 N.Y.S.2d 353 (Supreme Ct. 2005).

66. *Ragland v. Kentucky,* 191 S.W.3d 569 (Sup. Kentucky 2006).

number of gunshot residue (GSR) particles that indicates a positive result is not agreed.[67] "Based on the testimony of both the state's expert and the defendant's expert, it is clear that significant questions exist in the relevant scientific community concerning how many particles are required ... [I]t is also clear that scientists agree that the results will not determine if a person fired a gun, was present when a gun was fired or handled contaminated guns or ammunition. The scientists agree a positive test will only conclude a person has been in an environment of gunshot residue."[68]

# The Evolution from Junk Science into Real Science

Given the value and sophistication of DNA testing, the area of forensic identification technology has changed crime investigation remarkably. It has also affected public perceptions of the ability of science to help solve crimes. *See* Chapter 15. Below are some examples of new technologies being developed that may aid in crime investigation. The chances are good that these technologies, or others like them, will be accepted as science within the next few years.

## Can Your Smell Identify You?

The news recently reported that researchers have begun analyzing traces of scent that people leave behind them, hoping to develop a forensic technique to exploit one's smell as an identification device for airline security. The report states that researchers have isolated chemicals that evaporate off the body using an "electronic nose" that breaks the scent into chemical components:

> Researchers examined body odor samples of about 200 adults from Carinthia, a village in the Austrian Alps, chosen because no one from outside had settled there for many generations and the residents were mainly members of big families and genetically similar. Despite this the analysis showed each individual had a unique scent signature.... Dr. Silva Valussi, of the Forensic Science Service, said: "You can tell a lot about a person's lifestyle from the chemical markers in sweat. Getting it to a level of reliability where it can be used as evidence is the challenge.[69]

## Can Your Brain Waves Show If You Are Telling the Truth?

"Brain mapping" or "brain fingerprinting" is a process that uses electronic measurement of brain waves to detect guilty knowledge. Brain mapping can supposedly detect whether a suspect recognizes elements about a crime scene that someone not involved in the crime would not know. The theory is that certain parts of the brain respond

---

67. *Minn. v. Moua*, No. K5-05-7335 (Minn. Dist. 2006).
68. *Id.*
69. Richard Gray, *Scientists learn what every dog knows—that we all have a unique smell*," Telegraph.co.uk, January 21, 2007.

when someone sees something he or she recognizes. There is apparently no way to circumvent this process, as it is involuntary. "Brain fingerprinting" as it is called by Dr. Lawrence A. Farwell, its inventor,[70] is a process in which a suspect is shown a series or words or pictures relevant to a crime along with other irrelevant words or pictures. Electrical brain response [called MERMER] is measured through a headband equipped with sensors. The theory is that the brain will involuntarily "recognize" the words or pictures and the MERMER will show this recognition. The responses are coded by a computer, thereby theoretically removing human observational error.[71]

Farwell is not the only scientist involved in studying whether brain waves can reveal guilty knowledge. Researchers at the University of Pennsylvania have published extensively on their research on the measurement of functional magnetic resource imaging,[72] or fMRI, and the topic was presented at a symposium of the American Academy of Science in Boston on February 2, 2007. As stated by Ronald Barndollar, a former FBI polygrapher who has reviewed some of this experimental work: "fMRI has the potential to do for lie detection what DNA did for forensic serology."[73] This is discussed further in the chapter on polygraph.

## Can a Computer Identify Your Handwriting?

A similar phenomenon is occurring with handwriting analysis. Researchers at the State University of New York at Buffalo have been working for some years on a computer system that analyzes specified handwriting characteristics in an effort to demonstrate scientifically both that handwriting is unique and that it can be distinguished by computer. *See* Chapter 11.

These areas may lead courts of the future to resolve the controversy over reliability by applying the *Daubert* tests to these emerging technologies.

# Summary

In order to ensure that scientific or technical expert testimony is reliable, the court must first examine if the area of testimony is "science." Science is defined as a specific methodology of inquiry that involves developing an hypothesis, testing, replicating results, developing further hypotheses, and ruling out alternative explanations. The one form of forensic evidence that clearly adheres to the scientific method is DNA analysis. Other methods of forensic identification, such as fingerprint analysis, blood spatter analysis, eyewitness identification, and handwriting analysis, are based on scientific hypotheses, but the process of identification often includes an element requiring the judgment of the examiner, which cannot be an element of the scientific method. The scientific method assumes that the results of an experiment can be replicated by any other

---

70. http://forensic-evidence.com/site/Behv_Evid/Farwell.
71. *Id.*
72. Daniel D. Langleben, James W. Loughead, Warren B. Bilker, Kosha Ruparel, Anna Rose Childress, Samantha I. Busch, and Ruben C. Gur, *Telling Truth from Lie in Individual Subjects with Fast Event-Related fMRI, Wiley InterScience*, www.interscience.wiley.com, September 13, 2005.
73. Interview with the author, March 20, 2007.

scientist using the same methodology. This is one reason why courts have struggled with applying the *Daubert* tests to areas such as handwriting, where there is no set protocol for analysis, and fingerprint analysis, in which there is strong scientific methodology, but no final conclusion without an examiner's individual examination.

In addition to the identification forensics, there are other areas of science used in criminology, such as ballistics analysis, hair analysis, fiber analysis, comparison of shoeprints, lip prints and bite marks. In many cases, these methods can determine a class characteristic but cannot identify a particular person.

Much science that has been called "junk science" involves the effort to determine causation. Examples include damage from electromagnetic force fields and silicone breast implants. Plaintiffs are also attempting to prove causation for fibromyalgia and to prove damage caused by mold. These areas are much more difficult to prove using the scientific method than crime scene science, because they must account for all alternative explanations, which is often virtually impossible.

Even areas of forensic evidence that are scientifically trustworthy will be rejected by the courts if the expert is not qualified or attempts to testify to an experiment that does not meet the scientific method.

Junk science can become good science by experiment and time. The so-called junk science of anthropometry as a method of absolute identification is still used for other medical purposes. Although the leech as used for bloodletting has been discredited, leeches have been shown to aid in healing.

Scientists are developing computer models to evaluate handwriting, which would remove the subjective element and identify which aspects of handwriting can distinguish one writer's handwriting from another. Finally, new procedures called "brain fingerprints" and functional MRI promise to avoid the problems with polygraph and offer a failsafe method to show if a suspect is telling the truth. Will these theories cross the line from junk science to true science? Time will tell.

# Discussion Questions

1.  What is the scientific method and how does it operate?

2.  Why is the scientific hypothesis associated with causation of injury much more difficult than forensic evidence associated with identification? Explain with reference to the court opinion in *Black v. Food Lion*.

3.  What is the scientific hypothesis of identification through fingerprints, DNA, dental records, shoeprints, or lip prints? How can these hypotheses be proved?

4.  Why is it important for scientists to try to prove a scientific hypothesis is wrong?

5.  Are juries free to disregard forensic evidence?

6.  What is Anthropometry? What was its scientific hypothesis?

7.  What have been the results of efforts to prove that electromagnetic fields cause breast cancer, that silicone breast implants cause autoimmune disease or that smoking causes cancer? Why do you think these issues are still being debated today, even after many scientific studies?

8. Should gatekeepers be more suspicious of scientific tests generated specifically for litigation? Why or why not? What additional questions should the gatekeeper ask? Why not simply let the jury assess the credibility of the science at trial?

9. Can a jury decide that DNA evidence is not reliable and therefore reject the evidence?

10. Can a jury decide that the DNA expert was not qualified and therefore reject the evidence?

11. Assume the prosecution wanted to introduce lip print evidence. What would the trial court need to decide to admit the evidence under *Frye*? Under *Daubert*?

12. Suppose you were a juror in a tobacco liability case. Plaintiff's expert introduces his opinion that secondhand smoking causes cancer, backed by numerous studies. Defendant's expert testifies that not all people who are exposed to secondhand smoke get cancer, so this proves that secondhand smoke does not cause cancer. How is this case like the *Daubert* case?

13. Explain the scientific theories in the gatekeeping cases involving postmortem "hair banding," the lead composition of bullets, and psychological factors leading to false confessions. Does the fact that one trial court rejects such evidence under *Daubert* mean that another court will probably do the same thing in another case? Why or why not?

# Chapter 7

# Fingerprints

## Overview

The science of fingerprint identification rests upon two hypotheses:

- All fingerprints are permanent and unique and therefore can identify one individual compared with another.

- By visually examining certain detail on less than a complete fingerprint or a completely clear fingerprint, examiners can conclusively identify a subject.

Scientists agree that fingerprints are unique and cannot be easily altered. A typical fingerprint has approximately 200 distinguishing features, called ridge characteristics, which can appear in any one of a number of configurations. Fingerprint identification uses a similar principle as the probability statistics upon which DNA identification rests. That is, if one fingerprint has no visible characteristics that differ from another and a sufficient number of characteristics that appear identical in size, shape and location, the fingerprints came from the same source.

Fingerprint identification has been accepted as forensic evidence since the early 1900s.[1] Not until quite recently has there been any challenge to its reliability. However, a few scholars as well as one federal district court argued that fingerprint identification does not pass the *Daubert* tests for reliability because no scientific studies have been conducted outside the fingerprint community to verify the required minimum number of comparison points to declare a match.[2]

This case was later retracted, but it has spawned a large number of subsequent challenges to fingerprint identification under *Daubert* and similar state statutes. These challenges have uniformly failed.

There have been few reported cases of fingerprint identification errors, other than mechanical errors such as copying the wrong person's name on a file. One highly-publicized fingerprint identification error took place in 2004, in which a fingerprint that appeared in Madrid at the site of a train station bombing was incorrectly reported as iden-

---

1. *People v. Jennings,* 252 Ill. 534, 96 N.E. 1077 (1911).
2. *United States v. Plaza,* 179 F. Supp. 2d 492 (E.D. Pa. 2002); *vacated,* 188 F. Supp. 2d 549 (E.D. Pa. 2002). The two cases will be referred to as *Plaza I* and *Plaza II.*

ifying an attorney in Seattle, Washington, who happened to be a Muslim.[3] Most people believe this error was the result more of cutting corners in the haste to find a terrorist than any fault in fingerprint identification methods.

# Chapter Objectives

Based on this chapter, students will be able to:

1   Explain the scientific principle underlying fingerprint identification.
2   Appreciate the difference between class and individual characteristics of fingerprints and the three levels of detail in fingerprints.
3   Understand the process of lifting and comparing fingerprints.
4   Explain how fingerprints are compared using an AFIS database.
5   Explain the history of using fingerprints in court.
6   Apply each of the *Daubert* tests to fingerprint identification.
7   Identify errors in the initial identification of fingerprints in the Madrid bombing case.

# The Evolution of Fingerprint Identification

Fingerprinting is one of the oldest forms of forensic evidence, and has been routinely admitted in court to prove identity. Its predecessor was Anthropometry, which is discussed in a prior chapter. Anthropometry was a system developed by Alphonse Bertillon in which measurements of body dimensions, including the size of ears, were thought to create a unique profile of an individual's physical characteristics that could identify him to the exclusion of all others. Although Anthropometry did not prove discriminating enough for this task, the use of fingerprint comparison is based on the same principle: that no two people share the exact same fingerprints.

Scientists today agree that fingerprints are unique. This was confirmed by a government study in which 50,000 fingerprints consisting of all loop patterns from all white males were compared, and no two were identical:

> The goal of this study, which was comprised of two separate tests, was to determine the probability that fingerprints of two people could be identical. Donald Ziesig, an algorithmist at Lockheed Martin Information Systems who played an important role in developing the FBI's computer-based fingerprint system (the Automated Fingerprint Identification System, or AFIS), was a developer of the 50k x 50k study and explained in detail how it operated. The result of the first test, in which full-sized, one inch fingerprints were compared with each other, was that the probability of finding two people with identical fingerprints was one in ten to the ninety-seventh power.

3.  John Leyden, *FBI Apology for Madrid Bomb Fngerprint Fiasco*, The Register, May 26, 2004.

In the second test, the rolled prints were artificially cropped to the average size of latent prints so that only the center 21.7% of the rolled prints was analyzed, with the resultant conclusion that the probability of finding two different, partial fingerprints to be identical was one in ten to the twenty-seventh power.[4]

Some critics noted that this sample was restricted, and did not cover a wide spectrum of the population. However, no one has disproved the hypothesis that fingerprints are unique. Scientists have also concluded that most wounds will not eradicate a fingerprint; at most, a deep cut into the dermis layer may result in a scar, but the rest of the fingerprint will remain the same.

If you look at your own fingers, you will be able to see that each finger bears one of three primary patterns: loop, arch, or whorl, of which there are subgroups. There are two types of arches and loops and four types of whorls. There have been a number of studies done to determine the distribution of these major patterns in

> Class characteristics in fingerprints are the loop, arch and whorl and their variations.

the population. The loop pattern is most common—about 60% of people have this pattern. The whorl accounts for about 35% and the arch for about 5%.[5] These characteristics are therefore "class" characteristics. You can be excluded if your fingers all have loops and the print from the crime scene is a whorl. But if the crime scene print is a loop, that alone does not mean it is yours. It could belong is 60 out of 100 people chosen at random. Fingerprints also have fixed reference points called "deltas," which resemble triangles.

The principle that can identify a person's fingerprint depends upon much smaller characteristics that are called ridge characteristics or Galton points (after Sir Francis Galton, who identified them in the late 1800s). These are the patterns made by the raised lines on each print. Each fingerprint has from between 75 and 175 of these ridge characteristics on each finger.[6] Fingerprint examiners refer to three primary types of ridge characteristics: ending ridge, bifurcation, and ridge dot. Variations, such as an enclosure, island, crossover, bridge, and trifurcation are combinations of the three major patterns. The chart below taken from Ward's Natural Sciences includes five ridge characteristics:

- Bifurcation—where one friction ridge divides into two

- Enclosure—a single friction ridge that bifurcates and rejoins to continue as a single ridge

- Ending Ridge—a single friction ridge that terminates.

- Short Ridge—a single friction ridge that travels a short distance and terminates

- Ridge Dot—an isolated ridge unit whose length is approximately equal to its width.

> Level two and level three detail is used to identify fingerprints. Ridge Characteristics, such as bifurcations, ridge endings, and ridge dots, are level two detail. Pores are level three detail.

---

4. *Plaza I*, at 497.

5. Andre Moenssens, James Starrs, Carol E. Henderson and Fred E. Inbau, *Scientific Evidence in Civil and Criminal Cases*, 4th ed., Foundation Press, 1995, at 506.

6. *Id.*

Examiners also compare a final intricate level of detail—level three detail-which includes sweat pores and their structures.

## Patterns

### Loops

Characterized by one or more free recurring friction ridges and one delta. (When the hand from which the loop pattern originated is known, you may determine if the recurring ridges originate from the little finger side (ulnar loop) or the thumb side (radial loop).)

*Radial or Ulnar*

### Arches

Characterized by friction ridges lying one above the other in a general arching formation.

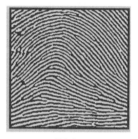

*Plain*

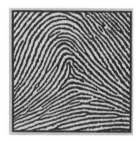

*Tented*

### Whorls

Characterized by one or more free recurring friction ridges and two points of delta.

*Plain*

*Double Looped*

*Central Pocket Loop*

*Accidental*

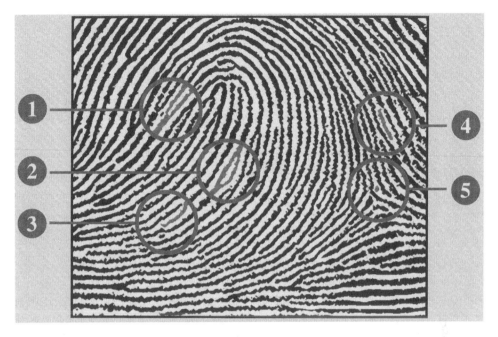

**Ridge Characteristics**

1. **Bifurcation**—The point at which one friction ridge divides into two friction ridges
2. **Enclosure**—A single friction ridge that bifurcates and rejoins after a short course and continues as a single friction ridge
3. **Ending Ridge**—A single friction ridge that terminates within the friction ridge structure
4. **Short Ridge**—A single friction ridge that only travels a short distance before terminating
5. **Ridge Dot**—An isolated ridge unit whose length approximates its width in size

© 2004 WARD'S Natural Science. Used with permission.

# The Process of Fingerprint Identification

## Obtaining the Crime Scene Print

Plastic fingerprints are those impressed in soft material, such as wax, putty, or dust. Visible prints are those plainly visible because they appear in colored substances such as blood, grease, or ink. Latent prints, which are not visible to the human eye, constitute the third type of prints.

Since the 1900s, fingerprint examiners have recovered latent prints by powdering surfaces, and then dusting the powder off with a small brush so as to differentiate the fingerprint image from its background. Light-colored powder was used for dark surfaces and dark-colored powder was used for light surfaces. The process of lifting the print can result in damaging or destroying the print. The most common damage is pressure distortion, which occurs when the print is being deposited. The shape of the surface on which the print has been deposited and the process used to develop and lift the print can cause other types of distortion.

Crime scene prints are often "latent," which means not visible to the human eye. They are colored to make them visible and then lifted and preserved for evaluation.

Investigators then photograph the resulting image, and lift the powdered image and transfer it to paper using clear tape. After classifying the fingerprint according to the prevailing classification system, examiners compare the ridge characteristics and minutia of the exemplar image taken from a suspect with those of the latent print.

## Taking Prints from a Suspect

Fingerprints are taken from criminal suspects using a two-part method. First, law enforcement officers apply ink to the suspect's finger and roll the inked finger on a piece of paper with boxes labeled for each finger of both the left and right hand.

Next, plain impressions are taken by pressing inked fingertips directly against the paper below the labeled boxes. This step insures against manual error and serves as a backup impression should the rolled print become smudged. You can see Ed Grant's inked prints later in this chapter. New technology is improving the process of taking prints from a suspect by using live scan computers.

## Comparing Ridge Characteristics and Minutiae

Even one difference between two fingerprints will disqualify an identification.

The process of identifying ridge characteristics and minutiae in one print and comparing them to another is how fingerprint examiners determine identification. If an examiner has two full prints which are clearly visible to compare, he can visually inspect them under magnification and decide if they match. Obviously, even one difference would disqualify the match, so he will search first for differences.

Although fingerprint identification today is frequently aided by computer searches, the basic search process can be done by visual inspection. The technician looks for four different elements:

- Likeness of general pattern type
- Qualitative likeness of the friction ridge characteristics
- Quantitative likeness of those characteristics, and
- Likeness of location of the characteristics.

The two most difficult challenges for the examiner are in determining when he has enough of a print from the crime scene for a valid comparison and how many characteristics to find in common to make an identification. Prints from a crime scene are frequently partial, badly blurred or smudged. You can see this on the prints from the Madrid bombing later in this chapter. Examiners use their skill and experience to make this judgment call. There is no agreed portion of a crime scene print—for example one-third or one-half of a total print—deemed acceptable for fingerprint identification among state and federal examiners.

There is also no agreed number of comparison points that must be found in common. "By tradition, though not be empirical studies, latent print examiners in the

United States have required a matching of at east six to eight characteristics in both prints for identity, though most experts prefer at least 10–12 concordances."[7] The FBI has no required minimum number for an identification. This fact led one federal court to decide that fingerprint identification was not scientifically reliable because it lacked an agreed standard number of comparison points to make an identification:

> Take an example where a latent print that possesses 8 matching points with a subject's inked print is compared by different examiners. The first examiner's criterion for identification is 8 points so he makes a positive identification. The second examiner's criteria is 9 points, therefore he is unable to make a positive identification. Is it wrong for the second examiner to report his findings? Many examiners feel that the second examiner should report that since he did not make a positive identification, the print is of no value.

> Is it wrong for the second examiner to provide detail that he found a significant number of matching points even though he did not make a positive identification? It would be better practice to state the facts of a comparison i.e. the print lacked the criteria for 100% positive identification, however 7 or 8 points match and there is a degree of probability the print was made by a particular person, rather than totally disregarding the print.[8]

Although it is possible for an overly-eager or unscrupulous examiner to call an identification based on a crime scene print with inadequate detail for evaluation, this does not invalidate the process of fingerprint identification. The same charges have been made about fraudulent DNA reports. When one watches a fingerprint examination, as I did, many of the theoretical objections that the court considered are put into perspective. In "real life," examiners typically compare far more points of similarity than 8 or 10.

In 1970, long before the legal challenge to fingerprinting in 2003, the fingerprint community set up a Standardization Committee, composed of 11 members with total experience of 250 years. After three years of work, it concluded:

> [T]here exists no valid basis, at this time, for requiring a predetermined minimum number of friction ridge characteristics in two impressions in order to establish positive identification. The decision on whether two prints under examination are made by the same digit is one that must be made ... on the basis of the expert's experience and background, taking into account, along with the number of matching characteristics, other factors such as clarity of the impressions, types of characteristics found, location of the characteristics in relation to the core or delta, etc.[9]

> "The decision on whether two prints under examination are made by the same digit is one that must be made ... on the basis of the expert's experience and background...."
> *Moenssens et al.*

The question then becomes: how many points of similarity are enough to call a match? Again, even one point of dissimilarity is enough to rule out a match. The question of the right number of points for a match was a major issue in a case we will examine that held fingerprint identification was unreliable under *Daubert*. In that case, the

---

7. *Id.* at 513–4.
8. *Id.* at 514.
9. *Id.* at 516.

court decided that the fact that there was no standard "required" number of points of similarity to declare a match meant that the process of fingerprint identification lacked standards and was therefore unreliable:

> In some state jurisdictions in the United States, and in some foreign jurisdictions, fingerprint examiners must find a minimum number of Galton points (characteristics on the fingerprint ridges) in common before they can declare a match with absolute certainty. The FBI switched from relying on a mandatory minimum number of points to no minimum number in the late 1940s. Mr. Meagher discussed the absence of a uniform standard prescribing a minimum number of points in common as a precondition of finding a match.

> Meagher testified that there is no single quantifiable standard for reaching an identification opinion because of differences in both the quantity of characteristics shown in the latent print and the quality of the image. For example, if a latent print shows a relatively small portion of a fingerprint but has a very clear image—one that allows clear identification of level three detail such as the shapes of ridges, locations of pores, and the like, a reliable identification may still be possible even with relatively few level two "points."[10]

I asked Christopher Grice, the fingerprint examiner in the *Grant* case, to respond to the controversy over looking for a specific number of ridge characteristics in common. "Two bifurcations appearing in prints being compared is not a point of identification," he says, "unless they have the same shape. A bifurcation can be y shaped or wine-glass shaped. It can have an acute angle or an obtuse angle. There is a myriad of shapes involving the width of the ridges themselves and in impressions of great clarity, even pore shapes."[11]

# The ACE-V Method of Fingerprint Comparison

## Analysis

> The ACE-V method consists of the following four steps:
> 1. Analysis
> 2. Comparison
> 3. Evaluation
> 4. Verification

The examiner must first analyze the crime scene print to determine if it is sufficient for identification purposes. Is it enough of a print and does it show enough clear ridge characteristics to be compared? What ridge characteristics can be identified on the print? Here are portions of testimony by an FBI expert in explaining the ACE-V method in the *Plaza I* case:

> In comparing latent and rolled prints, fingerprint examiners employ a process known as "ridgeology" or ACE-V, an acronym for "analysis," comparison," "evaluation," and "verification." Sergeant Ashbaugh testified that, during the analysis stage, examiners look at the unknown, or latent, print and note both the "anatomical aspects" of the fingerprint and the clarity of the

---

10. *Plaza I*, at 499–500.
11. Christopher Grice, interview March 12, 2007.

print. He described the analysis stage in some detail: Does it have first, second and third level detail or a combination? What is the clarity of the print? We would then look at all the ridge paths, all the ridge arrangements. We'd explore ridge shapes and we would note any red flags.

Red flags—I'll be very brief with this because it is a very large area—we would look for any lines running in the print that could have been caused by pressure, substraight [sic] or matrix smears. We would look for areas of fat ridges, possibly that could be caused by overlapping ridges. We'd look for differing amounts of pressure. We'd look for similar ridge characteristics close to each other. This could mean a double tap, two pressures and a [sic] again, an overlapping print. We'd look for shadows, shadow ridges in the furrows, which also could mean two prints deposited.

We'd look for misaligned ridges protruding into the furrow. We'd look for cross-over ridges running through the furrow and, of course, we'd look for inappropriate print outline.[12]

## Comparison of Prints

The examiner will compare the crime scene print with the inked print to determine if they match. Before the introduction of computer technology, the examiner visually compared prints side by side under a magnifier. Examiners have never used a method in which one print is superimposed on another to determine a match. This is simply TV theatrics. At the time of the Serra murder in 1973, for example, police detectives visually examined the latent print from the tissue box against the entire base of approximately 70,000 fingerprint cards in New Haven. No match was found.

The expert in Plaza I continued:

After analysis: We move on to comparison, and comparison is carried out in sequence or systematically and we start-first of all, we would look at first level detail, is the overall pattern configuration in agreement. And then we would look at-start at an area that is common to both the unknown and the known print. And we would start at a common area and we start systematically comparing all the various friction ridge arrangements and friction ridge shapes, including relative pore position, if it's at all possible.

The comparison is something that is very objective. We're dealing with physical evidence and if I discuss something in the ridge arrangement, I should be able to point to it, so it's a very objective process.[13]

## Evaluation

Once the comparison is complete, and we recommend that the whole print be compared, the next thing that we would do is then evaluate what we saw

---

12. *Plaza I*, at 498.
13. *Id.*

during comparison as far as agreement of the various ridge formations. And I break it down into actually two separate areas. The first area is, do I have agreement? If you say yes to that, if you form the opinion you have agreement, then you have to ask yourself, is there sufficient unique detail present to individualize?

That final decision is a subjective decision. It's based on your knowledge and experience and your ability. And that, if you say yes, I feel there's enough to individualize, then you formed an opinion of identification.

The conclusions that we recommend that are available to you at the end of identification, would be elimination, which usually would start very early in the identification process, identification, a situation where you have sufficient volume of unique details to individualize. And a situation where you have agreement, but you're unable to individualize or eliminate. And, in other words, you can't differentiate from others. And those are the three conclusions that we recommend that you can form.

## Verification

[All fingerprint identifications must be repeated by a second, independent investigator, who does not know the results of the first test.]

From there we move into the very last box, which deals with the verification, which is a form of peer review, and it is part of the scientific process. From this point the person actually starts right at the beginning and goes through the whole identification process again individually.

## Opinion

After utilizing the ACE-V and quantitative/qualitative processes, an examiner is ready to make a determination with respect to the latent print in question. The three options that the examiner has are described in one of two ways:

An Examiner can give one of three opinions: 1. identification, 2. elimination, or 3. inconclusive.

(1) identification, elimination, or "agreement but not enough to individualize — not enough to eliminate," or

(2) "absolutely him, absolutely not him, and absolutely I don't know," Whichever terminology is used, the result is the same — an examiner who makes a positive identification is determining that the latent fingerprint necessarily came from the individual in question, "to the exclusion of all other fingers in the world."

# The Automated Fingerprint Identification System "AFIS" Matching System[14]

The advent of computer technology has made the process of matching fingerprints quicker and it has expanded the number and geographic area of prints that can be searched. However, it has not eliminated visual examination by a human—both at the outset and after the computer gives its "results." The only step in the ACE-V process that does not depend upon the judgment and experience of the examiner is the "C" piece—Comparison. And it is important to note that even the computer comparison process requires the examiner to code information that goes into the computer and use his judgment in evaluating the scores the computer generates. The AFIS system does not generate one fingerprint "match." It generates a list of likely candidates in order of numerical score. The examiner can set the system to generate any number of candidates. The Connecticut Forensic Laboratory, for example, is set to generate 50 candidates.

The process of matching a latent print with prints in the database through an automated fingerprint identification system (AFIS) combines computer technology that marks all ridge characteristics (here called "minutiae") on a fingerprint (without regard to the type of minutiae). Early systems converted this data into an algorithm based on the number of characteristics on the field using an x/y axis. More modern systems can do a 360 degree search even if a print is scanned in upside down. It then searches its database of fingerprints that have been similarly coded and put into the system using the same algorithm.[15]

The fingerprints in the database come from inked fingerprint cards, referred to as "tenprints," that have been taken in conjunction with criminal investigations. Some databases also include prints taken by applicants for employment.

The FBI maintains an AFIS base of approximately 50 million cards. As each card contains 10 fingerprints, it contains 500 million prints. Most states have their own database on a computer system so that they can search within their own state. However, in order to search through the FBI database, states must adopt compatible software.

## Isolating the Print

The first step in matching a print is to get a copy of a latent print from a crime site. It is usually sent to the forensic lab by the officers who investigated the site. Once the print has been lifted, the examiner will scan it into a computer system and enter certain data that he obtains by visually examining the print, such as what finger the print came from or whether it is an arch, whorl, or loop. Typically a latent print will appear along with other prints—sometimes superimposed on other prints or partially masked. The latent print will typically not be straight up and down, as will the rolled print. It may be

---

14. This section is based on an interview at the Connecticut Forensic Laboratory with Christopher Grice and demonstration of fingerprint analysis using an AFIS system, August, 2005.
15. Grice interview, *supra*.

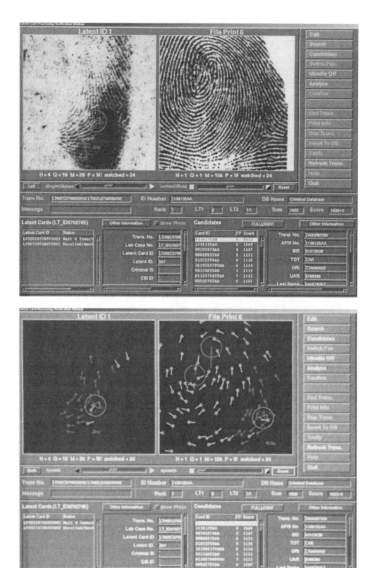

*AFIS screens, courtesy of Connecticut State Forensic Laboratory*

smudged and barely visible. It may be impossible to tell what finger it is from. The examiner will view the scanned print on a screen and isolate the portion that he wishes to match. Once isolated, this portion is then enlarged by the computer screen.

## Identifying the Ridge Characteristics

Once the print to be matched has been scanned in, the computer will automatically identify with yellow circles every minutiae point it identifies (ridge ending, branch, breaks, island, etc.). A typical print will have as many as 100 or more detectable minutiae points. The circle will have a "tail" pointing in the direction from which the minutiae is running, for example, in the direction of a ridge that ends with a ridge ending. It

CANDIDATE LISTS FOR LATENT SEARCH TRANSACTION


Searched Latent Data:

```
              Trans. No.: LT002L0507290005
                AFIS No.:
            Lab Case No.: LT_ID05016901
          Latent Card ID: LT002C0507290004
              Latent ID.: 001-L1
             Criminal SI:
                  CSI ID:
                     ORI: CT0000003
          Submitting ORI:
                Examiner: cwg
                 User ID: 1737
            Time Created: CURRENT
          Update User ID: 0
            Time Updated:
              Receipt ID:
       Miscellaneous No.:
                   Memo.: Theft from Auto
           Date of Crime:
              Crime Code: LFS
                     Sex: U
              Birth Year: 0
                TLI Flag:
           Contract Info:
            Pattern Type:
           Finger Number: 0
            Adj. Pttn. L:
            Adj. Pttn. R:
           Internal flag: 0
```


Tenprint Candidates:

| RANK | TRANS. NO | FP# | SCORE |
|------|-----------|-----|-------|
| 1 | 01042468AA | 2 | 2914 |
| 2 | 01042468AB | 2 | 2092 |
| 3 | 20201432AA | 4 | 1085 |
| 4 | 00226529AA | 3 | 1062 |
| 5 | 00508916AA | 4 | 1037 |
| 6 | 00294793AA | 4 | 1032 |
| 7 | 20215023AA | 4 | 1029 |
| 8 | 50117925AA | 1 | 1024 |
| 9 | 59911923AA | 1 | 1022 |
| 10 | 0410609752AA | 4 | 1010 |
| 11 | 00232070AA | 3 | 1009 |
| 12 | 0710675863AA | 4 | 998 |
| 13 | 0110246844AA | 3 | 996 |
| 14 | 00841993AA | 5 | 993 |
| 15 | 00419075AA | 1 | 988 |
| 16 | 0110420790AA | 4 | 987 |
| 17 | 1610712034AB | 1 | 979 |
| 18 | 00326599AA | 4 | 978 |
| 19 | 0110478931AA | 4 | 978 |
| 20 | 00298249AA | 1 | 974 |


Unsolved Latent Candidates:

| RANK | TRANS. NO | FP# | SCORE |
|------|-----------|-----|-------|


Print Time: 2005-07-29 15:02:43 (CAFIS -- Cogent Systems, Inc.)

*AFIS printout, courtesy of Connecticut State Forensic Laboratory* will also identify with a red circle what it sees as the "core," or center of the print and with a green triangle where it sees the "delta," which is a triangular area determined by the ridge flow.

When I observed a fingerprint comparison at the Connecticut Forensic lab, the computer identified approximately 60 of these points on the first print the examiner entered into the system. The system will also identify the "ridge count," which is the number of ridges between one minutiae to another. For example, if there are four ridges between a ridge ending and an island, the computer will mark this spatial relationship. The FBI database requires ridge counts for matching; the Connecticut system does not.

The examiner then looks at the latent print and removes yellow circles which in his judgment are not really minutiae, and he relocates yellow circles to the proper point of certain minutiae, again, using his judgment and experience. By restricting the search to the most prominent and strongest minutiae, the examiner reduces the amount of scanning the computer must do. Again, this is a judgment made based on the examiner's knowledge of typical patterns and decisions about where the computer has made a "mistake," possibly based on misreading woodgrain or scratches as being ridges.

The system then asks the examiner if he wants to search the latent print against any particular finger in the inked cards in the database. Only when the examiner is relatively sure that he is looking at a particular finger will he elect to restrict the search this way. It will also ask if the examiner wants to search prints with a certain direction of ridges.

## The Computer Search

In the print examination process that I watched, after the examiner had deleted and moved minutiae the computer had identified, there were 55 minutiae marked on the latent print and submitted for a match. It took about ten minutes to process. The screen produced the top ten prints, with "scores" ranging from 2914 to 1010. Christopher Grice of the Connecticut Forensic Laboratory estimates that the first candidate is the match about 75% of the time.[16]

In the case I observed, the latent print had 55 minutiae; the inked print had 94; 43 of the minutiae matched. *See* photograph below.

The examiner first looks at the number one print generated by the system and visually compares it to the latent print on the screen, and also to the actual latent print viewed through a magnifying glass. The list of prints in order of score helps speed up the search process, but the examiner may need to look at ten, twenty, or all fifty possible candidates in the comparison process.

One defendant appealed on the ground that the entire list of possible fingerprint matches had not been provided to his counsel in pre-trial discovery. The defendant had been the "second best" match and neither he nor the first match had a high score. The court held that the error was harmless as it would not have affected the outcome of the trial.[17]

A second example I watched did not result in a match. Although the computer found 10 prints with similar minutiae, the examiner could see on visual inspection (and so

---

16. Grice interview, *supra.*
17. *People v. Tims*, A092799, 2002 Cal. App. LEXIS 4154 (February 7, 2002).

could I) that the spatial relationship was slightly off, or one minutia was on one print and not the other. Although the number 1 print had a score similar to the number of ridge characteristic matches in the first case, on visual inspection, it was not a match. The examiner reviewed prints in order down to number 10, at which point the score had dropped to a very low number. He determined that there was no match in the system.

I watched two latent prints searched in the database; the entire process took about an hour and a half. Computer processing time is longer if the system is searching every finger; shorter if a particular finger is identified. The time is also shorter if the number 1 match is clearly the print; otherwise the examiner must review a number of potential matches.

Any latent print that cannot be matched is put in the "unsolved latent database" and is checked weekly against new prints that come into the AFIS system. In Connecticut, juvenile prints do not go into the system until the juvenile becomes 16.

It is obvious from this demonstration that it would be impossible for the computer to identify a match by itself—it does not identify minutiae by type and it does not distinguish between "important" minutiae and common ones. This is where the judgment of the examiner is important.

# Does Fingerprint Identification Pass the *Daubert* Test?

The first use of fingerprints in a criminal case was in England in 1902. The first such use in the United States occurred in 1911 in *People v. Jennings*.[18] The *Jennings* case actually held that fingerprints were "in such general common use" that the courts would take "judicial notice" of fingerprints as a method of identification. Here is a fairly typical analysis of the process many courts have used to determine that fingerprint expert testimony is admissible as generally accepted science:

### United States v. Abreu, 406 F.3d 1304 (11th Cir. 2005)

Appellant Jose Manuel Abreu appeals his conviction of possession with intent to distribute marijuana, in violation of 21 U.S.C. § 841, arguing that the district court erred in affirming the magistrate judge's order denying his motion to preclude expert testimony regarding fingerprint evidence, because the government failed to demonstrate that the testimony met the requirements of Rule 702 of the Federal Rules of Evidence. For the reasons that follow, we affirm.

\* \* \*

Abreu contends that the government failed to establish that its expert's testimony was the product of reliable principles and methods as required by Rule 702, and the district court should have at least held an evidentiary hearing on the issue.

\* \* \*

Abreu maintains that the admission of the expert testimony was "severely prejudicial" and was the most damaging evidence relied on by the government,

---

18. *Jennings*, 252 Ill. 534.

since it was the only direct evidence that placed Abreu in the storage room with the marijuana plants.

IL

In the present case, there is no dispute as to the qualifications of the expert or that the expert's testimony is relevant. Abreu, however, argues that the government failed to establish the reliability of the expert opinion. To assess the reliability of an expert opinion, the court considers a number of factors, including those listed by the Supreme Court in *Daubert:*

- whether the expert's theory can be and has been tested;

- whether the theory has been subjected to peer review and publication;

- the known or potential rate of error of the particular scientific technique; and

- whether the technique is generally accepted in the scientific community.

The *Daubert* factors are only illustrative and may not all apply in every case. The district court has wide latitude in deciding how to determine reliability. This court has not published an opinion regarding the admissibility and reliability of fingerprint evidence under *Daubert*. Other Circuits, however, have found that fingerprint evidence is sufficiently reliable and meets the standards of Fed. R. Evid. 702.

We agree with the decisions of our sister circuits and hold that the fingerprint evidence admitted in this case satisfied *Daubert*. Moreover, since district courts are given broad latitude in deciding how to determine the reliability of an expert opinion, we conclude from the record that the district court did not clearly err in giving greater weight to the general acceptance factor, as did the magistrate judge.

Additionally, the magistrate judge considered information presented by the government detailing the uniform practice through which fingerprint examiners match fingerprints and the error rate of fingerprint comparison. As a result, based on our review of the record, the district court correctly found that the magistrate judge did not apply the wrong legal standard or make a clear error of judgment.

Further, because the other evidence presented during Abreu's trial is sufficient to support the jury's verdict, any error committed by the district court in admitting the expert testimony regarding fingerprint evidence is not reversible error. Accordingly, we affirm Abreu's conviction.

Because most courts consider fingerprint identification to be generally accepted, they have not subjected it to the other factors in *Daubert*. The *Plaza* case and the *Mitchell* case before it were the first reported cases to conduct a full *Daubert* hearing on each of the specific tests of reliability.

## A Federal Trial Court Rules a Fingerprint Examiner May Not Give an Opinion about Fingerprint Identification

In 2002, a federal court in Philadelphia created quite a stir, when a federal district judge refused to allow an expert to give an opinion about a fingerprint match because the court examined each element of the *Daubert* test and decided that fingerprint testing failed. The court initially ruled that fingerprints did not meet the *Daubert* challenge and then reversed itself three months later. The first decision was based on a "cold record" of a similar *Daubert* hearing held in 1999 in a case called *United States v. Mitchell*.[19]

In 1991, Byron Mitchell was arrested and charged as a getaway driver in a robbery of an armored car. The primary evidence against him was testimony of Kim Chester, a female participant, who testified as an uncharged accomplice. The forensic evidence included two latent fingerprints found on the stolen getaway car and matched to Mitchell's thumb prints. Mitchell's first conviction was reversed based on the improper admission of an anonymous note found in the front seat of the getaway car that included the license plate of Mitchell's own vehicle.[20]

At his second trial, Kim Chester testified again. Two of the armored guards identified the getaway car and a fragment of the getaway car's license place, noted by a bystander, matched the stolen car that contained Mitchell's prints. Mitchell offered the testimony of three academics—Dr. David Stoney, of the McCrone Research Institute in Chicago, Professor James Starrs, of George Washington Law School, and Dr. Simon Cole, a postdoctoral fellow at Rutgers, who testified that fingerprint identification did not meet *Daubert*. The court conducted a five-day *Daubert* hearing to determine whether the government and defense experts could testify. The court then held that "the government's expert witnesses and Mitchell's expert witnesses could testify, but with the caveat that the latter could not testify to the question whether latent fingerprint identification is a 'science.'"[21] Mitchell was again convicted in February of 2000.

Mitchell again appealed and argued that it was error for the trial court to admit the government fingerprint identification under *Daubert*. The Third Circuit Court of Appeals reviewed each of the *Daubert* factors in detail, and concluded that fingerprint identification met *Daubert*. Although it held the trial court committed error by taking judicial notice of the "uniqueness and permanancy" of "human friction skin arrangements,"[22] it held it was harmless error and therefore upheld the conviction.

The appeals court in the *Mitchell* appeal decided that fingerprint identification as conducted by the FBI was reliable, based on several tests conducted by the government. It also held that the error rate was low and the trial court did not abuse its discretion in admitting the government fingerprint identification. This decision was in April of 2004.

After the *Mitchell* trials but before the second appeal was decided, another trial court in Philadelphia in the *Plaza* cases, relying on the identical one-thousand-page *Daubert* hearing transcript created in *Mitchell*, came to the opposite conclusion in an opinion dated January 7, 2002. Three months later, the trial court changed its mind and wrote another opinion accepting fingerprint identifications. We will examine these opinions in detail, as they illustrate how different courts can disagree on the meaning of the various tests in *Daubert*.

*Plaza* involved three defendants charged with committing four separate murders for hire in Puerto Rico and Pennsylvania. The murders were allegedly committed in furtherance of a gang-related drug conspiracy. The FBI recovered several latent prints on evidence connected to the murders. This evidence included fingerprints found in two separate vehicles allegedly used in the course of the crimes. In addition, latent prints were obtained from weapons and ammunition found in one of the vehicles.

19. *United States v. Mitchell*, 199 F. Supp. 2d 262 (E.D.Pa 2002), aff'd 365 F.3d 215 (3d Cir. 2004).
20. *State v. Mitchell*, 145 F.3d 572 (3d Cir. 1998).
21. *Mitchell*, 365 F.3d at 229.
22. *Id.* at 251.

Judge Pollack held a *Daubert* hearing using a "cold record" from *Mitchell,* but came to the opposite conclusion. He ruled for the first time that fingerprint evidence did not meet the federal evidentiary standard established in *Daubert.* The court determined that the government's experts could testify to the permanency and uniqueness of fingerprints. The experts could also point out places of comparison between the two sets of fingerprints. However, the fingerprint experts could not testify that the latent fingerprints matched those of the defendants. The prosecution relied upon the "match" testimony to convince juries of identification. Without this testimony, this ruling was a significant setback for the prosecution. The judge analyzed each of the following *Daubert* factors:

- Has the theory of fingerprint analysis been scientifically tested?
- Have the experiments been peer reviewed?
- Is there a quantifiable error rate?
- Are there controlling standards governing the process?
- Is fingerprint matching generally accepted by the scientific community?

## Whether the Theory or Technique Can Be Tested

This requires agreed standards. The basic problem the court found is that not all agencies agreed on the minimum number of ridge characteristics in common needed to make a match. The court reasoned that if the FBI used one standard and a state used a different one, then the "science" behind fingerprint identification was suspect.

The court was also troubled by the fact that fingerprint analysis contained a "subjective" evaluation in which the examiner looked at both prints and used his or her judgment to decide if they matched. The testimony at the *Mitchell* hearing used the term "subjective:"

*Plaza I*

\* \* \*

The significance of the fact that the determinations are "subjective" was explained by the further testimony of Dr. Stoney:

Now, by subjective I mean that it [a fingerprint identification determination] is one that is dependent on the individual's expertise, training, and the consensus of their agreement of other individuals in the field. By not scientific, I mean that there is not an objective standard that has been tested; nor is there a subjective process that has been objectively tested. It is the essential feature of a scientific process that there be something to test, that when that something is tested the test is capable of showing it to be false.[23]

Fingerprint identification is "subjective" insofar as it depends upon the experience, training and judgment of the examiner.

Christopher Grice, the fingerprint analyst from the *Grant* case, objects to the word *subjective* on the ground that it sounds as if the examiner makes arbitrary decisions: "My opinion on who the best candidate for president is would be subjective. The print itself is a physi-

---

23. *Plaza I,* at 507–8.

cal item that can be enlarged and studied and in that sense it is an object and objective. It is impossible to take subjective factors out of the thought process. Two doctors looking at the same cancerous tumor may give opposite treatments and diagnoses based on their training and experience. This does not mean that there is something unscientific about it if they both observed, studied and investigated the actual physical object, the tumor."[24]

## Peer Review

The prosecution argued that publications by examiners themselves about human error rates and the use of fingerprint testimony in courts equal "peer review." The court did not accept the argument. Peer review means review of the science, reasoned the court, not a review of error rates.

The prosecution also argued that fingerprint matching is peer reviewed because each examiner's test must be repeated by a second examiner. The court decided that peer review required review and replication by the scientific community, not the fingerprinting community and therefore decided there was no peer review.

### Plaza I

In his Mitchell testimony, Sergeant Ashbaugh voiced the same view. ACE-V "verification," he said, "is a form of peer review, and it is part of the scientific process." The difficulty is that if the opinion announced by a fingerprint examiner—"ident, non-ident," as Mr. Meagher expressed it—is, as both Mr. Meagher and Sergeant Ashbaugh acknowledged, "subjective," another opinion rendered by another examiner, whether in corroboration or in refutation, does little to put a "scientific" gloss on the first opinion, much less constitute "peer review" as described by Dr. Stoney.[25]

> Peer Review means a review by the scientific community, not fingerprint examiners, or a second fingerprint opinion.

## Rate of Error

The government argued that fingerprint identification, if done correctly, has an error rate of zero. However, it admitted that there is a risk of error by the examiner. The court reviewed the test relied upon in the Mitchell case in which the same prints were sent for evaluation by 53 law enforcement agencies. Thirty-four responded, and of those, 9 could not make an identification. The court decided this was too high an error rate.

## Controlling Standards

The court held that this *Daubert* requirement was also not met. How could there be controlling standards if different agencies could use a different number of ridge charac-

---

24. Grice interview, *supra*.
25. *Plaza I*, at 509.

teristics for a match? In addition, the determination involved a subjective judgment, over which there could be no control. Finally, the court said that the lack of a standard certification process meant that some fingerprint examiners could have learned on the job without any process for determining their proficiency. Therefore there were no controlling standards to be a fingerprint examiner.

*Plaza I*

> Controlling Standards. "there is no single quantifiable standard for rendering an identification opinion because of differences in both the quantity of characteristics shown in the latent print and the quality of the image." *Plaza I*

As described by the *Havvard* court, "there is no single quantifiable standard for rendering an identification opinion because of differences in both the quantity of characteristics shown in the latent print and the quality of the image." While there may be good reason for not relying on a minimum point standard—or for requiring a minimum number, as some state and foreign jurisdictions do—it is evident that there is no one standard "controlling the technique's operation …"[26]

## General Acceptance

Judge Pollack agreed that fingerprint matching is generally accepted in the "technical community" of examiners. However, he read the term to require general acceptance in the scientific community. As scientific studies had not been done, he decided that the testimony failed this test too. His solution was to permit the examiner to testify to his process of comparison, but refrain from giving his opinion about a match.

*Plaza I*

Since the court finds that ACE-V does not meet *Daubert's* testing, peer review, and standards criteria, and that information as to ACE-V's rate of error is in limbo, the expected conclusion would be that the government should be precluded from presenting any fingerprint testimony. But that conclusion—apparently putting at naught a century of judicial acquiescence in fingerprint identification processes—would be unwarrantably heavy-handed. The *Daubert* difficulty with the ACE-V process is by no means total.

The difficulty comes into play at the stage at which, as experienced fingerprint specialists Ashbaugh and Meagher themselves acknowledge, the ACE-V process becomes "subjective"—namely, the evaluation stage. By contrast, the antecedent analysis and comparison stages are, according to the testimony, "objective": analysis of the rolled and latent prints and comparison of what the examiner has observed in the two prints.

Up to the evaluation stage, the ACE-V fingerprint examiner's testimony is descriptive, not judgmental. Accordingly, this court will permit the government to present testimony by fingerprint examiners who, suitably qualified as "expert" examiners by virtue of training and experience, may

- describe how the rolled and latent fingerprints at issue in this case were obtained,

26. *Id.* at 513.

- identify and place before the jury the fingerprints and such magnifications thereof as may be required to show minute details, and

- point out observed similarities (and differences) between any latent print and any rolled print the government contends are attributable to the same person.

What such expert witnesses will not be permitted to do is to present "evaluation" testimony as to their "opinion" (Rule 702) that a particular latent print is in fact the print of a particular person.

The defendants will be permitted to present their own fingerprint experts to counter the government's fingerprint testimony, but defense experts will also be precluded from presenting "evaluation" testimony. Government counsel and defense counsel will, in closing arguments, be free to argue to the jury that, on the basis of the jury's observation of a particular latent print and a particular rolled print, the jury may find the existence, or the non-existence, of a match between the prints.[27]

Three months later, the Judge reconsidered his decision after a live *Daubert* hearing with fingerprint experts. His main reason for changing his mind was that the United Kingdom had abandoned its minimum number of Galton points and now requires no set number to declare a match. The U.K. had therefore adopted the same standard as used by the FBI. As to the subjective element of fingerprint evaluation, the judge simply said "[i]n short, I have changed my mind."[28] The second opinion did not rely on any new facts, except the change in UK fingerprint procedures. As the court did not give any reason for changing its opinion on testing, peer review, or error rate, the reversal appeared to rest primarily on the question of whether there was uniformity in the number of ridge characteristics required to make an identification.

## Other Cases on Fingerprints

Following the *Plaza cases*, a number of defendants have tried to convince courts to reject fingerprint identifications. These requests have uniformly failed. For example, the 7th Circuit federal court accepted fingerprint testimony over an objection by the defendant that it could not be effectively tested:

While an actual print taken in the field cannot be objectively tested, we are satisfied that the method in general can be subjected to objective testing to determine its reliability in application.[29]

A number of defendants have relied on the March 2000 solicitation by the National Institute of Justice for research to "determine the scientific validity of individuality in friction ridge examination based on measurement of features, quantification, and statistical analysis" to argue that the government has admitted there is no scientific proof of the process of fingerprint identification. This argument has also been rejected.[30]

---

27. *Id.* at 516.
28. *Plaza II* at 575.
29. *United States v. Mustapha*, 363 F.3d 666, 672 (7th Cir. 2004).
30. *United States v. Harvaard*, 260 F.3d 597 (7th Cir. 2001).

Other objections have also been rejected. In 1996, a defendant challenged a fingerprint identification when the expert admitted that original[31] prints were preferable to the copies on which he based his testimony. The court rejected that argument, and allowed the testimony.

# Changes in Fingerprint Identification Technology

As fingerprint identification technology changes, we can expect challenges similar to those that have followed changes in DNA test procedures. In one recent case, the court held that use of a "live scan" method for taking a suspect's prints had been proven to be reliable.

### *United States v. Lauder, 409* F.3d 1254 (10th Cir. 2005)

In May 2004, a jury in the United States District Court for the District of New Mexico convicted Weston Charles Lauder III on the following four counts related to the possession and distribution of illegal drugs.

\* \* \*

On appeal, Lauder alleges that ... (3) the district court erred in admitting fingerprint evidence. For the reasons set forth below, we affirm the district court's order of conviction and the resulting sentence.

On September 16, 2002, acting pursuant to a search warrant based on information supplied by a confidential informant, a Lea County Drug Task Force conducted a search of a residence in Hobbs, New Mexico. According to the warrant, the house belonged to Kena LaShawn Wright, but somebody referred to as "BL" also resided there. Upon arrival, the officers knocked on the door and announced they had a warrant to search the house. Although the officers heard footsteps running through the house, nobody answered the door. The officers then kicked open the door, entered the house, and found Weston Charles Lauder III lying face down and spread-eagle in the kitchen area. Nobody else was in the house.

During the search, the officers found large quantities of cocaine, crack, and money. In the master bedroom, for example, the search revealed approximately 124 grams of powder cocaine and $ 5,630 in the pocket of a brown sweatshirt that was hanging in the closet. There was also a blue jacket found in the closet that contained approximately 49.2 grams of crack cocaine and negligible amounts of marijuana in its hood. A dresser drawer contained six grams of crack cocaine and $ 295. The officers also retrieved a duffle bag containing men's clothing and a baggage claim tag in Lauder's name.

The officers searched the backyard and found, buried in the ground, $ 12,000 in cash and, separately, approximately 745 grams of powder cocaine that was wrapped in two plastic bags. The officers also searched Lauder's person. In Lauder's wallet they found several pieces of paper that contained the initials of numerous people written next to money amounts. According to the testimony of the arresting officer, the papers were consistent with drug ledgers that are

---

31. *State ex rel. Wilson*, CO-96-1339, 1996 Minn. App. LEXIS 1345 (December 3, 1996).

typically kept by people involved in drug distribution. Later witnesses, in fact, matched the initials found in Lauder's wallet to known drug dealers.

Following the search, the Task Force contacted the Drug Enforcement Agency and referred the case to the federal government for prosecution. Lauder was transferred to the DEA's custody in Las Cruces, New Mexico, whereupon a DEA agent recorded Lauder's fingerprints using a digital infrared scanner, referred to as the "live-skin[32] method," which, according to testimony given at trial, operates essentially like a copy machine. Lab analysis by the DEA determined that Lauder's digitally-obtained fingerprint matched a latent fingerprint that was found on one of the plastic bags containing cocaine and buried in the backyard.

* * *

Fingerprint Evidence

Lauder's third argument is that the district court erred in admitting fingerprint evidence tying Lauder to the cocaine buried in the backyard. Prior to trial, the government filed a motion *in limine* regarding the admissibility of fingerprint evidence it intended to use at trial. In the motion the government outlined the credentials of its fingerprint expert, Anna Zadow, and asserted her expert testimony was admissible under Federal Rules of Evidence 702 and 703.

* * *

Specifically, Lauder objected to the admission of fingerprint cards containing Lauder's known prints. The cards were created by technology referred to at trial as the "live-[scan] method." In essence, the live-[scan] method entails the use of a machine that records fingerprints much as a copy machine duplicates paper copies. The expert, Ms. Zadow, described it at trial:

> [It's a] digitally-captured system. It's what I will term live [scan] … because what it is, it's a plate, it's like a glass plate, and it has technology inside of it that when your finger is placed on a glass without ink, it will capture that friction ridged skin and it will appear to have black ink on it when you look on the computer monitor., … After you rolled your ten fingers, those are then printed out using a printer, a computer printer, and put on an 8 by 8 fingerprint card.

The government first attempted to have the cards admitted into evidence during the testimony of the DEA agent who took Lauder's fingerprints. The district court did not rule on the cards' admissibility at that time, telling the government that "your expert can determine admission." Zadow then took the stand and described the processes she followed in matching Lauder's known print to the latent print found on the plastic bag. On *voir dire* examination, Lauder attempted to show that the live-[scan] method involved new technology that lacked reliability.

Zadow admitted, for example, she was not aware of any testing done by a scientific body. Nor did she know its potential error rate, whether it has been accepted by the scientific community, or whether it had been subjected to peer review. However, Zadow stated the live-[scan] method has been in use for ap-

---

32. The court opinion apparently misspelled live-scan as live-skin.

proximately eight years and is routinely used by the FBI, DEA, United States Marshals Service, and numerous local police departments.

According to Lauder, the district court was required to make factual findings regarding the reliability of the live-[scan] method, which it did not do. Lauder argues further that the court's failure to make such findings amounts to reversible error under *Daubert*. If, in fact, *Daubert* established the applicable guideposts to this case, then Lauder's argument would have some appeal.... In our view, however, Lauder's reliance on *Daubert is* misplaced. Properly framed, the admissibility of the fingerprint cards is governed by the evidentiary rules regarding foundation and authentication, not *Daubert*.

Whether the live-[scan] method generated an accurate image is an authentication question unaffected by *Daubert*. The following thought experiment is illustrative: Suppose an expert relies on photographs taken by a new digital camera in forming her opinion. A district court would not be required to perform a *Daubert* analysis as to whether the photographs accurately reflected the subject matter depicted, even though digital technology is relatively new as compared to a traditional film camera.

Absent some specific objection to the technology underlying the digital equipment, a court is not required to take testimony as to how the equipment works. If the party opposing the exhibit has doubts as to whether the matter in question is what its proponent claims, the proper objection would arise under Rule 901, not Rule 702.

This is not to say, in the right case, the technology underlying the data collection equipment might be sufficiently cast into doubt to require a *Daubert* hearing. But every case involving equipment—whether it be computers, cameras, or speed guns—does not automatically require a *Daubert* hearing regarding the physics behind the operation of the machine.

* * *

We ... hold that the district court did not abuse its discretion in admitting the fingerprint cards into evidence. Trial testimony by the DEA agent and the expert, Zadow, provided evidence that Lauder's known fingerprint was properly recorded, that the live-[scan] method functioned properly when it recorded Lauder's print, and that the chain of custody was maintained.

If the fingerprint examiner has not personally taken the suspect's prints, he cannot be certain whose prints are on the card. One solution is to write in his report that the fingerprint he identified "was made by one and the same person who made the inked or live-scan print on the card in the name of [the suspect]."[33]

# Fingerprint Identification Mistakes

There have been relatively few fingerprint mistakes reported in cases, considering the widespread use of the procedure. A website called http://www.onin.com collects information about problem identifications, including the prominent example of a mistaken

---

33. Grice interview, *supra*.

fingerprint identification of a Portland, Oregon lawyer named Mayfield. His fingerprint was identified as being at the site of a Madrid railroad bombing in 2004. *See* photographs below.

Latent at site          Ouhnane          Mayfield

*Composite of Madrid prints, used with permission, onin.com*

*Daoud Ouhnane and latent Madrid prints enlarged, used with permission, onin.com*

In May of 2004, the FBI issued a formal apology, stating:

> The FBI identification was based on an image of substandard quality, which was particularly problematic because of the remarkable number of points of similarity between Mayfield's prints and the print details in the images submitted to the FBI.[34]

A subsequent article quoting fingerprint experts, expressed concern that using computers to determine fingerprint matches might lead to increasing errors:

> No statistics exist on false fingerprint matches in the United States, but mistakes are believed to be rare, in large part because all fingerprints are checked by human examiners who make the final decision on a match. But the federal database that tied Mayfield to the plastic bag in Madrid holds tens of millions of fingerprints. The computer compares curve angles and patterns to produce a list of possible suspects.

---

34. Leyden, *supra.*

"Obviously, the larger the database, the greater the possibility of two fingers having roughly similar sets of coordinates," Wertheim said. "It's an issue that has troubled some of us in the business." Once a computer identifies possible matches, the science of matching is much the same as it was when fingerprints were first used in a U.S. courtroom in Chicago in 1911: It is up to humans to review two blobs of squiggly lines and decide if they are the same.[35]

According to Mayfield's attorney, Spanish authorities had notified the FBI that they did not agree with the FBI's analysis. The Spanish authorities had pointed out only 7 points in common, whereas the FBI had found 15. Mayfield's fingerprints were on file because of his Army service. A federal judge in Portland threw out a case against Mayfield, after he had been jailed for two weeks as a material witness in the bombing. In December of 2006, Mayfield won a $2 million judgment based on the incident.

An Algerian, Daoud Ouhnane, was later identified as the true source of the fingerprint found on a plastic bag containing traces of explosives and seven detonators.

According to the New York Times:

Critics say the FBI has resisted using uniform standards for fingerprint identification. FBI officials say that human experience—rather than rigid and somewhat artificial indicators—is the best way to determine a fingerprint match, but critics say the FBI should insist that its examiners establish a set number of points of similarity on a print before they can declare a match.

The Seattle Times reported on June 4, 2004, that John Massey, the retired FBI agent who made the misidentification, had been reprimanded three times for false fingerprint identifications between 1969 and 1974.[36]

There will always be some level of human error in fingerprint matching. It is difficult to know how widespread this may be. One example is Rene Sanchez. In 2000, Rene Ramon Sanchez, an auto-body worker, had his fingerprints mistakenly placed on the official record of Leo Rosario. Sanchez had been arrested on three prior occasions for Rosario's crimes and once spent two months in custody before the mistake was corrected.[37]

In 2003, a Utah fingerprint examiner misidentified a fingerprint of the victim as that of her attacker. The problem came to light only when another examiner reviewed the prints in preparation for trial testimony:

"the staff found enough significant differences in the patterns, ridge flows, ridge counts and ridge points of the fingerprints they did not feel there was an identification of the fingerprints."[38]

Another misidentification case in Scotland led to much controversy in the fingerprint community. In 1966, the fingerprint of Detective Constable Shirley McKie was found on a candy tin inside the home of a murder victim in Scotland, despite her statement that she had not been in the home.[39] Fingerprints of one David Asbury were also found, and he was convicted of the murder. Nonetheless, McKie became an outcast

35. Andrew Kramer, *Fingerprint Science Not Exact, Experts Say,* Associated Press, May 21, 2004.
36. David Heath, *FBI's Handling of Fingerprint Case Criticized,* The Seattle Times, June 4, 2004.
37. Benjamin Weiser, *Can Fingerprints Lie? Yes, Man Finds to his Dismay,"* New York Times, May 31, 2004.
38. Loretta Park, *Bloody Prints Don't Match,* Ogden Standard Examiner, February 15, 2003.
39. Michael Specter, *Do Fingerprints Lie?"* The New Yorker, May 27, 2002.

among her colleagues because they felt she had undermined their case by testifying that she had not been in the house. She was subsequently charged and acquitted of perjury.

McKie then found Allan Bayle, a forensic official at Scotland Yard, who agreed the print was not hers. He was threatened with disciplinary action, but would not back down. "[I]n the end, McKie was acquitted of perjury charges and Bayle's statement helped challenge a system that had, until then, simply been taken for granted."[40]

# Fingerprints in the *Grant* Case

Ed Grant was identified in 1997 by a "match" of a latent print taken from a tissue box found in 1973 in the back of Serra's car to an inked print taken when Grant was arrested in a domestic dispute years later. His print was not number 1 on the AFIS report, but number 7. After Christopher Grice ruled out the first 6 candidates, he declared a match to Grant.

Grant's attorney pointed out that no expert could state when the fingerprint was deposited on the tissue box and that it might have occurred in a store. He did not dispute the fingerprint methodology or whether it identified Grant. The prosecution countered in its closing argument that the possibility of Grant's access to the box innocently at the Pathmark store where it was purchased was "essentially eliminated in this case."[41] There were numerous other prints in Serra's car, some of which belonged to Serra family members and some of which were not identifiable. The tissue box was found behind the driver's seat resting on the floor. *See* photograph in Chapter 1. Grant's counsel in his closing argument pointed out that it was improbable that Grant could have reached the box from the front seat and equally improbable that if the box had initially been in the front of the car that Grant would have placed it behind the driver's seat. His counsel also pointed out that there was another identifiable fingerprint—numbered LP4, on the exterior right window, that had never been identified.[42] The presence of other prints inside and outside the car, none of which could be matched to Grant, showed that he did not wipe away all prints. The question remains as to why only a single print identified to Grant was present at the crime site.

Based on that fingerprint, a blood sample from Grant was provided pursuant to court order. That was "matched" to the single spot of DNA on a handkerchief left at the crime scene. These were the two main pieces of forensic evidence used to convict Grant. One of Grant's arguments on appeal is that the fingerprint did not constitute probable cause to issue a search warrant for his blood. Were he to win this argument, the state would not be permitted to use the DNA evidence in a second trial. *See* Chapter 14.

## Should One Fingerprint Have Been Corroborated?

Grant did not argue on appeal that his conviction should be overturned because only one fingerprint allegedly placed him at the scene. However, the Connecticut Supreme Court has held that—absent any other corroborating evidence—evidence of a single fingerprint is insufficient to identify a defendant as a perpetrator. Where a defendant was convicted of kidnapping and robbery based on two of his fingerprints

---

40. *Id.*
41. Transcript, May 22, 2002.
42. *Id.*

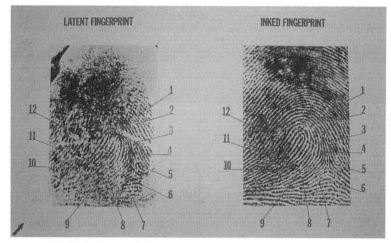

*Grant's latent and inked prints, exhibit 55.1*

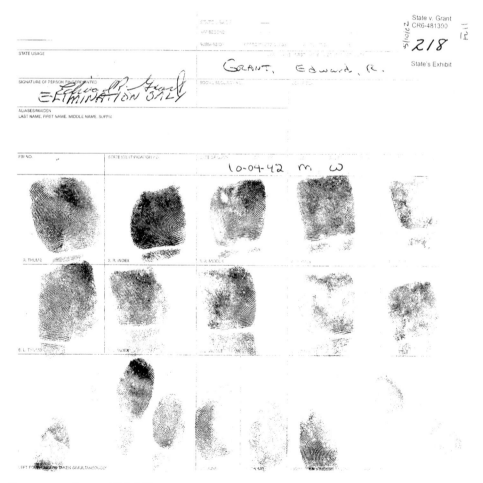

*Grants ten prints, exhibit 218*

found on the outside driver's window of the victim's car, the conviction was reversed because the only other evidence that connected the defendant to the crime scene was a general description of the perpetrator as a short, black male no more than sixteen or seventeen years old. The court agreed with the defendant's contention that the evidence against him was insufficient as a matter of law because of the "well-established rule that a conviction may not stand on fingerprint evidence alone unless the prints were found under such circumstances that they could only have been impressed at the time the crime was perpetrated.[43]

> The state was unable to present any evidence dating the defendant's fingerprints or otherwise limiting their impression to the circumstances of the crime. The state, however, has attempted to distinguish this case from those in which the rule has been applied on the ground that there was other evidence upon which the jury could have relied in reaching their verdict against the defendant. The evidence on which the state relies is the victim's description of one of the perpetrators as a short, black male no more than sixteen or seventeen years old.

> We are not persuaded by the state's argument. Although the description relied upon by the state arguably fits the defendant, it is far too general to provide any corroboration of the fingerprint evidence.[44]

Here is what another court concluded in reviewing other cases in its jurisdiction:

> Where the State has relied solely on fingerprint evidence to establish that the defendant was the perpetrator of the crimes charged, this Court has held that the defendant's motion to dismiss should have been granted.

> *See, e.g., State v. Bass*, 303 N.C. 267,278 S.E.2d 209 (1981) (where the only evidence tending to show that the defendant was ever at the scene of the crime was four of defendant's fingerprints found on the frame of a window screen on the victim's home, the State produced no evidence tending to show when they were put there, and the defendant offered evidence that he was on the premises at an earlier date);

> *State v. Scott*, 296 N.C. 519, 251 S.E.2d 414 (1979) (where the only evidence tending to show that defendant was ever in victim's home was a thumbprint found on a metal box in the den on the day of the murder, and the niece of the deceased testified that during the week, she had no opportunity to observe who came to the house on business or to visit her uncle.)

As [was] succinctly stated in *State v. Miller*:

> These cases establish the rule that testimony by a qualified expert that fingerprints found at the scene of the crime correspond with the fingerprints of the accused, when accompanied by substantial evidence of circumstances from which the jury can find that the fingerprints could only have been impressed at the time the crime was committed, is sufficient to withstand motion for nonsuit and carry the case to the jury. The soundness of the rule lies in the fact that such evidence logically tends to show that the accused was present and participated in the commission of the crime.[45]

---

43. *State v. Payne*, 186 Conn. 179 (1982).
44. *Id.* at 184.
45. *State v. Montgomery*, 341 N.C. 553, 461 S.E. 2d 732, 736–7 (1995).

The Supreme Court of Illinois agreed in a 1992 case: "defendant is correct in his assertion that in order to sustain a conviction solely on fingerprint evidence, fingerprints corresponding to those of the defendant must have been found in the immediate vicinity of the crime under circumstances as to establish beyond a reasonable doubt that they were impressed at the time the crime was committed."[46]

In *State v. Monzo*, the defendant was identified almost ten years after an assault based on a match of fingerprints left on the basement door trim of the victim's house and on her wallet to the defendant's prints found in an AFIS system. The door trim had been recently painted, which was circumstantial evidence that the defendant's print had been placed on the door after it had been painted, which was shortly before the attack. An expert also testified that the print on the wallet would have been fresh, as repeated handling of the wallet would have degraded the print or left overlapping prints on it. The defendant argued that he had been legitimately present in the house before the rape, performing odd jobs for her general contractor. He also argued that during one of those jobs, he may have touched her wallet when he handed it to her so that she could pay him. The defendant was convicted, lost his appeal and then petitioned for post-conviction relief based on a claim of ineffective counsel due to failure to investigate further alibi witnesses. The Ohio Court of Appeals denied the petition, holding that it was unlikely that further alibi evidence would have affected the jury's decision.[47]

Unlike the cases discussed above, the prosecution in *Grant* did offer more than one fingerprint. It presented the DNA evidence from the handkerchief and the testimony of a number of eyewitnesses. However, the eyewitness evidence was conflicting. Initially, one eyewitness conclusively picked Phil DeLieto out of a lineup. Dr. Lee testified that the blood was on top of the fingerprint and he could not say when the fingerprint was placed on the box. In addition, he conceded that in an earlier investigation, he concluded that the handkerchief was not related to the crime. All the expert witnesses agreed that it was impossible to tell *when* the fingerprint was placed on the tissue box or when the genetic material was placed on the handkerchief.

The combination of the fingerprint and the DNA evidence would doubtless have justified a court in ruling that the fingerprint itself did not need further corroboration. However, if Grant wins his appeal to exclude the DNA evidence, the state would have only one fingerprint and general eyewitness evidence on re-trial, facts very similar to those in *Monzo*.

## The Fingerprint Identification on Appeal

Grant has raised a related argument about the fingerprint identification in his appeal. He contends that the warrant to take his blood lacked probable cause because the fingerprint was on a moveable item and therefore did not link him to the crime scene. If the warrant lacked probable cause, then the state would have only the fingerprint to present as evidence and would not have been able to use the DNA evidence matched to his blood. Grant points out in his brief that Dr. Henry Lee testified at trial that the fingerprint was underneath the bloodstain—in other words the fingerprint was not made

---

46. *State v. Campbell*, 146 Ill. 2d 363, 586 N.E.2d 1261, 1271 (1992).
47. *State v. Monzo*, No. 97APA04-481, 1998 Ohio App. LEXIS 616 (February 17, 1998).

by a bloody finger, but covered by blood. Dr. Lee also testified that there is no way to date a fingerprint—the fingerprint could have been placed on the tissue box from a moment to months before the blood was added.

On this point, the appeal brief concedes that the location of Grant's fingerprint under the blood stain does not necessarily exonerate the defendant. Rather, Grant's lawyers argue that the relative location of the print made it impossible to conclude that there was probable cause to believe that Grant's print was impressed on the box at the time of the crime. For that reason, the defense contends, there was insufficient evidence to allow the police to secure a court order ("warrant") requiring Grant to submit to a blood test. Thus, the defense argues that the blood drawn from Grant pursuant to the warrant was impermissibly secured and was, therefore, inadmissible.

As to whether the fingerprint, by itself, is sufficient to show probable cause, the brief states that, given the fact that no one can state when the fingerprint was placed on the tissue box and given also that a tissue box is highly moveable, the fingerprint does not establish probable cause. In other words, even if the defense admits that the fingerprint is Grant's and therefore Grant touched the box at some point, there is no evidence that he touched the box *at the time of the crime* because the box is an easily moveable item. Grant's appellate brief says:

> This proves that the person whose fingerprint it is touched the outside of the box, but given the portability of the box, it does not even prove the tissue box was touched while [in the car] as opposed to at some other time prior to the tissue box being put [in the car.] Does the print on the tissue box provide probable cause that the person who made it is the [murderer]? Not if the fingerprint belongs to anyone who touched the box before the [murder] at any of its many prior locations before it ended up on the [car].[48]

His attorneys also argue that, as there was no fingerprint of Grant's anywhere on the car itself, including on the bloody steering wheel or any of the car handles, there is no way to place him in the car as a result of a fingerprint match on the tissue box.

The State argues that its probable cause affidavit was not misleading and even if it was, the result was harmless error. Grant's attorneys had moved before trial for a *Franks* hearing to ask the court to hear these issues; the motion was denied on January 7, 2002. Here is the standard for a *Franks* hearing, according to the State:

> Before a defendant is entitled to a Franks hearing, he "must make a substantial preliminary showing that the information was (1) omitted with the intent to make, or in reckless disregard of whether it made, the affidavit misleading to the judge, and (2) material to the determination of probable cause." Not all omissions, even if intentional, will invalidate an affidavit. An affiant may 'pick[]and choose[]' "the information that he includes in the affidavit and he may omit facts that he believes to be either immaterial or unsubstantiated. Cases like this one, which involve allegedly material omissions, are "less likely to present a question of impermissible official conduct" than those which involve allegedly material false inclusions.[49]

The State specifically rejects Grant's claims about omissions of information as follows: As to the issue of the fingerprint on the tissue box being under the blood and

---

48. Appellant Brief, *supra* at 26–27.
49. Appellee Brief, *supra* at 19–20.

therefore possibly placed there days before the commission of the crime, the state responds that even had "Dr. Lee's statement … been included in the affidavit, it would not have defeated a finding of probable cause because it was entirely consistent with the inference implicitly drawn by the issuing judge, based on the totality of the other information in the affidavit, that the defendant's bloodied and admittedly inexplicable fingerprint could have been deposited on the tissue box during the commission of the crime or its immediate aftermath."[50]

The appeal is not expected to be resolved until 2008.

# Summary

Fingerprint analysis is based on the hypothesis that all fingerprints are permanent and unique and that a trained examiner can compare fingerprints to determine whether or not they identify the same individual. This comparison can also be made by a jury by looking at an enlarged picture of fingerprints assuming the prints are sufficiently complete and clear. There are up to 200 "level two" ridge characteristics, such as bifurcations, ridge endings and ridge dots, that distinguish one person's fingerprint from another's. A full size fingerprint is approximately one inch square.

Examiners must use their judgment in matching a crime scene print that is less than complete or not completely visible. The process of lifting fingerprints from a crime scene can result in their becoming smudged or masked by other prints. An examiner typically will not attempt to identify a crime scene print of less than one-quarter of a full fingerprint or if there is insufficient detail. In addition, there is no set number of points that an examiner must find in common in order to declare a match. Although a commission in 1970 determined that such a set rule could not be established, the lack of "standards" led one district court in 2002 to declare that fingerprint identification was not reliable under *Daubert*. The court ruled that the examiner could point out similarities and differences to the jury, but could not offer an opinion about identity.

The advent of AFIS databases and computer searching has greatly decreased the time required to identify fingerprints, but it has not eliminated the need for an examiner with the training and experience to make the judgments about whether and when to determine a match. There have been very few reports of misidentification of fingerprints. The highly publicized case in which a fingerprint was misidentified to a Seattle attorney in connection with a political bombing in Madrid, Spain, was an embarrassment to the FBI and resulted in a large dollar settlement, but probably does not undermine the integrity of the fingerprint identification system.

Fingerprint identification has been accepted as forensic evidence since the early 1900s. The process of fingerprint identification requires Analysis, Comparison, Evaluation and Verification. It depends upon a comparison of ridge characteristics, such as ridge endings, ridge dots, and bifurcations, which must be identical in size, shape and location to declare a match. An examiner may make one of three conclusions: Identification; Exclusion; or Inconclusive.

---

50. *Id.* at 23–24.

The examiner must determine Exclusion if there is even one difference in ridge characteristics. If he determines that he does not have enough of a print or enough clearly visible ridge characteristics to compare, he would conclude Inconclusive. Only if he is satisfied, based on his training and experience, that the prints are identical, will he give the opinion: Identification.

Not until quite recently has there been any challenge to the reliability of fingerprint identification. However, a few scholars as well as one federal district court argued that fingerprint identification did not pass the *Daubert* tests for reliability because no scientific studies had been conducted outside the fingerprint community to verify the required minimum number of comparison points to declare a match.

This case was later retracted, but it has spawned a large number of subsequent challenges to fingerprint identification under *Daubert* and similar state statutes. These challenges have uniformly failed.

In *Grant*, the defense did not dispute that the fingerprint on the tissue box was Grant's, but argued there is no way for an expert to determine when the fingerprint was put on the box. Dr. Lee testified that the blood which appeared on the print was placed there after the print, which might mean that the print was placed on the box at some location and time other than at the crime. Grant used this argument to argue on appeal that the fingerprint was on a moveable item and therefore could not be used to establish probable cause to conclude Grant was in the car at the time of the crime in connection with the warrant to take Grant's blood. If Grant were to win his appeal on this issue, the prosecution would not be able to use the DNA results from Grant's blood in a subsequent trial. As of this writing, the appeal is pending.

# Discussion Questions

1. How do we know that no two fingerprints are alike?

2. How many points of comparison of ridge characteristics are required to match a fingerprint? How many do you think there should be?

3. Does your opinion change when you review the actual procedures used to compare fingerprints under an AFIS system such as that used in Connecticut?

4. On what grounds have courts thrown out fingerprint evidence?

5. What are some of the problems with lifting and examining latent fingerprints? Describe at least five different ridge characteristics.

6. Why did the court in *Abreu* hold that fingerprint identification met the *Daubert* standards?

7. Why did the trial court in *Plaza I* decide that fingerprint identification did not meet *Daubert*?

8. Why did Judge Pollack reverse himself in *Plaza II* and change that opinion?

9. What does the error in identifying the fingerprint in the Madrid bombing case say about possible errors in fingerprint identification?

10. How did the court in *United States v. Lauder* evaluate the "live scan" method of taking a suspect's prints under the *Daubert* standard?

11. How would you predict that future improvements in computer analysis of finger-prints, such as the possible "field testing" of fingerprints immediately at crime site will be evaluated under *Daubert*?

12. Do agree with Grant that the latent fingerprint found on the tissue box in Serra's car should not have been used to establish "probable cause" to issue a warrant for his blood?

13. Do you think Grant could be convicted if the DNA test on the handkerchief were excluded from the evidence at trial?

14. How does the trial in *Grant* compare with the cases that have held that a conviction may not be based on fingerprint evidence unless the evidence shows it could only have been impressed at the time the crime was perpetrated?

15. What might have happened if the jury had been told to use the standard cited above: *you must find proof beyond a reasonable doubt that the fingerprint identified from the tissue box could only have been impressed at the time the crime was committed?*

# Chapter 8

# DNA

## Overview

The ability of DNA profiling to identify the presence of a defendant at a crime scene has had an explosive effect on criminal trials. DNA typing is one of the newest forms of forensic identification and the most powerful. Its power stems from the wealth of knowledge scientists have generated in mapping the human genome—science for the sake of science, rather than for litigation. We can now examine a mere 13 sites on human chromosomes and, using probability statistics, identify a person with virtual certainty.

The scientific process by which DNA profiling has evolved has created pressure on other forms of forensic identification—such as fingerprints and handwriting—that rely on a scientific hypothesis, but combine examiner subjectivity. What are the implications of DNA profiling for other forensic disciplines? Can any other discipline duplicate the power of DNA?

The phenomenon of reversals of convictions due to newly-tested DNA is also a byproduct of DNA technology. Photos of convicts who have been cleared by DNA have caused the public to question the reliability of eyewitness identification, upon which many of the convictions have rested. Whether it will put pressure on juries to demand DNA evidence before they will convict is not yet known. However, the "CSI Effect," the desire of juries to expect scientific evidence connecting a defendant with a crime, is probably here to stay.

Grant's counsel believes that he might not have been convicted on a fingerprint alone. The DNA found on the handkerchief left in the garage, coupled with the fingerprint identification, was simply too overwhelming for the jury to ignore.

Will DNA testing lead to fewer erroneous convictions and more confidence in the criminal justice system?

## Chapter Objectives

Based on this chapter, students will be able to:

1. Explain the science of DNA testing and why testing of 13 loci can produce absolute identity.

2. Understand why DNA can absolutely rule out a suspect.

3. Describe the product rule.

4. Explain the Prosecutor's Fallacy.

5. Understand the issue of using the correct DNA database for the ethnicity of the suspect.

6. Explain how conditions in DNA testing laboratories can affect DNA tests.

7. Evaluate the reasons why courts have "judicially noticed" the science of DNA testing.

8. Explain how to challenge DNA test results.

9. Understand issues with mixed or contaminated samples.

10. Explain Polymerase Chain Reaction and why it is important to DNA testing.

11. Explain the difference between standard DNA tests and mitochondrial DNA testing.

12. Understand the court opinion in the gatekeeper challenge to STR DNA testing in the *Grant* case.

# The Process of DNA Profile Analysis

## What Is DNA?

The initials DNA stand for deoxyribonucleic acid, which is the material inside our chromosomes that controls our genetic makeup. All humans have 23 pairs of chromosomes—one pair inherited from the mother and one pair through the father. Both the egg and sperm contain only half the normal amount of chromosomes. The oocyte, or egg, contains 23 chromosomes and the sperm cell likewise contains 23 chromosomes. When the sperm fertilizes the egg, the cells merge and a full set of 46 chromosomes determines the genetic makeup of the offspring.

Chromosomes are made up of DNA, organized in a helix pattern, a ladder-like formation composed of sugars on each edge and four different proteins as the rungs of the ladder. These are adenine, thymine, guanine, and cytosine. Adenine pairs only with thymine and guanine pairs only with cytosine. They are organized in a pattern that repeats. These patterns vary by individual. By measuring where a pattern stops and begins a new repetition, scientists can distinguish one person's DNA from another.

At each genetic marker point on a chromosome, called a "locus," a person will have two genetic markers, called "alleles." One comes from the mother and one from the father. On the loci tested for DNA profiling, these alleles are of different lengths in different people.

# Location of DNA and MtDNA

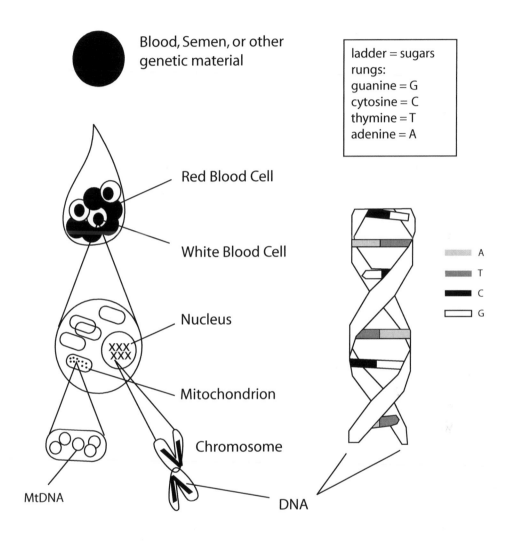

Blood, Semen, or other genetic material

ladder = sugars
rungs:
guanine = G
cytosine = C
thymine = T
adenine = A

Red Blood Cell

White Blood Cell

Nucleus

Mitochondrion

Chromosome

MtDNA

DNA

A
T
C
G

# DNA Typing—A Quickly Changing Technology

RFLP. Restriction
Fragment Length Poly-
morphism—an early
form of DNA testing.

DNA evidence has become the most respected forensic evidence in the shortest time of any forensic science. In 1944, Oswald Avery defined the concept of DNA (deoxyribonucleic acid) as the building block of human genetics. In 1953, Watson and Crick discovered the double helix model. In 1980, Botstein discovered small variations at the genetic level which he called restriction fragment length polymorphism. Shortened to its initials, it is RFLP. That technology was first applied in 1984 to detect alleles at various loci along a chain of DNA.

# The Principles of DNA Testing

DNA testing does not create a profile of the total DNA of an individual. All humans share 99.9% of their DNA in common. Of the .1% of DNA that varies, there are approximately 2,000,000 markers (called loci for the location on the chromosome) that differ from person to person. Some loci control individual characteristics, such as eye color, height or bone structure. Of these 2,000,000, there are about 2,000 markers that do not appear to control any known genetic variable. These are called "junk DNA" because their use is unknown. These junk DNA sites are used for testing because, as far as scientists know, they are distributed randomly through the population. Of these loci (sites), only 13 are tested in the typical DNA kit. How can a mere 13 markers out of 2,000,000 identify a person to a certainty of 1 in 300 million? The answer lies in statistics, which is another complexity involved in explaining DNA tests to a jury.

DNA testing can absolutely rule out or exclude a suspect. In the case of rapes, hospitals take samples of fluids from the vagina for testing in what is called a rape kit. If the DNA found in a rape kit does not match the suspect's, he is absolutely excluded as the rapist, or at least as the source of the semen found in the rape kit. The fact that rape kits are routinely collected and saved is one reason why a number of convicted rapists have been exonerated due to newly tested DNA technology that did not exist at the time that the accused was tried and convicted.

If the profile of the
defendant's DNA does
not match the markers at
all the loci tested from
the crime scene, the genetic
sample at the crime
scene did not come from
the defendant.

Today, no one disagrees that DNA is totally reliable in excluding a defendant as the source of the sample.

# Restriction Fragment Length Polymorphism (RFLP) Testing

Adenine pairs only with thymine and guanine pairs only with cytosine. The order of the chemical building blocks distinguishes different DNA strands. By measuring the number of repeating patterns of these four chemicals at a particular locus on the strand of DNA, scientists can create a DNA profile. And as the length of the strands differs among different people, a profile of one person's DNA strands will differ from another's. The earliest form of DNA testing looked for repeating patterns and marked the DNA whenever a repeat occurred. The chemicals are identified by their first letters; therefore a possible repeating pattern might look like this: AGCTCAATGC.

> STR. Restriction Fragment Length Polymorphism has been replaced by the discovery of loci where the fragment lengths were shorter and easier to measure, thus, Short Tandem Repeats (STR).

By using "restriction enzymes," scientists discovered that they could break DNA into smaller pieces at the places where a tandem repeat ended. RFLP testing involved applying an electrophoresic gel to the DNA sample. The gel would travel until it detected the end of a pattern. By using light, transfer of the pattern, and photography, scientists created a pattern that looks like a bar code in a supermarket. RFLP testing required at least a tablespoon of genetic material for testing. It was also expensive. The earliest court cases used RFLP testing and raised a number of issues about its reliability. Although RFLP testing has largely been superseded by a more efficient method called Short Tandem Repeat testing, the basic concept of identifying different length alleles is the premise of all DNA testing. Here is how one California court described the process:

*People v. Pizarro*, 110 Cal. App. 4th 530 (2003)

\* \* \*

Determination of a person's genetic profile using RFLP relies on the differences in length of certain DNA regions, or alleles. In *People v. Brown*, this court summarized the basis of variation between alleles and its utility to forensic DNA profiling. There, we analogized DNA to text:

The genetics of a human cell can be compared to a library, the genome, composed of 46 'books,' each a single chromosome. The 'text' contained in the books is written in DNA, the chemical language of genetics. The 'library' is compiled by the owner's parents, each of whom contributes 23 books, which are then matched up and arranged together in 23 paired sets inside the sacrosanct edifice of the nucleus. During embryonic development, the original library is copied millions of times so that each cell in the human body contains a copy of the entire library.

Twenty-two of the twenty-three paired sets of books are entitled 'Chromosome 1' through 'Chromosome 22'; externally, the two paired books of each set appear to be identical in size and shape. However, the 23d set, which contains information on gender, consists of one book entitled 'Chromosome X' (given by the mother) and one book entitled either 'Chromosome X' or 'Chromosome Y' (given by the father and determining the sex of the library's owner). The 22 sets comprising 'Chromosome 1' through 'Chromosome 22' address an enormous variety of topics describing the composition, appearance, and function of the owner's body.

In addition, they include a considerable amount of what appears to be nonsense. The two paired books of each set, one book from each parent, address identical topics, but may contain slightly different information on those topics. Thus, two paired books opened to the same page contain corresponding 'paragraphs,' but the text within those corresponding paragraphs may vary between the two books.

For example, within the paragraph addressing eye color, one book may describe blue eyes while the other book of the set may describe brown eyes.

The two corresponding, but potentially variant, paragraphs in the two paired books are called alleles. If, for a particular topic (i.e., at a particular region or locus on the DNA), the allele from the mother is A and the corresponding allele from the father is B, the genotype at that locus is designated AB. The text of two corresponding alleles at any locus may be identical (a homozygous genotype, e.g., AA) or different (a heterozygous genotype, e.g., AB). Regardless, one person's genetic text is, in general, extremely similar to another person's; indeed, viewed in its vast entirety, the genetic text of one human library is 99.9 percent identical to all others. As a result, the text of most corresponding paragraphs varies only slightly among members of the population.

Certain alleles, however, have been found to contain highly variable text. For example, alleles are composed of highly variable text when they describe structures requiring enormous variability. Also, some alleles appear to contain gibberish that varies greatly, or repeated strings of text that vary not in text but in repeat number. These variants (polymorphisms) found at certain loci render each person's library unique and provide forensic scientists a method of differentiating between libraries (people) through the use of forensic techniques that rely on the large number of variant alleles possible at each variable locus.... Since each person receives two alleles for each locus, the number of possible combinations is further increased.

When a sample of DNA—usually in the form of hair, blood, saliva, or semen—is left at the crime scene by a perpetrator, a forensic genetic analysis is conducted. First, DNA analysts create a genetic 'profile' or 'type' of the perpetrator's DNA by determining which variants or alleles exist at several variable loci. Second, the defendant's DNA is analyzed in exactly the same manner to create a profile for comparison with the perpetrator's profile. If the defendant's DNA produces a different profile than the perpetrator's, even by only one allele, the defendant could not have been the source of the crime scene DNA, and he or she is absolutely exonerated.

If, on the other hand, the defendant's DNA produces exactly the same genetic profile, the defendant could have been the source of the perpetrator's DNA—but so could any other person with the same genetic profile. Third, when the perpetrator's and the defendant's profiles are found to match, the statistical significance of the match must be explained in terms of the rarity or commonness of that profile within a particular population—that is, the number of people within a population expected to possess that particular genetic profile, or, put another way, the probability that a randomly chosen person in that population possesses that particular genetic profile. Only then can the jury weigh the value of the profile match.

# DNA Testing Improves with Short Tandem Repeats

As DNA testing progressed, scientists discovered certain loci (or locations) at which the alleles varied in length, but the variations were relatively short and easier to measure. These became known as Short Tandem Repeats. Short Tandem Repeat (STR) testing has replaced RFLP testing, not only because it is less expensive, but because once the FBI adopted STR, DNA profiles stored in its centralized CODIS database could not be "matched" by law enforcement from state agencies unless their testing used the same system.

> CODIS. Combined DNA Index System. The system stores profiles that can be matched to profiles created in connection with criminal investigations.

Most examiners who use the STR process examine the length of DNA alleles at 13 different possible sites, or loci. The results at each locus will show two alleles with lengths from a range of possible length alleles, varying from 8 possibilities (for site D13S317) to 23 possibilities (for site D18S51). The "length" of the repeats is measured using numbers from 4 to 51, which are what appear on a DNA report. A suspect will have two alleles at each locus— one from his mother and one from his father, unless both mother and father had the identical allele, in which case only one allele would appear.

The number associated with the length allele at each of the 13 loci determined from the suspect's genetic material is then compared with those of a sample taken from the crime scene. This comparison will either show one or more different length alleles between the samples, in which case they definitely do not match, or it will show that all tested alleles are identical. If they are identical, the next step is to calculate the likelihood of another person in the same racial group having that identical pattern of alleles at each of those 13 sites. This information then yields the likelihood of a "random match." The higher the denominator of the fraction, such as 1 over 300 million,[1] the less likely it is that anyone other than the defendant could have been the source of the DNA.

> Random Match Probability. The chance of selecting a random, unrelated person from the population who shares the same DNA profile found in an evidence sample.

# Polymerase Chain Reaction "Copies" Small DNA Samples

At the same time as STR testing was developing, another process was developed that could multiply an extremely small amount of genetic material into a specimen large enough to test. This is called Polymerase Chain Reaction, or PCR. A small bit of DNA is first separated into two linear halves of a ladder. Then it is combined with free molecules of adenine, guanine, thymine, and cytosine. In a process that involves heating and then

> PCR. Polymerase Chain Reaction is a system that copies a small piece of genetic material so that it is large enough for DNA testing.

---

1. 1 in 300 million is actually a smaller number than 1 in 10 million, as the number is a fraction. However, most people look at the size of the denominator of the fraction as the indicator of the rarity of a random match.

cooling the sample, the free molecules match up with their partners in the separated DNA fragment, thus creating a new fragment. This process is repeated until a "copy" of the original DNA fragment is of sufficient size to be DNA typed.

The PCR process was a significant development. RFLP testing requires 10–50 nanograms of genetic material—roughly the amount in a clump of pulled hair. STR testing can be done with .3–.5 nanograms, or a blood drop the size of a large pinhead, which can then be duplicated by using the Polymerase Chain Reaction system to create a large enough sample to test. A single strand of hair to which the root is attached would also be sufficient because the root contains genetic material. If the only sample is a hair shaft without a root, the only method of testing available is mitochondrial DNA testing, which will identify the DNA from the subject's mother only. *See* mtDNA at the end of this chapter.

# The Role of Statistics in DNA Profiling

In order to make DNA testing meaningful for identification, the scientist must first know the range of different alleles at a particular locus and how many people in the population have which allele. For example, if at a particular locus, there are 10 different variations in length of allele possible, but a test of 40,000 people showed that 99% of them had length #12, then the test is not much good for distinguishing one person from another. If you tested only the alleles at the locus D3S1358, almost 25% of the Caucasian population could be expected to have a number 15 allele. So that one fact, standing alone, would "include" the suspect, but would not be specific enough to identify the suspect, as 25 Caucasians out of 100 would share the same number 15 allele.

The reason that numbers for a "random match" can get to numbers such as 1 in a trillion is because of the "product rule." This rule states that the probability of a person having the exact same allele at all of the 13 loci tested is determined by multiplying the individual probability of a match at one allele, by the probability at the next allele, by the probability at the next, and so forth.

> The "Product Rule." If two events are independent and the probabilities of each event are known, then the combined probability is calculated by multiplying the individual event probabilities together.

To illustrate, assume you have a package of M&M's. The package contains 40 candies: 15 are red; 10 are yellow, 10 are green, and 5 are brown. Assume you reach into the bag, pull out an M&M, check its color, and then put it back in the bag. If you reached into the bag, the probability of pulling a red candy would be 15 divided by the total number of candies [40], or 3 in 8 [38%] If you wanted to determine the probability of drawing a red candy and then a green candy, you would need to multiply the first probability [38%] by the second probability [10 divided by 40, which is 1 in 4 or 25%] The product of 38% by 25% is 9.5%[ 38% times 25% is 9.5%] Multiply by the likelihood of next drawing a brown candy [12.5%] and the likelihood becomes about 1%. So, in just four probabilities, we have gone from 38% to 1%.

The following chart shows the chances of a "random match" occurring between a Caucasian suspect and any other Caucasian at each locus. The chances of this occurring at all of the loci together, which is the product of multiplying each probability by the next and so forth, becomes 5.01 times 10 to the 18th power, which equates to absolute identification.

| Locus | Chance of Random Match |
|-------|------------------------|
| CSF1PO | 0.132 |
| D2S1338 | 0.027 |
| D3S1358 | 0.076 |
| D5S818 | 0.147 |
| D7S820 | 0.063 |
| D8S1179 | 0.064 |
| D13S317 | 0.079 |
| D16S539 | 0.097 |
| D18S51 | 0.031 |
| D19S433 | 0.097 |
| D21S11 | 0.044 |
| FGA | 0.035 |
| TH01 | 0.079 |
| TPOX | 0.188 |
| vWA | 0.066 |
| combined | 5.01 x 10 to the 18th power |

## DNA Testing of Degraded Samples

If the genetic sample is too small to be tested, degraded, or contaminated, it may be impossible to get a clear DNA reading. If this happens, one or more of the markers may not appear on the DNA test results. But the test results will not falsely identify the defendant. In other words, it is not possible for a DNA test on a poor sample to misidentify a defendant by falsely creating his DNA pattern. However, if an evidentiary sample is contaminated with the defendant's DNA sample, the results could falsely implicate the defendant. This was one of the claims in the *Simpson* case. There have also been instances of a false match due to an analyst mislabeling the evidence tube as the defendant's reference sample.[2]

Even though defense lawyers may prove to the jury that a DNA sample was contaminated (either through negligence or intentionally), or that the laboratory was poorly equipped, none of those facts will turn a genetic sample that is not the defendant's into a test result that falsely implicates him.

2. The writer wishes to thank Jason Gilder, of Forensic Bioinformatic Services, for his review and comments on this chapter.

# The Use of DNA Evidence in Court

## The Expert Opinion in Court on a DNA "Match"

DNA is the only area of forensic individuation in which experts typically do not testify that a tested sample of DNA "identifies the suspect." Rather, the expert typically gives an opinion in terms of the likelihood of a random match, as opposed to certain identification. Unlike fingerprints or handwriting, a DNA expert typically does not testify that a DNA sample found at a crime scene absolutely came from the defendant. However, in the year 2006, one court approved an expert who testified that it can be concluded "to a reasonable scientific certainty that the evidence sample and the defendant sample came from the same person," adding that the defendant still can challenge the expert's conclusion in cross examination.[3]

## "Judicial Notice" of DNA Testing

As DNA has become more common in courtrooms, courts have "judicially noticed" DNA as a reliable scientific test. This means that no *Daubert* or *Frye* hearing would be required in order to admit DNA results. In 1999 the Kentucky Supreme Court ruled that the reliability of RFLP and PCR methods were sufficiently established so as to no longer require a *Daubert* hearing prior to its presentation to the jury. In that case, the defendant appealed his murder and first-degree burglary conviction. The only physical evidence was his blood on one of his shoes linked to the crime scene. The court held that even though the trial court took judicial notice of the validity of the underlying science of DNA, the evidence was still subject to challenges by the defense to its credibility and significance at trial.[4]

This case is an excellent illustration of the real limitations of DNA evidence. Let's say that the defendant did legitimate plumbing work at the victim's house weeks before a burglary occurred. Assume further that he accidentally cut himself in the bathroom, and left a bloodstain on the floor. The DNA analysis can establish that the blood on the bathroom floor came from the defendant. But in this example, the match is not incriminating. It does not tend to prove that the defendant committed the subsequent burglary. In this context, we see that although the science of DNA is now accepted and does not require a *Daubert* hearing, the significance of a "match" is always open to challenge.

## Avoiding the "Prosecutor's Fallacy"

If the DNA of the defendant matches the markers at each of the loci from the sample tested from the crime scene, the defendant is almost certainly the source of the genetic material at the crime scene. However, this does not prove that the defendant is guilty. It does not mean that the defendant was at the crime scene (the genetic material may have been planted) or that he was at the crime scene at the time of the crime. DNA testing cannot tell

---

3. *People v. Johnson*, 139 Cal. App. 4th 1135, 1146 (Cal. App. 2006).
4. *Fugate v. Kentucky*, 993 S.W.2d 931 (Sup. Ky. 1999).

when or under what circumstances genetic material was deposited. After all, the defendant may have deposited DNA, for example blood, under circumstances that show he was acting in self defense, or that an accident occurred, and so forth.

However, DNA can be powerful evidence. For this reason, courts are legitimately concerned with a phenomenon known as the "prosecutor's fallacy." That is the fear that the jury will conclude that if the profile shows the chance of a random match is 1 in 300 million, that means that the chance that the defendant is innocent is also 1 in 300 million.

> The Prosecutor's Fallacy. The chance that a jury will take the random match probability as representing the odds that the defendant is innocent.

In the Grant case, the DNA expert reduced the probability of a random match to 1 in 300 million, roughly the size of the population of the United States, even though the actual statistics were much higher. That is a policy set by the Connecticut Forensic Lab in an effort to reduce the statistic to a number that the jury can grasp.

## Early Court Challenges to DNA Test Results

DNA testing was first admitted in criminal courts in the late 1980s. The issues in early appeals included whether the RFLP method of DNA testing was reliable, challenges to laboratory conditions, concerns about a DNA profile "mis-identifying" a suspect if the sample were degraded or mixed, and concerns about the population statistics unfairly creating too high a likelihood of a random match. The issue of prejudice was also raised repeatedly.

Many of these objections were made in a federal court case in New Hampshire called *United States v. Shea*,[5] decided in 1997. The defendant, Anthony Mark Shea, was charged with robbery. The case is long and complex, but it illustrates a number of important issues about the use of DNA in the courtroom.

Here are the basic facts of the case, as reported by the court:

> Two men wearing masks and gloves broke into the Londonderry branch of the First New Hampshire Bank about an hour after closing on August 4, 1995. One of the robbers apparently cut himself when he entered the building, as bloodstains were discovered inside the bank and in a stolen minivan believed to have been used as a getaway vehicle.

> The government later charged Anthony Shea with the robbery and proposed to base its case in part on expert testimony comparing Shea's DNA with DNA extracted from several of the bloodstains. The government's expert, a forensic scientist employed by the FBI, used a method of DNA analysis known as Polymerase Chain Reaction ("PCR"), in determining that Shea has the same DNA profile as the person who left several of the blood stains at the crime scene and in the getaway vehicle. The expert also concluded that the probability of finding a similar profile match if a DNA sample were drawn randomly from the Caucasian population is 1 in 200,000.

Shea appealed on issues relating to the reliability of DNA testing, whether the statistical projections were correct, and the possible prejudice of reporting the statistical likelihood of a random match, referred to as the "prosecutor's fallacy."

---

5. *United States v. Shea,* 957 F. Supp. 331 (D. N. Hamp. 1997).

### 1. Reliability

First, Shea argued that the DNA evidence connecting him with the location of the bank robbery should be excluded because the RFLP method of DNA typing was unreliable. The court disagreed and wrote a detailed description of DNA, the testing of alleles, and the RFLP process.

### 2. Sample Size and Ethnic Database

Next, Shea contended that the testimony that the probability of finding another person whose DNA matched the sample was 1 in 200,000 should be excluded because the sample size from which the probability statistic was drawn was too small and was unreliable for other reasons.

The court explained in detail why it concluded that the statistical reasoning was correct. The court also explained that the expert had used separate databases to calculate the random match probability among the Caucasian population, the African-American population and the Hispanic population. The jury heard only the testimony applicable to Shea, who was Caucasian.

Although the early DNA cases frequently contained challenges that the prosecution should use a separate database for different races, on the theory that perhaps "random matches" would occur at different rates among the races, creation of larger databases and subgroups has resulted in accepted probability statistics based on race. However, other issues about using separate databases have arisen. See the discussion of the Pizarro case to follow.

### 3. Possible Prejudice

Finally, Shea argued that if the jury heard the 1 in 200,000 testimony, the result would be unduly prejudicial to him because the jury would automatically conclude he was guilty. In other words, he argued that the jury would hear the statistics as a probability of innocence as opposed as the probability of a random match. The court also rejected this argument. Finally, Shea contended that the prosecution should be required to calculate a "false match error rate" for the DNA laboratory industry to present to the jury. The court heard evidence that the FBI laboratory does not calculate such an error rate and ruled as follows:

> I reject Shea's argument because it is built on several flawed premises. First, I cannot accept Shea's contention that a laboratory or industry error rate is the best evidence of whether a test was properly performed in a particular case. Juries must decide whether a particular test was performed correctly based on all of the relevant evidence. The determination can never be precisely quantified because it will often depend in part on the subjective factors such as the credibility of the person who performed the test. At best, evidence of a laboratory's past proficiency should be considered as one of several factors in making this important judgment ...[6]

# The *Chischilly* Case—
# Arguments about Population Subgroups

Chischilly was a Navajo convicted of rape and murder. He appealed the use of DNA tests, arguing that substructuring within the Native American and Navajo populations invalidated the use of the product rule to determine the statistical probability of a

---

6. *Id.* at 344.

match. In other words, the product rule assumes that all loci are random, and this had not been proven for the Navaho subpopulation.

> [The defendant] asserts rather persuasively and with considerable scientific backing that where an individual's DNA sample is tested against samples from a population in which persons of that individual's ethnic group are underrepresented, calculations based on the product rule may tend to understate the probability that a random match would occur between the evidentiary sample and that individual's ethnic group.

> [He] called numerous experts who testified that the more homogenous a population remains through intermarriage, the less random the relationship becomes between the coincidence of certain sequences of alleles at different test sites across the two samples ... In analyzing the DNA evidence in this case, the FBI used its I-3 database, composed of DNA from Native Americans. Nevertheless, [defendant's] objection remains because his distinct tribe (Navajo) may be underrepresented in the I-3 database.... [7]

The appellate court held that the trial court did not abuse its discretion by admitting the expert testimony.[8] It added that the prosecution was careful to frame the evidence properly and the defense was adequately equipped to contest its validity. Also, the prosecution made sure the testimony referred to the probability of a random match, not the probability of the defendant's guilt or innocence.

> With regard to DNA evidence, there are two general tendencies that should be guarded against: (1) that the jury will accept the DNA evidence as a statement of source probability (i.e., the likelihood that the defendant is the source of the evidentiary sample); and (2) that once the jury settles on a source probability, even if correctly, it will equate source with guilt, ignoring the possibility of non-criminal reasons for the evidentiary link between the defendant and the victim.[9]

In another early case, a defendant was convicted of kidnap and rape of a woman whom he abducted at a highway rest stop. DNA testing showed that the defendant's semen was found in the rape kit and the victim's blood and hair were found in his trailer. At that time—1990—the trial court, in ruling the DNA evidence admissible, stated that there "currently are no written federal court opinions addressing the admissibility of DNA profiling."[10] After he was convicted, the defendant appealed on the ground that the government should be required to prove that DNA testing was reliable by a standard of beyond a reasonable doubt.[11] The court rejected this argument: "Although we realize that DNA evidence does present special challenges, we do not think that they are so special as to require a new standard of admissibility."[12]

---

7. *United States v. Chischilly*, 30 F.3d 1144, 1155 (9th Cir. 1994).
8. *Id.*
9. *Id.* at 1156.
10. *United States v. Jakobetz*, 747 F. Supp. 250, 255 (D. Vt.1990), aff'd 955 F.2d 786 (2d Cir. 1992).
11. *United States v. Jakobetz*, 955 F.2d 786, 796 2d Cir. (1992).
12. *Id.*

## Later DNA Challenges to Population Profiles

In 2003, the California Court of Appeals[13] addressed whether the prosecution commits error by introducing the statistical likelihood of a random match using an ethnic database that includes the defendant but where the ethnicity of the actual perpetrator is unknown. In this case, Michael Pizarro was tried and convicted of the rape and murder of his half-sister in deep woods in the middle of the night following a drunken party. Pizarro had refused to come home and his wife and half-sister went back to where he was last seen on the roadway to look for him. His half-sister disappeared and his wife returned home. The next day, the sister's body was found. Pizarro had meanwhile turned up at home, admitted he had seen the victim and taken her flashlight, later tossing it to her when she complained. He said this was the last he saw her.

Semen found in the victim's vagina was matched to Pizarro's DNA, using RFLP testing. The prosecution presented expert testimony that the likelihood of a random match, that is someone else other than Pizarro being the source of the semen, was 1 in 250,000, which was the likelihood of a random match in the Hispanic population.

On appeal, Pizarro contended that there was no evidentiary foundation introduced to prove that the perpetrator was Hispanic. Therefore, using the Hispanic database was prejudicial, as it planted in the jury's mind the idea that the perpetrator was Hispanic. The defense won this argument, even though had the state used the DNA base for the population at large, the likelihood would have been 1 in 1.1 million. In other words, using the Hispanic database was actually favorable to the defendant, as the match data in the general population was far more rare, implicating Pizarro to a much higher certainty than the Hispanic database. The court reversed Pizarro's conviction on the ground that a proper evidentiary foundation had not been established to introduce DNA statistics.

This case was later overruled by the California Supreme Court.[14] The effect of overruling the court's conclusion in *Pizarro* has no effect on the earlier case. It simply means that the court rejected the legal rule used by the appeals court that said a prosecutor must have independent proof of the perpetrator's ethnicity before using DNA statistics. However, the *Pizarro* case is still important because it shows how a tenacious defendant can use highly technical arguments about DNA evidence in order to appeal and possibly reverse a conviction:

Here are some relevant parts of the court's analysis:

*People v. Pizarro*, 110 Cal. App. 4th 530 (2003)

\* \* \*

Reduced to its simplest, this is a case of insufficient evidentiary foundation. The admission of DNA evidence to prove Pizarro's identity as the perpetrator raises foundational issues under both *Kelly* and the Evidence Code. Under *Kelly* and section 405, the analysis is one of reliability and trustworthiness.

\* \* \*

Generally, as in this case, DNA evidence consists of two distinct elements: the match evidence—evidence that the defendant could be the perpetrator; and the statistical evidence—evidence that a certain number of people in the population could be the perpetrator. These differ in both purpose and effect.

---

13. *People v. Pizarro*, 110 Cal. App. 4th 530 (Cal. App. 5th Dist. 2003).
14. *People v. Wilson*, 38 Cal. 4th 1237, 136 P.3d 864 (2006).

The purpose of the match evidence is to establish that the defendant's genetic profile resembles or "matches" the perpetrator's genetic profile. The effect of the match evidence is to directly incriminate the defendant by establishing that he genetically matches the perpetrator and therefore could be the perpetrator.

Using a physical profile as an analogy, the match evidence might be that the defendant, like the perpetrator, has black hair, blue eyes, and a 5-foot 8-inch stature. Because the defendant shares the same physical profile and therefore resembles the perpetrator, the defendant could be the perpetrator. Thus, the match evidence deems the defendant a possible perpetrator, but does not establish his identity as the perpetrator.

Using a physical profile as an analogy requires the assumption that physical features, like genetic features, are essentially immutable, such that the perpetrator could not have changed the color of his hair and so on.

The statistical evidence gives the match evidence its weight. It is an expression of the rarity of the perpetrator's profile, the size of the pool of possible perpetrators, and the likelihood of a random match with the perpetrator's profile. Specifically, the purpose of the statistical evidence is to establish how few people in the relevant population genetically match the perpetrator.

The relevant population is the population of possible perpetrators—the perpetrators' population. Thus, the statistical evidence informs the jury of the frequency with which the perpetrator's genetic profile occurs in the perpetrators' population (i.e., the number of people in that population whose profiles are considered to be the same as the perpetrator's profile).

The effect of the statistical evidence is to indirectly incriminate the defendant by allowing the jury to infer that because the defendant is one of the few people who genetically match the perpetrator, he is likely to be the actual perpetrator. Unlike the match evidence, the statistical evidence itself does not consider or rely upon the defendant; it is a statement regarding the perpetrator (his profile and his population) and it is the same regardless of who the defendant is.

Continuing the physical profile analogy, the evidence might be that 1 in 10,000 Hispanics have black hair, blue eyes, and 5-foot 8-inch stature. From this statistical evidence, the jury may infer that because the defendant is one of the few Hispanics who possess these traits, he is likely to be the actual perpetrator.

* * *

These foundational preliminary facts regarding the perpetrator's traits must be established by independent proof. In other words, the description of the perpetrator—whether genetic or physical—must be based on evidence of the perpetrator's traits. A sketch artist creates an artistic representation of the perpetrator from an eyewitness's description of the perpetrator's physical features. Then the defendant is held up to that sketch to determine whether he possesses the perpetrator's traits. If the defendant happens to match the sketch of the perpetrator, the match provides evidence against him.

If the description of the perpetrator is instead based on evidence of the defendant's traits—which are simply assumed to be the same as the perpetrator's— the defendant no longer enjoys the presumption of innocence. It is as though the sketch artist sits with the defendant, sketches him as the perpetrator, and the prosecution introduces the sketch at trial as evidence that the defendant looks exactly like the perpetrator. The defendant's traits fill out the perpetrator's description with facts that are not in evidence, and the perpetrator's traits are "proved" by what is in effect a presumption that because the defendant possesses certain traits, the perpetrator also possesses those traits.

Such a presumption operates as a substitute for proper evidence of the perpetrator's traits, thereby lightening the prosecution's burden of affirmatively proving the defendant's identity as the perpetrator and undermining the defendant's presumption of innocence. The logic is this: the defendant is the perpetrator; the defendant possesses certain traits; therefore, the perpetrator also possesses those traits. The defendant's guilt is the premise rather than the ultimate conclusion sought by the prosecution.

\* \* \*

In this case, the FBI and the prosecution committed this fundamental violation by relying on defendant's traits, rather than on independent proof of the perpetrator's traits, to establish the preliminary facts necessary to render the DNA evidence relevant. Specifically, the FBI relied on proof of defendant's genetic profile to establish the preliminary fact of the perpetrator's genetic profile, and the prosecution relied on proof of defendant's ethnicity to establish the preliminary fact of the perpetrator's ethnicity.

This improper reliance on defendant was founded on and legitimized by the underlying assumption that defendant was in fact the perpetrator and thus could be substituted for the perpetrator for the purpose of demonstrating relevance and admissibility. In sum, reliance on defendant's traits added unproved traits to the perpetrator's profile and provided an illegitimate foundation for the admission of the DNA evidence.

In summary, we think prosecutors have three options in presenting profile frequencies:

(1) establish that the perpetrator more likely than not belongs to a particular ethnic population, then present only the frequency in that particular ethnic population;

(2) present only the most conservative frequency, without mention of ethnicity; or

(3) present the frequency in the general, nonethnic population.

These options promote the goals of admitting only relevant evidence and eliminating unjustifiable and potentially prejudicial references to ethnicity and race.

\* \* \*

The judgment is reversed.

The issue of whether the perpetrator is known to be Caucasian, Hispanic or African American prior to the DNA test was raised two years later in *People v. Prince.* The DNA expert had testified:

Based on an FBI database, that in the Caucasian population, the DNA from the mask was 1.9 trillion times more likely to match Princes' DNA rather than some unknown, unrelated person. In the Hispanic population, it was 2.6 trillion times more likely, and for the African-American population, it was about 9.1 trillion times more likely.[15]

The court held that "because three ethnic databases were used ... there was a greater chance that, by luck, the perpetrator's ethnic group was included ... Using three ethnic databases does not cure the core problem or render the statistics relevant ... nothing in Smith's testimony shows that the frequencies from the three populations extrapolate to the general population."[16]

However, the court held that there was sufficient non-DNA evidence to establish that the suspect was Caucasian, so the profile frequency statistics from the Caucasian database were relevant and properly admissible. This case affirmed the earlier holding in *People v. Pizarro*[17] that "DNA profile frequency evidence cannot be used to prove that a defendant committed a crime if the profile statistics are based on the assumption that the defendant and perpetrator belong to the same ethnic group."

## *People v. Wilson*

In a subsequent case, the California Supreme Court overruled the *Pizarro* case[18] to the extent that it required independent proof of the suspect's ethnicity before introducing statistical probability of a random match. It decided that the prosecution did not commit error by introducing the statistical likelihood of a genetic DNA match for the three most common population groups in the United States: Caucasian, African-American, and Hispanic. The court also disagreed that the jury should hear statistics for only one ethnic group:

> "We disapprove of *Pizarro* to the extent it concludes that evidence regarding any particular population group is inadmissible absent sufficient independent evidence that the perpetrator was a member of that group."
> *People v. Prince*

> Excluding probability evidence about any but the most likely group could deprive the jury of potentially crucial evidence. If, for example, the jury believed it 51 percent likely the perpetrator was Caucasian, providing it with the probability only for Caucasians would leave it uniformed regarding the 49 percent possibility the perpetrator was of some other population group.... We approve *Pizarro I* to the extent they condemn admitting evidence of the odds solely regarding the defendant's population group. But we disapprove *People v. Pizzaro* to the extent it concludes that evidence regarding any particular population group in inadmissible absent sufficient independent evidence that the perpetrator was a member of that group.[19]

---

15. *People v. Prince*, 134 Cal. App. 4th 786, 800 (Cal. App., 5th Dist. 2005); depublished 42 Cal. Rptr. 3d 1 (Cal. 2006) later proceedings, 2006 Cal. LEXIS 6182 (Cal. April 19, 2006).

16. *Id.*

17. *Pizarro*, 110 Cal. App. 4th 530.

18. *Wilson*, 38 Cal. 4th 1237.

19. *Id.* at 1250–1251.

## "Cold Hit" DNA

Cold Hit DNA. Where a suspect is identified based on his DNA profile in a database.

As the *Pizarro* case shows, defendants will continue to challenge the admission of DNA profiles using new strategies. In 1996, a fifteen-year-old girl was abducted at knifepoint while on a pay phone and raped. She escaped and although she was unable to identify her assailant from 576 photographs, she described the truck her assailant had been driving. Investigators were unable to find a suspect. In 2001, five years later, the sexual assault kit was submitted to the Department of Justice Regional laboratory CODIS [Combined DNA Index System] system, which contained more than 200,000 offender DNA profiles. The rape kit profile matched a suspect, Michael Johnson, then in prison for another crime. The victim was still unable to identify Johnson, but evidence that Johnson's truck matched the victim's description and that Johnson had tattoos matching her description was introduced in court, along with the DNA match. Johnson was convicted.

On appeal, Johnson argued that the database search presented different statistical issues than a "confirmation" match and therefore should have been excluded without a *Kelly* hearing. The court held that the CODIS search was used merely as an "investigative tool," and therefore was not subject to the *Frye* "general acceptance" standard, which was applicable in that court:

> In our view, the means by which a particular person comes to be suspected of a crime—the reason law enforcement's investigation focuses on him—is irrelevant to the issue to be decided at trial, i.e., that person's guilt or innocence, except insofar as it provides *independent* evidence of guilt or innocence. For example, assume police are investigating a robbery. The victim identifies "Joey" as the perpetrator. The means by which "Joey" becomes the focus of the investigation—the eyewitness identification—is relevant because that identification is itself evidence of guilt.

> Suppose instead that a surveillance camera captures the robbery on tape. Police use facial recognition software to check the robber's facial features against driver's license photographs. When the computer indicates a match with "Joey," officers obtain his name and address from DMV records, then go to his house and interview him. In the course of the interview, "Joey" confesses.

> Whether the facial recognition software is discerning and accurate enough to select *the* perpetrator, or whether it declared a match involving many different people who resembled "Joey," or how many driver's license photographs were searched by the software, is immaterial: what matters is the subsequent confirmatory investigation.[20]

The court also rejected Johnson's argument that the jury should hear the probability of finding his particular DNA profile in the CODIS database.

---

20. *People v. Johnson*, 139 Cal. App. 4th 1135, 1150 (Cal. App 2006).

## Mixed Samples

If the sample is contaminated, the report should show the DNA of different contributors. One recent court accepted a report on a mixed sample as follows:

> The judge's findings that Cellmark's methodology in reporting tests of a mixed sample with an identifiable primary contributor in the same way it reports tests of a single source sample conforms to the recommendation of the NRC [National Research Council], and that Cellmark's methodology in dealing with the presence of mixtures or technical artifacts is generally accepted within the scientific community, were made with record support and well within his discretion.[21]

However, the defense in *People v. Pizarro* convinced the court that the DNA evidence was inadmissible because the finding of a match at one of the loci was based on only one possible hypothesis, which was not explained to the jury. The prosecution did not explain to the jury the possibility that the "bands" at that locus could have excluded the defendant under certain hypothetical situations.

> The alleles at locus D2 showed only two bands—consistent with a single source. However, it was obvious from all the other alleles than there was DNA both from the perpetrator and the victim in the semen sample. Therefore, unless the perpetrator and the victim had identical DNA alleles at D2, one would have expected to see 3 or 4 bands at the D2 locus. The defense argued that there were other explanations that might point to the true perpetrator's DNA being hidden behind the two bands.
>
> ...
>
> The prosecution failed to carry its burden of demonstrating that the FBI used a proper scientific procedure to determine the perpetrator's D2 genotype. Reference to defendant's genotype to prove the perpetrator's genotype was improper, and use of band-intensity analysis to prove the perpetrator's genotype required *Kelly* first-prong scrutiny of that method. Thus, the FBI's method of discerning the perpetrator's D2 genotype constituted improper procedure under *Kelly's* third prong.[22]

# DNA Evidence in the *Grant* Case

The DNA evidence in the *Grant* case was restricted to a test of one small spot on a handkerchief found in the garage next to some keys that belonged to Serra's car. The police theory was that Grant drove Serra's car looking for his own; he finally found his car, and dropped both her keys and his handkerchief when he got back into his own car. The prosecution used a DNA expert to testify that one small red stain on the handkerchief was consistent with Grant and the chance of a random match was 1 in 300 million. The defense did not contest this finding.

---

21. *Commonwealth v. Gaynor*, 443 Mass. 245, 820 N.E.2d 233 (2004).
22. *Pizarro*, 110 Cal. App. 4th 530.

## DNA Report Summary - II

| Item | NH # | Lab # | D3S1358 | vWA | FGA | D8S1149 | D21S11 | D18S51 | D5S818 | D13S317 | **D7S820** | **D3S1358** | D16S539 | THO1 | TPOX | CSF1PO | **D7S820** | **Amel.** |
|---|---|---|---|---|---|---|---|---|---|---|---|---|---|---|---|---|---|---|
| | | | ------blue------ | | | ------green------ | | | ------yellow------ | | | ------blue------ | | ------green------ | | | ------yellow------ | (both) |
| E. GRANT BLOOD | - | 74-2 | 15,16 | 14,16 | 21,25 | 13,15 | 30,30.2 | 12,15 | 11,12 | 11,13 | 8,9 | 15,16 | 11,13 | 9,3 | 8 | 10,12 | 8,9 | X,Y |
| Handkerchief cutting 10/01/01 | 6 | 6-1G4 | 15,16 | 14,16 | 21,25 | 13,15 | 30,30.2 | 12,15 | 11,12 | 11,13 | NR | 15,16 | 11,13 | 9,3 | 8 | NR | NR | X,Y |
| Philip DELIETO blood | - | 2004 | 16,18 | 16,19 | 24 | 8,12 | 29,34.2 | 12,18 | 12,13 | 11,13 | 8,10 | | Cofiler | Test | Not | Done | | X,Y |
| Selman TOPCIU blood | - | 1000 | 15,17 | 16,17 | 20,23 | 14,15 | 30,32.2 | 12,17 | 11,12 | 12 | 9,11 | 15,17 | 9,12 | 6,9 | 8,9 | 10,11 | 9,11 | X,Y |
| Penny SERRA (blood fr/ bra) | 3 | 3 | 17,18 | 14,18 | 23,25 | 13 | 29 | 14 | 11,12 | 11,14 | 8 | 17,18 | 8,9 | 7,8 | 11 | 10,12 | 8 | X |

Header spans: ------Profiler Plus Loci------ | ------COfiler Loci------

NOTE: Results are combined from Profiler Plus and COfiler data. **Amelogenin** & two loci, **D3S1358** and **D7S820** are included in each kit. Results at those loci are in columns with **bold** headings.

NR = No DNA detected above the threshold for calling the alleles, due to degraded nature of the sample.

*Grant's DNA report, trial exhibit 254*

## Electropherograms : Edward Grant Blood : Lab # 74-2
### Profile Plus Loci (scale: 0-300 rfu)

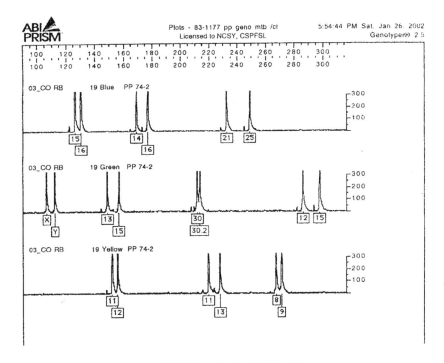

### CofilerLoci (scale : 0-600 rfu)

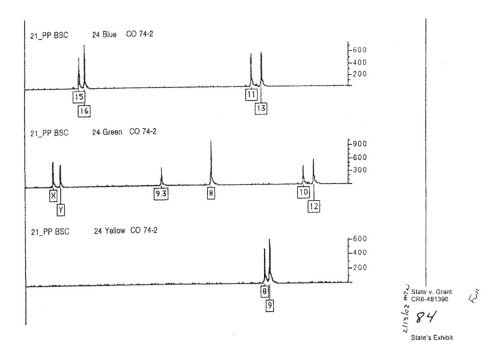

*Grant's electropherogram, trial exhibit 84*

> "Something is not right about the handkerchief ..." *Grant's counsel.*

Rather, the defense concentrated on the condition of the handkerchief, its uncertain chain of custody, and the unlikely fact that only one drop of blood had not degraded beyond the point of being able to test. After the crime, the handkerchief went to local and state police labs, to a lab at Yale, to Pond Lily in New Haven, and through the mail to DuPont Corporation in Delaware. Then Detective Beausejour drove it to an army lab in Natick, Massachusetts. It then came to rest in a big box in a converted men's room with no temperature control. The state expert testified that age, heat, humidity, bacteria and moisture all may affect a sample in degradation.[23]

Each lab cut a chunk of the handkerchief to test, so that by the time Grant was arrested, it resembled Swiss cheese. Although the defense said "something was not right about the handkerchief," in the closing arguments, echoing Henry Lee's testimony about the bloody glove in the *Simpson* case, this argument required the jury to believe that someone deliberately tampered with the blood evidence on the handkerchief. There was no testimony that anyone with access had such a motive.

The state used two common DNA tests kits: Cofiler and Profiler Plus. These tests measure the length of the alleles at 13 different locations, or loci, on the DNA strand. The expert who testified for the state about the DNA testing was Dr. Carl Ladd. A second expert on population statistics testified about the significance of the profile, Dr. Kenneth Kidd, a professor of genetics and psychiatry at Yale University. Grant's attorneys did not present their own expert, but relied on cross examination of the state's witnesses.

Ladd gave a statistic for the likelihood of a random match fitting Grant's DNA profile as found on the handkerchief to be 1 in 300 million, which is roughly the population of the United States. Dr. Kidd testified that the actual probability based on the FBI data base for Caucasians was one in 4 trillion, 20 billion. Using a similar database from Florida, the likelihood would be 1 in 6 trillion 910 billion. He added that the likelihood if he used the Hispanic population would be slightly more common.[24] Kidd testified: "I consider it virtually certain that the DNA sample came from the same individual as the blood sample identified as Grant."[25]

When asked to explain in lay terms what a number such as 6 trillion means, Kidd replied: "It basically means if you took the genes at the frequency they exist in the population ... today, and randomly recombined them to generate a whole new set of people, you would have to generate approximately four trillion people before you found one that matched this profile."[26]

Dr. Kidd used statistics for the Caucasian population (which Grant is), although he acknowledged that the likelihood would be more common if he used the Hispanic population (which at least the parking lot attendant said the perpetrator was).

The prosecution asked Kidd what would happen if he dropped two of the alleles from the Grant test, and Kidd replied that the likelihood of a random match would be 1 in 11 billion rather than 1 in 4 trillion. This is a sizeable difference, but 11 billion is still considerably larger than the population of the earth.

---

23. Transcript, May 13, 2002 at 22.
24. Transcript, May 17, 2002 at 119.
25. *Id.* at 120.
26. *Id.* at 121.

Kidd also stated that he was unaware if the source of the DNA on the handkerchief were blood or other genetic material, such as mucus. "By the time it's analyzed, it's pure DNA, and there is nothing in that aspect of the analysis that says what the source of that DNA was."[27]

## Porter DNA Hearing in *Grant* Case

Although DNA had already been judicially noticed as valid science in Connecticut, the defense asked for a *Porter* hearing, contending that PCR/STR testing was not yet reliable. The Court wrote a detailed opinion in which it held that PRC/STR met the *Porter* tests and was admissible.

Here are parts of the court's opinion in the evidentiary hearing

*State v. Grant,* CR6-481390, Ct. Supr. Ct., April 9, 2002

\* \* \*

> "Given these specific findings, the court concludes that the STR technique used by the Laboratory is valid. It is admissible under Code of Evidence §7-2 and the *Daubert/Porter* test. The court cannot find that its probative value is outweighed by undue prejudice." *State v. Grant*

The Laboratory's general method of DNA typing is Polymerase Chain Reaction (PCR). Dr. Ladd referred to the PCR method as "molecule Xeroxing." PCR takes a small amount of DNA and copies it in a process known as amplification. Hypothetically, the method allows a scientist to take a single DNA molecule and create 10 million exact copies. Dr. Ladd's testimony is consistent with the description of the PCR process set forth in *State v. Pappas,* 256 Conn. 854, 869, 776 A.2d 1091 (2001).

The STR technique is, in Dr. Ladd's words, "[t]he latest generation of PCR tests." STR, as mentioned, is an acronym for Short Tandem Repeat. There are certain regions, or loci, of the DNA where multiple copies of identical DNA sequence are arranged in direct succession. In those loci the four nucleotides are repeated one after another, in tandem. The repeats in these loci distinguish one person from another.

The initial task of the forensic scientist seeking to identify the contributor or source of biological material—such as a bloodstain found at a murder site—is to extract the DNA from the sample in question. The PCR amplification process is then used to generate enough material to detect the DNA profile of that sample.

Most genes exist in multiple forms called alleles. When the STR technique is employed, the alleles are separated through a process known as electrophoresis—involving the application of an electric current to a gel containing the DNA in question—so that the individual components of the DNA can be determined. For these purposes, the Laboratory uses two commercial kits, named (by their manufacturer) Profiler Plus and Cofiler. Profiler Plus, the most widely used STR kit in the United States, amplifies nine STRs plus gender. Cofiler amplifies six STR's. There is some overlap because two STRs are amplified by both kits. Use of both

27. *Id.* at 125.

kits amplifies a total of thirteen STRs plus gender. In addition, the overlap serves as a quality control.

> "What happens when a match is achieved? National guidelines permit the positive identification of the matching suspect as the source or contributor of the evidentiary sample." *State v. Grant*

The STRs in the evidentiary sample—here the bloodstains found at the murder scene—are compared with the STRs of the suspect. (In this case, a sample of Grant's blood was seized pursuant to a search warrant.) Many suspects are definitively excluded by this process. Nationally, this happens in about one-quarter to one-third of the cases in which this analysis is used.

In some cases, the evidentiary sample is so degraded or contaminated that no reliable result can be obtained. In still other cases, there is a genetic match. Degradation or contamination of the evidentiary material may preclude the detection of a result, but these factors will not result in a false match. No amount of degradation or contamination will change one person's DNA profile into another's.

What happens when a match is achieved? National guidelines permit the positive identification of the matching suspect as the source or contributor of the evidentiary sample. The laboratory is more conservative and merely calculates the probability of a coincidental match in the general population. Another way of looking at this is that the laboratory calculates the expected frequency of two individuals having the same genetic profile as the evidentiary sample.

* * *

Although the STR technique is of relatively recent vintage and has not been considered in any discovered Connecticut decision, it has already found broad acceptance in our nation's courts. Beginning with *Commonwealth v. Rosier*, numerous appellate courts have held STR evidence to be legally admissible. Three state courts of highest jurisdiction have held that the STR technique satisfies the *Daubert* test of scientific validity used in those states. A fourth state court of highest jurisdiction has held that the STR technique satisfies the 'general acceptance' test famously promulgated in *Frye v. United States* used in that state.

* * *

> "There is overwhelming evidence that the STR technique has gained general acceptance. This conclusion should end the court's inquiry, and the conclusions derived from that methodology should be held admissible." *State v. Grant*

There is overwhelming evidence that the STR technique has gained general acceptance. This conclusion should end the court's inquiry, and the conclusions derived from that methodology should be held admissible.

In the event that a reviewing court should disagree with this conclusion, the remaining factors identified by *Pappas* will briefly be considered. The court makes the following additional findings.

1.  The STR technique has been repeatedly tested, both by the Laboratory and by other scientific Researchers and has just as repeatedly been found reliable.

2.  The technique has repeatedly been subjected to peer review and publication.

3. The known or potential rate of error is low to nonexistent when the technique is properly employed.

4. Strict, well-defined standards govern the technique's operation.

5. The prestige and background of Ladd, the expert witness supporting the evidence, is impressive.

6. The technique in question relies on objectively verifiable criteria rather than subjective interpretations and judgments by the testifying expert. Professional experience and judgment are used in the analysis, but this is frequently the case with respect to scientific evidence. (As the State points out, the acceptance of X-ray technology is well established, but experts can nevertheless disagree about the meaning of a particular X-ray image.) STR analysis itself is based on objectively verifiable criteria.

7. Ladd, the testifying expert, can present the data and methodology underlying his scientific testimony in such a manner that the fact finder can reasonably and realistically draw its own conclusions therefrom.

8. The technique was originally developed for research purposes rather than for in-court use. It is now used for a multitude of purposes, including sexual offender data bases and the identification of human remains (as in the aftermath of the World Trade Center attack), in addition to in-court testimony.

Given these specific findings, the court concludes that the STR technique used by the Laboratory is valid. It is admissible under Code of Evidence §7-2 and the *Daubert/Porter* test. The court cannot find that its probative value is outweighed by undue prejudice.[28]

As you can see from the opinion, the court held that STR testing of DNA is good science and an expert may testify.

# What Objections Are Left to Refute DNA Profiles?

Today, few defendants argue that DNA testing is, of itself, objectionable. Therefore, defense objections must be restricted to the specifics of each case. The defense can always attack in the following ways:

1. hire an expert to review the prosecution's DNA report to find any possible areas for objection,

2. challenge the training and experience of the DNA investigator,

3. challenge the laboratory conditions or present evidence of fraud in the lab,

4. challenge the chain of custody of the genetic evidence,

5. argue that the test cannot show when the DNA was deposited,

6. remind the jury of the prosecutor's fallacy—a DNA match does not equal guilt,

---

28. *State v. Grant*, Memorandum of Decision re Motions to Preclude Evidence re: Relevancy and Lack of Sufficient Chain of Custody (No. 57) and Defendant's Motion to Preclude All Evidence Relating to STR/DNA Testing Conducted at the Connecticut State Forensic Laboratory (No. 74), No. CR6-481390, April 9, 2002.

7.  argue that the DNA may have been either innocently transferred to the crime scene or may have been "planted" at the site by someone with a motive to frame the defendant.

## Review the Prosecution's DNA Report for Case-Specific Anomalies

> Blobs, noise and stutter on a DNA chart can mask the true alleles.

Typically, the defendant in a case involving DNA will not hire a DNA expert to review the DNA reports created by law enforcement and offered by the prosecution. Although the public defender did contact an independent DNA expert in the *Grant* case, that expert did not testify at trial. One expert estimates that the software needed to even open the files provided by crime laboratories in discovery costs over $18,000.[29] Forensic Bioinformatic Services argues that defendants should focus on "case-specific issues and problems that greatly affect the quality and relevance of DNA test results, rendering DNA evidence far less probative than it might initially appear."[30] They discuss issues such as mixtures, which led the court in *Pizarro* to throw out the DNA test results. They also explain how to identify degraded samples, how to interpret imbalances in which the peak height of one allele at a locus varies by more than 30% of the height of another, and how to identify "blobs, noise, and stutter," all of which appear to be alleles, but actually may mask a true allele. This company markets a software system which enables defendants to analyze a DNA profile without hiring an expert.

## Planting

In the *Grant* case, defense counsel did not argue that the DNA on the handkerchief sample was not Ed Grant's. However, Attorney Brian Carlow in summation said "something is not right with the handkerchief."[31] His objections were chiefly that the crime scene photos did not clearly show the handkerchief, that the small spot tested was the only spot on the handkerchief that had not degenerated past the point of testing, and that the chain of custody of the handkerchief did not account for long periods when it was in a basement exposed to heat.

Even if the DNA did come from Grant, Attorney Carlow pointed out that no one could testify as to when the DNA got on the handkerchief. He was raising a doubt that perhaps the police, in an effort to solve a high-profile cold case, may have had a motive to plant a drop of blood on the old handkerchief after the fingerprint on the tissue box led to the arrest of Ed Grant.

In order to win a planting argument, the defense must show some motive for planting, as well as some evidence to substantiate this claim. As seen below, both were introduced in the *Simpson* trial.

---

29. Forensic Bioinformatic Services, www.bioforensics.com/Frames/intro.html, last visited February 28, 2007.
30. *Id.*
31. Transcript, May 22, 2002.

# The Planting Argument in the *Simpson* Case

Although many Americans believed that the jury in the *Simpson* case ignored DNA evidence that clearly pointed to Simpson's guilt, the defense raised legitimate questions about many items of forensic evidence.

> "The defense challenge to the DNA evidence was not an effort to confuse or obfuscate. It was well-grounded in science and was supported by considerable evidence."[32]

In some cases, they argued, the evidence was planted. In some cases, blood at the site that was supposedly Simpson's was actually mixed with Nicole's, or had chemical preservatives consistent with having come from a stored sample. The prosecution tried Simpson for the murder of his wife and a waiter in the walkway in front of her home. Simpson denied the charge and said that he was in Chicago the night of the murders. He explained a cut on his hand as having occurred when he learned by telephone in Chicago of Nicole's murder and dropped and broke a glass. Blood evidence was collected from the murder site and from inside Simpson's Ford Bronco. Evidence seized in Simpson's home included a bloody glove and a sock with a blood spot on it. Here is a summary of the forensic evidence in the case, as reported by William Thompson:

> The Bundy Crime Scene—Although most of the blood at the crime scene matched victims Nicole Brown Simpson ("NBS") and Ronald Goldman ("RG"), DNA profiles consistent with O.J. Simpson ("OJS") were found in five blood drops on the Bundy walkway and in three blood stains from the rear gate.

> The Rockingham Glove—The right-hand glove found at Simpson's residence was saturated in blood. Although the great majority of the blood matched the victims, three tiny samples taken from near the wrist notch produced profiles consistent with a mixture of DNA from OJS and one or both victims. However, the portion of the DNA mixture that could be consistent with Simpson's DNA (but not the victims') consisted of a single genetic marker (allele) that is quite common.

> The Sock—In Simpson's bedroom, police collected a pair of dark, finely woven socks. One of these socks was later found to have a large bloodstain at the ankle that contained a DNA profile consistent with NBS. Three additional samples from the same sock (two from the leg area, one from the toe) contained minute amounts of material containing DNA consistent with OJS.

> The Bronco—Blood samples were collected from Simpson's Bronco on two occasions: shortly after the crime on June 14, and over two months later on August 26, 1994. Most of the samples were consistent only with OJS. But three small smears of blood collected from the console in August contained profiles consistent with a mixture of DNA from OJS, NBS, and RG.

> According to prosecution experts, a sample collected from the console in June also showed a mixture of DNA from OJS and RG, although a defense expert testified that this result was inconclusive because a control had failed during the assay. A sample collected from the steering wheel in June had a profile consistent with a mixture of DNA from OJS and a second, unknown person. DNA

32. William C. Thompson, *"Proving the Case: The Science of DNA: DNA Evidence in the O.J. Simpson Trial,"* 67 U. Colo. L. Rev. 827 (1996).

of NBS might (or might not) have been included in this mixture as well. Finally, a sample from the carpet contained a profile consistent with NBS.

Rockingham Blood Drops—Blood drops on Simpson's driveway, and in the foyer of his house, contained DNA consistent with his profile.[33]

The prosecution's theory of the case was that Simpson murdered Nicole and Goldman on June 12, 1994 with a knife that was never found and was himself cut in the attacks. He left blood drops at the crime site, in his car, and on his driveway as he returned to his house, disposed of his bloody clothes and knife, but neglected to discard a bloody glove and one sock with blood on it. He then flew to Chicago.

According to Thompson's article,[34] blood was drawn from Simpson the day after the crime and was not logged in immediately, but driven to Simpson's home and handed to a criminalist three hours later. Some blood was shown to be missing from one of the vials taken from Simpson. The sock was inventoried and examined three times with no mention of any bloodstain. Dr. Lee testified that the bloodstain had been placed on the sock and pressed into the wool while it was lying flat. Simpson's blood drops on the back gate at Nicole's were not collected until July 3, 1994. A photograph taken on June 13 showed no blood on the gate. The samples contained undegraded DNA, which would be unusual given the heat and sunlight exposure. In his article, Thompson, one of Simpson's lawyers, states that in his opinion, the jury did not ignore the DNA evidence, but accepted the defense theories that explained it or neutralized it:

> A major reason for O.J. Simpson's acquittal was that the defense successfully neutralized the "overwhelming" DNA evidence against him by offering plausible alternative explanations for all of it. The defense challenge to the DNA evidence was not an effort to confuse or obfuscate. It was well-grounded in science and was supported by considerable evidence. The failure of the prosecution to rebut several key elements of the defense attack inevitably left the jurors with reasonable doubts about the DNA evidence.[35]

The Simpson defense had hard evidence to support its planting argument: inconsistent photographs, a racist detective, blood samples that contained preservatives that should not have, undegraded blood when it should have been degraded, missing blood from collected vials, and poor laboratory and chain of custody procedures.

In contrast, the defense in the *Grant* trial had only one of these arguments: a genetic sample that should have been degraded but wasn't. Unfortunately, it had no plausible explanation other than an unknown party who might have wanted to solidify the fingerprint evidence against Grant. With no person to point to, the defense was unsuccessful.

## Objections Based on Poor Laboratory Procedures

Today most testing is done by a few large laboratories, including Cellmark labs.[36] Some labs under the control of law enforcement agencies have been criticized for shoddy methods, lack of training, and in some cases, the outright fraudulent reporting of results in order to obtain convictions. In August of 2005, for example, the Illinois State Police can-

---

33. *Id.* at 828–830.
34. *Id.*
35. *Id.* at 856–857.
36. This was the case in *State v. Grant.*

celed its contract for DNA analysis with the Bode Technology Group after finding that it failed to recognize semen on rape kit evidence in 22% of the cases that had been re-checked by police scientists.[37] The state police director notified the Justice Department and other states, at least 10 of which also had contracts with the same forensic laboratory. The canceled contract had called for payment of $7.7 million over three years.

The Houston DNA laboratory was shut down in 2003 based on findings of sloppy work, although a grand jury failed to indict anyone after reviewing 1,000 felony cases that relied on questioned DNA evidence.[38]

A federal investigation of the Massachusetts state police crime laboratory in 2007 found that the lab entered incomplete genetic profiles into its computerized databases, entered the same genetic profile under two different identification numbers, and in one case, waited nearly eight months to confirm a tentative match. The state had begun its own investigation after discovering that a technician failed to report matches to police departments in 11 sexual assault cases, making it impossible for prosecutors to pursue charges.[39]

Defendants also may object to admission of DNA where the procedures in the lab were inadequate. This objection was made in 1996 in a bank robbery case where hairs of the defendant found in a ski mask were tested using the PCR method of DNA replication. The defendant appealed his conviction arguing that the lab procedures were inadequate, that there was no external testing, the DNA samples were not "double blind" tested, and there was no record of errors made. The court decided that the PCR method was reliable and that the lab was accredited to do PCR testing and did double-reading tests of its results. Any objections about the quality of the lab went to the weight of the evidence, not its admissibility. Defendant was free to try to discredit the lab on cross examination, but could not exclude the testimony.

# DNA Identification Mistakes

As with fingerprints, there is rarely a claim of a DNA error. However, in October of 2000, Andre Moenssens, the same professor who has written about handwriting and fingerprint analysis, identified an error in the United Kingdom in April of 1999 in which a suspect was arrested for a burglary based on a match at 6 loci.[40] According to Moenssens, the suspect was a man with advanced Parkinson's disease, who could not drive and could barely dress himself. He lived 200 miles from the site of the burglary. His blood sample had been taken when he was arrested, and then released, after hitting his daughter in a family dispute.

> It is only when the suspect's solicitor demanded a retest using additional markers, after the suspect had been in jail for months, that further testing was done. This testing, using a total of 10 loci, showed an exclusion at the additional four loci.

---

37. Gretchen Ruethling, *Illinois State Police Cancels Forensic Lab's Contract, Citing Errors*, The New York Times, August 20, 2005.

38. *Grand Jury Blasts Houston Police DNA Lab*, October 17, 2003, cnn.com.

39. *Federal Probe Finds problems with state crime lab*, Associated Press, The Boston Herald, February 1, 2007.

40. Andre A. Moenssens, *A Mistaken DNA Identification? What Does it Mean?* http://forensic-evidence.com/site/EVID/EL_DNAerror.html, updated October 2000.

The interpretation of the original test's results, given by law enforcement officials, was proven to be inaccurate. The suspect was then released from custody.[41]

The British adopted a ten loci DNA test shortly thereafter.

# *Daubert* Hearings on Mitochondrial DNA

> Mitochondrial DNA.
> A DNA profile extracted from the mitochondria in the cytoplasm outside the cell nucleus. The resulting profile will reveal alleles inherited only from the mother.

The newest DNA technology is mitochondrial DNA, which is found within circular structures surrounding the cellular nucleus that provide a cell with energy. DNA is found only in the nucleus of a cell; mitochondria are found in the surrounding mitochondrion. Mitochondrial DNA can be extracted from much smaller samples of genetic material, including degraded material. A hair root, for example, is required for DNA analysis, but mtDNA can be obtained from a hair shaft. It can likewise be extracted from skeletal remains. The mitochondria does not contain a full set of chromosomes; only the 23 chromosomes contributed by the mother are present. For this reason, mtDNA can exclude a defendant, but cannot be used to identify a defendant.

During his testimony about the blood spatter in the *Grant* case, Dr. Lee explained the difference between nuclear DNA testing and mitochondrial DNA. He stated that neither test had been available in 1973 to test the nasal hairs found on the handkerchief:

Lee: You have to destroy the hair to do mitochondrial DNA. You don't have to destroy the hair to do nuclear DNA.

Q: Am I correct that if you have a very small hair you may not have enough to do?

A: Any DNA.

Q: That's correct. Okay. If you do nuclear and you get no result, then you would be precluded from doing mitochondrial because you might not have enough?

A: Nuclear, we look at tissue because in body cell we have nucleus, those nucleus basically from, one DNA from father, one from mother, when the sperm fertilize the egg, now you have two piece of DNA, so our whole body, the tissue all have the same DNA, especially in cytoplasm, the cell, the energy house, cytoplasm have something called mitochondrial DNA which only maternity link from mother, not from father because when sperm fertilize the egg, the tail stay outside, the father mitochondrial DNA is in the tail and it fall off and that's why we can't trace the father. So, with mitochondrial DNA we could only say from the mother, and all the brothers and siblings all have the same mitochondrial DNA; but nuclear DNA, everybody is different except for identical twins.[42]

Mitochondrial DNA has been admitted in court, although it has been challenged as true science, just as in the early days of DNA.

---

41. *Id.*
42. Transcript, May 9, 2002 at 60–61.

In *State v. Pappas*,[43] the Connecticut Supreme Court held that mtDNA was admissible and that questions concerning contamination and matching criteria could be raised before the jury as to the weight of the evidence. The police found two head hairs on a sweatshirt left near the scene of a robbery and compared the mtDNA to hairs from the defendant's head. The tests showed that the defendant could not be excluded as the source of the hairs.

In 2003, a defendant who had been convicted of rape[44] filed a motion for a new trial based on mtDNA testing of some hairs that had been offered in evidence against him at the trial.[45] The victim testified that she had been drinking at an East Hartford bar on November 8, 1996 and was accosted by the defendant, Mark Reid, as she was walking home in the early morning hours. She stated that he pulled her into a nearby park, raped her, threatened to kill her and eventually let her go. The jury heard the victim's eyewitness identification from a photo array and testimony by a state expert about three hairs found on the victim's clothes after she was admitted to the hospital. One was on her jeans, another on a sock, and another on her panty. The expert testified that the hairs were recovered by combing or scraping down the clothing surface. The victim declined to be examined and therefore no rape kit was available.

The expert testified at trial that the three hairs were Negroid pubic hairs and were microscopically similar to those of the defendant. Reid was convicted.

In his motion for a new trial based on newly-discovered evidence, Reid argued that mtDNA tests performed by Dr. Terry Melton showed that he was excluded as the source of the hairs. She stated that mtDNA "can eliminate an individual as a contributor of samples. Its primary difference from nuclear DNA testing is that mtDNA is not a unique identifier; unlike nuclear DNA which is found at the center of the human cell, and which is inherited from both parents, only maternal lineage exhibits the same mitochondrial profile."[46] Although the state argued that the pubic hairs were likely those of the victim, and therefore did not exonerate Reid, the expert admitted that neither gender nor the race of a possible contributor could be determined by mtDNA testing. However, the mtDNA did match a buccal swab taken from the victim.

In order to win the motion for a new trial, Reid had to prove that the mtDNA results were newly discovered evidence that was not available at the time of trial and that it was likely to produce a different result in a new trial. The court reviewed the trial transcript and concluded that the eyewitness identification appeared credible and not unduly influenced by the fact that the victim had been told the police had a suspect or by the fact that Reid's photo was added by the police to the photo array because one officer said the description stated by the victim "sounds like Mark Reid."

However, the only forensic evidence at trial was the three hairs:

> That evidence, stressed by the State, was, if accepted by the jury, immensely supportive of the victim's identification, and cannot be dismissed now as being unnecessary simply because it is impossible to quantify what weight the jury might have placed on it.

> Simply put, at the criminal trial, the identification by the victim was presented to the jury along with strong circumstantial evidence provided by the [state's] expert testimony which, if accepted, furnished powerful support for the vic-

43. *State v.* Pappas, 256 Conn. 854, 776 A.2d 1091 (2001).
44. *State v. Reid,* 254 Conn. 540, 757 A.2d 482 (2000).
45. *State v. Reid*, CV020818851, 2003 Conn. Super. LEXIS 1496 (May 14, 2003).
46. *Id.* at *38.

tim's identification; guilty verdicts resulted. At a retrial, the victim's identification would not have the support of such circumstantial evidence in view of the new mtDNA evidence excluding petitioner as the source of the pubic hairs.... Although the former jury had to have accepted the victim's identification in order to convict, it did so in a proceeding where it was presented with expert testimony circumstantially supporting that identification.[47]

Reid's motion for a new trial was granted, and the case was subsequently dismissed.

## The *Scott Peterson* Case

Mitochondrial DNA was also used in the California conviction of Scott Peterson for the murder of his wife, Laci. A strand of dark hair found on Scott Peterson's boat probably came from his dead wife, in the opinion of a DNA expert who testified at the trial. The hair was significant because Laci had apparently never been on the boat and was unaware that her husband even had bought it. Constance Fisher, the DNA expert stated:

> Mitrochondrial DNA cannot be used to point to an individual to the exclusion of all others, as nuclear DNA can be.... It is less discriminating.[48]

Mitochondrial DNA was tested because the hair did not have a root, which would have permitted standard DNA testing. The expert stated that about one out of 112 Caucasian people would have the same mitochondrial makeup. Clearly, the test would not exclude Laci. It was consistent with her DNA. The jury was free to infer that it was probative of whether Laci was on the boat, and whether she was killed on the boat.

Peterson was convicted, entirely on circumstantial evidence, including testimony by his girlfriend that he had told her he was not married.[49]

# Summary

The principle of DNA testing is that each person has a unique DNA profile. Scientists have proved this in the process of mapping the human genome. Currently, most DNA testing is done by examining the length of "alleles" at different locations or "loci" on specified chromosomes. These 13 loci have alleles that differ in length from person to person, but do not control for any known genetic trait. Thus, scientists assume that the length of an allele at each loci is independent from the length at any of the other 12.

The advent of the Polymerase Chain Reaction (PCR) method of copying small amounts of DNA in order to yield a sample large enough for testing has vastly increased the ability of investigators to link crime scenes with suspects. DNA from a single hair root, for example, can yield a valuable DNA profile. Mitochrondrial DNA, the latest form

---

47. *Id.* at *80.
48. *Peterson Testimony Focuses on Hair*, Associated Press, September 9, 2004.
49. Catherine Crier Exclusives, *The Lacy Peterson Case,* http://www.courttv.com/trials/peterson/crierexclusives.html.

of DNA matching, can extract DNA from the mitochrondria in a cell, which yields the DNA markers passed through the mother's line. Although it is less discriminating, MtDNA can be used in cases where DNA can no longer be extracted due to degradation or size of sample.

The force of DNA testimony results from application of the "product rule," which permits analysts to measure the statistical likelihood of having a particular length allele at one locus, by the likelihood at the next locus, and so forth. In the *Grant* case, Dr. Carll Ladd, of the Connecticut Forensic Laboratory, testified that the likelihood of a "random match," someone other than Grant being the source of the sample, was 1 in 300 million. The figure of 1 in 300 million is used by the Forensic Laboratory whenever the denominator of the number exceeds 300 million, which is roughly the population of the United States. Using the FBI database for Caucasians, Dr. Kenneth Kidd testified that the actual probability was 1 in 4 trillion, 20 billion.

Early challenges to the admissibility of DNA evidence in court included issues such as subsets of the database and application of probability statistics. Many courts have judicially noticed the reliability of DNA testing. In the *Grant* case, the defense asked for a *Porter* hearing, arguing that the STR method of DNA testing was not yet reliable. The court held a hearing and denied the motion to exclude the test results.

Objections to the laboratory conditions where DNA has been tested generally do not affect admissibility, unless the defense can show that results from the laboratory have been fraudulently altered. A contaminated or degraded DNA sample will not mis-identify a defendant, although it may result in an inconclusive profile, or a lack of identifiable alleles at certain loci.

Defendants can still challenge DNA results based on the specifics of their case, and software is now available that can help the defense analyze the DNA profile created by the prosecution. Such challenges include the training and experience of the DNA investigator, the chain of custody of the genetic evidence, and the possibility of innocent or purposeful transfer of the defendant's genetic material to the specimen to be tested.

# Discussion Questions

1. How do probability statistics affect DNA expert testimony?

2. What is the CODIS? How does it affect how state law enforcement conducts DNA tests?

3. What are some differences between the history of use of fingerprint matching and DNA matching?

4. In the *Simpson* trial, the jury heard testimony from experts that blood drops at the scene of Nicole's death matched Simpson's DNA. They also heard testimony that blood on a sock found in Simpson's bedroom matched the DNA of Nicole. The jury acquitted *Simpson*. What must the jury have concluded about the DNA evidence?

5. Explain the process of PCR. Why was it a major step forward in DNA testing?

6. What is mitochondrial DNA? Why is a mtDNA match not as good as a DNA match?

7. Do most courts decide that deficiencies in lab conditions mean that DNA evidence should not be admitted? Why or why not?

8. What percentage of DNA is common among all humans? How many potential junk DNA loci could be tested? How can 13 sites create a reliable match?

9. What is the Prosecutor's Fallacy and why do defendants worry about it?

10. If there is no eyewitness evidence identifying the race of the defendant, can the prosecution introduce DNA statistics based solely on the defendant's ethnicity? Explain.

11. What possible objections can a defendant make to DNA evidence?

12. What was the objection to the DNA tests that Grant asserted in the gatekeeper hearing? What is the objection he asserted in his appeal of his conviction? How do they differ?

# Chapter 9

# Eyewitness Identifications

## Overview

Testimony by experts who present scientific studies to cast doubt on eyewitness identifications is a relatively recent phenomenon. Eyewitness recollection is affected by factors that anyone would suspect—such as distance from the suspect, the amount of time they looked at the suspect, and the amount of time between the crime and attempting to make an identification. Studies show that the reliability of identifications is also affected by level of stress, witness expectations, and conduct by the administrator of lineup procedures. Witnesses may also respond to perceived danger to themselves, such as in the situation where a weapon is pointed at them.

Many experts have called for changes in eyewitness identification procedures to increase the reliability of identifications. One court threatened a stern jury instruction about eyewitness identification errors unless law enforcement adopted procedures that made it clear to witnesses that the suspect might or might not be in the lineup. As this issue becomes better known, lineup and photo array identifications doubtless will improve.

The trend of the cases is to exclude expert misidentification testimony that is simply general in nature and not supported by specific scientific studies. Due to the possible prejudice, courts are also likely to ban such experts where there is other evidence identifying the defendant. Where, however, the expert testifies to a matter of high relevance, such as prejudicial lineup procedures, we are likely to see more and more courts admit this testimony. Eyewitness expert testimony is a good example of scientific research that is not yet generally accepted but that meets the *Daubert* standards of testing, peer review, and error rate.

In the *Grant* case, there were a number of eyewitnesses who testified to seeing a man running after a woman in the garage, driving a car really fast in the garage, and checking out of the garage at the attendant booth. No one actually saw the murder. Composite sketches were made shortly after the crime, and one eyewitness identified Phil DeLieto in a lineup. DeLieto was later eliminated as a suspect due to his blood type and alibi. There were many reasons to question the reliability of the eyewitnesses, but no expert testimony was presented.

# Chapter Objectives

Based on this chapter, students will be able to:

1. Explain the scientific challenges to the reliability of eyewitness identifications.

2. Understand how lineup procedures can affect the reliability of eyewitness identifications.

3. Identify proposed reforms to combat eyewitness unreliability.

4. Distinguish the different ways courts have ruled on admitting expert testimony that challenges the reliability of eyewitness identification.

5. Understand the relationship between false identifications and DNA exonerations.

6. Appreciate legal issues with admitting composite sketches at trial.

When a witness identifies a suspect as the person who committed a crime, his testimony is direct evidence — the gold standard in criminal trials. The direct evidence of a personal identification is viewed by most people as far more powerful than a wealth of circumstantial evidence, facts which a jury must knit together by inference to conclude that a defendant is guilty.

> This is likely due to the fact, as the Supreme Court has observed, that 'despite its inherent unreliability, much eyewitness identification evidence has a powerful impact on juries.... All evidence points rather strikingly to the conclusion that there is almost nothing more convincing than a live human being who takes the stand, points a finger at the defendant, and says, 'That's the one!' Yet, studies have repeatedly shown a roughly forty percent rate of mistaken identifications. In spite of this, nearly 80,000 suspects are targeted every year based on an eyewitness identification.[1]

Psychologists have shown through repeated experiments that eyewitness identifications are fragile and fallible. Their accuracy depends, not just on the lighting conditions or whether the witness normally wears eye glasses, but on the ability of the brain to perceive, store and retrieve information. Some of the factors that affect memory — such as the length of time the witness viewed the suspect or the time between the viewing and a later identification — are obvious to a juror. These issues have been held to be within the common knowledge of jurors by courts that exclude expert testimony on eyewitness identification problems. Other courts have noted the disagreement about experts on such issues as whether witnesses are subject to suggestions at lineups or photo arrays that change their memory of a perpetrator and have therefore concluded that such testimony is not generally accepted.

But the growing body of knowledge about how an eyewitness's memory of a face can be manipulated by later information or unconscious expectations or prejudices has demonstrated the need for testimony to educate and caution jurors. As one court said: "Today, there is no question that many aspects of perception and memory are not within the common experience of most jurors, and in fact, many factors that affect memory are counter-intuitive."[2] Others have used their "bully pulpit" to threaten stern

---

1. Henry F. Fradella, *Why Judges Should Admit Expert Testimony on the Unreliability of Eyewitness Testimony*, 2006 Fed. Courts. L. Rev. 3, 5 (June 2006).
2. *United States v. Smithers*, 212 F.3d 306, 316 (6th Cir. 2000).

jury instructions cautioning jurors about the fallibility of eyewitness identifications un-less local law enforcement adopts better lineup and identification procedures.[3]

Here is but one example of the psychological process of "misremembering." A photograph of two men stand-ing and conversing in a subway car was shown to a wide variety of subjects. One person in the photo was a black man. The other was white. The white man was holding a razor. Over half of the subjects reported that the black man had been holding the razor. "Effectively, expecta-tions and stereotypes cause people to see and remember what they want or expect to see or to remember."[4]

> "Today, there is no ques-tion that many aspects of perception and memory are not within the com-mon experience of most jurors, and in fact, many factors that affect mem-ory are counter-intuitive."

The recent phenomenon of exonerations of prisoners based on newly-tested DNA evidence reveals that a majority were convicted based on er-roneous eyewitness testimony. The Innocence Project, which successfully freed over 197[5] defendants by early 2007, reported that approximately 75% to 85% of the convictions of innocent people were cases of mistaken eyewitness identification.[6]

# Why Is Eyewitness Testimony Unreliable?

Here are some of the psychological phenomena that affect eyewitness identifications.

- Expectations. A person's expectations influence the way he encodes details about an event in his mind. This was the factor at work in the experiment above with the white man holding the razor.

- Exposure to post-event misinformation can lead an eyewitness to encode the in-formation into the original memory. Jennifer Thompson's eyewitness identifica-tion of Ronald Cotton as her rapist led to his conviction. Cotton had been ap-prehended based on an anonymous tip that he resembled the artist's sketch based on the victim's description. Cotton was subsequently exonerated based on DNA, and the real rapist, Bobby Poole, was apprehended. Even though Jennifer Thompson now knows that it was Poole, and not Cotton, who raped her, she still "sees" the face of Ronald Cotton as her rapist.[7]

- Stress. Contrary to popular belief, the stress of being exposed to a violent crime does not heighten perception and memory. "When people are concerned about personal safety, they tend to focus their attention on the details that most di-rectly affect their safety, such as weapons and aggressive acts, and not on the personal characteristics of the suspect."[8] This has been called the "weapon focus" factor.

---

3. *State v. Ledbetter*, 275 Conn. 534, 881 A.2d 290 (2005).
4. Fradella, *supra* at 15, citing Elizabeth F. Loftus, *Eyewitness Testimony* 22 (1979).
5. Comments of Barry Scheck, The Innocence Project, March 19, 2007, University of Hartford.
6. www.InnocenceProject.org.
7. WGBH Educational Foundation, *What Jennifer Saw*, available at www.pbs.org/wgbh/pages/frontline/shows/dna.
8. Fradella, *supra* at 13.

> Some factors that affect reliability of an eyewitness identification are witness expectations, exposure to post-identification confirmation, stress, and confidence level.

- Confidence Level. The reported confidence level of an eyewitness in his identification does not correlate with the rate of accuracy of his identification. Put another way, the confidence of an eyewitness that he has made a correct identification is not a good predictor of its accuracy, yet this is one factor likely to strongly impress a jury.

## The Effect of Lineup and Photo Array Procedures

The procedure used to identify a suspect may mislead an eyewitness into choosing someone, rather than no one. Information conveyed verbally or unconsciously by authorities during an identification can also influence whether the eyewitness makes an identification and how confident the eyewitness feels about that identification. Gary Wells, a psychologist who has conducted experiments in eyewitness identification, described a test of eyewitness identification error in 1993.[9] He summarized his findings as follows:

1. Victims under high stress are more likely to make mistakes in identification.

2. When a victim is not cautioned that the perpetrator might NOT be in the lineup, the victim tends to pick the person who looks the most like the perpetrator rather than concluding that the perpetrator is not present (the relative-judgment process).

3. In archival police lineups, eyewitnesses to actual crimes identified a known-innocent "filler" 24% of the time from live lineups.

4. Words, attitude, and even the presence of police at a line-up can influence the outcome.

> The "relative-judgment process." Witnesses will choose a person who best fits their memory of the perpetrator, rather than choosing no one.

An experiment was conducted in which a "staged crime" was shown to 200 witnesses.[10] The "perpetrator" was in the first lineup but not in the second one. Over 50% of the witnesses chose the correct perpetrator in the first lineup and 25% of them chose the person who looked the most like the actual perpetrator. In the second lineup, in which the correct candidate was not present, 38% of the witnesses chose the next closest person. This shows that witnesses will choose a person who best fits their memory of the perpetrator, rather than choosing no one.

Using "sequential lineups," in which the witness is not able to compare one suspect against another, improves accuracy because the witness is not as tempted to choose the "best" candidate simply to make an identification.

Wells analyzed 30 studies including over 4,000 participants. He concluded that sequential lineups reduce false identifications, but also reduce accurate ones.[11]

---

9. Gary L. Wells, *Cover Story: Eyewitness Identification Evidence: Science and Reform*, 29 Champion 12 (April 2005).

10. *Id.*

11. *Id.*

Another psychologist recommends that after viewing each person in a sequential lineup, the witness should be asked how certain he is of his identification. "Obtaining a statement of confidence level before other information can prevent contamination of a witness's judgment, thereby increasing the reliability of an identification. Since confidence level at the time of initial identification is a powerful force in determining both the admissibility of an out-of-court identification and the weight accorded to it by the trier of fact, it should be self-evident why an uncontaminated statement of high confidence should be obtained at the time of an initial identification.[12]

## What Happens If the Administrator Knows Who the Suspect Is?

An administrator who knows which candidate is the suspect may consciously or unconsciously convey that knowledge to the eyewitness. Such feedback can affect whether the eyewitness picks any candidate and the perceived confidence level in the accuracy of his choice. Experiments have shown that the behavior of the administrator of the lineup influenced the outcome. In one experiment,[13] 352 people who made wrong identifications were put into two groups. One group received feedback that confirmed their choice; ("Good, you identified the actual suspect"); the other received no feedback. Later, both groups were asked how certain they felt about their identification, and how good a view they got of the gunman's face. The group that were "confirmed" by the administrator were 35% more certain of their identifications than the other group. The first group also were more likely to say they got a clear view of the perpetrator's face.

This led Wells to conclude that the administrator of the lineup should not know which person in the lineup is the suspect (a "double-blind" administrator). The witness will stop looking for "cues" from the administrator.

> An administrator who knows which candidate is the suspect may consciously or unconsciously convey that knowledge to the eyewitness.

## Proposed Lineup Reforms

Wells proposed the following reforms:

1. Strict controls over lineups.

2. Double blind lineups.

3. Sequential lineups.

4. Securing certainty statements from witnesses at the time of the identification.

5. Requiring detailed recording of the witness's statements or response to the lineup.

6. Some sort of probable cause before putting a suspect into a lineup.

7. Training police about eyewitness problems.

---

12. Fradella, *supra* at 20–21.
13. Wells, *supra*.

8. Improving how "fillers" are selected.

9. Warning instructions to juries.

10. Education for judges.[14]

## One Court "Encourages" Lineup Reforms

Courts recognize that law enforcement has no strong incentive to spend the money for more complex identification procedures and the training to improve lineups. The Connecticut Supreme Court understood this in an appeal based on a prejudicial identification. It delivered both a set of guidelines for fair lineups and a threat if they were not followed. In *State v. Ledbetter*,[15] the police stopped a car based on a description from a knifing victim in an incident that occurred 20 minutes earlier. The police then lined up the defendant and his companions from the car on the sidewalk and asked the victim if he could identify his assailant. The victim identified Ledbetter, who was subsequently convicted.

On appeal, Ledbetter argued that the trial court improperly admitted the identification. The Connecticut Supreme Court held that the identification process was not unnecessarily suggestive and comported with federal and Connecticut constitutional protections. However, the court ruled that in the future, in any eyewitness identification in which an administrator failed to instruct the witness that the perpetrator might or might not be present, the defendant would be entitled to the following jury instruction:

> In this case, the state has presented evidence that an eyewitness identified the defendant in connection with the crime charged. The identification was the result of an identification procedure in which the individual conducting the procedure either indicated to the witness that a suspect was present in the procedure or failed to warn the witness that the perpetrator may or may not be in the procedure.
>
> Psychological studies have shown that indicating to a witness that a suspect is present in an identification procedure or failing to warn the witness that the perpetrator may or may not be in the procedure increases the likelihood that the witness will select one of the individuals in the procedure, even when the perpetrator is not present. Thus, such behavior on this part of the procedure administrator tends to increase the probability of a misidentification.

> "Studies have shown that indicating to a witness that a suspect is present or failing to warn the witness that the perpetrator may or may not be in the procedure increases the likelihood that the witness will select one of the [*cont.*]

> This information is not intended to direct you to give more or less weight to the eyewitness identification evidence offered by the state. It is your duty to determine whether that evidence is to be believed. You may, however, take into account the results of the psychological studies, as just explained to you, in making that determination.[16]

This case affected police lineups in Connecticut immediately. The Connecticut state police were given a

---

14. *Id.*
15. *Ledbetter*, 881 A.2d 290.
16. *Id.* at 579–80.

individuals, even when the perpetrator is not present." *Proposed Connecticut Jury Instruction.*

written set of procedures including a standard statement to be read to witnesses prior to viewing photographic arrays of suspects. The following witness instructions must be given to each witness, who must sign and write any comments about the identification at the bottom:

1.  I will ask you to view a set of photographs.

2.  It is as important to clear innocent people as to identify the guilty.

3.  Persons in the photos may not look exactly as they did on the date of the incident, because features like facial or head hair can change.

4.  The person you saw *may or may not* be in these photographs.

5.  The police will continue to investigate this incident, whether you identify someone or not.[17]

The Officer Instructions for Eyewitness Identification[18] require that officers read the witness instructions out loud and have the witness initial each line. The officer must avoid "words, gestures, or expressions which could influence the witness's selection. If practical, especially during a photo array, take a position where the witness cannot see you.... If the witness makes an ID, refrain from making any comment on the witness's selection."[19] The procedures require the officer to date and time the identification procedures, name all those present and the subjects and sources of all photos used. The array must be preserved.

The process of assembling a photographic array requires that at least six to eight photos be used and displayed in an array folder. Photographs should be all color or all black and white, similar in type or style, and any "mug shot" detail shall be masked from view. Each photograph should resemble the suspect, and witnesses must view the array separately.

The Connecticut State Police rarely use lineup identifications,[20] but procedures revised as of January 2006 prescribe how to conduct lineups as well as photo arrays. A suspect in custody may not refuse to appear in a lineup, but has the right to counsel, if charged with a crime. The administrator must use at least four other persons in the lineup.[21]

# Court Challenges to Eyewitness Identification

The courts have been divided on admitting experts who challenge the validity of eyewitness identifications. The trend in courts that use *Daubert* is toward admitting expert testimony. However, courts that use the general acceptance test often do not admit it. The courts that exclude such testimony have given a variety of reasons:

---

17. Connecticut State Police, Witness Instructions for Photo Identification, DPS-213-C (New 05/05).

18. Connecticut State Police, Officer Instructions for Eyewitness Identification, DPS-212-C (Rev. 10/05).

19. *Id.*

20. Interview with Trooper Peter Valentin, Connecticut State Police, January 2007.

21. Connecticut State Police, Regulation 19.3.1 *Suspect Identifications*, Revised January 2006.

- The issue of eyewitness fallibility is within the common knowledge of jurors so no expert testimony is needed.
- The expert is not properly qualified.
- The testimony is general in nature and not supported by specific scientific research.
- Proper cross-examination can reveal any errors in the eyewitness identification.
- Scientific research demonstrating memory issues is not generally accepted.

## Common Knowledge

Expert testimony is not permitted if the issue is one where an expert's opinion would not aid the jury because the jury can understand and appreciate its significance, using common knowledge. A number of courts have rejected eyewitness experts on this ground, as the defense can cross-examine the eyewitness to explore reliability.

In 1999, the Connecticut Supreme Court held in *State v. McClendon*[22] that the trial court did not err when it refused to admit testimony by expert Michael Leippe, who questioned eyewitness identification and memory retention. It decided that Lieppe's testimony was about common knowledge and would not help the jurors resolve the case.

> Leippe testified in general terms about memory retention and the various circumstances that can deter memory and recall. He testified, among other things, that the confidence of any eyewitness does not correlate to the accuracy of observation, that variables such as lighting, stress and time to observe have an impact on accuracy, that leading questions and the repetition of testimony can increase an eyewitness's confidence but not accuracy, that people remember faces best when they analyze many features and characteristics of the face rather than just one, that misleading police questions can alter memories, and that the most accurate descriptions are given immediately after a crime.[23]

A Connecticut court[24] affirmed a conviction in which the defendant's eyewitness expert was excluded. The expert had been prepared to testify on:

- The effect of stress on memory.
- The weak correlation between accuracy of eyewitness testimony and confidence level.
- The unreliability of aural identifications.
- The phenomenon of unconscious transference.

The dissent in that case addressed the common knowledge objection this way:

> Although most people believe that they possess a strong intuitive grasp of the workings of memory, numerous studies demonstrate that 'commonsense' notions may not accurately reflect the true state of affairs ...[25]

---

22. *State v. McClendon*, 248 Conn. 572, 730 A.2d 1107 (1999).
23. *Eyewitness Identification Testimony Properly Excluded, Conn. Supreme Court Rules*, 3–5 Mealey's Daubert Rep. 11 (1999).
24. *McClendon*, 730 A.2d 1107.
25. *Id.* at 1122.

A Texas appeals court also rejected the common knowledge objection: "while jurors might have their own notions about the reliability of eyewitness identification, that does not mean they would not be aided by the studies and findings of trained psychologists on the issue."[26]

## Testimony Would Not Be "Useful" for Jury

The Eight Circuit Court of Appeals ruled that eyewitness expert testimony was not needed where the photographic spreads were not impermissibly suggestive and where the expert intended to testify only to the general reliability of eyewitness identifications. "In fact, the district court specifically instructed the jury to weigh the strength of [the witnesses'] eyewitness identifications by considering various reliability-related factors, including the length of time the witness observed the person, the prevailing conditions such as distance and visibility, and the strength of later identifications."[27]

Where an eyewitness had been cross-examined about his ability to perceive, remember and identify the suspect and the jury instructions had cautioned the jury about the reliability of eyewitness identifications, it was not reversible error to exclude a defense memory expert.[28] Another court refused to reverse a conviction for bank robbery based on the refusal to provide the defendant with the services of a psychologist to testify about the unreliability of eyewitness identifications. The standard for providing an expert to an indigent defendant was "whether a reasonable attorney would have engaged an eyewitness expert in this type of case. The answer is probably not."[29] In addition the court found no prejudice to the defendant in his ability to cross examine the eyewitness.

## Testimony Is Not Supported by Scientific Research

A federal district court in Virginia admitted expert testimony on some issues involving eyewitness identification and rejected others. In *United States v. Lester*,[30] the defendant was charged with robbery of a convenience market involving a handgun. The cashier and a customer both saw the perpetrator. The customer described him as a black skinned male, 6'1" tall wearing shorts and a blue short-sleeved shirt. The cashier disagreed, and said he was a skinny black male, 5'6" tall, wearing black pants and a black T-shirt. Investigators suspected Cornelius Lester and put his photo in a photo array with five other men who resembled him. The customer identified him with 100% confidence; the cashier also identified him with 90% confidence.

The defense sought to suppress the identifications and moved to introduce the testimony of Dr. Brian Cutler, an eyewitness expert. In the *Daubert* hearing, Cutler identified six factors that might affect the validity of the identifications:

1. Cross-race recognition.
2. Time the witness is exposed to the perpetrator.

---

26. *Nations v. Texas*, 944 S.W.2d 795, 798 (Tex. App, 3rd Dist 1997).
27. *United States v. Martin*, 391 F.3d 949 (8th Cir. 2004).
28. *United States v. Carter*, 410 F.3d 942 (7th Cir. 2005).
29. *United States v. Sims*, 617 F.2d 1371, 1375 (9th Cir. 1980).
30. 254 F. Supp. 2d 602 (E.D. Va. 2003).

3. "Weapon focus," the tendency to look at the weapon and not the perpetrator.

4. The effect of stress on the witness at the time of the crime.

5. Retention interval.

6. The relation between the witness's confidence level and accuracy of identification.

The court said it must evaluate three factors to decide whether to admit the expert:

- How significant is the eyewitness identification to the state's case?

- Are the factors the expert will testify about both relevant to the case and beyond the common knowledge of the average juror?

- Does the prejudice of admitting the expert testimony outweigh the probative value?

Because the case against the defendant was based almost exclusively on eyewitness identification and because the two witnesses gave inconsistent descriptions, the expert testimony had probative value. As to factor 1—cross-racial identification—the court denied the testimony because Dr. Cutler's opinion was conclusory and not backed up with concrete evidence. As standard juror instructions instruct the jury that it should evaluate the amount of time the witness had to observe the perpetrator, the court ruled that the expert's testimony on factor 2—time to observe—was within common knowledge.

The last four factors were beyond the knowledge of the average juror, and the expert backed them up with studies and statistics. Therefore the court allowed them. This case shows that courts require that the expert opinion be both beyond common knowledge and also based on specific research.

In case of *United States v. Smithers,* the defendant was convicted of bank robbery based almost entirely on the eyewitness identification in court of three witnesses. Two of those witnesses had been unable to identify the defendant from a photo spread. The defendant's offer of eyewitness expert testimony had been denied by the trial court. The appeals court relied on an earlier case to provide the correct test for admitting eyewitness testimony and reversed the defendant's conviction for robbery because the expert had been excluded:

**United States v. Smithers, 212 F.3d 306 (6th Cir. 2000)**

\* \* \*

On appeal, this Court applied the four prong test for expert testimony articulated in *United States v. Green:* (1) that the witness, a qualified expert, (2) was testifying to a proper subject, (3) which conformed to a generally accepted explanatory theory, and (4) the probative value of the testimony outweighed its prejudicial effect.

Applying that standard, the Court noted that the offered testimony would have been based on "a hypothetical factual situation identical" to the facts of the case and would have explained: (1) that a witness who does not identify the defendant in a first line-up may "unconsciously transfer" his visualization of the defendant to a second line-up and thereby incorrectly identify the defendant the second time; (2) that studies demonstrate the inherent unreliability of cross-racial identifications; and (3) that an encounter during a stressful situation decreases the eyewitness's ability to perceive and remember and decreases the probability of an accurate identification.

\* \* \*

Courts' treatment of expert testimony regarding eyewitness identification has experienced a dramatic transformation in the past twenty years and is still in a state of flux. Beginning in the early 1970's, defense attorneys began to bring expert testimony into the courtroom. Then, courts were uniformly skeptical about admitting such testimony, elaborating a host of reasons why eyewitness experts should not be allowed to testify. In the first case to address the issue, *United States v. Amaral*, the Ninth Circuit held that the district court did not err in excluding expert testimony regarding eyewitness identification because cross-examination was sufficient to reveal any weaknesses in the identifications.

After that decision, a series of cases rejected similar evidence for a variety of reasons.... This trend shifted with a series of decisions in the 1980's, with the emerging view that expert testimony may be offered, in certain circumstances, on the subject of the psychological factors which influence the memory process.

State court decisions also reflect this trend. Indeed, several courts have held that it is an abuse of discretion to exclude such expert testimony. This jurisprudential trend is not surprising in light of modern scientific studies which show that, while juries rely heavily on eyewitness testimony, it can be untrustworthy under certain circumstances. [footnote]

> [footnote] A plethora of recent studies show that the accuracy of an eyewitness identification depends on how the event is observed, retained and recalled. Memory and perception may be affected by factors such as:
>
> > (1) the retention interval, which concerns the rate at which a person's memory declines over time; (2) the assimilation factor, which concerns a witness's incorporation of information gained subsequent to an event into his or her memory of that event; and (3) the confidence-accuracy relationship, which concerns the correlation between a witness's confidence in his or her memory and the accuracy of that memory. Other relevant factors include: (4) stress; (5) the violence of the situation; (6) the selectivity of perception; (7) expectancy; (8) the effect of repeated viewings; (9) and the cross-racial aspects of identification, that is where the eyewitness and the actor in the situation are of different racial groups.
>
> * * *
>
> Social science data suggests, however, that jurors are unaware of several scientific principles affecting eyewitness identifications.
>
> * * *
>
> This ignorance can lead to devastating results. One study has estimated that half of all wrongful convictions result from false identifications. And "it has been estimated that more than 4,250 Americans per year are wrongfully convicted due to sincere, yet woefully inaccurate eyewitness identifications." A principal cause of such convictions is "the fact that, in general, juries are unduly receptive to identification evidence and are not sufficiently aware of its dangers."
>
> Many jurists agree that eyewitness identifications are the most devastating and persuasive evidence in criminal trials.... Ju-

rors tend to overestimate the accuracy of eyewitness identifications because they often do not know the factors they
should consider when analyzing this testimony.

## Eyewitness Expert Testimony Lacks General Acceptance under *Frye*

A New York trial court, in *State v. Legrand*,[31] excluded a psychologist's opinion
about the correlation between a witness's confidence in his identification and the accuracy of the identification, the impact of post-crime information on his level of confidence, and the weapon focus accuracy. The court held a pretrial hearing and concluded that the expert testimony did not satisfy the *Frey* test of general acceptance,
which is still used in New York. The state's expert had introduced a contradictory
study showing a strong relationship between confidence of identification and its accuracy. Even the defense expert admitted that there is no consensus among psychologists
as to the weapon focus effect on identifications. As in the *Grant* case, the defendant in
*LeGrand* was not identified and arrested until years after the crime had been committed—in this case, seven years.

### *State v. Legrand*, 747 N.Y.S.2d 733 (2002)

Seeking the admission of expert testimony concerning eyewitness identification, the defendant has requested a pretrial ruling allowing such evidence at his
retrial, following the declaration of a mistrial, on a charge of Murder in the
Second Degree. Specifically, what is sought to be introduced is the testimony of
a psychologist, Professor Roy S. Malpass, Department of Psychology, University of Texas at El Paso, with regard to:

(1) the confidence-accuracy correlation;

(2) post-event information and confidence malleability; and

(3) weapon focus.

For the reasons set forth below, this application is denied.

\* \* \*

At the outset, in order to avoid any misapprehensions, I believe it is necessary to recognize that these subjects or concepts are commonly defined as
follows:

(1) Confidence-accuracy correlation refers to "the relation between
the accuracy of an eyewitness's identification and the confidence that
[the] eyewitness expresses in the identification"

(2) Postevent information refers to the proposition that "eyewitness
testimony about an event often reflects not only what [the eyewitness]
actually saw but information they obtained later on" ...

(3) Confidence malleability refers to the proposition that "an eyewitness's confidence can be influenced by factors that are unrelated to
identification accuracy"; and

31. *State v. LeGrand*, 196 Misc.2d 179, 747 N.Y.S.2d 733 (2002).

(4) Weapon focus refers to "the visual attention that eyewitnesses give to a perpetrator's weapon during the course of a crime."

## FACTUAL AND PROCEDURAL BACKGROUND

At approximately 7:00 AM on June 15, 1991, a taxicab driver, Joaquin Liarano, was stabbed to death. Witnesses had heard the cab crash into a parked automobile, observed the victim and his assailant fighting both inside and outside the cab, saw the victim repeatedly being stabbed, and watched as the assailant then took property from the cab and fled the area. Almost immediately, they called 911; police officers responded to the scene, and the victim was taken to a hospital, where later that morning he died.

That same day one of the witnesses was taken to the 26th precinct and shown photographs; however, he did not make an identification. The next day, that witness, and another witness, were shown additional photographs, but neither witness made an identification. Five days later, on June 20th at the Police Artist Unit, four witness—Pazmino, Foote, Gonzalez and Gomez—were present and a composite sketch was prepared. This sketch was incorporated into a wanted poster and circulated; however, for the next seven years no suspects were identified.

On April 5, 1998, the defendant was arrested in connection with burglary charges within the confines of the 26th Precinct, leading to a detective reopening the 1991 homicide investigation.... Thereafter, on May 9, 1998, Pazmino viewed a photo array, containing the defendant's photograph, and identified the defendant as the person who had committed the 1991 homicide. Then, on August 17, 1998, the detective traveled to Florida, where he displayed the photo array to Foote and Gonzalez. Each selected the defendant's photograph—to Foote it was a "close match"; to Gonzalez, it was similar.

A lineup was held on February 3, 1999, where the defendant was identified by Pazmino, which led to the defendant's indictment in April 1999. Just prior to the April 2001 trial, there was a defense motion seeking permission to call an eyewitness expert. The trial justice reserved decision until after Pazmino's testimony, and then after argument denied the application.

At that trial, Pazmino identified the defendant, as did Foote, noting that he was a "striking match." Gonzalez pointed out the defendant, stating that "it looks like he gained more weight." Other witnesses, including Gomez, did not identify the defendant. Because of the jury's inability to reach a unanimous verdict, a mistrial was declared, and the case was ultimately sent to me for retrial.

\* \* \*

In addressing the general acceptability of the proffered expert testimony, it is not necessary that I determine whether the eyewitness identification discipline, in its entirety, is generally accepted. Rather, the issue that I must decide is whether the proposed testimony of the defense's witness, Dr. Malpass, which specifically addresses the confidence-accuracy correlation, postevent information and confidence malleability, and weapon focus, is generally accepted as reliable within relevant psychological community

\* \* \*

[The court determined that the testimony was both relevant and beyond common knowledge.]Thus, having affirmatively dealt with three parts of the Frye test, I will now turn to the last outstanding issue under Frye, which is whether the proffered expert testimony has gained general acceptance within the relevant psychological community.

## I. CONFIDENCE-ACCURACY CORRELATION

First turning to the proffered expert testimony on confidence-accuracy, Dr. Malpass testified that twenty-five years of research has led psychologists to conclude that "there is a statistically significant, but very small correlation" between the confidence eyewitnesses express in the accuracy of their identifications, and the actual accuracy of those identifications.

> "86.7% of the respondents found the proposition that 'an eyewitness's confidence is not a good predictor of his or her identification accuracy' to be reliable." *State v. Legrand*

Dr. Malpass further testified that, according to a survey conducted by Saul M. Kassin, V. Anne Tubb, Harmon M. Hosch and Amina Memon, entitled "On the 'General Acceptance' of Eyewitness Testimony Research: A New Survey of the Experts," American Psychologist (2001), this relationship between confidence and accuracy is generally accepted within the relevant psychological community. This is based on the finding that 86.7% of the respondents found the proposition that "an eyewitness's confidence is not a good predictor of his or her identification accuracy" to be reliable.

… Moreover, Professor Leippe testified, "that 'we don't always know what factors are influencing' an eyewitness," and that "a controversy existed in the area of the statistical probability of false identification, the one kind of information inaccessible to the average juror." Thus, it is evident that there is no consensus on the confidence-accuracy correlation.

… For the foregoing reasons, I conclude that the confidence-accuracy correlation has not yet achieved general acceptability within the relevant scientific community.

## II. POSTEVENT INFORMATION AND CONFIDENCE MALLEABILITY

Turning now to the proffered expert testimony on postevent information and confidence malleability: The defense seeks to introduce evidence "regarding studies investigating the impact of various types of suggestion, such as that involved in lineup and photo array procedures and post-identification feedback suggesting the identification was correct, on the witness's recollection of a perpetrator's appearance."

The defense further seeks to introduce evidence "that witnesses exposed to this type of post-event information tend to incorporate it into their memory of the actual event, that witnesses' confidence levels in an identification are higher when they chose a person pointed to by suggestion in an identification procedure, and that witnesses' confidence levels are enhanced by their receipt of post-event information which suggests to them that their initial identification was correct."

\* \* \*

The defense relies on the Kassin survey, according to which, 93.7% of the respondents found the proposition on postevent information, that "eyewitness testimony about an event often reflects not only what they actually saw but information they obtained later on", to be reliable. Moreover, according to the

survey, 95.2% of the respondents found the proposition on confidence malleability, that "an eyewitness's confidence can be influenced by factors that are
unrelated to identification accuracy", to be reliable.

\* \* \*

More significantly, this apparent general consensus, as to the reliability of these
propositions on postevent information and confidence malleability, is undermined by the survey's failure to adequately represent the relevant community
of researchers in the eyewitness identification discipline, and the low response
rate, of only 34.4.%, from the people, to whom the questionnaire was sent.
And, of course, as noted earlier, the survey failed to give an adequate description of who the respondents were, and their particular position in the forensic
eyewitness identification debate.

For the foregoing reasons, I conclude that this proposed testimony on postevent
information and confidence malleability, which includes the "Mock Witness
Paradigm" experiment, has not been generally accepted.

### III. WEAPON FOCUS

Finally, turning to weapon focus: Dr. Malpass testified concerning the effect of
"weapon focus" on the accuracy of eyewitness identifications. Relying solely on
Steblay's meta-analysis, he testified that it was generally accepted within the
relevant psychological community that "witnesses to a crime in which the perpetrator is displaying a weapon tend to focus their attention on the weapon,
and therefore are less accurate in identifying the perpetrator, relative to witnesses in equivalent situations where no weapon is displayed".

\* \* \*

However, the allegedly general acceptability of this conclusion, which was
drawn from Steblay's meta-analysis, does not adequately represent the majority of studies on weapon focus. According to the study, only six of the
nineteen tests, which made up the meta-analysis, found a weapon focus effect, even though the mean effect size for the group of tests indicated otherwise.

\* \* \*

For the foregoing reasons, I conclude that this proposed testimony on weapon focus is not generally
acceptable.

### LABORATORY vs. REALITY

One of the fundamental underpinnings of the disagreement concerns the question of whether it is

> Weapon focus effect is
> not generally accepted.
> Only six of the 19 tests
> found a weapon focus
> effect. *State v. Legrand*

generally acceptable for experts to extrapolate their research findings from laboratory studies to the testimonies of actual eyewitnesses in real life criminal events.

\* \* \*

Dr. Ebbesen has written that "not much is known about how these factors
[stress, unconscious transference, confidence, retention interval, exposure du-
ration, lineup fairness, racial similarity, and weapon focus] do interact" to affect eyewitness identification, which has, in turn, led to the question, "if not
much is known, one wonders how defense experts can draw the sweeping conclusions that they do?"

Even Dr. Malpass testified that the research on the psychological state of witnesses (e.g., stress) is "messy", and therefore, he is unable to determine its application to a given situation. Thus, not only do the stress or arousal levels in the experimental studies dramatically differ from the real world, but there is apparently a lack of understanding of how that difference in stress or arousal levels will affect a witness's accuracy.

\* \* \*

> Dr. Malpass testified that the research on the psychological state of witnesses (e.g., stress) is "messy." *State v. Legrand*

To allow this testimony to be received at trial would require jurors to determine whether the expert evidence is generally accepted as reliable, which is the role of the court, not the jury. And absent general acceptability, as Chief Justice Kaye once noted, "it is not for a court to take pioneering risks on promising new scientific techniques, because premature admission both prejudices litigants and short-circuits debate necessary to determination of the accuracy of a technique."

CONCLUSION

Accordingly, for the foregoing reasons, the defense motion to admit the proffered expert testimony on eyewitness identification is, in all respects, denied.

## Is There an Alternative to Expert Testimony on Eyewitness Reliability?

Wells, whose studies were reported earlier, does not favor using experts to explain the unreliability of eyewitness identifications. He acknowledges that an expert can explain what happens to eyewitnesses statistically, but the expert cannot state that those eyewitness phenomena happened in a particular case. Wells cautions there are only about 50 eyewitness identification scientists who could be potential experts, but well over 77,000 eyewitness identification cases per year. "The cost of expert testimony, and the arbitrariness with which cases will receive this benefit, make this solution ineffective given the magnitude of the problem."[32]

Wells argues instead for improvement in lineup procedures to minimize the rate of false identifications.

# Eyewitness Errors in Exoneration Cases

As we will see in the chapter on Exonerations based on newly-tested DNA evidence, many of these defendants were convicted primarily based on mistaken eyewitness identification. The Innocence Project maintains a website[33] on which it reports the details of the exonerated. Herman Atkins served more than eleven years of a forty-five year sen-

---

32. Wells, *supra* at 10.
33. http://www.innocenceproject.org.

tence for rape based on an eyewitness identification. The victim was raped at gunpoint in the shoe store where she worked. She identified Atkins after she saw a poster of him in the police station based on unrelated charges. After seeing the poster, she picked Atkins out of a lineup. But she was wrong.[34]

Jennifer Thompson, who wrongly identified Ronald Cotton as the man who raped her when she was a college student, is now an activist for eyewitness reform. Thompson's identification of Cotton exemplifies the problems with lineups.[35] She was raped by a black man who broke into her college apartment in 1984. Throughout the attack, she made a concerted effort to memorize his face. Thompson managed to escape after telling her attacker that she needed a glass of water. When she first spoke with police, she learned that a man with a similar description had committed a second rape shortly after hers. Based on an anonymous tip that a man named Ronald Cotton, who worked at a local seafood restaurant, resembled the composite sketch, the police put his photograph, along with five other men with similar appearance, into a photo array.

Thompson was told that the man who raped her might or might not be in the array. She chose Cotton. And then the police said to her "We thought this might be the one," because Cotton had a prior conviction for raping a 14-year-old-white girl he knew. From that point forward, Thompson was convinced the face she saw in the photo was the face of her rapist.

The second rape victim identified a different suspect, so prosecutors made the decision to try Cotton for just the rape of Thompson and not to tell the jury about the other rape. The police found a small piece of foam rubber under Cotton's bed that could have matched a piece of foam rubber left in Thompson's apartment. They also found a flashlight similar to the one she described. But there was little forensic evidence—no fingerprints, no hair. Blood typing of semen samples proved inconclusive. However, Cotton had given investigators three different false alibis, which hurt his credibility. Cotton did not take the stand, but his demeanor hurt him anyway. One juror said "he had no change of emotions for eight days. He never changed his facial expression. This was extremely strange to me and, as time went by, I expected to see him react and I never did. And so he seemed more guilty and guiltier and guiltier as time went by."[36] Cotton was convicted and sentenced to life.

While in prison, Cotton became convinced that a fellow inmate—Bobby Poole—was actually the rapist. Poole had bragged of the crime to another inmate and the two looked very much alike. Two years later, Cotton was granted a new trial on the ground that the jury should have heard about the second rape, in which the victim did not identify him. However, she changed her mind and identified Cotton at trial. Poole testified that he did not rape anyone. Cotton was convicted a second time, and sentenced to serve two life sentences. Here is what Thompson said at the second trial about seeing Poole:

> I never remember looking at Bobby Poole, thinking, 'Oh, I've got the wrong person!" I mean, "I've made a huge mistake." Now I remember that never—that never entered my head. It just didn't. Again, I thought, "Oh, this is just a game. This is just a game they're playing."[37]

---

34. *Id.*
35. WGHB educational foundation, supra.
36. *Id.*
37. *Id.*

Eight years later, Cotton's case came to the attention of a law professor, Rich Rosen, who noticed that there was no physical evidence of Cotton in Thompson's apartment. Given the length of time he had been in the house and the nature of the assaults, this surprised him. He asked for testing of the DNA from Thompson's rape. It excluded Cotton. However, it did match Poole, whose DNA had been entered into a database where samples from 20,000 violent offenders were kept.

Thompson's initial identification of Cotton from the photo array had been confirmed by the investigators, who said they thought "this might be the one." Thompson admits that she felt a lot of pressure because her eyewitness testimony would be crucial to the trial. Cotton was released, and as of 1997, was working in the lab that had tested his DNA.

Thompson's initial identification of Cotton was reinforced to the extent that even today, she admits that she still sees Cotton's face as her rapist, even knowing now that he was not the man who raped her. Here is the ending from a program produced by Public Broadcasting System Station WGBH called "What Jennifer Saw:"

> **Ronald Cotton:** What would I say to Miss Thompson? Well, I would like to know how she feels right now. What—what does she have to say in her own words, you know, to me?

> **Jennifer Thompson:** I have to accept the answer that's been given to me and put faith in our system that the DNA tests, the science, tells me we had the wrong guy. I just wish I had some answers. I still see Ronald Cotton. And I'm not saying that to point a finger. I'm just saying that's who I see. And I would love to erase that face out of my mind. I would do anything to erase that face out of my mind, but I can't. It's just—it's in my head. Sometimes it's more fuzzy than others because my mind now says, "Well, it's Bobby Poole," But it's—it's still the face I see.[38]

# Eyewitness Identification in the *Grant* Trial

No one saw Grant murder Serra. Although the state introduced either live testimony or written statements from five witnesses who stated that they saw Grant, the testimony was about seeing a man running after a woman, seeing a man running with "something shiny" in his hands, seeing a man driving by "fast" in a car, and a description of a man who handed a bloody parking ticket to a parking attendant.

No witness at trial was asked to identify Ed Grant in person. Of course, Grant looked much different in 2002 than he had in 1973. Also, none of the eyewitnesses were shown a photograph of Grant from 1973, although the photograph was presented to the jury and to several other witnesses, and the prosecution commented on the "uncanny resemblance" between the composite and Grant's 1973 photo in its closing remarks.

Here is a summary of the eyewitness statements. Jane Merold and Gary Hyrb were smoking marijuana on level ten on their lunch break from their jobs. Shortly before 1 pm as they were going down to level nine to return to work, they saw a blue car traveling fast up to level ten. Merold testified that she saw a car come careening by in the garage. She said she did not see who was driving. Hyrb went to the police that afternoon and gave a statement to Detective Donald Beausejour. Hyrb described the driver as a white male, 21

---

38. *Id.*

*Lineup photo, trial exhibit 207*

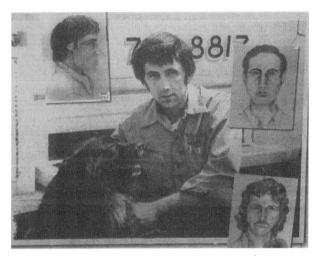

*Grant and composite drawings, trial exhibits 222.1, 208, 216, and 41.1*

*Selman Topciu, trial exhibit 1067*

to 27 years old, 180 pounds, medium build, 5 feet, 10 inches tall, with collar length black or brown hair, a neat mustache and wearing dark trousers and a white shirt.[39] In the meantime, detectives had questioned Phil DeLieto, Serra's former fiancé. Later that evening, Hyrb picked Phil DeLieto's photo out of an array and later identified him in a lineup. Unfortunately, he had seen DeLieto on his way into the station, so his identification may well have been compromised.[40]

Timothy Woodstock and his cousin Frederick Petzold had parked their car on level eight to go shopping. As they returned shortly before 1 pm, they could see through the half level wall to a commotion on the next floor up. Woodstock said he saw a female chased by a white man, heard a long scream and a few seconds after the couple disappeared from sight, he saw the man running back to the blue Buick Electra, carrying a shiny object that was five to six inches long. Woodstock described the man as in his 20's, 5 feet, 8 inches tall, slim build, fair complexion, medium length black hair combed slick with hair tonic. The man had no facial hair and was wearing light green trousers, a white or light colored "golf-type" shirt and black dress shoes.[41]

Petzold said the man was in his early 20's, slim, slightly taller than 5 feet, 9 inches, with dark hair and an olive or darker skin tone, possible Hispanic. The man was wearing a blue short-sleeve shirt.[42] Both Woodstock and Petzold worked with a sketch artist to develop composite drawings.

Christopher Fagan, the parking lot attendant who took a bloody parking ticket from the perpetrator as he fled the scene, was deceased at the time of trial. His statement was admitted as an exhibit, in which he testified that the perpetrator was 21, with olive skin, perhaps Puerto Rican or Italian, with black medium length hair. Fagan said the driver spoke in a foreign accent. When Fagan asked if the driver needed assistance, he said "no thank." Fagan remembered two numbers from the license plate, but no match was ever made. He said the driver was in a green or blue Chrysler or General Motors vehicle that may have had the letters MR or MH in the license plate. The car Grant drove at the time—an orange Jeep Wagoneer—did not match the description of the car he was driving in the garage.[43] Selman Topciu, a later suspect, drove a brown Buick with registration number HN5533.[44] No eyewitness expert testified at trial.

The police initially suspected DeLieto, because they believed that the perpetrator was someone known to the victim and that the murder was a crime of passion. They seriously interviewed Phil DeLieto, Selman Topciu, and Anthony Golino. All of these men apparently looked close enough to the composite sketch to lead investigators to question them further. DeLieto had type O blood, which was the type found throughout the crime scene.[45] In 1992 and 1993, DQ Alpha DNA tests were done on the blood samples from Phil Delieto and Selman Topciu, another suspect. DQ Alpha is one locus now included in standard DNA testing. The test excluded DeLieto as the source of the blood in the garage, but it included Topciu, along with about 5% of the population.[46] De Lieto also had an alibi that was confirmed by investigators.

39. Appellant Brief at 6.
40. Transcript, May 6, 2002 at 122–26.
41. Appellant Brief at 2.
42. Id.
43. Transcript May 20, 2002 at 172.
44. Appellant Brief at 15.
45. 45% of the population has O type; 40% has A, 11% B and 4% A/B.
46. Appellant Brief at 16.

Although this evidence was not presented to the jury, Golino was actually arrested for the murder and not until the eve of trial, when blood testing excluded him, was he released from suspicion. Golino actually created a disturbance at Grant's trial, shouting that Grant was innocent too.[47]

At trial, the defense presented "third party culprit" evidence that the real killer could have been DeLieto or Topciu. DeLieto had been excluded in 1993 by the DQ Alpha DNA test, but Topciu had not. The DNA testing done pursuant to a warrant for Grant's blood identified him as the source of the blood on the handkerchief and excluded both DeLieto and Topciu. However, by that time, none of the other crime scene blood could be tested.

The evidence against Topciu connected him with Serra. First, he had been a patient in a dental practice where Serra had worked, and two bills for dental service, sealed and stamped but not postmarked, were found in the visor of the car Serra was driving.[48] No one could give any explanation as to how the bills got there, but Serra's father testified that they had not been there when his daughter had picked up the car from him that morning. The bills inside, dated May 1 and April 20, would have been typed by Serra to be sent to Topciu. A co-worker of Serra's at the dentist's office said that she recalled seeing Topciu at a diner where she and Penney would go for lunch.[49] A photo of Topciu from 1973 was introduced into evidence as well as photos of his left wrist, showing what defense lawyers called a very noticeable scar.[50] Topciu also spoke with a foreign accent. However, two different Connecticut superior court judges refused to issue arrest warrants for Topciu in 1994 and 1995 due to lack of probable cause.[51]

At the trial, the prosecutor showed the jury the "uncanny similarity"[52] between the artist's sketch and Ed Grant's photograph at the time.

As you will see from the Closing Statements as the end of this book, each party argued that the eyewitness identifications helped his case. But when the jury considered the forensic evidence, the discrepancies in the eyewitness identification probably didn't seem that important.

## Does the Composite Sketch Identify Grant?

Police artists frequently make a composite sketch based on a description by an eyewitness shortly after a crime has occurred. Traditionally, composite sketches were made by police artists, but this required a trained artist and sufficient time to create the sketch. Today, many police departments use composite kits that contain hundreds of plastic overlays that can be combined for an eyewitness to examine.[53] These sketches are often circulated in canvassing for witnesses or suspects, publicized in newspapers or on TV in an effort to locate a suspect.

47. Colleen Van Tassell, *supra*.
48. Appellant Brief at 14.
49. *Id.* at 15.
50. *Id.* at 16.
51. Appellee Brief at 29.
52. Transcript May 22, 2002.
53. James Lang, *Hearsay and Relevancy Obstacles to the Admission of Composite Sketches in Criminal Trials*, 64 B.U.L. Rev. 1101 (November 1984).

Traditionally, composites were not admissible at trial, as once a suspect is arrested, the eyewitness can appear in person to identify the suspect. When a party tried to admit a composite as evidence of identity, as the prosecution did in the *Grant* case, some courts ruled the sketch inadmissible as hearsay.

Federal Rule of Evidence 801(d)(1)(C) and similar state laws now provide that a prior identification made in person or based on a photograph is admissible as proof of identification at trial if the witness is present in court and subject to cross examination. The witness is referred to in the rule as a "declarant," indicating that he has "declared" a statement:

> A statement is not hearsay if ... [t]he declarant testifies at the trial or hearing and is subject to cross-examination concerning the statement, and the statement is ... one of identification of a person made after perceiving him.

In 1970 a New Jersey trial court decided that this rule would also permit admitting a composite sketch into evidence provided that the witness upon whose description it was based testifies at trial and is subject to cross-examination.[54]

In the *Grant* case, two composite sketches were introduced in court, although no eyewitness was asked if the photograph of Ed Grant taken around 1973 was the man they saw. A photograph of the lineup that included Phil DeLieto and a photograph of Selman Topciu were also introduced as trial exhibits.

The prosecution claimed on Closing Arguments that the photograph of Ed Grant looked just like the composites. The defense claimed just the opposite. If the eyewitness descriptions had been a major part of the state's evidence, it is conceivable that the parties would have relied on eyewitness experts. After all, the eyewitnesses saw only fleeting images of a man either running after a woman at some distance, or driving by driving very fast, or in the case of the parking lot attendant, handing a bloody ticket to him when leaving the garage. Was it more likely that Christopher Fagan was looking at the bloody ticket than at the suspect's face? With such strong forensic evidence, the issue of eyewitness reliability was not important enough to create reasonable doubt.

# Summary

Testimony by experts who present scientific studies to cast doubt on eyewitness identifications is a relatively recent phenomenon. Eyewitness recollection is affected by some obvious factors that anyone would suspect—such as distance from the suspect, the amount of time they looked at the suspect, and the amount of time between the crime and attempting to make an identification. Studies show that the reliability of identifications is also affected by level of stress, witness expectations, and conduct by the administrator of lineup procedures. Witnesses may also respond to perceived danger to themselves, such as in the situation where a weapon is pointed at them. This issue, called "weapon focus" tends to undermine the credibility of eyewitness identifications.

Many experts have called for changes in eyewitness identification procedures to increase the reliability of identifications. One court threatened a harsh jury instruction about eye-

---

54. *State v. Ginardi,* 111 N.J. Super. 435, 268 A.2d 534 (1970), aff'd, 57 N.J. 438, 273 A.2d 353 (1971).

witness identification errors unless law enforcement adopted procedures that notified witnesses that the suspect might or might not be in the lineup. As this issue of eyewitness error becomes better known, lineup and photo array identifications doubtless will improve.

The trend of the cases is to exclude expert testimony that is simply general in nature and not supported by specific scientific studies. Due to the possible prejudice, courts are also likely to ban such experts where there is other evidence identifying the defendant. Where, however, the expert testifies to a matter of high relevance, such as weapon focus, supports the testimony with scientific studies, and in cases such as *Lester* where the eyewitness identification is the major evidence against the defendant, we are likely to see more and more courts admit this testimony.

Eyewitness error has figured in many convictions of people later exonerated due to DNA testing. One example is the case of Ronald Cotton, who was misidentified by Jennifer Thompson. Cotton looked like the real rapist—Bobby Poole, who was later identified by DNA as the real rapist. Thompson, now an advocate for eyewitness identification reform—says that even though she knows now that Poole, not Cotton, was the rapist, she still "sees" Cotton in her mind. This shows how powerful the mind can be in encoding false information.

In the *Grant* case, there were a number of eyewitnesses who testified to seeing a man running after a woman in the garage, driving a car really fast in the garage, and checking out of the garage at the attendant booth. No one actually saw the murder. Composite sketches were made shortly after the crime, and one eyewitness identified Phil DeLieto in a lineup. DeLieto was later eliminated as a suspect due to his blood type and alibi. There were many reasons to question the reliability of the eyewitnesses, but no expert testimony was presented.

# Discussion Questions

1. What is the "common knowledge" about the validity of an eyewitness identification?

2. How do experts challenge that common knowledge?

3. What experiments have experts done to challenge eyewitness identifications?

4. What were the six factors the expert identified in *United States v. Lester* that affect the validity of eyewitness identifications?

5. How did Connecticut change its lineup procedures following the case of *Ledbetter*? What other changes would you suggest?

6. Do you agree with Wells that the solution to the problem of eyewitness identification error is not expert testimony? Why or why not?

7. Why did the court in *State v. Legrand* decide that eyewitness expert testimony did not meet the *Frye* test of general acceptance?

8. How do the frequency of eyewitness misidentifications in exoneration cases affect your view of the reliability of eyewitness identifications?

9. What is your opinion of the eyewitness testimony in *Grant*? How does the fact that Phil DeLieto was identified by one eyewitness affect your conclusion?

10. Do you think the composite sketches of Grant should have been admitted at the trial? Why or why not?

# Chapter 10

# Blood Spatter Analysis

## Overview

Blood spatter analysis is based on mathematics and physics, which can be used to determine the velocity and angle with which blood has hit a surface, as well as the direction from which it came. Experts can also determine what type of impact caused the blood, based on the size of the blood drops.

Once these basic facts are known, however, the job of the analyst becomes more complex. There may be blood drops from more than one source that are intermingled. As the analyst attempts to reconstruct the likely position of people and objects, the science of blood spatter analysis moves into a more speculative realm.

Most courts accept the reliability of blood spatter analysis. However, some courts have refused to let experts testify about blood spatter, when the conclusion of the expert seems speculative. Some experts are permitted to testify as to a hypothetical set of facts, but are not permitted to conclusively relate the reconstruction to the defendant.

Experts are generally not permitted to testify about experiments they conduct to recreate the crime scene unless the court is satisfied that the conditions are exactly the same. Some police investigators have not been permitted to testify about crime scene blood on the theory that they lack training and experience in blood spatter.

Blood spatter experts are frequently used when a defendant offers a version of facts, typically one in which the victim was the aggressor, which the blood spatter shows is inconsistent with the facts.

Blood spatter analysis was important in reconstructing the facts in the *Grant* case, particularly the answer to how Serra's car was found on the 8th level of the garage, but her car keys and the handkerchief were found on the 7th level. However, as the testimony of Dr. Lee at trial showed, the analyst may derive a different conclusion once he knows additional facts about the case. In this sense, there is much more to blood spatter analysis than "pure science."

# Chapter Objectives

Based on the chapter, students will be able to:

1. Understand and explain how the measurement of blood spatter can identify angle and speed.

2. Explain the difference between low, medium and high velocity blood spatter.

3. Define cast off, arterial spurt, and transfer pattern.

4. Explain methods blood spatter experts use to reconstruct events at a crime scene.

5. Explain legal issues with admissibility of blood spatter testimony at trial.

6. Identify the reasoning behind cases that hold blood spatter testimony is reliable and those that hold it is not.

7. Find ways in which blood spatter testimony can refute a defense of self defense.

8. Explain why the court in *Crawford v. County of Dauphin* admitted some blood spatter testimony and refused to admit other testimony.

9. Distinguish the blood spatter issues in the case of Sam Sheppard from those in the *Simpson* case and the *Grant* case.

# What Is Blood Spatter?

Most people think that blood spatter [that's spatter, not splatter] evidence is basically a matter of physics. The scientist measures the blood spots, determines the speed by which they were deposited and from what direction, and then can reconstruct the crime.

> Spattered blood is defined as a random distribution of bloodstains that vary in size that may be produced by a variety of mechanisms. The quantity and size of spatters produced by a single mechanism can vary significantly, depending on the quantity of available blood.... Spatter is created when sufficient force is available to overcome the surface tension of the blood.[1]

In practice, the process is not so simple or certain. Here is what Louis L. Akin, a licensed professional investigator with 23 years' experience in crime scene reconstruction says:

> [Blood spatter analysis is the term] most commonly used to describe the process of examining bloodstains at crime scenes for the purpose of determining what happened to who by whom.... However, the procedure is far more akin to a tracker reading a trail sign than a hematologist working in a lab. The analyst interprets the evidence at the scene just as if it were tracks in the sand.

> In fact, the analyst uses every item of evidence at the scene, as well as the autopsy reports, the police reports, witness statements, and knowledge that he

---

1. Stuart H. James and Jon J. Nordby, *Forensic Science, An Introductionto Scientific and Investigative Techniques,* 2nd ed, CRC Press at 195.

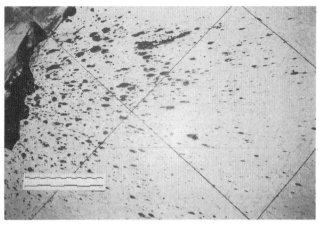

*Low velocity blood spatter, courtesy Connecticut State Police, Department of Records*

brings to the scene himself such as knowledge about the dynamics of the behavior of blood, knowledge of guns and ballistics, and knowledge of wounds to the human body. The analyst looks at the evidence, and based on what he sees in the blood spatter patterns and other evidence, makes a pronouncement about what he, or she, believes happened. Seen in this light, blood stain analysis is more of an art than a science and is always open to interpretation.[2]

This does not mean that the laws of physics are not important in the reconstruction, but it does mean that if the scientist is influenced by facts beyond the pattern of blood spatter itself, the results are going to be influenced by those facts.

## Blood Spatter Analysis— What Are the Scientific Hypotheses?

All blood pattern analysts agree on certain fundamentals based on science and mathematics.

A free falling drop forms a sphere or ball. The sphere breaks up when it strikes another object or when acted upon by some other force. The angle of impact can be determined by looking at the shape of the drop. A drop of blood striking a surface at right angles will produce a nearly circular stain. As the angle decreases, the stain appears more elongated. Therefore, the shape of blood drops can indicate the angle of impact. The tail of blood spatter drops will point in the direction of travel.

> The shape of drops of blood reveals angle of impact and direction of motion.

> The size of blood drops reveals speed of travel and possible weapon.

Therefore, just looking at the drops can tell the angle of impact and the direction from which the blood was moving.

Another part of the analysis of blood spatter involves the fact that blood travels through the air at different speeds, depending upon the force with which the blood is

---

2. Louis L. Akin, *Interpretation of Blood Spatter for Defense Attorneys—Part II: Velocities of Blood Spatter,* 29 Champion 26, 28–29 (May 2005).

expelled from the body. The resulting size of the droplets will determine the speed, and therefore can be linked to the kind of weapon or object that produced the blood flow.

Blood spots are typically grouped into three types, depending on the different velocities at which the blood travels:

- Low velocity stains are produced by a force less than 5 feet per second (fps), which is the force of gravity. The resulting blood drops are 4 mm or larger and circular.

- Medium velocity stains result from a force between 5 fps and 25 fps. They are 1 to - 3 mm in size. This kind of stains are commonly believed to result from blunt force trauma such as caused by a fist or baseball bat.

> Patterns can determine source and position of people and objects.

- High velocity spatter is produced by a force of greater than 100 fps. Those stains are generally less than 1 mm. This pattern is usually the result of a gunshot or explosive. As the drops are small, they do not travel far because of the resistance caused by the surrounding air.[3]

The size of the blood drops coupled with the impact pattern they create can help the investigator determine the object that caused the bleeding. In addition to the size of the drops, the analyst must examine the pattern of the drops:

- The first pattern is called "**arterial spurt.**" Arterial spurts are squirted arcs of blood caused by blood being pumped from the left ventricle of the heart. It starts with low pressure, increasing and decreasing with the rhythm of the heart muscle, and generally is concentrated near the victim, who typically dies quickly from blood loss.

- **Cast-off patterns** typically result from blood being thrown off a weapon. After the first penetration, the assailant may yank a bloody knife blade out of the victim. As he does so, the victim's blood is cast off the blade, forming a pattern on items in the surrounding environment: perhaps a ceiling. Successive stab wounds will add to the number of separate spatter patterns. Analysis of these patterns can help determine how many blows were struck. The total will be one more than the spatter patterns, as the first blow will not create cast-off. The pattern tends to be oval or elliptical as the weapon is swung in an arc. One of the most useful conclusions from cast off analysis is based on finding a pattern in a place that is inconsistent with the defendant's version of what happened. For example, if the suspect says he was defending himself from attack, but has blood cast-off on the bottom of his shoes, the suspect was probably on his knees bending over a prone victim when the bleeding occurred.

- A **transfer pattern** occurs when a wet, bloody surface contacts another surface. The resulting pattern may indicate the source of the bloody surface. This is frequently the case with bloody fingerprints or handprints.

Investigators can reconstruct the crime by placing people and things at the scene based on the spatter patterns:

> There is a mathematical correlation between the length and the width of these blood splatters that can be measured. We can then determine what angle they came in at and by using a set of strings and thumbtacks and a large protractor

---

3. Nordby and James, *supra* at 196.

we are able to reconstruct the scenes of crimes many times and actually place people where they were at the time they were injured … or shot.[4]

Of course, most blood scenes are not neat, and a variety of patterns can occur together, combined with smears or swipes as the victim or suspect touches blood, struggles, or wipes blood off on clothes or objects. Spatter patterns can help determine the location of objects, including the parties. For example, if a victim is surrounded by blood, but there is no blood under the body, the victim was probably killed in place.

Clotting time outside the body ranges from 3 to 15 minutes, so spattered clots indicate that time passed from initial bleeding. Coughing of clotted blood may indicate post-injury survival of the victim. Drying begins at the outside of the drop and proceeds inward. Drying time is affected by the surface type, amount of blood present and climate.[5]

## Methods of Determining Patterns

Blood spatter experts testify about the meaning of blood spatter patterns based on three methods of analysis.

- The first is an examination of the crime scene—generally by looking at photographs—and theorizing facts about the crime based on the patterns. This was the method used by Dr. Lee, who testified for the prosecution in the *Grant* case, which we will examine later.

- The second is by actually visiting the crime scene and measuring the distance from various points at the scene to the blood droplets, and drawing conclusions about the angles of impact and type of weapon.

- The third method is by attempting to duplicate the blood patterns by experiments. One court opinion[6] criticized the "reenactment" method of blood spatter analysis as follows:

  … blood spatter experiments are conducted using old blood received from blood banks. The blood is put into plastic bags and containers and dropped to the ground, or plastic bags filled with blood are strapped to one of the "scientists" before they run into an object, such as a wall.…

  This sort of analysis does not take into account factors such as the thickness of a victim's skin, or the presence of a large blood vessel, bone or hair that may impede or accelerate the loss of blood by the victim. Also, blood spatter will look more circular if it falls on a hard, smooth surface, tending to become ragged at the edges if it falls on a rough or porous surface.[7]

> Blood spatter analysis requires linking the blood pattern to other known facts about the crime.

4. *State v. Moore*, 458 N.W.2d 90, 96 (Minn. 1990).
5. Hugh Berryman, "Laboratory Demonstration of the Replication of Blood Stain Patterns, Southern Institute of Forensic Science, 2005.
6. *State v. Rogers*, 119 Idaho 1047, 1055, 812 P.2d 1208, 1216 (1991).
7. James and Nordby, *supra* at 192.

# Is Blood Spatter Expert Testimony Reliable?

Most courts have held that the science of blood stain shape, size, and movement is reliable in explaining the speed or trajectory of blood. However, expert testimony linking the blood spatter pattern to conclusions about how a crime occurred have sometimes been rejected on a number of grounds:

- The "expert" was not qualified to give an opinion. This has occurred most frequently when the expert was a police officer or criminologist without formal training.
- The opinion was speculative concerning the positions of people at the crime scene.
- The "expert" conducted his own experiment in attempting to reconstruct the crime, which went beyond testimony about the scene itself.

## Reliability Rulings

A Texas court in 2004 concluded that the trial court erred in holding that blood spatter analysis was sufficiently reliable, in the absence of any testimony concerning the validity of the scientific techniques or whether they had been verified. On appeal, the court acknowledged that the parties had conducted a hearing on the testimony outside the jury's hearing, but said it was restricted to the qualifications of the expert, not the reliability of blood spatter testing itself. The court then concluded that blood spatter testimony meets the Daubert tests, as well as the test of reliability in Texas: "To be considered reliable, evidence derived from a scientific theory must satisfy three criteria:

- The underlying scientific theory must be valid;
- The technique applying the theory must be valid; and
- The technique must have been properly applied on the occasion in question.... This three-criteria test is not limited to novel scientific evidence; it applies to all scientific evidence.... The proponent of the scientific evidence has the burden to prove its reliability by clear and convincing evidence.[8]

The court reviewed cases from around the country and prior *Daubert* hearings on blood spatter evidence. It decided to take judicial notice of the scientific reliability of blood spatter testimony:

the reliability of a scientific theory or technique can be judicially noticed in three ways: (1) when it is a matter of common knowledge, (2) when widely available court decisions show that reliability has been litigated elsewhere in fact-finding forums to a degree sufficient for the appellate court to conclude that reliability is well-established, and (3) when a prior determination of reliability has been made by an appellate court whose pronouncements are binding in the jurisdiction.[9]

In reviewing court decisions that had determined reliability, the court explained the scientific basis for blood stain interpretation:

---

8. *Holmes v. Texas*, 135 S.W.3d 178, 195 (Tex. App. 2004).
9. *Id.* at 187.

The geometric Blood Stain Interpretation is a method used to reconstruct the scene of the crime. Blood stains are uniform in character and conform to the laws of inertia, centrifugal force and physics. Study of the blood pattern along with its size and shape helps determine the source of the blood and any movement that might have occurred after the bloodshed began, including subsequent violent attacks upon the victim.[10]

However, as recently as 1991, some courts questioned the reliability of blood spatter analysis. Some judges caution that blood spatter testimony may not be as "scientific" as its proponents claim. For example, in *State v. Rogers*,[11] the dissent stated: "If one reviews an article on blood spatter, it becomes quite clear that this is a new science in need of further research before it may be properly relied upon in a court of law. For example, as recently as 1983, an article on the subject concluded that "[b]ackwards spatter of blood from gunshot wounds is a complex phenomenon which we do not presently understand completely." ... Some experts have even testified that back spatter of blood from gunshot wounds does not exist."[12]

## Crime Reconstruction

Although *Holmes v. Texas* found no court that had held blood spatter analysis to be unreliable, courts have excluded blood spatter experts and have held blood spatter analysis inadmissible *as applied*. In particular, courts have refused to admit expert conclusions or opinions based on the expert's lack of qualifications or on his experiments with blood stains. For example, in *Franco v. Texas*,[13] the court held a police officer was not qualified to testify about the blood spatter in relation to the defendant's actions. In that case, a police officer testified that the blood spatter in the case showed that Franco was the aggressor and did not act in self defense. The court stated:

"We can envision some circumstances where the trier of fact may quite properly be aided by some evidence of blood spatter analysis, but we are dubious of the claim in this record that blood spatter evidence can determine the aftermath of a violent incident of bloodshed and to try to determine the location of individuals before, during and after bloodshed and to try to determine, perhaps, a sequence of events that occurred based upon the bloodstain evidence at the scene."[14]

In this case, Carl, the victim had been beaten with a cast iron skillet and stabbed seven or more times. The police arrested the defendant Franco based on a truck that had been stolen from the victim. Franco gave the following statement to police:

At the police station, Franco made a statement which was tape recorded. Franco said that Carl picked him up on the Andrews Highway and offered him a ride that Saturday night. They drove to Carl's home and went inside. Inside, Carl asked Franco to come to his bedroom where he attempted to take Franco's jeans off, ripping them in the process. Franco said that a struggle

---

10. *Id.*
11. 119 Idaho 1047, 812 P.2d 1208 (Ida. 1991).
12. *Id.* at 1055, 1216.
13. *Franco v. Texas*, 25 S.W.3d 26 (Tex. App. 2000).
14. *Id.* at 29.

began and moved from the bedroom, down the hall, and into the kitchen. Franco, who is 5'6" tall and weighing 130 pounds, insisted that he was defending himself against Carl, who was about 6' tall and weighed around 200 pounds.

When they entered the kitchen, Franco said he grabbed a frying pan and hit Carl in the head. Franco admitted that the handle broke off the pan when he hit Carl. Then Franco picked up a knife and stabbed Carl. Franco said that he stabbed Carl "everywhere because he kept comin' at me." Franco also stated that he kicked Carl in the head, and kept kicking Carl because he tried to get up. Franco did not leave the house until Carl stopped moving. When he left, Franco took Carl's wallet and pick up truck. Throughout his statement, Franco maintained that he only acted in self-defense. Franco stated that he was not injured in any way during the altercation.[15]

> The testimony of a police officer would give the evidence an aura of reliability which could lead the jury to conclusions which were actually based on mere speculation.

At trial, a police officer testified that the blood stains painted a scenario in which Franco was the aggressor and the movement of the victim and Franco was away from the exit rather than toward the exit. Franco appealed, stating that the trial court did not conduct a "*Kelly*" hearing outside the jury's presence or require the state to show that the blood stain testimony was reliable. The court agreed that this was error, adding that the testimony of a police officer would give the evidence an aura of reliability which could lead the jury to conclusions which were actually based on mere speculation. However, the court held that the error did not affect the verdict and so affirmed Franco's conviction.

The Georgia Supreme Court came to a similar result. It held that the expert should not have been allowed to reconstruct the crime, but that the error was harmless:

> An expert's testimony on issues to be decided by the jury is not admissible where the conclusion of the expert is one which jurors would ordinarily be able to draw for themselves. In the instant case it was permissible for Detective Gill to testify about his observations of the physical evidence at the Coleman residence. It was likewise allowable for him to assist the jury by stating his opinion that, based on his experience and training in the field of criminal investigation and crime scene reconstruction, the physical evidence was consistent with a hypothetical sequence of events surrounding the shooting.

> Detective Gill should not have been allowed, however, to offer his factual conclusions concerning the victim's and defendant's locations when the victim was shot and whether she was holding a knife when shot. These conclusions were not beyond the ken of the jurors, once they were apprised of the physical evidence and the permissible conclusions of Detective Gill.[16]

The solution for the expert appears to be to give a "hypothetical opinion" rather than state with certainty based on the facts of the crime that he can tell what the defendant or the victim did. Given the technical nature of the testimony, however, it is doubtful that a jury could understand a lesson in both physics and mathematics sufficiently to draw its own conclusions about who stood where at the time of the crime.

---

15. *Id.* at 27.
16. *Coleman v. State*, 257 Ga. 313, 313, 357 S.E.2d 566, 567 (1987).

The investigator can also use blood spatter analysis to corroborate and disprove a witness's statement. For example, in *Smith v. Virginia*,[17] the court held that blood spatter testimony was reliable in the murder trial of James Smith for the murder of Tracey Chandler, who was found in Smith's bedroom, lying on her back on the bed with her feet on the floor. Chandler had six bullet wounds, including one behind her right ear, in the right side of her chest, in her mouth, in her right hand, and above her left and right knee caps.

Smith testified that he killed Chandler in self defense when she attacked him with a needle during an argument over his drug use. The expert for the prosecution testified, based on blood spatter analysis, that Chandler was not standing when she was shot, thereby disproving Smith's defense. The court stated that blood stain pattern analysis is a reliable science, composed of the application of principles of physics, chemistry, biology and mathematics. The court also noted that the state of Minnesota had concluded that blood spatter science may be appropriate for judicial notice, which would mean that the proffering party would not need to prove the *Daubert* factors, although he would still need to prove that the testifying expert was qualified by experience or education to testify.

In the *Smith* case, investigators found 18 drops of blood on the leg of Chandler's pants and determined they were her blood. All but two of the spots were circular in shape, which indicated that the blood struck her pants at a perpendicular angle. As there was no impact spatter on her pants below the knees, on the back of the pants, or on her shirt, the expert concluded that she was not standing when she was shot. At trial the expert explained the science to the jury: ..."when a bullet enters the body and blood leaves the body through the entry wound, the type of blood stain is known as impact spatter. The blood under these conditions, following 'the path of least resistance,' exits the entry wound in a conical pattern, and eventually falls to the ground. The greater the force of the impact, the smaller the droplets of blood that are expelled from the wound. [The expert] testified that when these droplets strike a surface at a perpendicular angle, the resulting blood stain is circular. If the resulting blood stain is elliptical in shape, it may be concluded that the blood droplet struck the surface at an angle."[18]

On cross examination by the defense, the expert agreed that it was possible that the blood spatter on the pants could have come from Chandler's hand, but concluded it was unlikely because the bullet had entered the back of her right hand and exited at her palm. As exit wounds cause more spatter than entry wounds, the expert testified he would have expected to see more spatter on Chandler's pants and spatter below her knees and above her waistline.[19]

A number of factors can affect the blood patterns and mislead investigators. This is where the art and experience enter the picture. For example, blood that falls on different textures may result in different size droplets than normal. Drops can fall on top of each other, thus inflating their actual size. Blood patterns may support more than one plausible theory of the crime; yet the investigator may see only the most obvious one.[20]

In another case in which there were two drops of the victim's blood on the defendant's pants, the defense offered three different theories as to how the blood was de-

17. 265 Va. 250, 576 S.E.2d 465 (2003).
18. *Id.* at 252, 467.
19. *Id.*
20. Akin, Part I, 29 Champion 38 (April 2005).

posited: they resulted from the defendant kneeling over the already-wounded victim, the victim and defendant had shaved and cut up vegetables together—perhaps this resulted in the blood spatter—or the defendant may have mistaken the victim's pants as his own.[21] The jury probably saw this as grasping at straws. In any event, they convicted the defendant of murder.

Another common scenario when the defendant has the victim's blood on his body or clothes is to argue that he came upon the scene when the victim was already dead and got blood on his body or clothes by touching or trying to help the victim. This was the defense in the case of Jeffrey Hall, tried and convicted of killing his girlfriend with a knife. He tried to convince the jury that he came upon the scene and found his girlfriend in a pool of blood and got blood on his clothes by dragging her body to get help. He ran to a neighbor's house holding the murder weapon, which he said he found by the body.

A criminalist who analyzed both the clothing and the murder weapon testified that the blood patterns on the defendant's clothes could only have been produced by blood spatter at a great velocity and could not have resulted from mere contact.[22] He also testified that certain blood on the defendant's pants was consistent with wiping a bloody knife on them. In addition, course blue fibers were identified on the knife, which were consistent with the defendant's corduroy pants. The court held the expert testimony was admissible:

> [T]he evidence offered to show the reliability of the bloodstain analysis included: (1) Professor MacDonnell's considerable experience and his status as the leading expert in the field; (2) the existence of national training programs; (3) the existence of national and state organizations for experts in the field; (4) the offering of courses on the subject in several major schools; (5) use by police departments throughout the country in their day-to-day operations; (6) the holding of annual seminars; and (7) the existence of specialized publications.[23]

# Challenges to Expert Qualifications

Frequently the defense will argue that the expert—generally a police officer—is not qualified to give the opinion. For example, in *State v. Halake*,[24] the court held that a police officer who testified that blood spatter on the victim's pants was "consistent with" gunshot blood spatter he had observed at other scenes, was held not qualified to give that opinion. The prosecution tried to rephrase the question so that the officer was not asked to testify about the actual crime scene, but instead about differences between the blood pattern from a gun shot victim and one who bleeds as the result of blunt force. The appellate court reversed the trial court's decision that a police officer who had observed one hundred crime scenes could testify to the limited question of whether the blood spots on the defendant's pants were consistent

21. *State v. Halake*, 102 S.W.3d 661, 672 (Tenn. Crim. App. 2001).
22. *State v. Hall*, 297 N.W.2d 80 (Iowa 1980).
23. *Id.* at 85.
24. 102 S.W.3d 661.

with blood spatter that the officer had observed as a result of other gun shot wounds.[25] The prosecution's attempt to qualify the officer as a "lay person" who could testify to his prior experience with gun shot wounds, but not offer an expert opinion was, in the appellate court's view, still prejudicial to the defendant and likely to be construed as expert testimony by the jury. It held the officer not qualified to testify as an expert.

## Blood Spatter "Experiments" Inadmissible

Here is one case that decided certain experiments by the expert and his conclusions based on it were not reliable:

*Crawford v. County of Dauphin, 1:CV-03-0693.* 2006 U.S. Dist. LEXIS 15818 (M.D. Pa. April 4, 2006)

\* \* \*

On January 9, 2006, plaintiff filed a motion *in limine* to preclude the expert testimony of blood splatter expert Herbert L. MacDonnell. After the matter was fully briefed, on January 30, 2006, we issued an order directing a *Daubert* hearing on the admissibility of MacDonnell's testimony before this court. A hearing was held on the afternoon of March 16, 2006. After the hearing both parties further briefed the matter and it is now ripe for our decision. For the following reasons we find that MacDonnell's proffered testimony is largely admissible under *Daubert*. However, we will preclude MacDonnell from testifying about his demonstrative of medium blunt force trauma overlaid onto human prints.

\* \* \*

A court may qualify a witness as an expert based on his knowledge, skill, experience, training, or education. Fed. R. Evid. 702. In this case, neither the parties, nor the court, dispute that based on MacDonnell's professional and academic credentials, he qualifies as an expert in bloodstain pattern analysis and latent finger print identification.

\* \* \*

Rather, it is the second prong, the reliability of MacDonnell's proffered testimony as applied to the facts of this case, that is the subject of the parties' dispute.

\* \* \*

In addition to those factors enumerated in *Daubert*, the United States Court of Appeals for the Third Circuit continues to apply a series of factors it enumerated prior to the *Daubert* decision.

\* \* \*

[T]he factors *Daubert* and *Downing* have already deemed important include:

---

25. *Id.* at 670.

(1) whether a method consists of a testable hypothesis;

(2) whether the method has been subject to peer review;

(3) the known or potential rate of error;

(4) the existence and maintenance of standards controlling the technique's operation;

(5) whether the method is generally accepted;

(6) the relationship of the technique to methods which have been established to be reliable;

(7) the qualifications of the expert witness testifying based on the methodology; and

(8) the non-judicial uses to which the method has been put.

\* \* \*

Plaintiff asserts that MacDonnell's expert testimony should be barred for several reasons. First, plaintiff argues that MacDonnell's methodology lacks reliability. Second, Crawford contends that the equipment used by MacDonnell to simulate a medium velocity blunt force trauma was never sufficiently demonstrated to have been calibrated, standardized, verified or ensured reliable by other methods. Likewise, plaintiff asserts that there is no known error rate for MacDonnell's methodology of simulating medium velocity blunt force trauma blood splatter [sic] on a human palm print.

Next, plaintiff notes that MacDonnell's methodology in determining that medium velocity blunt force trauma blood splatter could repose in the valleys of a human print and the results of the subject test have never been published and subject to peer review. Plaintiff also argues that MacDonnell's methodology lacks general acceptance in the scientific community.

Finally, Crawford contends that MacDonnell's methodology and results in simulating the medium velocity blunt force trauma blood splatter on a human print were the product of subjective observations and methodologies.

The defendants initially assert that the "experiment" conducted by MacDonnell was not conducted in order to create data, but rather was a demonstration of known scientific principles of which MacDonnell was already aware, i.e., the relative sizes of blood splatter created by medium velocity impact as compared to the width of valleys of a human print. Essentially, defendants contend that although comparing the size of the blood splatter on the latent print via Mac-Donnell's blood splatter "experiment" is uncommon, comparing two known measurements does not involve unproven scientific method.

We agree with the defendants that MacDonnell sufficiently established that his testimony will be based on comparing the sizes of two objects. At the hearing, MacDonnell testified and cited numerous publications, which state that the size of blood splatter from medium velocity impact is in the range of 1 to 3 mm in diameter. MacDonnell testified that he measured the spacing between ridges on Crawford's print with a microscopic ruler as 0.53 mm. We agree with the central underpinning of the defendants' argument. Mac-Donnell's testimony will be based on the comparison of two sizes: (1) the range of sizes of microscopic blood splatter as generally accepted in the scientific community and (2) the size of the distance between the ridges of Crawford's print.

\* \* \*

Therefore, we must turn to the reliability of Mac-Donnell's proffered testimony. We find that the expert qualifications of MacDonnell in the areas of blood splatter and finger print analysis and the wide publication of medium velocity blood splatter sizes along with his personal measurements of the space between the ridges on Crawford's print make his testimony regarding the two sizes reliable enough to be admissible for purposes of *Daubert*.

> MacDonnell is Precluded From Presenting His Demonstrative of Medium Blunt Force Trauma Over His Own Handprint.
> *Crawford v. County*

We now turn to the issue of whether MacDonnell should be allowed to present his demonstration of the medium velocity blunt force trauma blood splatter as measured against his own print. For the following reasons we will preclude MacDonnell from presenting the demonstrative to the jury.

Defendants argue that the device MacDonnell used to create the medium force trauma has been widely used by blood splatter experts and that at the hearing there was testimony regarding how high-speed strobe photography measured the device at 25 feet per second, the speed of medium velocity impact. The defendants also argue that it makes little difference that MacDonnell produced the blood splatter over his own hand print as he could have also easily produced the splatter on a blank piece of cardboard and compared it to the distance between ridges on Crawford's palm print.

\* \* \*

We find that defendants have failed to produce by the preponderance of the evidence that MacDonnell's demonstrative has sufficient indicia of reliability.... [W]e find that use of MacDonnell's own print and the circumstances on the whole of how he created his demonstrative lack the controls necessary to ensure reliable results. Although MacDonnell used his own print, which is presumably within the average of adult size, a demonstrative of Crawford's own print would be less confusing and more helpful to a jury.

Furthermore, the court is convinced that defendants failed to adequately demonstrate by a preponderance of the evidence that the demonstrative sufficiently captured the numerous factors at play at the scene of the crime, including the trajectory of the splatter, passage of time, climate, etc.

Because we cannot find by a preponderance of the evidence that MacDonnell's demonstrative offers sufficient indicia of reliability to be helpful to a jury, and because we find that the demonstrative might confuse a jury of the relevant issues we will preclude MacDonnell from testifying about the demonstrative.

The court ordered that McDonnell could testify about the relative sizes of medium blunt force trauma blood spatter and the size of the space between ridges in the defendant's print, but was barred from presenting his experiment using his own handprint.[26]

---

26. *Id.*

# The *Sam Sheppard* Case —
# Blood Spatter in a Brutal Killing

On July 4, 1954, Marilyn Sheppard, the wife of a prominent osteopathic physician in Cleveland, Ohio, was found bludgeoned to death in her bed. Her husband, Dr. Sam Sheppard, was arrested for her murder, and convicted of second degree murder and sentenced to life in prison. Sheppard maintained that he was downstairs when he heard his wife call out. He rushed upstairs and confronted a bushy-haired stranger, who knocked him out. After he regained consciousness, he followed the stranger out to his backyard, where he was again knocked out on the shore of the Lake Erie beach. Sheppard said that when he regained consciousness, he called his brother, who took him to the family osteopathic hospital for treatment. The story of the bushy-haired intruder was turned into a popular TV series called "The Fugitive," and later made into a film.

Sheppard was tried for murder and convicted. Blood spatter testimony was critical to Sheppard's conviction. The prosecutor's blood spatter expert testified that Marilyn Sheppard was beaten where her body was found, on the bed. A defense expert testified that she had been bludgeoned elsewhere and her body repositioned on the bed and argued that she had been sexually assaulted by an unknown assailant. An additional piece of evidence was introduced late in the trial — a lamp that supposedly matched a blood stain on Marilyn's pillow and could have been the murder weapon. A recent book on the Sheppard case concludes that this evidence was not disputed by the defense, although "the impression on the pillow was actually much smaller than the harp of the lamp that the government displayed."[27]

In addition to blood spatter in the bedroom, there was a trail of blood drops leading out of the bedroom, blood found on Sheppard's watch, which was in a green bag outside his house, and blood on his pants. The prosecution attempted to type the blood, but it was inconclusive.

In *Mortal Evidence,*[28] Dr. Cyril Wecht analyzes the blood evidence in the Sheppard case. At the time of the crime, the only blood test available was blood typing — A, B, AB, or O. Many pieces of blood-stained evidence were examined, but the only one tested was the bed sheet on which Marilyn Sheppard was lying. It was type O, which was consistent with Marilyn's. None of the blood leading out of the house, the blood on Marilyn and Sam Sheppard's watches or the blood spatters found on the bedroom wall, were tested. Sheppard hired Dr. Paul Kirk, a professor of biochemistry and a criminalist at the University of California, to review the evidence.

Dr. Kirk, according to Wecht, found large amounts of spatter on the wall to Marilyn's right, the east wall, which also included a closet door. These were low-velocity drops, as opposed the high velocity spatter found throughout the rest of the room. Dr. Kirk concluded that the blood on the east wall must have been thrown off the murder weapon during its backswing, and based on the patterns, concluded that the murderer was left-handed.[29]

---

27. Jonathan L. Entin, *Being the Government Means (Almost) Never Having to Say You're Sorry: The Sam Sheppard Case and the Meaning of Wrongful Imprisonment,* 38 Akron L. Rev. 139, 148 (2005).
28. Cyril Wecht, Greg Saitz with Mark Curriden, *Mortal Evidence,* Prometheus Books, 2003.
29. *Id.* at 132.

Kirk also found an area in the corner where the north and east walls met where there was no blood. He concluded that the blood was blocked by the body of the killer, who must have been standing at the foot of the bed on the east side, and would therefore have been covered with the blood spatter himself.[30]

At the first trial, Mary Cowan, a laboratory analyst at the corner's office, had testified that the blood on the watchband of Sheppard's watch, found in a green bag outside the house, was spatter. However, Kirk believed the blood looked more like smear that had been transferred by contact with something bloody, perhaps the hand of the killer.

Kirk also examined the blood trail leading out of the house. He disagreed that the stains came from blood dripping off the murder weapon and conducted experiments using different tools dipped in blood. Almost all of them shed all drops within fifteen feet and the drops were always small. But the blood trails in the house were longer and bigger. Kirk concluded that the killer was injured and the trail was in his blood,[31] the same conclusion that Henry Lee would draw in the case of *Grant*.

Sheppard moved for a new trial after his conviction on the ground of newly discovered evidence in the form of blood spatter experiments conducted by Kirk that were consistent with Sheppard's innocence. He argued that the prosecution had sealed off his house and that he had been denied access in order to conduct the experiments earlier. The court denied the motion on two grounds: first, it did not believe that Sheppard was refused access to his home to conduct these experiments prior to trial, and second, even if Sheppard had conducted such experiments, they would have been inadmissible because they were speculative and con-ducted under circumstances that were not similar to the conditions at the crime scene.[32]

> Sheppard's blood experiments, conducted after his conviction, were not newly-discovered evidence and would not be admissible at trial because the conditions under which they were undertaken were unreliable.
> *State v. Sheppard*

Kirk's experiments involved the drying time for the blood on the watch, a series of experiments during which different instruments were used to strike a "skull" made of wood, rubber and plastic, evaluation of the "agglutination" of blood drops on the wardrobe and walls of the bedroom, and an examination of the blood trail.[33] He also offered his opinion that the murderer was left-handed, which had been argued to the jury at the trial.[34] The court reported Kirk's conclusions as follows:

> [Kirk] describes the distribution of blood on the walls, defendant's bed and the radiator. By determining the point of origin, he gives the opinion that the head of the victim was essentially in the same position during all of the blows from which blood was spattered on the defendant's bed; that her head was on the sheet during most, if not all, of the beating that led to the blood spots; that probably all of the blood drops on the east wall were thrown there by the back swing of the weapon used; and that the blows on the victim's head came from swings of the weapon "which started low in a left hand swing, rising through an arc, and striking the victim a sidewise angular blow rather than one brought down vertically."

---

30. *Id.*
31. *Id.*
32. *State v. Sheppard*, 100 Ohio App. 399, 128 N.E.2d 504 (1955).
33. *Id.*
34. *Id.* at 415, 514.

He then explains the *cause of distribution* and comes to the conclusion based on his experiments as described in Appendix I and his observation of the blood distribution in the bedroom that the blows were struck by a left-handed person. He then proceeds to explain the impact spatter, and the throw-off drops of certain weapons, and decides that the blood spots on the doors of the bedroom were drops made by the back-throw of the lethal weapon, and that a very large spot on the wardrobe door could not have come from the back-throw of the weapon.

This spot measured about one inch in diameter. He then expostulates that "this spot could not have come from impact spatter. It is highly improbable that it could have been thrown off a weapon," and that "it almost certainly came from a bleeding hand.—The bleeding hand could only have belonged to the attacker.[35]

The Ohio Supreme Court affirmed Sheppard's conviction[36] in 1956, finding that there was sufficient evidence for the jury to have found guilt beyond a reasonable doubt. In a dissenting opinion, Judge Taft said he would have reversed Sheppard's conviction because in his opinion, it was impossible for the jury to have used the blood evidence on Sheppard's pants to conclude guilt:

[T]he state established by its evidence facts and circumstances which cannot be reconciled with any reasonable hypothesis except that of defendant's innocence. For example, there was admittedly blood on the knee of defendant's pants which could have gotten there when he discovered his wife after she had been killed, because the knee was at about the height of the bed which was covered with her blood.

However, there was admittedly no other blood on those pants, although the evidence indicates without contradiction that defendant's wife's blood spurted all over the room. Certainly there would have been blood all over the pants of defendant if he had been her assailant.[37]

Although Sheppard lost all of his appeals and his motion for a new trial, he petitioned for a writ of *habeas corpus* on the ground that he was denied a fair trial due to pretrial publicity. The U.S. Supreme Court reversed his conviction on this ground in June of 1966.[38] Sheppard was acquitted on retrial later that year and died in 1970.[39]

Twenty-five years after Sheppard's death, his son filed a civil suit to declare Sheppard innocent, which is a higher standard than "not guilty." A finding of innocence was then required in order to sue for damages for wrongful imprisonment.[40] Sheppard's son hired Dr. Mohammad Tahir, an expert in DNA, to review the evidence once more. Tahir discovered that the bloodstains on Sheppard's pants were not from Marilyn, and as Sheppard had no open wounds right after the murder, the blood must have come from a third person. Tahir excluded Sheppard as the source of the sperm found in Marilyn's vagina and also excluded him as the source of the bloodstain on his pants.[41]

Sheppard's defense team suspected that the murderer was Richard Eberling, a workman who had been in the Sheppard house shortly before the murder. When Eberling

35. *Id.*
36. *State v. Sheppard*, 165 Ohio St. 293, 307, 135 N.E.2d 340, 350 (1956).
37. *Id.*
38. *Sheppard v. Maxwell*, 384 U.S. 333 (1966).
39. Entin, *supra.*
40. Wecht, Saitz with Curriden, *supra* at 129.
41. *Id.*

died in 1998, his autopsy showed a half-inch scar on the inside of his left wrist. Again, similar to the *Grant* case, the defense was looking for a wound that would have created enough blood to make the bloody trail.

In January of 2000, with both Sheppard and Eberling deceased, the jury refused to rule for Sheppard's estate that he had been innocent. Notwithstanding the new blood spatter evidence, a pregnant woman had died, and her husband was a womanizing socialite. In the end, it appeared that science could not overcome character evidence.

*Serra and spatter on stairs, trial exhibit 1.2*

*Spatter in garage and handkerchief, trial exhibit 6.3*

# Blood Spatter Testimony in the *Grant* Case

The initial crime scene, the 10th floor stairwell of the Temple Street garage leading to the elevator penthouse, was covered with blood from Serra, on her dress and on the floor. The police found her car on the 8th floor. A white handkerchief with dried blood and some other kind of paint-like stain was found on the ground of the 7th floor, about

9 feet from a set of car keys which had blood on the keys and on the white plastic key holder.[42] The investigating officer, Vincent Perricone, initially thought the keys had been thrown down from the 8th floor, where the car was located, to the 7th.[43]

The keys were subsequently lost and were therefore not introduced at trial. No testing for blood was done on them. Former Detective Louis Ranciato testified that he discovered a trail of blood leading from the Buick Serra drove, which was parked on the 8th floor, down various staircases and ramps leading down through the 7th, 6th and 5th floors, then going across the 5th floor and back up the stairs ending on the 7th floor about 10 feet from where the bloody keys and handkerchief were found. The length of the trail was about 360 feet. It was photographed, and the photos were introduced at trial.

Serra's car, parked on the 8th floor, had visible blood on the driver's side door, window, handle, steering wheel, and seat. There was also blood covering a fingerprint found on a Pathmark-brand box of tissues found on the floor behind the driver's seat as well as other blood stained areas on the box where bloody fingers had touched it, but no identifiable prints were present.[44]

The police theorized that Grant, following the murder in the 10th floor stairwell, ran around looking for either his car or Serra's. He apparently found Serra's and then drove around looking for his own. He stopped her car on the 8th floor, and walked around the garage looking for his own car and leaving a trail of blood. When he finally found his car on the 7th floor, he dropped Serra's keys and his handkerchief, entered his car and left the garage. Police believed that Grant was wounded in the struggle in the stairwell, perhaps with his own knife, perhaps with the bread knife that Serra's mother testified she had given her daughter for a picnic. No knives were ever found.

The blood from the trail was typed and determined to be type O. Penney Serra was type A. There was no DNA testing at the time of the crime in 1973. By the time of trial almost thirty years later, none of the blood evidence had survived to the point of DNA testing except a small portion of a handkerchief which was found on the ground near Serra's car. Serra's blood was found only at the initial crime scene. Type O blood was identified on the Pathmark tissue box, on 5 of 6 tape listings of blood from the Buick as well as on several items taken from the Buick. Type O was also identified on the handkerchief. No typing was done on the parking ticket. Type O was also identified in 3 of 4 tape liftings from the blood trail. About 45% of the U.S. Caucasian population has type O blood. Both Grant and Selman Topciu, a patient of the dentist for whom Serra worked as bookkeeper and whose bills were found in the visor of the Buick, had type O blood.

In 1988, a tape lift of blood from the car was tested using an early form of DNA testing known as DQ Alpha and was found to have the profile 1.2,3. Five percent of the Caucasian population with Type 0 blood have profile 1.2,3. As Topicu was determined to have this profile, he continued to be investigated for the murder. Dr. Henry Lee, director emeritus of the Connecticut Forensics Laboratory, examined photos of the blood-like stains on the driver's side and stated that the stains on the metal trim were consistent with medium velocity impact blood spatters. He explained: "means some-

42. Appellant Brief at 4–5.
43. *Id.*
44. *Id.* at 11.

body hand maybe move, like move the hand, now it's not the contact, it becomes spatter. If I have some liquid or blood on my hand, I'm doing that, deposit on exterior surface of the window and the car, so that's called medium velocity."[45]

Lee was asked on cross examination whether he could measure the size of the blood stain from the photos, and he said he could not: "since there is no close-up, just a distance photo, I could only see transfer of blood."[46] He further identified stains on the left portion of the driver's seat as drop-like patterns. However, he acknowledged on cross examination that his opinions were limited to what he could see on the photographs and that he did not see a photo of the blood trail, the handkerchief or the keys.

Lee had been asked fourteen years earlier to complete a detailed analysis of the crime scene. He reviewed the police reports, the photographs, and toured the scene. He also completed an exercise in which similar cars were driven through the garage to attempt to validate the timeline from entrance to exit of Grant's car.

Lee determined in 1988 that Serra had been chased to and stabbed in the 10th floor stairwell. He concluded that either Serra and the perpetrator had been acquainted and the meeting at the top of the garage had been pre-arranged or they did not know each other and the meeting was by chance. Lee also concluded that the blood on the Buick meant the perpetrator had been injured on his left hand before he entered the driver's door. He concluded that there was no direct connection between the handkerchief and the crime.[47]

The prosecution called Lee to testify at trial to establish a link between Serra, her car, and the suspect. The location of the car was a secondary crime site and as the handkerchief and fingerprint were found there, the state needed to link them to the crime.

The defense, on cross examination, attempted to show that Lee never viewed the actual crime scene, and relied on reports of witness accounts from in the original police report.

Lee stated that as part of his reconstruction, he took cars and drove them around the garage to see if they could meet the timing of the crime. However, he did not reach any conclusions because the garage had been altered after the murder and prior to Lee's examination. Lee denied relying on witness statements, stating "I have to base on my independent result of police officers[48] [statements and records]. Here is the process of reconstruction as he explained it:

> My reconstruction basically the first group is the police report. Second group is reexamination of the physical evidence. Third group is interpretation of the photograph. The fourth section, talk about reenactment. The fifth is conclusion. [My] conclusion basically [is] based on my interpretation of the photograph, look[ing] at the scene and reexamin[ing] evidence. So witnesses, I did not use their statement[s] to put my report together.[49]

Although Lee stated that he did not allow witness statements to affect his reconstruction, it is clear that he did allow the DNA testing on the handkerchief to alter his conclusion as to whether the handkerchief was connected to the crime.

By the time Grant was arrested, none of the blood spots from the car or trail could be DNA typed, as they had all degraded beyond the point of being tested. The only

---

45. Transcript, May 9, 2002 at 77.
46. *Id.*
47. *Id.* at 47.
48. *Id.* at 88.
49. *Id.*

DNA test linking Grant to the crime was that on some genetic material found on a small spot on the handkerchief, which could have been blood, nasal mucus, or some other form of genetic material.[50]

> Lee connected the hand-kerchief with the crime based on a hypothetical question.

At trial, Lee was called as an expert witness to testify about the blood on the tissue box and his reconstruction of the crime based on the blood trail. Lee testified that the bloody fingerprint resulted from blood being placed over the existing fingerprint. On cross examination, he said that he could not tell when the fingerprint had been put on the tissue box. It could have been hours, days, or months. As to the other blood stains on the box, Lee testified that the person who picked up the box must have picked it up and then turned it around in order to leave a thumb print where it was located.[51]

Lee testified that the photos he examined did not include a photo of the handkerchief or keys and the blood trail was in black and white. The prosecution then presented Lee with a detailed "hypothetical" in order to have Lee recreate the crime scene. Counsel asked Lee to assume the following:

- Serra's car was found on level 8 parked skewed.
- There was O type blood in the car and no A type.
- A trail of blood starts at the driver's side door and runs down to 7A, down to 6A, across to the next stairway.
- It then goes down to 5, comes up from 5 to 6, 7 and ends with a large number of drops which increase in number and closeness to each other right next to the space where Serra's car is parked.

Counsel then asked Lee, "Is the car and the blood trail connected?" Lee said it was. He was then asked if the handkerchief was connected:

> The handkerchief on the seventh floor and the key looks like a direct line. The blood drops in this area, which suggest the vehicle more likely parking this side and if those, in fact, those keys have blood, handkerchief we know have type O blood, and those blood drops, I don't know those drop, they lift it or not, if those are type O, and, again, shows continuous. [Dr. Lee is an original speaker of Chinese.]

> Q: Given the additional information that you learned since 1988 concerning the DNA on the handkerchief, the identity of the fingerprint, the fact that the fingerprint owner has O and the DQ Alpha 1.2, 3, which is from a spot inside the car, and all of this stuff about the blood trail, is that handkerchief connected to that crime, to the car itself in this case?

> A: Indicative this handkerchief is associate to the car, associate to this crime.

Lee was then asked if the bloody ticket helped him reconstruct the crime. He replied, "Judge from all that evidence we have, this is a multiple location crime scene. It's not a single location on the tenth floor where the victim was stabbed, it's kind of continuation of the crime scene involving tenth floor, tenth level, ninth level, seventh level, five, six level, and then finally exits Frontage Road exit."[52]

---

50. *Id.* at 10.
51. Transcript, May 9, 2002 at 36.
52. *Id.* at 46–47.

Counsel then asked Lee why he said there was no connection with the handkerchief back in 1988. Lee replied that he was looking for paint on the handkerchief to associate with a garage. Also "we found type O human where victim is type A. I cannot make an association between—that's not victim's blood type."[53] So at the time, Lee was assuming the blood trail was the victim's, not the perpetrator's, and the blood type ruled this out. Lee did not change his testimony that the blood on the tissue box was over, not under, the fingerprint linked to Grant.

Counsel then asked Lee if he had an opinion on the amount of pressure used to make the fingerprint, but all he could say is that the fingerprint was a "stationary contact," not a sliding motion.

The defense concentrated on the discrepancy between Lee's written report in 1988 that decided the handkerchief was not connected to the crime and his subsequent reversal of that opinion at the time of trial. Lee's reconstruction did not add much to the original speculation in the police report. He had reviewed only black and white partial photographs, had done no testing on any of the blood, and did not give any opinion as to where the perpetrator may have been injured.

In the end, the jury apparently did not believe that these two facts created reasonable doubt: first, that Dr. Lee initially did not connect the handkerchief with the crime scene, and second, that he testified the fingerprint on the tissue box had been placed on it before blood was smeared on top.

# Summary

Blood spatter analysis depends upon mathematics and physics, which can be used to determine the velocity and angle with which blood has hit a surface, as well as the direction from which it came. The major variable in this type of analysis is the surface upon which the blood adheres, which can distort the size and shape of the drops somewhat.

Once these basic facts are known, however, the job of the analyst becomes more complex. There may be blood drops from more than one source that are intermingled. As the analyst attempts to reconstruct the likely position of people and objects, the science of blood spatter analysis moves into a more speculative realm.

Most courts accept the reliability of blood spatter analysis. However, some courts have refused to let experts testify about blood spatter, when their conclusion seems speculative. Some experts are permitted to testify as to a hypothetical set of facts, but are not permitted to conclusively relate the reconstruction to the defendant.

Blood spatter experts are frequently used when a defendant offers a version of facts, typically one in which the victim was the aggressor, which the blood spatter shows is inconsistent with the facts.

Experts are generally not permitted to testify about experiments they conduct to recreate the crime scene unless the court is satisfied that the conditions are exactly the same. Even in the case of Lee's review of the Serra murder in 1988, he could not dupli-

53. *Id.*

cate the conditions in the garage at the time of the crime, due to alterations in the garage itself, among other factors.

Blood spatter testimony figured prominently in the conviction of Sam Sheppard for the murder of his wife, and his motion for a new trial based on experiments on blood conducted by an expert was denied. Blood spatter analysis also was important in reconstructing the facts in the *Grant* case, particularly the fact of how Serra's car was found on the 8th level of the garage, but her car keys and the handkerchief were found on the 7th level.

# Discussion Questions

1. What information can examination of blood drops at a crime scene tell an investigator?

2. What would an investigator conclude if blood spatter drops were 3 mm in size versus if they were less than 1 mm in size?

3. How many wounds would likely have been inflicted if the investigator finds 4 cast-off patterns on the wall behind where the perpetrator stood?

4. What is a transfer pattern and what can it tell the investigator?

5. Why are courts likely to refuse to admit experiments with blood spatter in which an expert tries to duplicate crime scene conditions? What were the similarities between the blood spatter experiment in *Crawford v. County* and *State v. Sheppard?*

6. On what grounds have trial courts refused to admit blood spatter opinion testimony from police? Explain the reasoning of the court in *Franco v. Texas.*

7. Have the courts all agreed that blood spatter analysis is reliable? Why or why not?

8. Are there any subjective elements to analyzing blood spatter? What are they?

9. Why did Sam Sheppard hope that blood spatter analysis would constitute newly discovered evidence?

10. How was blood spatter analysis relevant in the *Grant* case?

# Chapter 11

# Handwriting Analysis

## Overview

Handwriting experts have testified in courts for many years about authorship and forgery. The basic premise used by handwriting experts is that handwriting, like fingerprints, is unique to the individual. Therefore, a person cannot disguise his or her handwriting from an expert who examines both a sample of the person's genuine handwriting and a purported forgery. Handwriting analysis is frequently used in courts to establish a number of issues:

1. Did an individual write a particular document in his or her "normal writing"?

2. Did an individual forge the writing of another person?

3. Did an individual write a document, attempting to disguise his or her normal writing?

The methods used to determine common authorship were developed by Albert S. Osbourne, in the early 1900s and have remained virtually unchanged. The examiner first views the suspected document and exemplars of the natural handwriting of the suspected author. If the examiner determines that he has enough writing to compare, he will first look for obvious differences, which might rule out the suspected author. Such differences include such "macro" features as line slant, pen pressure, and the like. If the suspect cannot be ruled out, the examiner will then proceed to examining "micro" features, such as the size and shape of particular letters. There is no set number of similarities that an examiner must find to determine a match.

Courts have admitted handwriting testimony for many years, but when confronted with the *Daubert* tests, some courts have determined that handwriting identification is not reliable. Experts cannot state which characteristics are most important, nor can they state that if a writer of a known document has x number of similarities, there is given probability that the writer wrote the questioned document.

All this may change with the advent of computer programs designed to compare questioned documents. One computer system has determined that handwriting is unique, by looking for a certain number of macro and micro features. In essence, it is similar to DNA testing in that it does not look at all possible match points, but the sample it examines is large enough to make probability estimates of common authorship.

Handwriting may well be a type of forensic science that does not meet *Daubert,* but that will lead to a form of computer analysis that will meet the tests in the near future.

# Chapter Objectives

Based on this chapter, students will be able to:

1. Explain the different purposes for which handwriting comparison can be used.

2. Explain the scientific hypotheses about intra-writer and inter-writer handwriting.

3. Identify the different opinions a handwriting expert may give about common authorship.

4. Identify the 21 basic areas of macro-characteristics experts look for in traditional handwriting analysis.

5. Understand the subjective elements of traditional handwriting analysis.

6. Explain the process involved in comparing handwriting as a forensic investigative device.

7. Explain how the admissibility of handwriting expert testimony has been viewed by the courts before and after *Daubert* and after the *Kuhmo* decision.

8. Evaluate whether traditional handwriting experts should be able to point out similarities and differences but not give an opinion as to authorship.

9. Evaluate the issues, including publicity and notoriety, which affected handwriting analysis in both the *Hauptmann* and the JonBenet Ramsey ransom notes.

10. Explain how traditional handwriting analysis may be both generally accepted and yet still fail the remaining *Daubert* tests.

11. Evaluate the process of handwriting comparison when done by computer and compare with traditional handwriting analysis.

# What Is Handwriting Analysis?

The purpose of handwriting analysis is to determine whether a particular individual wrote a questioned document, based on examination and comparison of characteristics in his handwriting and that in the questioned document:

> The main goal of all forensic identification, including handwriting identification, is individualization. Individualization is the establishment that a person or object now held is the same person or object associated with a past event in a particular way, to the exclusion of all other candidates.[1]

Handwriting expert testimony can range from the routine cases, such as whether a defendant forged a check by "copying" the handwriting of someone else, to the highly dramatic. The best known handwriting cases have been ransom notes, in which the suspect has tried to disguise his writing. From the famous kidnapping of the Lindbergh baby, in which Bernard Hauptmann was executed based on evidence that included testimony about his authorship of the ransom note—to JonBenet Ramsey, in which officials have been un-

---

1. Michael Risinger, *Handwriting Identification,* in *Modern Scientific Evidence: The Law and Science of Expert Testimony,* 2d ed. 2002 at 42.

able to conclude that any known suspect wrote the ransom notes, attempts to identify ransom notes continue to intrigue.

Handwriting testimony has also undergone a transformation from the early days. At one point, the only "expert" permitted to testify in court was someone who had actually seen the writer's normal handwriting. Today, experts are people who generally have no first-hand knowledge of the writer, but have applied certain theories to determine authorship.

## Handwriting Analysis Is Subjective

Even handwriting experts agree that there is no identifiable "system" for analyzing handwriting and that the process depends on training and experience. Although the American Board of Forensic Document Examiners was established in 1977,[2] whose members include the American Society of Questioned Document Examiners,[3] there is no formal training to become a handwriting examiner. Most examiners have been trained at forensic laboratories.

> Unfortunately, as yet there is no program of reputable courses offered or training available in Canada or the United States to private persons who wish to enter the discipline. As a result, the few qualified private practicing examiners are, frequently, former employees of government forensic laboratories whose personal facilities for performing the work may be inadequate and may vary substantially.[4]

Some argue that the 1910 text called *Questioned Documents*, written by Albert S. Osborn, is the definitive text on handwriting analysis. However, the book is currently out of print,[5] so it is doubtless not being used in any current training programs.

Handwriting analysis is subjective. Unlike fingerprints, there is no agreed upon number of points of comparison required to declare a "match." No one claims that handwriting analysis is a "science," although it has been called a "technique." After the *Daubert* standards were extended to "technical" experts by the Supreme Court in *Kuhmo*, some courts have attempted to apply these standards to handwriting. Most cases, however, seem to continue to accept handwriting expert testimony, even when it is challenged. The question we will examine is "why?" There appear to be three main reasons:

1. Handwriting expert testimony has been admitted since the early 1800's and therefore continues to be admitted because of its longevity.

2. Handwriting is "generally accepted" within the litigation community.

3. As the jury can examine the handwriting for themselves, there is little fear of prejudice from the expert opinions.[6]

> No one claims that handwriting analysis is a "science," although it has been called a "technique."

---

2. *See* http://www.abfde.org.

3. *See* http://www.asqde.org.

4. Roy A. Huber and A. M. Headrick, *Handwriting Identification: Facts and Fundamentals*, CRC Press 1999, at 7.

5. Based on a search of amazon.com; later texts by the same author are available.

6. *United States v. Starzecpyzel*, 880 F. Supp. 1027 (S.D.N.Y. 1995).

Handwriting is one of those "unique" human characteristics that has been accepted as part of common wisdom. As we will see, there has never been a scientific study to confirm this common perception; nonetheless experts on handwriting have been permitted to testify in court both before and after *Daubert* virtually without challenge. Yet, how do we know that it is true that handwriting is unique? How does one become an expert in identifying handwriting? What techniques and methods do they use? Exactly how do they determine that a particular piece of handwriting originated from a particular person? What is the threshold of identification? And especially, what makes it possible to say with authority that this handwriting was produced by person A attempting to appear as if it were written by person B?

## The Role of Training and Experience

Kenneth Zercie, Assistant Director of the State of Connecticut Forensic Science Laboratory, has spent over twenty years examining handwriting. He believes handwriting can be individualized and handwriting analysis is "relatively reliable as long as basic rules are followed."[7]

## Is Handwriting Analysis a Reliable "Science?"

The scientific hypothesis underlying handwriting analysis has multiple components:

1. Each person's handwriting is unique.

2. Each writer will exhibit small variations within his writing.

3. Handwriting changes with age and over time and is affected by alcohol, drugs, and tiredness.

4. Handwriting is consistent from one piece of writing by one author to the next, assuming the pieces are written close together in time.

5. A certain number of similarities between one sample and another supports the conclusion of common authorship.

6. By examining a sufficient number of samples of a sufficient quality of writing, an expert can determine:

   - If two pieces of undisguised writing were written by the same person. For example, is a will written by person A genuine, based on other exemplars of person A's handwriting?

   - If one person has attempted to forge another person's signature or handwriting. For example, did person A forge person B's signature on a check?

   - If one person, attempting to disguise his or her handwriting, can be identified from the disguised handwriting. For example, did person A write a ransom note or bank robbery note, attempting to avoid detection by disguising his handwriting?

7. By experience and training, an expert is in a better position to make these determinations than is a lay person.

---

7. Interview with the author, November 17, 2006.

# Is There Any Proof That Handwriting Is Unique?

Whether each person's handwriting is unique would require a study of a large number of individuals. In addition, the study would need to determine which specific characteristics to include in the test. As there are literally hundreds of variations in handwriting, this might prove an impossible task. See some of the variables discussed below. Also, many Americans learned handwriting under a common instructional method in school. It is not known to what extent this promotes similarity of handwriting.

Students frequently cannot write all the letters of the alphabet in upper and lower case cursive script. Many do not write in cursive at all. Handwriting is becoming rare, as computer technology puts typewriting within the abilities of almost every writer. Some predict that in the future, there will be no handwriting experts, as documents will all be in type. Even signatures will rely on mechanical reproduction.

Some efforts have been made to study handwriting differences in large populations. A study was reported in 1977 that studied the characteristics of handwriting of 200 writers.[8] Almost 20 years later, Mary Wenderoth Kelly, a forensic document examiner with the Cleveland Forensic Laboratory and Vice President of the American Board of Forensic Document Examiners, referred to the 1977 study as evidence of the uniqueness of handwriting and was unable to recall any more recent studies.[9]

The Connecticut Forensic Lab began a study in 2001 of 2,500 samples consisting of a letter and address on an envelope. The random samples were coded by age of writer, part of the country, sex, educational level, and handwriting method they learned in school. The study looked at the cursive letter "Q" and found that there were no identical Qs in the sample.[10]

More recently, a computer program developed by Cedar-Fox has evaluated a number of characteristics of handwriting and determined that handwriting is unique, with a confidence level of over 90%. See the discussion at the end of this chapter.

> A computer program developed by Cedar-Fox has evaluated a number of characteristics of handwriting and determined that handwriting is unique, with a confidence level of over 90%.

# What Characteristics Are Most Useful in Distinguishing Handwriting?

Even if one accepts on faith that handwriting is unique, which characteristics are the most important in matching one sample of handwriting to another? As we have seen with fingerprints, there are three class characteristics—arch, loop and whorl. Are there certain "class characteristics" that handwriting examiners look at first? These would be characteristics shared by all handwriting, such as slant, alignment, connections, consistency of habits, and the frequency with which a given habit occurs. Is this the complete list? Should another factor be listed? A large sample size would perhaps answer this question.

---

8. J. Muehlberger, et al, *A Statistical Examination of Selected Handwriting Characteristics*, 22 Journal of Forensic Science 206 (1977).

9. *Starzecpyzel*, 880 F. Supp. at 1034.

10. Zercie, *supra*.

What number of class characteristics must be found to "match" before the examiner will proceed to individual characteristics, rather than declaring exclusion? Again, there is no specific answer. Which characteristics are more rare and therefore more likely to distinguish between writers? We don't know. How many ways can one write a lowercase, cursive "e" or "i"? We do not know.

Most examiners tend to agree that one's handwriting can change over time, so it is important to evaluate two pieces of handwriting written over a short period. Illness, being tired or intoxicated can also affect one's handwriting, as one can attest simply from common knowledge. How does the examiner account for these variations?

In DNA testing, the examiner [or rather the DNA test kit] knows the relative frequency of different length alleles at each loci tested and also knows that the DNA sites do not control a specific genetic trait. If they did control a specific trait, they might not be truly independent. Many brown eyed people, for example, have brown hair. Therefore, if one were to test for the genes for eye color and hair color, one could not create independent statistics for the likelihood of a random match, as those two genes would not occur in mathematical random fashion. Because the loci in DNA testing are not associated with any known trait, there is not much possibility that an allele of a particular length at locus #1 would always occur with an allele of a particular length at locus #2. Is the same thing true for handwriting? In other words, are people who slant their letters to the right more likely to connect their letters? Again, no studies have been performed to answer this question.

## Are More Common Characteristics Required in Disguised Writing?

Finally, is less skill needed to determine a match between two exemplars where the writer is not trying to disguise his handwriting than to determine a forgery (attempt to copy another's writing) or a ransom note (attempt to disguise one's own writing)? Logic would indicate that it is far more difficult to determine writing when the author is deliberately trying not to write normally.

# The Traditional Handwriting Analysis Process

## Gathering Exemplars

The process of comparison varies depending on whether the person suspected is available or not. If the person is available, such as in the case of Patty Ramsey, the examiner will ask the suspect to write an exemplar of his or her "normal" handwriting. Generally, the expert will ask the suspect to write at least three exemplars of some length, on the theory that the suspect may try to write differently at the beginning, but will eventually lapse into familiar patterns. Many experts prefer ten exemplars written no more than six months prior to the questioned document.[11] In examining a known

---

11. *Id.*

writing compared with a questioned document, they will first examine the questioned document to see if it is sufficient to continue investigating. There must be a sufficient amount of writing that is neither highly stylized nor in block letters.

## Examine Pictorial Similarities

The next step is to make a general observation of pictorial similarities. Do the letters look alike? Are they in a similar style? Is the spatial relationship and slant similar? Is the format the same, either cursive, printing, or a combination? Are there obvious letter stylistics in common? At this point, an examiner may eliminate the suspect as the author of the questioned document.

## Look for Individualizing Characteristics

If not, then the examiner will look for individualizing characteristics, beginning with the first letter and working forward. More than one person can share an individualizing characteristic. Therefore, the issue of when the examiner has seen enough characteristics to make a conclusion is highly subjective.

## Forgeries

When the questioned document is suspected to be a forgery, an examiner looks for a variety of indications. First, the writer was attempting to copy someone else's signature, and so was actually "drawing," not writing. This will be evident in the small motor skills, neuromuscular responses and subconscious activity associated with drawing. Signs indicating forgery include: a lack of "feathering" on the introductory stroke. A writer will not touch the paper first with the writing instrument before beginning to write, as will someone who is drawing. The forger will also demonstrate abrupt pen lifts and an attempt to keep the signature on a baseline.[12]

## Disguise

The second issue is whether the examiner is trying to match two pieces of writing, both of which were supposedly written without any effort at disguise, or whether one of the pieces of handwriting (as in a ransom note) was purposefully disguised. The task of comparing similarities between two pieces of undisguised writing is much simpler than to compare a sample of "normal" handwriting to one where the suspect is trying to disguise it. In that case, the examiner must determine how a person who writes as the suspect normally writes would write if that suspect were trying to disguise his or her handwriting. One can see immediately that this is a far more complex task. The theory is that even in a disguised writing, the suspect would still retain certain characteristics of his or her normal writing. But which ones?

---

12. *Id.*

## The Handwriting Expert's Opinion

There are 21 basic areas which handwriting experts examine to determine handwriting matches.

In rendering an opinion, a handwriting expert is limited to these conclusions:

- Common authorship;
- High probability;
- Probable;
- Inconclusive;
- No evidence.

# What Characteristics Do Experts Look For?

According to one author, there are 21 basic areas which handwriting experts examine to determine handwriting matches.[13]

**1. Elements of Style.** This includes arrangement, placement and balance of text, dimensions and uniformity of margins, interlinear spacing, parallelism of lines, character and position of interlineations, depth of indentions, paragraphing, use of numerals and symbols in monetary amounts, location and nation of hearings, location of signatures, and style, size and position of addresses.

**2. Class of Allograph.** Cursive (letters are connected); script (letters are disconnected); hand lettering or block lettering; and composites of the above.

**3. Connections.**

**4. Design of Allographs** and their construction, such as capitalization or use of two or more forms for the same letter.

**5. Dimensions,** such as relative heights.

**6. Slant, slope.**

**7. Spacing.**

**8. Abbreviations.**

**9. Alignment.**

**10. Commencements and terminations.**

**11. Punctuation and diacritics.**

**12. Embellishments,** such as flourishes.

**13. Writing quality** and how legible the writing is.

**14. Line continuity.** Does the writer lift the pen or write continuously.

**15. Line quality,** from smooth to erratic.

**16. Pen control,** determined from ink level, pen position.

---

13. Huber and Headrick, *supra* at 136–138.

17. **Writing movement**, such as clockwise or not, more straight lines or curves.

18. **Consistency.**

19. **Persistency.**

20. **Lateral expansion.** Is the writing spread out or contracted?

21. **Word proportions.** Is the writing vertical or horizontal?

# The Admissibility of Handwriting Expert Testimony

Before the advent of the "expert" in handwriting analysis, courts accepted testimony concerning handwriting only from a witness who had actually seen the author write. So, for example, a witness who had seen a person write his will would be permitted to testify that the signature was, in fact, the testator's handwriting. Jurors would also be permitted to review the handwriting and make their own judgments.[14]

In 1836, a court in Massachusetts first allowed an expert to testify, stating that "it couldn't be any worse than what was traditionally relied on."[15] This is hardly a strong endorsement of handwriting analysis. This concept of relative benefit was echoed in 1995 by a New York court that accepted handwriting testimony as "nonscientific" expert testimony:

> While handwriting analysis may not be as scientifically accurate as fingerprint identification, it is, on the whole, probably no less reliable than eyewitness identification which is often made after a quick glance at a human face.[16]

## Handwriting Analysis after *Daubert* but before *Kuhmo*

Many people believed that the *Daubert* decision applied only to forensic testimony based on science. If a "technique" were involved, then *Daubert* would not apply. The Supreme Court clarified this issue in the *Kuhmo* case, when it held that the *Daubert* standards applied to techniques too—in that case testimony about the cause of a tire defect. Before the *Kuhmo* case was decided, however, a New York case called *United States v. Starzecpyzel*[17] evaluated handwriting testimony under the *Daubert* test. It found that handwriting failed *Daubert*, but it admitted it anyway because it was a technique, and at that time, *Daubert* did not apply to techniques. Its analysis of handwriting under *Daubert*, however, would prove helpful to later courts after *Kuhmo* was decided.

In *Starzecpyzel*, a husband and wife were charged with stealing paintings from the wife's elderly aunt by forging her name on deeds of gift.[18] The expert compared 224

---

14. D. Michael Risinger with Michael J. Saks, *Science and Nonscience in the Courts: Daubert meets Handwriting Identification Expertise*, 82 Iowa L. Rev. 21, 24 (October 1996).

15. *Id.* citing *Moody v. Rowell*, 34 Mass. 490 (1835).

16. *Starzecpyzel*, 880 F. Supp. 1043.

17. *Id.*

18. *Id.*

samples of the aunt's known handwriting with her signature on two deeds made out to one of the defendants and determined that the deed signatures were not genuine. He pointed out to the jury that the letter "E" was slanted to the right in 219 of the genuine signatures but not on the deeds. Also, the "l" in "Ethel" was lower than the "B" in "Brownstone" in all 224 known signatures, but not on the deeds. The court said that this testimony would be helpful to the jury as it would save them the time of examining all the signatures themselves, but that the jury could come to its own conclusion after the similarities and differences were pointed out.

The court compared handwriting analysis to other nonscientific technical testimony such as carpenters, auto mechanics, drug sale experts, money laundering experts, pipe fitters, and dog trainers,[19] and found them of similar benefit:

> The problem arises from the likely perception by jurors that FDEs [forensic document examiners] are scientists, which would suggest far greater precision and reliability than was established by the *Daubert* hearing. This perception might arise from several sources, such as the appearance of the words "scientific" and "laboratory" in much of the relevant literature, and the overly precise manner in which FDEs describe their level of confidence in their opinions.[20]

The court was convinced that handwriting testimony would not meet *Daubert* based on a number of factors: the lack of studies demonstrating its reliability, the lack of peer review, and the lack of controlling standards. By far the most important factor to the court was the fact that the handwriting expert who testified at the *Daubert* hearing, Mary Kelly, a handwriting expert for the Cleveland police with over 10 years' experience, was unable to explain any objective standards for handwriting analysis. Here is an example of her testimony in the hearing:

> Q: [Osborne states that] a slight but persistent difference [in] slant in two documents of considerable length may be evidence that the writings are by two different writers, while a pronounced difference might be the result of intended disguise. What would be the difference between a slight but persistent difference and a profound difference in slant?

> \* \* \*

> A: He is using it as a comparative between two different writers ...

> Q: What degree of measure might be slight?

> A: ... I wouldn't quantify it.

> \* \* \*

> Q: To make that precise, let me give you an example. Suppose, let us say, that if we look at a known writing and a reasonably fair sample of known writing by a particular writer, that the writer's small L is always slanted between say 8 to 12 degrees to the right, you find that in an adequate sample of known writing, is there some numerical standard which a document examiner would apply to determine what degree of slant in the questioned document would lead to the conclusion that the questioned document is by a different author? Would you need 14 [degrees], 17, 19, is the real question.

> \* \* \*

19. *Id.* at 1042.
20. *Id.*

A: I would say as a general rule, no, your Honor; there is no numerical measurement of that kind of slant.

The court stated that if the *Daubert* standards were applied, handwriting analysis would fail the test. However, it allowed the testimony anyway as "non-scientific" expert testimony on the ground that it would be helpful to the jury. This case was decided before *Kuhmo Tire v. Carmichael*,[21] in which the Supreme Court held that *Daubert* also applies to non-scientific testimony.

## Admissibility after *Kuhmo*

After *Kuhmo*, handwriting analysis must pass the Daubert tests as a "technique." Therefore, one would assume that the New York courts would reject handwriting testimony, based on the detailed analysis under *Daubert* from the *Starzecpyzel* case. Yet, the Second Circuit Court of Appeals, which governs the New York court in *Starzecpyzel*, ruled in the *Brown* case that handwriting expert testimony is admissible under *Daubert*.[22] In that case, the defendant was charged with drug trafficking, and an expert testified that a mailing receipt was in his handwriting. The Second Circuit did not address the *Daubert* factors at all. It approved the trial court's admission of the testimony based on the grounds that other federal appellate courts were accepting it, and that the Second Circuit had "routinely alluded to expert handwriting analysis without expressing any reservation as to its admissibility." In addition, the court stated that if the admission of the testimony had been in error, it was "harmless beyond a reasonable doubt," and therefore had not contributed to a wrongful conviction of the defendant.[23]

The standard for appeal from the trial judge's decision whether to admit or deny an expert is "abuse of discretion." Therefore, unless the trial court was "clearly erroneous," the appeals court will generally let the trial court's decision stand.

So far, all the federal appellate courts to address the issue have accepted handwriting testimony after *Daubert* and *Kuhmo*. Most of them conclude simply that handwriting testimony is "generally accepted" and therefore do not conduct a point-by-point *Daubert* analysis. The courts do not require a finding of controlling standards or error rate. One 2002 case admitted handwriting testimony, stating that it met *Daubert*.[24] However, the reason given was that handwriting testimony has a long history, is generally accepted in the expert community, and that it is primarily to draw the jury's attention to similarities between a known exemplar and a contested sample. Compared to the analysis in the cases above, this is not a rigorous *Daubert* analysis.

> Most courts that admit handwriting testimony conclude simply that handwriting testimony is "generally accepted" and therefore do not conduct a point-by-point *Daubert* analysis.

Most of the cases that discuss *Daubert* have been those where a defendant's writing is compared to his natural handwriting, either from exemplars or documents taken from another source. One example is drug shipments addressed by the defendant to himself or

---

21. 526 U.S. 137 (1998).
22. *United States v. Brown*, No. 03-1542, 152 Fed. Appx. 59 (2d. Cir. 2005).
23. *Id.*
24. *United States v. Crisp*, 324 F.3d 261 (4th Cir. 2003).

others. Others were based on a defendant accused of mailing an envelope containing a white substance to President Bush,[25] or where a defendant filed false tax returns.[26]

## Disguised Writing

The issue of comparing handwriting where the defendant is attempting a disguise is much more difficult. "Of course, where someone attempts to mimic the handwriting of another, there is a suppression of "ordinary' inter-writer differences, which makes the [examiner's] task more difficult."[27] No court appears to have drawn a distinction between expert testimony where disguise is alleged versus the person's "natural handwriting." However, experts acknowledge that even one person's handwriting will vary because no one person will write exactly the same way when repeating. [inter-writer differences]. The same issue arises when the defendant is alleged to have forged the signature of another.

> To determine whether or not a signature is genuine is a very different problem from that of determining who actually wrote a forged signature. It is not often that the writer will put enough of his own writing qualities into it to identify himself. From this meager evidence it is of course just as presumptuous to say that the suspected writer did not write it.[28]

## Rejections Based on Lack of Expert Qualifications or "Common Knowledge"

The courts that have rejected handwriting expert testimony have generally done so on the following grounds where:

1.  The expert was not qualified.

2.  As the jury could see for itself the similarities and differences, the expert would not be permitted to give an opinion as to authorship

3.  The expert did not explain his methodology in any detail.[29]

In one case, the expert testified that he had looked at two pieces of handwriting under a microscope and evaluated them based on "consistency, variation style, and peculiar or identifying characteristics."[30] The expert had also testified earlier that "there is no scientific methodology. It's a misnomer. There's not a scientific method in the sense of being a formal procedure. There is an analysis based upon the study of handwriting marks, including their length and width, the document, and sequence."[31] The court held that this was not sufficient to admit the testimony.

---

25. *United States v. Lewis,* 220 F. Supp. 2d 548 (S.D. W. Va. 2002).
26. *United States v. Hernandez,* 42 Fed. Appx. 173 (10th Cir. 2002).
27. *Starzecpyzel,* 880 F. Supp. at 1032.
28. *Id.* at 1043.
29. *Dracz v. American General Life Insurance Co.,* 426 F. Supp. 2d 1373 (M.D. Ga. 2006).
30. *Id.*
31. *Id.*

A few courts have barred handwriting testimony as not reliable in unique situations, such as one case in which a court barred expert testimony regarding printing by a defendant who learned to write in China.[32]

## Reliability and Error Rate

Is handwriting comparison reliable? One court examined four studies attempting to distinguish between the results of experts versus lay people. Here is what it said.

> Mr. Cawley testified that there has been at least one empirical study concerning the reliability of handwriting comparison, conducted for the FBI by Moshe Kam. According to Mr. Cawley, the Kam study determined that a document examiner could do what he said he could do, i.e., compare a known document and a questioned document and offer an opinion about whether the writer of the known document was the writer of the questioned document.
>
> \* \* \*
>
> [T]he Kam study concluded that document examiners had an error rate of 6.5% and laypersons had an error rate of 38.6%.... [there were 4 studies.] The first study found that experts outperformed non experts but that the best non experts did about as well as the experts.
>
> The second study found the rate of true positives to be almost identical for experts and non-experts, while experts committed fewer false positives.
>
> The third study found an unexplained 40% improvement in laypersons' ability to avoid false positives. The fourth study tested the ability to determine whether a signature is genuine or not. Experts and laypersons had similar ability to detect forgeries....[33]

In another federal court case, the court rejected expert testimony because the government had failed to meet its burden of showing that it was reliable based on reliability testing.[34] The defendant was convicted of sending a white power through the mail addressed to President Bush. The defendant was charged with mailing five letters from Kanawha County, West Virginia, between January 2 and January 11, 2002, each of which contained a white power, a cigarette butt and a note. Four were identical copies and said "If I were you [sic], I'd change my attitude." The fifth note was sent to a private citizen, with a note saying "it is on." The return address on each envelope said "Gloria Fields," with her address incorrect. Ms. Fields admitted, however, that the notes were in her handwriting and that she had sent them to the defendant, her former boyfriend, Edward Lewis.

The defendant, Edward Lewis, moved to exclude the handwriting testimony before trial. The court denied the motion. On appeal, Lewis argued that the court failed to hold a *Daubert* hearing. The court agreed that the trial court could not refuse to apply the *Daubert* factors:

---

32. *United States v. Saelee,* 162 F. Supp. 2d 1097 (D. Ala. 2001).
33. *Id.* at 1102.
34. *Lewis,* 220 F. Supp. 2d 548 (S.D. W. Va. 2002).

While district courts have considerable leeway in determining how to assess reliability, they do not have the discretion to simply abandon their gate-keeping function by foregoing a reliability analysis.... Significantly, 'in a particular case the failure to apply one or another of [the *Daubert* factors] may be unreasonable, and hence an abuse of discretion." [citing *Daubert*]

\* \* \*

Handwriting analysis proposes a theory that each person's handwriting is unique, and involves a method by which a trained expert can identify each writing's author. The sufficiency of that theory and method can be tested through the basic factors set forth in *Daubert*.[35]

"In a particular case, the failure to apply one or another of [the *Daubert* factors] may be unreasonable, and hence an abuse of discretion."
*United States v. Lewis*

The expert in the *Lewis* case was John W. Cawley, III. Since 1977, he had been a forensic document analyst at the U.S. Postal Service, received a certificate after a two-year training with the post office and one year of internship training. He had testified approximately seventy times in the past. He attended annual meetings of the American Society of Questioned Document Examiners and passed annual proficiency tests with a 100% rating. He also referred to the Kam studies as demonstrating error rate, but didn't know of any other reliability studies, except for some vague references to some in other countries. The court decided that Cawley's statement that handwriting identification had been proven though studies was "inadequate to demonstrate testability and error rate."

The court was also troubled that Cawley and his fellow examiners always got 100% on their proficiency tests and always agreed with the first examiner when checking his results. Cawley also stated that twenty-five samples were necessary to compare handwriting, but could not say why.

Although the court decided that the handwriting evidence did not pass *Daubert*, it upheld the conviction because of the mass of other evidence that supported Lewis's guilt.

In *United States v. Crisp*, another bank robbery case,[36] the court admitted handwriting testimony about a note the defendant slipped to another convict in jail where he was awaiting trial. It asked the other man to lie and give him an alibi for the crime, stating "you know if you don't help me I am going to get life in prison, and you ain't going to get nothing. Really it's over for me if you don't change what you told them." Based on samples of the defendant's handwriting that the police got from his girlfriend, an expert with the North Carolina Bureau of Investigation testified that the defendant had written the note.

The trial held a *Daubert* hearing, but it did not strictly apply the criteria. First, it stated that all the other circuit courts admitted handwriting examiner testimony. The expert had twenty-four years' experience and referred to the Kam studies as evidence of error rates. His opinion that the defendant had written the note was based on the following:

... Among the similarities ... were the overall size and spacing of the letters and words in the documents; the unique shaping of the capital letter "L" in the name

35. *Id.* at 550–552.
36. *Crisp,* 324 F.3d 261.

"Lamont"; the spacing between the capital letter "L" and the rest of the word; a peculiar shaping to the letters "o" and "n" when used in conjunction with one another; the v-like formation of the letter "u" in the word "you"; and the shape of the letter "t," including the horizontal stroke.

Currin [the expert] also noted that the word "to-morrow" was misspelled in the same manner on both the known exemplar and the Note. He went on to testify that, in his opinion Crisp [the defendant] had authored the Note.[37]

> "handwriting comparison analysis has achieved widespread and lasting acceptance in the expert community."

The court concluded that the testimony was admissible given the fact that "handwriting comparison analysis has achieved widespread and lasting acceptance in the expert community ..." Here, Currin merely pointed out certain unique characteristics shared by the two writings. Though he opined that Crisp authored the Note in question, the jury was nonetheless left to examine the Note and decide for itself whether it agreed with the expert.[38]

Judge Michael, of the three judge panel, wrote a scathing dissent in this case. A dissent is not law that later cases must follow, but it does show what the courts could do to conduct a genuine *Daubert* hearing. Judge Michael first observed that the government has made no progress after *Daubert* in demonstrating that handwriting analysis complies and that "it should not be given a pass in this case."[39] Here is Judge Michael's evaluation of the *Daubert* factors.

1. **Has the science been tested?** ... it appears that no one has ever assessed the validity of the basic tenets of handwriting comparison, namely, that no two individuals write in precisely the same fashion and that certain characteristics of an individual's writing remain constant when the writer attempts to disguise them.

2. **Has there been peer review and publication?** Those within the field have failed to engage in any critical study of the basic principles and methods of handwriting analysis, and few objective outsiders have taken on this challenge.... Indeed, the field ... relies primarily on texts that were written fifty to one hundred years ago.

3. **What is the error rate?** The court looked at the few studies, including one that shows almost 25% of examiners misidentified the author of a forged document, and concluded the error rates were "disquieting to say the least."

4. **Are there standards or controls?** There does not seem to be any list of universal, objective requirements for identifying an author.... the results are "only as good as the unexaminable personal database of the practitioner and the practitioner's not-fully-explainable method of deriving answers." [quoting *Lewis*]

5. **Is the science generally accepted?** ... general acceptance of handwriting analysis appears to come only from those within the field ... and those within the field have not challenged or questioned its basic premises."[40]

On the other hand, the Ninth Circuit federal appellate court ruled that admitting the testimony of a handwriting expert, including an opinion as to authorship, was not error, where the trial court applied all the *Daubert* factors and found the testimony reliable.[41]

---

37. *Id.* at 271.
38. *Id.*
39. *Id.* at 272.
40. *Id.* at 280–281.
41. *United States v. Prime*, 431 F.3d 1147 (9th Cir. 2005).

**United States v. Prime, 431 F.3d 1147 (9th Cir. 2005)**

* * *

Between April and June 2001, Prime, along with three coconspirators, David Hiestand ("Hiestand"), Juan Ore-Lovera, and Jeffrey Hardy, sold non-existent items on eBay, purchased items using counterfeit money orders created by the group, sold pirated computer software, and stole credit card numbers from software purchasers. To facilitate this operation, Prime and his cohorts used a credit card encoder to input the stolen data on their own credit cards, set up post office boxes under false names, manufactured false identifications, and used a filter bank account to hide proceeds of the crimes.

At trial, numerous victims testified as to the details surrounding how they had been defrauded by Prime's various scams. In addition, co-conspirators Hiestand and Hardy both extensively testified as to the details of the conspiracy, implicating Prime in all of the crimes charged. The prosecution also elicited the expert opinion of Kathleen Storer ("Storer"), a forensic document examiner with the Secret Service. She testified that Prime was the author of as many as thirty-eight incriminating exhibits, including envelopes, postal forms, money orders, Post-it notes, express mail labels and postal box applications.

Prime took the stand in his own defense and claimed that despite all of the evidence linking him to the various scams, including admissions that his fingerprints were on several items linked to the crimes, he was simply attempting to engage in legal entrepreneurial ventures. Prime also confirmed that he had previously been convicted of first and second degree theft, two counts of possession of stolen property in the second degree, and forgery. The jury found Prime guilty on all counts.

Prime moved for a new trial based on the improper submission of extrinsic evidence to the jury. The district court denied the motion, and this appeal follows.

## ADMISSIBILITY OF EXPERT TESTIMONY

Prime moved *in limine* to exclude Storer's expert testimony. The court held a *Daubert* hearing where both sides were allowed to offer voluminous materials and expert testimony regarding the reliability of the proposed testimony. After careful consideration, the court denied the motion, and Storer testified that, in her opinion, Prime's handwriting appeared on counterfeit money orders and other incriminating documents. On appeal, Prime contends that the admission of expert testimony regarding handwriting analysis was unreliable under *Daubert*, and thus the court abused its discretion by allowing Storer to testify.

* * *

1. Whether the theory or technique can be or has been tested.

Handwriting analysis is performed by comparing a known sample of handwriting to the document in question to determine if they were written by the same person. The government and Storer provided the court with ample support for the proposition that an individual's handwriting is so rarely identical that expert handwriting analysis can reliably gauge the likelihood that the same individual wrote two samples.

The most significant support came from Professor Sargur N. Srihari of the Center of Excellence for Document Analysis and Recognition at the State University of New York at Buffalo, who testified that the result of his published research was that "handwriting is individualistic."

With respect to this case in particular, the court noted that Storer's training credentials in the Secret Service as well as her certification by the American Board of Forensic Document Examiners were "impeccable." The court also believed that Storer's analysis in this case was reliable given the "extensive" 112 pages containing Prime's known handwriting.

2. Whether the technique has been subject to peer review and publication.

The court cited to numerous journals where articles in this area subject handwriting analysis to peer review by not only handwriting experts, but others in the forensic science community. Additionally, the Kam study, *see infra,* which evaluated the reliability of the technique employed by Storer of using known writing samples to determine who drafted a document of unknown authorship, was both published and subjected to peer review. The court also noted that the Secret Service has instituted a system of internal peer review whereby each document reviewed is subject to a second, independent examination.

3. The known or potential rate of error.

In concluding that the type of handwriting analysis Storer was asked to perform had an acceptable rate of error, the court relied on studies conducted by Professor Moshe Kam of the Electrical and Computer Engineering Department at Drexel University. Professor Kam's studies demonstrated that expert handwriting analysts tend to be quite accurate at the specific task Storer was asked to perform—determining whether the author of a known writing sample is also the author of a questioned writing sample.

When the two samples were in fact written by the same person, professional handwriting analysts correctly arrived at that conclusion 87% of the time. On the other hand when the samples were written by different people, handwriting analysts erroneously associated them no more than 6.5% of the time. While Kam's study demonstrates some degree of error, handwriting analysis need not be flawless in order to be admissible.

Rather, the Court had in mind a flexible inquiry focused "solely on principles and methodology, not on the conclusions that they generate." As long as the process is generally reliable, any potential error can be brought to the attention of the jury through cross-examination and the testimony of other experts.

4. The existence and maintenance of standards controlling the technique's operation.

The court recognized that although this area has not been completely standardized, it is moving in the right direction. The Secret Service laboratory where Storer works has maintained its accreditation with the American Society of Crime Laboratory Directors since 1998, based on an external proficiency test. Furthermore, the standard nine-point scale used to express the degree to which the examiner believes the handwriting samples match was established under the auspices of the American Society for Testing and Materials ("ASTM"). The court reasonably concluded that any lack of standardization is not in and of itself a bar to admissibility in court.

5. General acceptance.

The court recognized the broad acceptance of handwriting analysis and specifically its use by such law enforcement agencies as the CIA, FBI, and the United States Postal Inspection Service.

Given the comprehensive inquiry into Storer's proffered testimony, we cannot say that the district court abused its discretion in admitting the expert handwriting analysis testimony. The district court's thorough and careful application of the *Daubert* factors was consistent with all six circuits that have addressed the admissibility of handwriting expert testimony, and determined that it can satisfy the reliability threshold.

Conviction AFFIRMED.

## Expert May Point Out Differences, but Not Give an Opinion

Some courts have required that an expert simply point out similarities and dissimilarities between two pieces of handwriting, without giving an opinion as to authorship. The theory is that the expert is educating the jury to make up its own mind, when it looks at the handwriting itself.[42] This was the same restriction put on fingerprint experts in the first of the *Plaza* cases. That opinion was later retracted, so the ruling is no longer good law.

### United States v. Hines, 55 F. Supp. 2d 62 (D. Mass. 1999)

This case raises questions concerning the application of *Daubert v. Merrell Dow Pharmaceuticals, Inc.*, to technical fields, that are not, strictly speaking, science.... " Johannes Hines ("Hines") is charged under 18 U.S.C. §2113 for allegedly robbing the Broadway National Bank in Chelsea, Massachusetts on January 27, 1997. The government's principal evidence consisted of the eyewitness identification of the teller who was robbed, Ms. Jeanne Dunne, and the handwriting analysis of the robbery note. In connection with the latter, the government offered Diana Harrison ("Harrison"), a document examiner with the Federal Bureau of Investigations, to testify as to the authorship of a "stick-up" note found at the scene of the crime.

Hines sought to exclude the handwriting analysis. This testimony, defense claims, notwithstanding its venerable history, does not meet the standards of *Daubert* and *Kumho*. In the alternative, if the court permitted the jury to hear the handwriting testimony, Hines sought to have his expert—Professor Mark Denbeaux ("Denbeaux")—testify as to the weaknesses of the methodology and the basis of Harrison's conclusions. The government, on the other hand, argued for its handwriting expert under the applicable tests, and rejects Denbeaux.

\* \* \*

Our evidentiary rules put a premium on firsthand observations. Opinion testimony is disfavored except under certain circumstances; hearsay is gener-

---

42. *Brown*, 152 Fed. Appx. 59.

ally excluded. The jury is to draw reasonable inferences from the firsthand data. When an expert witness is called upon to draw those inferences, several concerns are raised. The rules give expert witnesses greater latitude than is afforded other witnesses to testify based on data not otherwise admissible before the jury. In addition, a certain patina attaches to an expert's testimony unlike any other witness; this is "science," a professional's judgment, the jury may think, and give more credence to the testimony than it may deserve.

Accordingly, the trial court is supposed to review expert testimony carefully. The court is to admit the testimony not only where it is relevant to the issues at bar, the usual standard under Fed.R.Evid. 401, but when certain additional requirements are met under Fed.R.Evid. 702.

The first requirement has to do with the necessity for the testimony: expert testimony may be admitted where the inferences that are sought to be drawn are inferences that a jury could not draw on its own. The inferences may be the product of specialized information, for example, beyond the ken of the lay jury.... For example, the subject looks like one the jury understands from every day life, but in fact, the inferences the jury may draw are erroneous. (As I describe below, eyewitness identification, and testimony about battered women syndrome fits uniquely into this category.)

The second requirement concerns the nature of the inferences to be drawn. In outlining the standards for admissibility, the *Daubert* Court noted the difference between information gleaned in a scientific setting and information presented in a courtroom. In the former, the decision makers are professionals; there is no need to come to a definitive conclusion; the decision making process comports with certain rules established by the professional scientific community. In the courtroom, the decision makers are lay, a jury; there is a need to come to a definitive conclusion; the decision making process has to satisfy norms of due process and fairness. In our tradition, for example, the adversary system and party examination and cross examination are central.

\* \* \*

Moreover, if the *Daubert* standard takes into account the unique trial setting—how well the lay trier will understand the testimony after examination and instructions—*Kumho* plainly does as well. In fact, cross examination and limiting instructions may be more effective in "technical" fields because they are more accessible to the jury, than fields with the charisma of science.

Again, a mixed message: Apply *Daubert* to technical fields, even though the scientific method may not really fit, but be flexible. Moreover, in this setting, because few technical fields are as firmly established as traditional scientific ones, the new science/old science comparison is less clear. The court is plainly inviting a reexamination even of "generally accepted" venerable, technical fields.

Handwriting analysis is one such field. The Harrison testimony may be divided into two parts: Part 1 is Harrison's testimony with respect to similarities between the known handwriting of Hines, and the robbery note. Part 2 is Harrison's testimony with respect to the author of the note, that the author of the robbery note was indeed Hines. I concluded that Harrison could testify only as to the former.... Hines challenges Harrison's testimony under *Daubert*/Kumho. If I were to give special emphasis to "general acceptance" or to treat *Daubert/Kumho* as calling for a rigorous analysis only of new technical fields, not traditional ones, then handwriting analysis would largely pass muster. Handwriting analysis is perhaps the prototype of a technical field regularly admitted into evidence. But, if I were to apply the *Daubert/Kumho* standards rigorously, looking for such things as empirical testing, rate of error, etc., the testimony would have serious problems.

\* \* \*

According to Denbeaux, handwriting analysis by experts suffers in two respects. It has never been subject to meaningful reliability or validity testing, comparing the results of the handwriting examiners' conclusions with actual outcomes. There is no peer review by a "competitive, unbiased community of practitioners and academics."

\* \* \*

I do not believe that the government's expert, Kam, and the studies he has cited suggest otherwise. While Kam has conducted several interesting and important tests, purporting to validate handwriting analysis, they are not without criticism. They cannot be said to have "established" the validity of the field to any meaningful degree.

\* \* \*

Handwriting analysis typically involves reviewing two samples, a known sample and an unknown one, to determine if they are similar. Both defense and government experts agree that unlike DNA or even fingerprints, one's handwriting is not at all unique in the sense that it remains the same over time, or uniquely separates one individual from another.

> "Both defense and government experts agree that unlike DNA or even fingerprints, one's handwriting is not at all unique in the sense that it remains the same over time, or uniquely separates one individual from another."
> *United States v. Hines*

Everyone's handwriting changes from minute to minute, day to day. At the same time, our handwriting is sufficiently similar to one another so that people can read each other's writing. Given that variability, the "expert" is obliged to make judgments—these squiggles look more like these, these lines are shaped more like these, etc. And those judgments are, as Harrison conceded, subjective.

When a lay witness, the girlfriend of the defendant for example, says "this is my boyfriend's writing," her conclusion is based on having been exposed to her paramour's handwriting countless times. Without a lay witness with that kind of expertise, the government is obliged to offer the testimony of "experts" who have looked at, and studied handwriting for years. These are, essentially, "observational" experts, taxonomists—arguably qualified because they have seen so many examples over so long. It is not traditional, experimental science, to be sure, but Kumho's gloss on *Daubert* suggests this is not necessary. I conclude that Harrison can testify to the ways in which she has found Hines' known handwriting similar to or dissimilar from the handwriting of the robbery note; part 1 of her testimony.

Part 2 of the Harrison testimony is, however, problematic. There is no data that suggests that handwriting analysts can say, like DNA experts, that this person is "the" author of the document. There are no meaningful, and accepted validity studies in the field. No one has shown me Harrison's error rate, the times she has been right, and the times she has been wrong.

**There is no academic field known as handwriting analysis. This is a "field" that has little efficacy outside of a courtroom. There are no peer reviews of it. Nor can one compare the opinion reached by an examiner with a standard protocol subject to validity testing, since there are no recognized standards. There is no agreement as to how many similarities it takes to declare a match, or how many differences it takes to rule it out.**

\* \* \*

[T]he issue here is not only the validity and reliability of the expert testimony, but its validity and reliability in the context of this lay proceeding. Harrison's account of what is similar or not similar in the handwriting of Hines and the robber can be understood and evaluated by the jury. The witness can be cross examined, as she was, about why this difference was not considered consequential, while this difference was, and the jury can draw their own conclusions. This is not rocket science, or higher math. [footnote]

> [footnote] ... I am persuaded for now that the testimony involves more than just identifying what is similar and what is different in the same way a lay person would. It involves taking the next step—which this or that similarity matters, that it equals a general pattern. Presumably, the expert is helped in drawing general patterns by the numbers of exemplars she has seen, just like the spouse identifies the husband's handwriting because she has seen it numbers of times.

\* \* \*

The Court faced a similar issue in *United States v. McVeigh,* ...:

> The problem with ... handwriting is that there is no testing of the— no verification-type testing of these opinion results; and in addition, there has never been within the discipline of people who practice this skill—there has never been any agreement on how to express the results. There is no standardized nomenclature, you know.

> Therefore, it seems to me that we should draw the distinction between somebody getting on the stand and saying 'Yeah, written by the same person,' or 'no, not written by the same person,' vs. 'these are the similarities or these are the dissimilarities'; and the jury can decide.

**I find Harrison's testimony meets Fed.R.Evid. 702's requirements to the extent that she restricts her testimony to similarities or dissimilarities between the known exemplars and the robbery note. However, she may not render an ultimate conclusion on who penned the unknown writing.**

\* \* \*

This solution might be an ingenious compromise by courts that are unwilling to apply the strict *Daubert* standards. "But their solution may be, at root, another attempt to evade the difficult question of whether handwriting experts offer genuine expertise."[43]

---

43. Jennifer L. Mnookin, *Comment: Scripting Expertise: The History of Handwriting Identification Evidence and the Judicial Construction of Reliability,* 87 Va. L. Rev 1723, 1838 (December 2001).

In addition, one court said that the fact that handwriting has been accepted for years as "generally accepted" does not mean that it should be generally accepted now.[44]

# Does Scholarly Disagreement Show Lack of General Acceptance?

Although the court in *Prime* may be right that there has been little challenge among examiners themselves, a few professors have engaged in a long-standing debate about the validity of handwriting examination. Three law school professors, D. Michael Risinger, Mark P. Denbeaux, and Michael J. Saks, have publicly questioned[45] the opinion that handwriting analysis is valid with a fellow professor, Andre Moenssens. Moenssens has defended handwriting analysis as valid under "Osbornian" principles of identification and has referred to the Kam studies as support for their reliability.

Moenssens has argued that using the following procedures would ensure reliability.[46]

- Accepted processes are stated in a professional literature.
- There are professional societies and associations to train and provide further education to examiners.
- Required courses of study and training.
- Education is supervised by prominent professionals in the discipline.
- A program of clinical experience supervised by such professionals.
- Any expert must show aptitude and proficiency by passing an examination board.
- The opposing party can retest the same materials with its own expert.

Risinger and his colleagues challenge the conclusion that handwriting analysis is "science," and give their definition as follows:

> Science requires standardization of the conditions.... and a formal analytical system for their organization. A central condition that must be present is theoretical reproducibility of observation (two observers in the same position could perceive the same thing) with strong favor given to reports of observations that can be practically repeated by multiple observers ...

> A scientific hypothesis is a statement about inter-relationships between items or categories that is formulated in such a way that it can be subjected to empirical testing ...

> ... handwriting identification ... doesn't even make it into the category of "science" in any tenable modern sense.... To apply the label "science" to the enterprise in general or to the practice of individual practitioners in particular would deprive the term of any defensible meaning.[47]

---

44. *Saelee*, 162 F. Supp 2d. at 1105.
45. D. Michael Risinger, Mark P. Denbeaux, and Michael J. Saks, *Brave New "Post-World"—A Reply to Professor Moenssens*, 29 Seton Hall L. Rev. 405 (1998).
46. *Id.* at 444.
47. *Id.* at 440–441.

Risinger and his colleagues maintain that Moenssens' standards will not screen out unreliable experts because all the "tests" would be supervised and conducted within the handwriting community itself—a community with a vested interest in ensuring that the field be accepted.

## Will the Courts of the Future Insist on All of the *Daubert* Factors?

The dissent in the *Crisp* case from the 4th Circuit and the majority opinion in the *Prime* case from the 9th Circuit each applied the *Daubert* factors to handwriting analysis and came to opposite conclusions. At present, most courts that use *Daubert* are continuing to admit handwriting experts, at least if the expert is experienced and can articulate his process of examination. Some restrict the expert testimony to a comparison of samples without an opinion about authorship. However, a scholarly debate continues to rage as to whether the reliability of handwriting analysis should be proved by independent scientists, rather than the document examiners themselves. This was the same argument made about fingerprint comparison in the *Plaza* cases. The argument that "generally accepted" is not the same as "generally admitted" will doubtless continue to be raised in handwriting cases.

# Will Computer Handwriting Analysis Meet the *Daubert* Test?

The primary objections to handwriting analysis are that its scientific hypotheses have not been tested, that is, no one can prove what characteristics of handwriting are unique, either individually or in combination, or what number of characteristics could positively identify a writer. That may change with the advent of computer technology that can develop an objective set of characteristics to review and a large enough number of characteristics so that conclusions based on probability analysis could be an reliable as DNA analysis.

In 1999, the National Institute of Justice funded a project to determine if computers could prove, first, that handwriting is unique and second, that a sample of handwriting could be identified based on a computer program search of exemplars provided by a writer.

The results of the study were published in the Journal of Forensic Science in 2002.[48] The study included three copies of an identical handwriting sample from each of approximately 1,500 writers, randomly selected among gender, age and ethnicity. The writing sample was a short letter to a doctor that incorporated 156 words, each letter of the alphabet at least once in each of upper and lower case, punctuation, all ten numerals and distinctive letter and number combinations.

The study examined both variations within the three samples for each writer (within-writer variance) and variations among all the writers (between-writer variance).

---

48. Sargur N. Srihari, Sung-Hyuk Cha, Hina Arora and Sangjik Lee, *Individuality of Handwriting*, Journal of Forensic Sciences, July 2002, available at www.cedar.buffalo.edu/publications.

The study examined 11 "macro features," which are listed below correlated with the terminology used in conventional handwriting analysis:

| Terminology from HW Analysis | Macro-Feature |
|---|---|
| pen pressure | 1. entropy of grey values |
| | 2. grey-level threshold |
| | 3. number of black pixels |
| writing movement | 4. number of interior contours |
| | 5. number of exterior curves |
| stroke formation | 6. number of vertical slopes |
| | 7. number of horizontal slopes |
| | 8. number of negative slopes |
| | 9. number of positive slopes |
| slant | 10. slant |
| word proportion | 11. height |

The computer study also used certain "micro-features," such as gradient, structural and concavity, all of which are based on the individual shape of letters. Cursive writing, for example, would have a greater number of interior contours and fewer exterior contours, whereas the opposite would be true for hand printing.

According to the authors, "in order to validate individuality among $n$ writers, we would have to determine whether the samples form $n$ distinct clusters, where samples of the same writer belong to the same cluster and samples of different writers belong to different clusters." The article reports: "Taking an approach that the results are statistically inferable over the entire population of the U.S., we were able to validate handwriting individuality with 95% confidence."[49]

In addition, the authors concluded that their software could determine the writer of a questioned document. The authors also analyzed the data to determine if they could identify the writer of the three samples based on their proximity in the criteria evaluated to each other. The prototype consisted of all of the exemplars written by all subjects, except for one exemplar removed from the set to "match." They report: "using character-level features of all eight characters of the word 'referred' in the exemplar, the correct writer was identified in 99% of the cases when all possible pairs of writers were considered. When there are five possible writers, the writer of the test document is correctly assigned with a 98% probability."

"Based on a few macro-features that capture global attributes from a handwritten document and micro-features at the character level from a few characters, we were able to establish with a 98% confidence that a writer can be identified." The computer screen below shows the results of analyzing the sample with the Cedar-Fox system.

The authors also attempted to determine whether two documents were written by the same writer. This process involved evaluating both within writer and between-writer distances. The verification accuracy was about 96%

The authors have marketed their system under the name Cedar-Fox. It has been used by law enforcement on a limited basis. As of this writing, no handwriting testimony based on the system has yet been introduced in court or evaluated judicially for reliability.

---

49. *Id.* at 16.

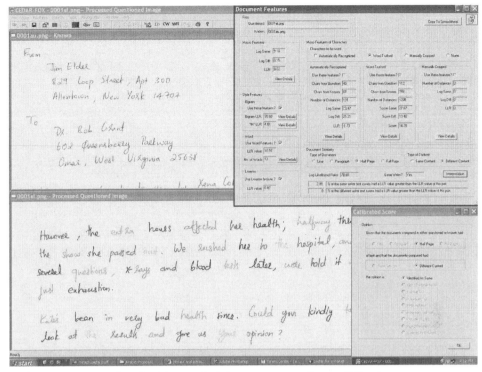

*Cedar-Fox computer handwriting analysis image, courtesy Sargur Srihari*

# Ransom Notes — From Lindbergh to JonBenet — Has Anything Changed?

In 1935, Bruno Richard Hauptmann was convicted of one of the most notorious kidnapping-murders in history. He was accused of climbing up a ladder at the home of Charles A. Lindbergh, the famous aviator, and kidnapping his almost two-year-old boy. On the window sill was a letter demanding a $50,000 ransom and referring to later instructions to come. The note said:

Dear Sir!

Have 50.000$ redy 25.000$ in 20$ bills 15.000in 10$ bills and 10.000$ in 5$ bills. After 2–4 days we will inform you were to deliver the Mony.

We warn you for making anyding public or for notify the polise the child is in gute care.

Idication for all letters are singnature and 3 holes.

The "signature" was two interlocking circles. The area within the overlap was solid red. The rest of the circles were outlined in blue. Three square holes pierced the symbol in a horizontal line.[50]

---

50. Dr. Henry Lee and Dr. Jerry Labriola, *Famous Crimes Revisited — From Sacco-Vanzetti to O.J. Simpson,* StrongBooks, 2001, at 114.

The note led to negotiations, and a number of additional notes. Hauptmann was captured at the meeting point for the supposed payoff. Eventually, it was determined that the baby died shortly after the kidnapping.

The nation followed the ordeal through the news. At the trial, Albert S. Osborne, the famous author of the text referred to by every handwriting expert, testified that the notes were written by Hauptmann. He stated that his conclusion was "irresistible, unanswerable and overwhelming."[51] The testimony against Hauptmann included three experts who testified he wrote the kidnapping notes, one of whom said the address of the package used to send the baby's sleeping suit was Hauptmann's. Hauptmann called John Trendley, a documents examiner from St. Louis, who said he did not believe Hauptmann wrote the ransom notes.

Hauptmann appealed his sentence, arguing, among other things, that the trial court gave a prejudicial instruction on the handwriting issue by emphasizing Osborne's testimony:

> A very important question in the case is, did the defendant, Hauptmann, write the original ransom note found on the window sill, and the other ransom notes which followed? Numerous experts in handwriting have testified, after exhaustive examination of the ransom letters, and comparison with the genuine writing of the defendant, that the defendant Hauptmann wrote every one of the ransom notes, and Mr. Osborne, Senior, said that the conclusion was irresistible, unanswerable and overwhelming. On the other hand, the defendant denies that he wrote them, and a handwriting expert, called by him, so testified. And so the fact becomes one for your determination. The weight of the evidence to prove the genuineness of handwriting is wholly for the jury."[52]

Hauptmann also appealed on the ground that the trial court failed to give three jury instructions that he had proposed, which instructions stated that handwriting testimony was "proof of low degree," that it was "most unsatisfactory, very inconclusive, most unreliable and of the lowest probative force," and that a jury was not bound to accept an expert opinion. The court rejected the appeal. It said that although a judge in an earlier decision had referred to handwriting experts as of "a low order of testimony," the statement was not complete without the entire sentence, which defendant had not asked to charge:

> "Handwriting is an art concerning which correctness of opinion is susceptible of demonstration ... Without such demonstration the opinion of an expert in handwriting is a low order of testimony."
>
> *State v. Hauptmann*

> Handwriting is an art concerning which correctness of opinion is susceptible of demonstration, and I am fully convinced that the value of the opinion of every handwriting expert as evidence must depend upon the clearness with which the expert demonstrates its correctness ... Without such demonstration the opinion of an expert in handwriting is a low order of testimony."[53]

"Some authors and advocates argue that our legal system victimized Bruno Hauptmann because of the admission of questionable evidence: expert handwriting testimony. This controversy extends far beyond this infamous case, reaching the acade-

51. *State v. Hauptmann*, 115 N.J.L. 412, 180 A. 809 (Ct.App. N.J. 1935).
52. *Id.* at 432, 822.
53. *Id.* at 434, 823.

mic and judicial forum."[54] In reviewing a new book called "Using Great Cases to Think About the Criminal Justice System," the authors note that Hauptmann could not afford to hire a lawyer and his lead defense was paid by the Hearst newspapers, which stood to profit handsomely from the public's purchase of its papers.[55] Hauptmann's appeal was denied and he was executed on April 3, 1936. His wife continued to declare that he was innocent.

In the year 2000, further evidence came to light casting doubt on whether Hauptmann had been guilty of the kidnapping. One of the claims was that "a document examiner for the U.S. Army and Secret Service" had concluded that Hauptmann was not the author of the ransom notes.[56]

## Who Wrote the JonBenet Ramsey Ransom Note?

JonBenet Ramsey was a six-year old found murdered on December 26, 1996 in her basement in Boulder, Colorado. The case, which as of this printing, has not been solved, became famous because of its bizarre circumstances, the charges that the police compromised the crime scene, and the attempts to determine who wrote the ransom note. The note was found by Patsy Ramsey, JonBenet's mother, on the kitchen steps in the early morning of December 26. Patsy called 911 just before 6 a.m. JonBenet's body was found nearly seven hours later in the basement by her father at 1 p.m.

The ransom note was handwritten in printing on paper from a pad found in the basement. The note was addressed to "Mr. Ramsey" and demanded $118,000 in ransom money. It was signed "Victory! S.B.T.C." The following is the text of the note:

Mr. Ramsey,

Listen carefully! We are a group of individuals that represent a small foreign faction. We respect your business but not the country that it serves. At this time we have your daughter in our possession. She is safe and unharmed and if you want her to see 1997, you must follow our instructions to the letter.

You will withdraw $118,000.00 from your account. $100,000 will be in $100 bills and the remaining $18,000 in $20 bills. Make sure that you bring an adequate size attaché to the bank. When you get home you will put the money in a brown paper bag. I will call you between 8 and 10 am tomorrow to instruct you on delivery. The delivery will be exhausting so I advise you to be rested. If we monitor you getting the money early, we might call you early to arrange an earlier delivery of the money and hence a earlier pickup of your daughter.

Any deviation of my instructions will result in the immediate execution of your daughter. You will also be denied her remains for proper burial. The two gentlemen watching over your daughter do not particularly like you so I advise you not to provoke them. Speaking to anyone about your situation, such as Police, F.B.I., etc., will result in your daughter being beheaded. If we

---

54. Simone Ling Francini, *Expert Handwriting Testimony: Is the Writing Really on the Wall?*, 11 Suffolk J. Trial & Appeal Adv. 99 (2006).

55. Jonathan L. Entin, *Book Review: Using Great Cases to Think about the Criminal Justice System*, 89 J. Crim. L. & Criminology 1141 (Spring 1999).

56. Jesse Leavenworth, *Questions Linger about 'Crime of the Century,'* The Hartford Courant, February 6, 2000.

catch you talking to a stray dog, she dies. If you alert bank authorities, she dies. If the money is in any way marked or tampered with, she dies. You will be scanned for electronic devices and if any are found, she dies. You can try to deceive us but be warned that we are familiar with Law enforcement countermeasures and tactics. You stand a 99% chance of killing your daughter if you try to out smart us. Follow our instructions and you stand a 100% chance of getting her back. You and your family are under constant scrutiny as well as the authorities. Don't try to grow a brain John. You are not the only fat cat around so don't think that killing will be difficult. Don't underestimate us John. Use that good southern common sense of yours. It is up to you now John!

Victory!

S.B.T.C.

The immediate reaction to the ransom note was that it was a decoy to mislead the investigation. First, the note was three pages in length—far longer than required to state a ransom demand and of a length that would take considerable time to write. As it was written on paper found in the Ramsey home, the idea that an intruder would enter the home and write such a long note, risking detection, appeared ridiculous. The dollar amount was the same as Ramsey's year end bonus and it was much too small to indicate a real kidnapping. Authorities suspected that JonBenet had been murdered by a family member and the note was a ruse to make it look like a kidnapping gone bad.[57]

As the JonBenet case shows, document analysis can include both handwriting and the content of the writing itself. Examiners have pointed out that the ransom note contained word choice and phrasings that would be highly unusual in a real kidnapping. For example, the note says that two men are "watching over" Ramsey's daughter. This sounded more like language from the Bible than a kidnapper, in the opinion of one author. He also noted that the phrase "and hence a earlier pickup of your daughter," used a word that is quite uncommon—hence. Yet the Ramsey's Christmas message at church used the word "hence."[58]

Police hired four handwriting experts and the Ramseys hired two. All of them concluded that Patsy Ramsey did not write the note, with a likelihood ranging from 4 to 4.5 out of 5 that she was excluded as the writer:

> Both parties agree that the Ransom Note is not an ideal specimen for handwriting analysis, primarily due to the type of writing instrument, a broad fiber-tip pen, used to draft the note. This type of pen distorts and masks fine details to an extent not achievable by other types of pen, as for example a ball point pen.

> In addition, the stroke direction used to construct certain letters and subtle hand printing features, such as hesitations and pen lifts, are difficult to ascertain because of the pen used in the Ransom Note. Finally, the handwriting in the original Ransom Note showed consistency throughout the entire writing.

> One of the most common means to disguise one's handwriting is to attempt to make the script erratic throughout the text. In sum, for the above reasons,

---

57. Mark McClish, *Statement Analysis, JonBenet Ramsey Ransom Note,* http://www.statementanalysis.com/ramseynote.

58. *Id.*

the Ransom Note is not an ideal specimen for handwriting analysis. Nevertheless, the writer does not appear to have been trying to disguise his or her handwriting.[59]

The handwriting note became an issue in a lawsuit filed by Robert Wolf against John and Patsy Ramsey. Wolf was a local journalist who was investigated for a short time based on information from his girlfriend that he had been acting suspiciously. The Ramseys wrote a book and appeared on TV, denying their involvement in the murder and commenting that Wolf had been investigated as a suspect. Wolf then sued for libel stating that he had been falsely accused of murder. In order to win his case, Wolf needed to show that the Ramsey's had acted with "actual malice" in accusing him as a suspect. The term actual malice in libel law means that the person making the statement knew it was untrue. The only way the Ramseys could know that Wolf was not the murderer was if one of them was in fact the murderer. Therefore, whether John or Patsy Ramsey wrote the ransom note, and knew that Wolf was not the murderer, was critical to Wolf's lawsuit.

Wolf claimed that Patsy Ramsey killed JonBenet in a fit of anger, possibly for wetting the bed, and smashed her head against the bathroom floor or tub. He then alleged that Patsy set up a cover-up to look like an intruder had killed JonBenet and wrote the ransom note. Two handwriting experts testified for Wolf on a motion by the Ramseys to dismiss the case. Both concluded the ransom note was written by Patsy Ramsey. The court ruled the first expert, Cina Wong Epstein, was unqualified because she had not taken any courses or tests. The second expert, Gideon Epstein, failed to provide any methodology for his conclusions. He was allowed to point out differences and similarities, but was not permitted to give his opinion that Mrs. Ramsey wrote the notes. Below is the court's analysis of the handwriting expert testimony.

### Wolf v. Ramsey, 253 F. Supp. 2d 1323 (N.D. Ga. 2003)

Plaintiff ... asserts that his retained experts believe Mrs. Ramsey to be the author of the Ransom Note. Indeed, Gideon Epstein and Cina Wong, the handwriting experts proffered by plaintiff, opine that they are "100 percent certain" Mrs. Ramsey wrote the Ransom Note. In contrast to the experts relied upon by defendants and by the Boulder Police Department, however, neither of these experts have ever seen or examined the original Ransom Note.

* * *

Defendants' experts base their conclusion that Mrs. Ramsey is not the author of the Ransom Note on the "numerous significant dissimilarities" between the individual characteristics of Mrs. Ramsey's hand printing and of that used in the Ransom Note. For example, defendant asserts Mrs. Ramsey's written letter "u" consistently differs from the way the same letter is written throughout the Ransom Note. Plaintiff's experts respond that this variation may be due to a conscious effort by Mrs. Ramsey to change her handwriting or to her heightened stress level.

In support of their conclusion that Mrs. Ramsey authored the Ransom Note, plaintiff's experts assert that there are similarities between letters found in the Ransom Note and exemplars and that the note contains proof-reader marks of

---

59. *Wolf v. Ramsey*, 253 F. Supp. 2d 1323, 1334 (N.D. Ga. 2003).

the kind often used by newspaper reporters and journalists. Plaintiff also notes that Mrs. Ramsey was a journalism major in college.

Other experts believe the Ransom Note may have been authored by other people. In addition to Mrs. Ramsey, there were other individuals "under suspicion" who had their handwriting analyzed and who were not eliminated as the possible author of the Ransom Note. For example, forensic document examiner Lloyd Cunningham cannot eliminate plaintiff as the author of the Ransom Note. Plaintiff's ex-girlfriend has also testified that she was "struck by how the handwriting in the note resembled [plaintiff's] own handwriting" and believes that he is the note's author.

\* \* \*

Defendants argue that the opinions of plaintiffs' expert should not be admitted because the field of forensic document examination is not sufficiently reliable. In their Brief in Support of the Motion in Limine, defendants argue that the "science" of handwriting analysis does not meet the reliability standards of Rule 702: as the theoretical bases underlying this science have never been tested; error rates are neither known nor measured; and the field lacks both controlling standards and meaningful peer review.

In examining defendants' contention, the Court notes that both parties agree that the field of forensic document examination is premised on the assumption that no two persons' handwriting is exactly alike; instead, each person has a unique handwriting pattern that allows the person to be identified through a comparison of proper handwriting specimens. Forensic document examination involves the subjective analysis and assessment of writing characteristics found in a person's handwriting or hand printing style, by examination of subtle and minute qualities of movement such as pen lifts, shading, pressure and letter forms.

Handwriting identification is an inexact endeavor that "cannot boast absolute certainty in all cases." Two or more handwriting experts can reach different conclusions of authorship, even when examining the same questioned document and handwriting exemplars.

Forensic document examiners are generally trained through a "guild-type" apprenticeship process, in which supervised trainees study methods of document examination described by the field's leading texts. The only recognized organization for accrediting forensic document examiners is the American Board of Forensic Document Examiners .

\* \* \*

The most reliable method of forensic document examination occurs when an examiner compares both historical writings and requests exemplars to the questioned document.

The recognized method for forensic document analysis occurs in several important steps. First, the expert determines whether a questioned document contains a sufficient amount of writing and enough individual characteristics to permit identification. After determining that the questioned document is identifiable, the expert examines the submitted handwriting specimens in the same manner. If both the questioned document and the specimens contain sufficient identifiable characteristics, then the expert compares those characteristics often through the use of a chart.

For example, the slant of the writing, the shapes of the letters, the letter connections, the height of the letters, the spacing between letters, the spacing between words, the "I" dots and "t" crosses are aspects of handwriting that can be used for comparison. Next, the expert weighs the evidence, considering both the similarities and the differences of handwriting, and determines whether or not there is a match.

> "Ignoring differences between characteristics is a frequent cause of error in handwriting identification." *Wolf v. Ramsey*

Ignoring differences between characteristics is a frequent cause of error in handwriting identification. Similarly, dismissing differences as merely the product of intentional disguise is another common mistake made in the analysis. In addition, an examiner should not know the identity of the comparators and should consult more than one comparator to increase the reliability of his or her analysis.

In addition to a recognized methodology, there are some accepted standards that should be employed when engaging in handwriting analysis. One standard is that the genuineness of the historical writing or request [sic] exemplar must be verified; that is, the forensic document examiner should ensure the purported author is the true and historical writing is indeed the author. [sic] In addition, any differences between the questioned document and the comparison writings are generally considered to be more significant than are similarities, when attempting to determine whether someone is the author of a questioned document.

The reason that similarity, by itself, is not dispositive is because most people are taught handwriting as children from the same or similar "notebook styles" and, therefore, many people will share common handwriting characteristics called "class characteristics."

The existence of even one consistent fundamental difference between writings, however, has historically been viewed as a legitimate basis for concluding that two writings were not produced by the same person. Finally, it is generally accepted that consistent characteristics present over the course of a long writing should be viewed as genuine characteristics of the author's handwriting, and not the product of an attempt to disguise.

\* \* \*

The Reliability of Epstein's Proffered Testimony.

Although the Court has concluded, as a general matter, that Epstein is qualified to testify as a forensic documents examiner, it must still determine the parameters of his expertise with regard to the opinions he seeks to offer. Specifically, Epstein claims that he can state, with absolute certainty, that Mrs. Ramsey is the author of the Ransom Note. The Court, as gatekeeper, must therefore examine the methodology that he puts forward in support of such a categorical conclusion. First, Epstein states that he used the standard methodology of forensic document examiners when assessing the Ransom Note and Mrs. Ramsey's writing samples.

He initially determined that he had a sufficient amount of handwriting by Mrs. Ramsey to allow an examination. He then proceeded to examine the submitted materials for similarities and dissimilarities. After conducting the examination, he then determined that the original writing and the exemplars matched to a "one hundred percent" degree of certainty. Finally, he consulted other forensic document analysts who approved of his methodology and result.

Defendants move to exclude the testimony of Epstein because they assert that the methodology he employed does not meet the accepted standards of handwriting analysts. In particular, defendants argue that Epstein's opinions are not reliable because he did not consult the original Ransom Note, original handwriting exemplars of Mrs. Ramsey, nor original course-of-business writings of Mrs. Ramsey.

\* \* \*

Epstein's failure to consult the originals should go to the weight of his testimony, but should not bar its admission, completely. To hold otherwise could create a perverse incentive for individuals not to allow an opponent access to original documents, in order to render those expert's opinions inadmissible.

In short, the Court is satisfied as to Epstein's ability to testify concerning perceived similarities and differences in Mrs. Ramsey's known handwriting and the Ransom Note. Any criticism of Epstein's analysis by defendants goes to the weight of his testimony.

Of more concern to the Court, however, is the reliability of Epstein's ultimate conclusion concerning the identity of the writer of the Note. As noted, Epstein claims that he is "100 percent certain that Patsy Ramsey wrote the Ransom Note," and in his professional opinion "there is absolutely no doubt she is the author."

Nowhere in the submissions provided by plaintiffs is there any attempt to show by what methodology Mr. Epstein reaches a conclusion of absolute certainty that a given person is, in fact, the writer of a questioned document. Defendants persuasively argue that Epstein was unable to identify any unique characteristics of Mrs. Ramsey's handwriting that were mimicked in the Ransom Note. Instead, Epstein bases his conclusion on perceived similarities between the two. Yet, as noted by defendants, Epstein never indicates how many similarities or what kind of similarities are required before he can reach absolute certainty, 50% certainty, or no certainty, at all.

> "Epstein never indicates how many similarities or what kind of similarities are required before he can reach absolute certainty, 50% certainty, or no certainty, at all."
> *Wolf v. Ramsey*

Further, as defendants also note, whenever encountering any differences between the known writing of Mrs. Ramsey and the Ransom Note, Epstein finds refuge in the explanation that Mrs. Ramsey must have been trying to disguise her handwriting.

While it is, of course, possible that differences between known writing and questioned documents are the result of a known writer's efforts to disguise her handwriting, it is just as plausible that the differences can occur because the known writer is not the author of the questioned matter. On that issue, Epstein offers no hint of the methodology that he employs to distinguish between disguised writing and writing that is simply being provided by two different people.

The underlying notion behind *Daubert*, and all good science, is that a given premise or principle should be capable of being tested to determine whether the principle is, in fact, sound. Thus, if Epstein indicated, for example, that whenever a writer of known material has x number of similarities, there is a given probability that the writer wrote the note—and if this methodology had been tested by reliable means in the past—then Epstein would have shown reliability in the methodology that he used to reach a determination of the likelihood of his conclusion.

As it is, however, Epstein's explanation for his conclusion seems to be little more than "Trust me; I'm an expert." *Daubert* case law has indicated that such an assertion, which seems to be based more on intuition than on scientific reasoning, is insufficient.

Accordingly, the Court concludes that while Epstein can properly assist the trier of fact by pointing out marked differences and unusual similarities between Mrs. Ramsey's writing and the Ransom Note, he has not demonstrated a methodology whereby he can draw a conclusion, to an absolute certainty, that a given writer wrote the Note.

In a bizarre coda to the dispute over who wrote the ransom note, police finally apprehended a suspect, John Mark Karr, in the fall of 2006. Karr had been obsessed with the JonBenet case and had made certain statements that he had been present at her death but that it had been an accident. In no time, a website appeared that compared Karr's handwriting from his high school yearbook to the ransom note, concluding "There is now no doubt that John Mark Karr wrote the JonBenet Ramsey ransom note. From the bottom kick on every 't' to the top loop of the 'a' to the concave of the semi-oval on the 'h', the handwriting samples match up almost perfectly."[60]

Karr's DNA was compared to the DNA samples found on JonBenet, and he was determined not to be a match.[61] The State of Colorado dropped all charges against Karr on March 12, 2007.[62] Clearly, Karr did not write the ransom note.

# Summary

The methods used to determine common authorship were developed by Albert S. Osbourne, Sr., in the early 1900s and have remained virtually unchanged. The examiner first views the suspected document and exemplars of the natural handwriting of the suspected author. If the examiner determines that he has enough writing to compare, he will first look for obvious differences, which might rule out the suspected author. Such differences include such "macro" features as line slant, pen pressure, and the like. If the suspect cannot be ruled out, the examiner will then proceed to examining "micro" features, such as the size and shape of particular letters. There is no set number of similarities that an examiner must find to determine a match.

Courts have admitted handwriting testimony for many years, but when confronted with the *Daubert* tests, a few courts have determined that handwriting identification is not reliable. Experts cannot state which characteristics are most important, nor can they state that if a writer of a known document has x number of similarities, there is a given probability that the writer wrote the questioned document. Courts that follow the general acceptance test frequently admit handwriting testimony. Some courts that follow *Daubert*, permit the expert to point out similarities and differences to the jury, but not give an opinion as to authorship.

---

60. http://www.powerwurks.com/john_mark_karr_handwriting.php.
61. *No DNA match, no JonBenet Charges*, CNN.com, March 17, 2007.
62. *People v. Karr*, No. 2006 CR 1244, People's Motion to Quash Arrest Warrant.

Handwriting experts have analyzed ransom notes in at least two highly publicized cases: the kidnapping and murder of the son of John Lindbergh and the murder of JonBenet Ramsey. Questions still remain as to whether Bernard Hauptmann really wrote the Lindbergh baby ransom note. Handwriting experts have disagreed as to whether John or Patsy Ramsey wrote the note found at the time of their daughter's death, but a content analysis of the style and words of the note raises many questions as to whether it was part of a hoax. The court in a libel case against Patsy Ramsey evaluated whether handwriting expert testimony met the *Daubert* test, and concluded that the methodology was not reliable enough to permit an expert to give his opinion about authorship. The most he could do was point out similarities and differences to the jury.

All this may change with the advent of computer programs to compare questioned documents. One computer system has determined that handwriting is unique, by looking for a certain number of macro and micro features. In essence, it is similar to DNA testing in that it does not look at all possible match points, but the sample it examines is large enough to make probability estimates of common authorship. The system has also demonstrated the ability to determine the writer of an unknown document.

Handwriting may well be a type of forensic science that does not meet *Daubert* but that will lead to a form of computer analysis that will meet the tests in the near future.

# Discussion Questions

1. What are the scientific hypotheses of handwriting analysis? Have any of these hypotheses been proved?

2. When was Osborne's *Questioned Documents* published and why do you think it is still viewed as an authority today?

3. Name at least three different purposes for which handwriting analysis can be used.

4. What are at least two assumptions in handwriting analysis?

5. What are the similarities and differences between fingerprint and handwriting evidence?

6. What are the subjective elements of handwriting analysis?

7. What are the main reasons why courts have admitted handwriting testimony?

8. How does the computer evaluating methodology developed by Cedar-Fox change your views about the scientific validity of handwriting comparison?

9. What effect did the *Kuhmo* case have on whether a *Daubert* hearing is required for handwriting testimony?

10. Does the disagreement among scholars demonstrate that handwriting analysis is not generally accepted?

11. Is the compromise strategy of allowing the expert to point out similarities and differences, but not give an opinion a good idea? Refer to the opinion in *United States v. Hines* in your answer.

12. Do you agree with the court in *United States v. Prime* that handwriting analysis meets *Daubert? Why or why not?*

13. How would you expect computer technologies such as that developed by Cedar-Fox to change handwriting analysis and admissibility?

14. What are the similarities and differences between the analysis of the ransom notes in the *Hauptmann* and *Joneses Ramsey* cases? How do these cases show what has changed in handwriting analysis from 1930 to today?

# Chapter 12

# Polygraph Testimony

## Overview

Polygraph has been one of the longest-running types of forensic evidence. The court cases about admitting polygraph are almost always about whether a defendant can introduce a polygraph that supports his innocence. Polygraph was rejected in 1923 in the *Frye* case because it was held not to be "generally accepted." This case set the standard for forensic expert testimony for many years and is still the test in some states, including New York.

A second well-known forensics case also dealt with polygraph—*State v. Porter* in Connecticut. That case examined polygraph more carefully and seemed to be persuaded that polygraph might meet the *Daubert* tests. However, the court decided to maintain its rule that polygraph is inadmissible in court because of the possible prejudice to the defendant. In essence, the court feared that a jury, confronted with scientific evidence that proved the defendant told the truth when he said he had no involvement in the arson, would substitute the polygraph for the jury's own judgment instead of weighing all of the other facts.

Polygraph has definitely improved since the *Frye* case. Today, the combination of a well-trained examiner and computer technology to evaluate the results gives more assurance of reliability. However, the major concerns are error rates and the possibility that suspects can change the polygraph reading by using techniques called countermeasures.

New Mexico is the one state that admits polygraph and it has adopted strict rules that must be followed. The federal courts do not ban polygraph *per se*, or automatically, but most cases reject it unless both parties have agreed in advance that the test results will be admissible.

Newer technologies involving measuring brain wave response to questions similar to polygraph show real promise for identifying truth or deception, while removing concerns about countermeasures.

## Chapter Objectives

Based on this chapter, students will be able to:

1. Explain the process of polygraph and how it works.
2. Distinguish between "control questions" and "relevant questions."

3.  Evaluate data involving the reliability of polygraph and understand the difference between a false positive and a false negative.

4.  Identify uses outside of the court system where polygraph is accepted as valid.

5.  Describe the legal issues in court opinions about whether polygraph should be accepted.

6.  Explain the legal argument that admitting polygraph would deprive the jury of its right as the finder of fact.

7.  Explain the defense argument that admitting polygraph is part of the U.S. Constitutional rights to present a defense.

8.  Distinguish between polygraph and fMRI.

# The History of Polygraph in Court

> Inadmissible *per se* means that polygraph is inadmissible as a matter of law, without proof by the objecting party.

The landmark *Frye* case in 1923 dealt with the admissibility of an early version of the polygraph. At that point, the Supreme Court decided that polygraph was not "generally accepted" by scientists and therefore should not be admitted.[1] Over eighty years later, the state of Connecticut adopted the *Daubert* test in a case that also involved the admissibility of polygraph— *State v. Porter.* In *Porter*, the defendant wanted to introduce polygraph testimony to prove that he was not lying when he said he had no involvement in an arson. Connecticut had a per se rule against admitting polygraph, which means that polygraph was not admissible for any purpose as a matter of law. Porter tried to change this rule by presenting evidence that polygraph was reliable. The court actually agreed that polygraph probably would meet the standards for reliability. Despite its error rate, the court felt that juries could weigh this issue for themselves. However, the court refused to change the rule of *per se* inadmissibility because it held that the prejudicial effect of testimony on the issue of whether the defendant was lying or telling the truth was greater than its probative value.

> Stipulation. A formal agreement on the record between counsel for both sides agreeing to facts, terms or conditions at trial.

Polygraph is inadmissible in criminal trials in most states. Those states that make exceptions generally do so in only where the prosecution and defense stipulate, or agree, that the test will be admissible before the defendant takes the test.

The major change made by the court in *Daubert* was to state that general acceptance was only one criterion for admission. An expert could testify about a science that was not generally accepted so long as it met other tests for reliability, the type of tests that govern science generally. On its face, this loosened the standard for admissibility— more science rather than less should have been admissible after *Daubert*. Even if not all scientists agree that polygraph is a valid method to assess truthfulness, if polygraph has

---

1. *Frye v. United States*, 293 F. 1013 (Ct. App. D. C. 1923).

been subjected to scientific inquiry and reliability and error rate can be quantified, then presumably it would be admissible. The jury could decide if the error rate was too high, or if the defendant had been able to manipulate the results in some way, but the judge would not be able to keep the jury from hearing the testimony. Therefore, even if scientists did not generally agree that polygraph was reliable, it could be admitted if it passed the other tests designed to show reliability. This has not been the case. Most courts continue to hold that it is not generally accepted. Was this intended by the *Daubert* decision?

Why is polygraph viewed as reliable in government employment screenings, police investigations, parole monitoring, FBI work and a variety of other applications,[2] but not in criminal trials?

# What Is a Polygraph?

A polygraph, also called a "lie detector," is a graph developed by asking a subject a series of questions and measuring certain body changes in heart rate, blood pressure, sweat glands, and breathing. The American Polygraph Association (APA) describes it as: "a scientific test that collects physiological data from a person for the purpose of detecting reactions associated with dishonesty."[3] The polygraph instrument collects physiological data from at least three systems in the human body. Conventional rubber tubes that are placed over the examinee's chest and abdominal area will record respiratory activity. Two small metal plates, attached to the fingers, will record sweat activity, and a blood pressure cuff, or similar device, will record cardiovascular activities.

## Scientific Hypothesis of Polygraph

The polygraph is based on the following hypothesis:

> The polygraph technique is based on the premise that an individual's conscious attempt to deceive engenders various involuntary physiological changes due to an acute reaction in the sympathesis parts of the autonomic nervous system.[4]

> Hypothesis: a conscious attempt to deceive results in involuntary physiological changes that can be measured by the polygraph.

The *Porter* case contains an excellent explanation of exactly how polygraph works:

**State v. Porter, 241 Conn. 57, 698 A.2d 739 (1996)**

\* \* \*

Modern polygraph theory rests on two assumptions:

(1) there is a regular relationship between deception and certain emotional states; and

(2) there is a regular relationship between those emotional states and certain physiological changes in the body that can be measured and recorded.

---

2. www.polygraph.org/Press/FAQ.htm.
3. www.polygraph.org/Press/GAQ.htm.
4. *United States v. Alexander*, 526 F.2d 161 (8th Cir. 1975).

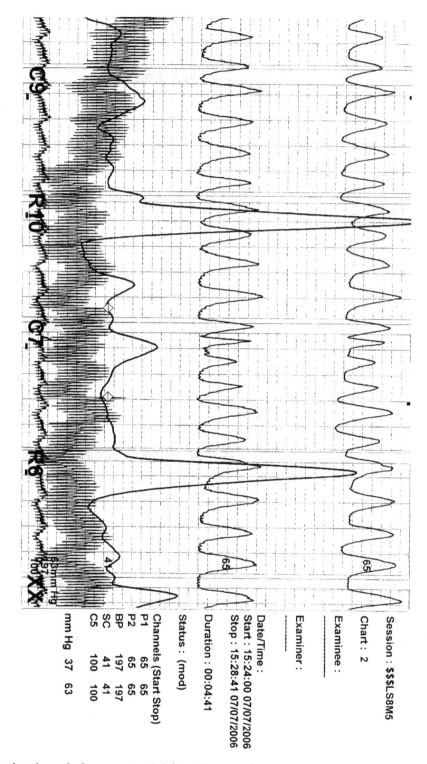

*Sample polygraph chart, courtesy Leighton Hammond*

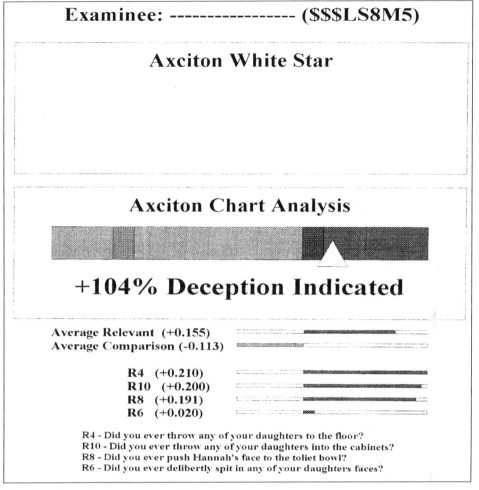

*Sample polygraph report, courtesy Leighton Hammond*

These physiological changes include fluctuations in heart rate and blood pressure, rate of breathing, and flow of electrical current through the body, and they are measured by a cardiosphygmograph, a pneumograph and a galvanometer, respectively. These instruments, bundled together, form the basis of most modern polygraphs.

There is no question that a high quality polygraph is capable of accurately measuring the relevant physical characteristics. Even polygraph advocates, however, acknowledge that "no known physiological response or pattern of responses is unique to deception."

Indeed, "there is no reason to believe that lying produces distinctive physiological changes that characterize it and only it.... There is no set of responses—physiological or otherwise—that humans omit only when lying or that they produce only when telling the truth.... No doubt when we tell a lie many of us experience an inner turmoil, but we experience similar turmoil when we are falsely accused of a crime, when we are anxious about having to defend ourselves against accusations, when we are questioned about sensitive topics—and, for that matter, when we are elated or otherwise emotionally stirred."

Thus, while a polygraph machine can accurately gauge a subject's physiological profile, it cannot, on its own, determine the nature of the underlying psychological profile. "The instrument cannot itself detect deception."

The polygraph examiner, therefore, is responsible for transforming the output of a polygraph machine from physiological data into an assessment of truth or deception. This mission actually involves two separate tasks. First, the examiner must design and implement a polygraph test in such a way that the physiological data produced is properly linked to a subject's deceptiveness, and not just to his nervousness or other unrelated emotional responses. Second, even if the data produced is linked to a subject's deception, the examiner must interpret the data, that is, grade the test, correctly.

> The polygraph instrument measures the fear of detection rather than deception *per se.*

The "control question test" is the polygraph method most commonly used in criminal cases to link physiological responses to deception. The control question test is based on the theory that fear of detection causes psychological stress. Under that test, therefore, the "polygraph instrument is measuring the fear of detection rather than deception per se."

In the control question test procedure, the polygrapher first conducts a pretest interview with the subject wherein the accuracy and reliability of the polygraph are emphasized. This is done to aggravate the deceptive subject's fear of detection while calming the innocent subject, which is crucial given that the test's efficacy is based entirely on the subject's emotional state.

> There are three categories of questions: neutral; relevant; and control.

All exam questions are then reviewed with the subject, in order to minimize the impact of surprise on the test results and to ensure that the subject understands the questions. The actual control question test consists of a sequence of ten to twelve questions, repeated several times. There are three categories of questions: neutral; relevant; and control. All questions are formulated by the polygrapher conducting the examination based on a review of the facts of the case.

A neutral question is entirely nonconfrontational and is designed to allow the polygrapher to get a baseline reading on the subject's physiological responses. A neutral question addresses a subject's name, age, address, or similar topic.

A relevant question is accusatory and directed specifically at the subject under investigation. "For example, in an assault investigation, a relevant question might be: 'On May 1, 1986, did you strike Mr. Jones (the alleged victim) with any part of your body?'"

> The control question is a general question designed to get the subject to lie.

A control question concerns "an act of wrongdoing of the same general nature as the main incident under investigation," and is designed to be "one to which the subject, in all probability, will lie or to which his answer will be of dubious validity in his own mind." Control questions "cover many years in the prior life of the subject and are deliberately vague. Almost anyone would have difficulty answering them truthfully with a simple 'No.'"

In an assault case, a control question might be: "Did you ever want to see anyone harmed?" Although few people honestly could deny these control questions categorically, they are "presented to the subject in a manner designed to lead him to believe that admissions would negatively influence the examiner's opinion and that strong reactions to those questions during the test would produce a deceptive result."

The theory behind the control question test is that "the truthful person will respond more to the control questions than to the relevant questions because they represent a greater threat to that person. For the same reason the deceptive person will respond more to the relevant questions than to the control questions."

Thus, in order for the test to work properly, both truthful and deceptive examinees must have particular mind sets during the exam. "The innocent examinee [must fear] that the polygraph examiner will pick up his deception [on the control question] and incorrectly conclude that he is also being deceptive about the relevant question." As a result, the innocent subject's physiological responses to the control question, stemming from this fear, will be greater than those to the relevant question, which the subject can answer honestly.

A guilty subject, however, will be more worried about having his crime and deception exposed by the relevant question than he is about any control question issues. Accordingly, his physiological responses—prompted by his fear of detection—will be greater with regard to the relevant question than to the control question.

Under the control question test, the absolute measure of the subject's physiological responses to each question is unimportant. For example, the mere fact that a subject has a strong response to a relevant question can simply be indicative of nervousness and does not, by itself, indicate deception. Instead, the polygrapher looks to the relative strength of the responses to the control and relevant questions in order to determine truth or deception. The art of the polygrapher lies in composing control and relevant questions that elicit the appropriate relative responses from truthful and deceitful parties.

> The polygraph scores the relative strength between the control and relevant questions.

A control question exam ordinarily pairs relevant and control questions with some neutral questions interspersed. For example, a typical progression would be:

1. (Neutral) Do you understand that I will ask only the questions we have discussed?

2. (Pseudo-Relevant) Regarding whether you took that ring, do you intend to answer all of the questions truthfully?

3. (Neutral) Do you live in the United States?

4. (Control) During the first twenty-four years of your life, did you ever take something that did not belong to you?

5. (Relevant) Did you take a ring from the Behavioral Sciences Building on July 1, 1985?

6. (Neutral) Is your name Joanne?

7. (Control) Between the ages of ten and twenty-four, did you ever do anything dishonest or illegal?

8. (Relevant) Did you take that diamond ring from a desk in the Behavioral Sciences Building on July 1?

9. (Neutral) Were you born in the month of February?

10. (Control) Before 1984 did you ever lie to get out of trouble or to cause a problem for someone else?

11. (Relevant) Were you in any way involved in the theft of that diamond ring from the Behavioral Sciences Building last July?"

The entire sequence is normally gone through three times, after which the examiner scores the result to attempt to reach a determination of truthfulness or deception.

The most common technique for scoring polygraph charts is pure numerical grading.... If an analysis of the first three charts produces inconclusive results, the examiner will often repeat the question sequence twice more. After that, however, further repetitions are generally considered meritless, as the subject will have become habituated to the test questions and, therefore, will no longer have sufficiently strong emotional responses for polygraph purposes.

* * *

There is, however, little standardization of polygraph test procedures. With the polygraph test, each administration of a control question test is necessarily different, with appropriate control and relevant questions chosen and formulated by each individual examiner. As a result, a battle of the experts over polygraph evidence cannot simply address whether "the" test was properly administered.

In the case of the control question test, for example, the experts will have to debate both whether the standardized control question test format was properly observed, and whether the particular, nonstandardized questions involved, as chosen by the examiner, were theoretically sound. The latter point will require an in-depth examination of the polygrapher's credentials. This additional layer of controversy will cause the qualification and questioning of experts to consume even more courtroom time than it ordinarily does.[5]

Although there are a number of other methods of formulating polygraph questions, the Control Question Test, or CQT, remains the most common. According to one commentator:

The most popular form of testing is the CQT. Here, the examiner asks three different types of questions: neutral, control, and relevant questions. The neutral questions are asked to ascertain the subject's chart readings when answering honestly. The control questions are intentionally stress-inducing, designed to elicit a sharp increase in the subject's physiological response. Control questions usually are closely related to the type of crime of which the subject is accused, and are designed to result in an untruthful response. The polygraph measures the stress produced by the uncertainty of how to answer

5. *State v. Porter*, 241 Conn. 57, 60–73, 698 A.2d 739, 743–749 (1996).

the control question. Finally, relevant questions are those that go directly to the issue at hand.

In other words, the control question is designed to force a reaction in an innocent person, either by leading him to lie or forcing him to admit to prior wrongdoing.[6]

# The Importance of Experience and Training

Most polygraph today is measured and scored by computer. A polygrapher may still score the data printout manually, or as a cross check. The process of computer analysis removes one of the objections to polygraph being subjective. If the subject answers even one of the relevant questions deceptively, he will "fail" the test.

I interviewed Leighton Hammond, former President of the Connecticut Polygraph Society, about his experience with polygraph.[7] Hammond says that he agrees with the computer scoring 95% of the time. When he does not, he does his own scoring of the test, which involves looking at the three measures for each question and comparing the reaction for the relevant question to the immediately preceding control question.

Most polygraphers recognize that it is the experience and training of the polygrapher in interviewing the subject and formulating the questions that results in reliable results. The polygrapher must spend time both establishing a relationship with the subject and carefully creating the control questions. No matter how heinous the charged crime, the polygrapher must find "something good" in the subject. Says Hammond, "If he likes, fishing, I like fishing." A judgmental or harsh attitude will get poor results.

A typical polygraph examination done in the private sector takes about two hours, of which only about 10 minutes is the actual administration of the test. The "pre-test period" is therefore crucial. During this phase, the examiner will seek to put the subject at ease, draw the subject out on some neutral topic, and then discuss the questions to be asked and familiarize the examinee with the testing procedure.

The examiner is therefore the most essential component of the polygraph testing process. This individual is responsible for almost every variable vital to the examination's success: properly screening the subject, establishing a trusting relationship with the subject, thwarting attempts to manipulate the polygraph results through physical countermeasures, stimulating physiological changes, and accurately analyzing the test results. The failure to execute properly any of the above tasks seriously undermines the precision of the test results.

The control questions take time and a good understanding of the subject. The object is to develop a question to which the subject will say "no," but will be lying. The control question is vital to reading the report, as an innocent person will generally show a strong reaction to the control question, whereas a deceptive person will typically show less of a response than to the relevant question.

---

6. Timothy B. Henseler, *A Critical Look at the Admissibility of Polygraph Evidence in the Wake of Daubert; The Lie Detector Fails the Test,* 46 Cath. U.L. Rev 1247 (Summer 1997).

7. Interviews with Leighton Hammond, former President, Connecticut Polygraph Society, October–November, 2006.

Hammond may begin with a control question such as "prior to today, have you ever lied to anyone?" If the subject says "no," he will then ask further questions to uncover lies, even minor ones, that the subject has told. Hammond will finally ask, "Other than the lies you have told me about just now, have you ever lied to someone?" The subject, unwilling to add yet another lie to the list, will simply say "no." The truthful person will be distressed, because he or she will know that there are still lies that are undisclosed. The deceptive person, on the other hand, won't care about the control questions because he is prepared to lie on all the questions and is more focused on the relevant question, the one related to the crime.

> Experience and training in polygraph are needed to:
>
> • screen the subject
> • establish a trusting relationship
> • formulate "control" questions
> • thwart attempts at countermeasures
> • correctly analyze results.

Other strategies an experienced polygrapher might use are to ask the subject "What questions would you like me to ask you?" According to Hammond, a guilty man accused of having an affair with another woman will say, "Ask me if I really loved my wife," rather than "Ask me if I cheated on my wife." In other words, he will make up a related question that he thinks he can answer truthfully.[8]

For this reason, many conclude that polygraph is more an art than a science:

> Retired CIA polygraph examiner John Sullivan, noting that polygraph is more art than science, opines that polygraphers at various agencies range from "Rembrandts" to "finger-painters."

Drew Richardson, a retired FBI scientist and polygraph critic, has observed, "polygraphers are involved in the detection of deception ... to the extent that one who jumps from a tall building is involved in flying."[9]

## Use of Polygraph in Law Enforcement

Polygraph is used extensively by law enforcement in investigation of crimes. Sometimes an officer will ask a suspect if he is willing to take a polygraph. Sometimes a suspect will volunteer. Attorneys for criminal defendants will sometimes ask their clients to take a polygraph and use it in the process of negotiating a plea agreement with the prosecution. As long as the jury is not informed in any way about a defendant's taking or refusing to take a polygraph, the polygraph is not illegal.

## Use of Polygraph outside of Criminal Investigation

A large number of polygraphs are performed in connection with applicants for law enforcement. Here is another example of the actual polygraph test for a police appli-

---

8. *Id.*
9. George W. Maschke, *Art or Not, Polygraphy doesn't Do the Job,* The Washington Post, June 27, 2006.

cant.[10] This test has no "relevant" question, as the subject is not suspected of a crime. The questions are designed to see if the subject has ever committed an act that would make him or her unfit for duty. As you can see, the test itself is very short:

Is your first name Lawrence? Yes.

Have you ever detected a serious undetected crime? No.

Have you ever committed a sexual crime you could have been arrested for? No.

Have you ever stolen anything worth over $100 in value? No.

Have you told the complete truth to the best of your knowledge? Yes.

Hammond estimates that of the 700 polygraphs he administered in 2006, about three-quarters were of police applicants. He estimates that 80% of those applicants were deceptive. The most common areas about which police applicants lie are minor domestic disputes, repeated larcenies, and drug use.[11]

Despite the strong reservations of courts to admitting polygraph, it continues to be used in many other areas. A recent commentator has pointed out that outside of the courtroom, polygraph tests are used more commonly than fingerprints and handwriting. The author refers to a survey of psychologists in which the majority found polygraph to be reliable and more accurate than other psychological evaluations that are routinely admitted in court:[12]

In 2003, the National Academy of Sciences reviewed over one hundred studies on the scientific validity of the polygraph and found a median accuracy of eighty-six percent. One study from more than thirty-five years ago compared the accuracy of polygraph tests with fingerprint identification, handwriting analysis, and eyewitness identification, and concluded that the polygraph test was as accurate as any of the other forensic techniques, and far more accurate than an eyewitness identification.[13]

The American Polygraph Association states that polygraph is used in government pre-employment screening, homeland security investigations, commercial theft investigations, for monitoring of convicted sex offenders and for those on parole. For example, under Florida state laws, when sentencing a sex offender to probation or community control, a judge must order the offender to undergo periodic polygraph examinations to obtain information necessary for risk management and treatment and to reduce the sex offender's denial mechanisms.[14]

The Employee Polygraph Protection Act of 1988[15] prohibits use of polygraph in commercial businesses, with certain exceptions such as those noted above. In 2004, the Justice Department sought to have senior federal prosecutors take a polygraph to find who leaked the name of a confidential informant in a Detroit terrorism[16] case.

---

10. Michael Alison Chandler, *The Moment of Truth: Polygraph Firm Banks on Separating Fact from Fiction,* The Washington Post, December 8, 2005.

11. Hammond interview, *supra.*

12. Rick Simmons, *Conquering the Province of the Jury: Expert Testimony and the Professionalization of Fact-Finding,* 74 U. Cin. L. Rev. 1013, 1044 (Spring 2006).

13. *Id*. at1045.

14. Florida Statutes Section 948.03(b)(1).

15. 29 U.S.C. 2001 et. seq.

16. Eric Lichtblau, *Investigators Seek Lie-Detector Tests in Terrorism Case,* New York Times, Sept. 4, 2004.

## Role of Training and Experience

In addition to concerns about the parts of the polygraph process that require judgment by the examiner, some question whether an individual examiner has enough training and experience to make those judgments. One examiner has stated that he believes that an examiner does not become fully competent until he or she has conducted 500 exams.[17]

The APA reports as of 2007 there were 29 states and 3 counties which have laws requiring training or certification for polygraph examiners. Most states require formal instruction, an in-training period and successful completion of a licensing examination.[18]

# Common Objections to the Reliability of Polygraph

> Countermeasures are methods used by subjects to manipulate polygraph results, such as holding their breath.

The three most common objections to polygraph are:

1. subjectivity in the process,

2. error rates in the results, and

3. the possibility that a subject can trick the test through "countermeasures."

## Error Rate

There is much controversy over the error rate in polygraph. This is no doubt due, in part, to the fact that valid results often depend on the experience of the examiner, both in formulating questions and assessing results. Nevertheless, a number of studies have been performed attempting to validate polygraph.

The error rate is the extent to which a subject gives an answer which is not deceptive and the detector identifies it as deceptive (false positive) or vice versa (false negative). This is explained further by the American Polygraph Association:

> While the polygraph technique is highly accurate, it is not infallible and errors do occur. Polygraph errors may be caused by the examiner's failing to properly prepare the examinee for the examination, or by a misreading of the physical data on the polygraph charts. Errors are usually referred to as either false positives or negatives. A false positive occurs when a truthful examinee is reported as being deceptive. A false negative is when a deceptive examinee is reported as truthful.
>
> Some research shows that false negatives occur more frequently than false positives; other research studies show the opposite conclusion. Since it is recognized that any error is damaging, examiners use a variety of procedures to identify the presence of factors which may cause false readings and to insure an unbiased review of polygraph records.[19]

---

17. Hammond, *supra.*
18. www.polygraph.org/faq.cfm.
19. *Id.*

There is no general agreement about what the error rate is. Accuracy rates have been quoted between 60 and 85%. The American Polygraph Association cites figures of 80% and above. It has reviewed 80 studies involving 6,380 polygraph examinations or sets of charts from examinations, and twelve studies of 2,174 field examinations, providing an average accuracy of 98%. Researchers also conducted studies involving the reliability of independent analyses of 810 sets of charts from laboratory simulations, producing an average accuracy of 81%.[20]

> "Polygraph errors may be caused by the examiner's failing to properly prepare the examinee for the examination, or by a misreading of the physiological data on the polygraph charts." *www.polygraph.org/faq.cfm*

One reason for disparities in error rates may be the statistical base used; another is the method of conducting the studies. Most important, according the APA, is that some statisticians identify an "inconclusive" response as an incorrect decision, thus inflating the error rate. The APA website points out that if 10 polygraph examinations are administered and the examiner is correct in 7 decisions, wrong in 1 and has 2 inconclusive test results, the correct accuracy rate as 87.5% (8 definitive results, 7 of which were correct). Critics of the polygraph technique would calculate the accuracy rate in this example as 70% (10 examinations with 7 correct decisions). Those who use polygraph testing do not consider inconclusive test results as negative, and do not hold them against the examiner.

The APA believes that error rates are controllable by proper training of examiners and protective procedures as follows:[21]

- An assessment of the examinee's emotional state.
- Medical information about the examinee's physical condition.
- Specialized tests to identify the overly responsive examinee and to calm the nervous.
- Control questions to evaluate the examinee's response capabilities.
- Factual analysis of the case information.
- A pre-test interview and detailed review of the questions.
- Quality control reviews.

Hammond believes that the accuracy rate is 96–97%, assuming the test is properly conducted. He admits, however, that there is no way to determine how the examination has been conducted, as there is no independent review.[22]

The American Medical Association states an error rate of 75–97%, but the rate of false positives is often sufficiently high to preclude its use as the sole arbiter of guilt or innocence:

> It is established that classification of guilty can be made with 75% to 97% accuracy, but the rate of false positives is often sufficiently high to preclude use of this test as the sole arbiter of guilt or innocence.... The effect of polygraph testing for theft and fraud associated with employment has never been measured, nor has its impact on employee morale and productivity been deter-

---

20. *Id.*
21. *Id.*
22. Hammond interview, *supra.*

mined. Much more serious research needs to be done before polygraph should be generally accepted for this purpose.[23]

The *Porter* case reviewed error rate and concluded that polygraph studies show troubling results:

**State v. Porter, continued**

\* \* \*

The word "validity" has two meanings in the polygraph context: for the purposes of this discussion, they will be labeled "accuracy" and "predictive value." Courts generally do not specify to which concept they are referring when they address polygraph issues. Maintaining this distinction is essential, however, if one is to evaluate fairly the validity of the polygraph test.

The "accuracy" of the polygraph test itself has two components: sensitivity and specificity. The polygraph's sensitivity is its ability to tell that a guilty person is, in fact, lying. If the polygraph test had a 90 percent sensitivity, then it would correctly label a deceptive subject as being deceptive 90 percent of the time. Thus, the test would incorrectly label a deceptive subject as being truthful 10 percent of the time; this mislabeling is called a "false negative" error.

The polygraph's specificity is its ability to tell that an innocent person is, in fact, being truthful. If the polygraph test had an 80 percent specificity, then it would label a truthful subject as being truthful 80 percent of the time. The test would thus incorrectly label a truthful subject as being deceptive 20 percent of the time; this mislabeling is called a "false positive" error. It is generally agreed in the literature, by both advocates and critics, that polygraphs have greater sensitivity than specificity; that is, that false positives outnumber false negatives.

There is wide disagreement, however, as to what the sensitivity and specificity values actually are for a well run polygraph exam. Dozens of studies of polygraph accuracy have been conducted. They fall into two basic types, namely, laboratory simulations of crimes and field studies based on data from polygraph examinations in actual criminal cases. The variance in expert opinion regarding polygraph accuracy arises from disagreements as to which methods and which studies within each method are methodologically valid.

Polygraph supporters base their accuracy estimates on both laboratory simulation and field studies. These advocates acknowledge that field studies are theoretically preferable for establishing the polygraph test's field accuracy, but they conclude that serious methodological difficulties inherent in such studies, such as establishing the actual guilt or innocence of the study subjects, make most of these studies unreliable. They think, however, that laboratory studies, when designed to approximate field conditions and when carefully conducted, can provide useful and valid data.

Department of Defense, although acknowledging that more research needs to be done, concluded after a thorough review of the literature that there was no "data suggesting that the various polygraph techniques and applications ... have high false positive or high false negative error rates." United States Department of Defense, The Accuracy and Utility of Polygraph Testing (1984) p. 63.

---

23. Journal of the American Medical Association, Vol. 256, No. 9, September 5, 1986, available at http://jama.ama-assn.org/cgi/content/abstract/256/9/1172.

Critics, however, view the existing body of polygraph studies quite differently. First, although polygraph detractors agree with the advocates that most field studies are invalid due to methodological concerns, they disagree as to which tests are valid. David Lykken, a prominent polygraph critic, has concluded from the field tests he deems valid that the polygraph has a sensitivity of 84 percent and a specificity of only 53 percent.

Another critic has concluded that reliable field studies indicate that there is "little or no case" for using the polygraph, and that "polygraph lie detection adds nothing positive to conventional approaches to interrogation and assessment...."

After its own thorough review of the polygraph field studies, the United States Office of Technology Assessment concluded that "the cumulative research evidence suggest that ... the polygraph test detects deception better than chance, but with significant error rates."

Moreover, polygraph critics argue that laboratory simulation studies are almost completely invalid. They point out that, although the accuracy of the control question test turns entirely on the subject having the "right" emotional responses, the emotional stimuli in the laboratory are completely different from those in the field ...

Even if one accepts Raskin's field study estimates of accuracy over those of the polygraph critics, polygraph evidence is of questionable validity. Raskin's 87 percent sensitivity indicates a 13 percent false negative rate. In other words, 13 percent of those who are in fact deceptive will be labeled as truthful. Moreover, Raskin's 59 percent specificity indicates a 41 percent false positive rate. In other words, 41 percent of subjects who are, in fact, truthful will be labeled as deceptive.

> "It is generally agreed in the literature, by both advocates and critics, that polygraphs have greater sensitivity than specificity; that is, that false positives outnumber false negatives." *State v. Porter*

The U. S. Supreme Court ruled that a defendant in a military trial has no Constitutional right to present polygraph evidence in his defense. One of the reasons it used to support a rule banning polygraph in military trials was the lack of reliability. Justice Stevens dissented, arguing that he believed that polygraph was reliable:

*United States v. Schaeffer,* 523 U.S. 303 (1998)

* * *

Dissent by: Stevens, J.

There are a host of studies that place the reliability of polygraph tests at 85% to 90%. While critics of the polygraph argue that accuracy is much lower, even the studies cited by the critics place polygraph accuracy at 70%. Moreover, to the extent that the polygraph errs, studies have repeatedly shown that the polygraph is more likely to find innocent people guilty than vice versa. Thus, exculpatory polygraphs—like the one in this case—are likely to be more reliable than inculpatory ones.

Of course, within the broad category of lie detector evidence, there may be a wide variation in both the validity and the relevance of particular test results. Questions about the examiner's integrity, independence, choice of questions, or training in the detection of deliberate attempts to provoke misleading physiological responses may justify exclusion of specific evidence. But such questions are properly addressed in adversary proceedings; they fall far short of justifying a blanket exclusion of this type of expert testimony.

There is no legal requirement that expert testimony must satisfy a particular degree of reliability to be admissible. Expert testimony about a defendant's "future dangerousness" to determine his eligibility for the death penalty, even if wrong "most of the time," is routinely admitted. Studies indicate that handwriting analysis, and even fingerprint identifications, may be less trustworthy than polygraph evidence in certain cases.

And, of course, even highly dubious eyewitness testimony is, and should be, admitted and tested in the crucible of cross-examination. The Court's reliance on potential unreliability as a justification for a categorical rule of inadmissibility reveals that it is "overly pessimistic about the capabilities of the jury and of the adversary system generally. Vigorous cross-examination, presentation of contrary evidence, and careful instruction on the burden of proof are the traditional and appropriate means of attacking shaky but admissible evidence." … [footnote]

> [footnote] One study compared the accuracy of fingerprinting, handwriting analysis, polygraph tests, and eyewitness identification. The study consisted of 80 volunteers divided into 20 groups of 4. Fingerprints and handwriting samples were taken from all of the participants.
>
> In each group of four, one person was randomly assigned the role of "perpetrator." The perpetrator was instructed to take an envelope to a building doorkeeper (who knew that he would later need to identify the perpetrator), sign a receipt, and pick up a package. After the "crime," all participants were given a polygraph examination.
>
> The fingerprinting expert (comparing the original fingerprints with those on the envelope), the handwriting expert (comparing the original samples with the signed receipt), and the polygrapher (analyzing the tests) sought to identify the perpetrator of each group. In addition, two days after the "crime," the doorkeeper was asked to pick the picture of the perpetrator out of a set of four pictures.
>
> The results of the study demonstrate that polygraph evidence compares favorably with other types of evidence. Excluding "inconclusive" results from each test, the fingerprinting expert resolved 100% of the cases correctly, the polygrapher resolved 95% of the cases correctly, the handwriting expert resolved 94% of the cases correctly, and the eyewitness resolved only 64% of the cases correctly.
>
> Interestingly, when "inconclusive" results were included, the polygraph test was more accurate than any of the other methods: The polygrapher resolved 90% of the cases correctly, compared with 85% for the handwriting expert, 35% for the eyewitness, and 20% for the fingerprinting expert.[24]

There is also the possibility of intentional error. In 2004, Adrienne LaMorte, a former Connecticut state trooper, sued the State of Connecticut for removing her from the polygraph unit after she complained about a fellow examiner who had flunked his

---

24. *United States v. Schaeffer*, 523 U.S. 303, 332–335 (1998).

courses at polygraph school but was passed anyway. LaMorte alleged that the other examiner had graded potential suspects in sexual assault cases as being truthful, when the polygraph results indicated the opposite. She won her suit for wrongful demotion and was awarded $216,000.[25]

## Countermeasures

Websites instructing how to beat a polygraph exam abound.[26] One says it can train a subject to fool a polygraph in a mere 15 minutes of training. Hammond responded that only about 1% of subjects he tests try to use countermeasures. He addresses the issue head-on in the pre-interview by stating "if you try to use countermeasures, I will see it on my screen, but please go ahead and try." He adds that the only way the website instructions would be helpful is if the subject had access to a polygraph and could practice, which is almost impossible. Further, subjects are unsure when to adopt the countermeasure during the test, which defeats the purpose.

The most common forms of countermeasures are:

1. slowing down breathing rate.
2. tightening the anal sphincter muscles.
3. taking beta blockers.
4. creating pain when a question is asked.

This is what the *Porter* court concluded about countermeasures:

### State v. Porter, continued

Countermeasures are also a concern with regard to polygraph validity. A countermeasure is any technique used by a deceptive subject to induce a false negative result and thereby pass the test. For a countermeasure to work on the control question test, all it must do is "change the direction of the differential reactivity between the relevant and control questions...."

\* \* \*

It may be true that "subjects without special training in countermeasures are unable to beat the polygraph test, even if they have been provided with extensive information and suggestions on how they might succeed ..."

\* \* \*

Yet as one polygraph supporter, Charles Honts, concedes, "studies have indicated that [expert-conducted] training in specific point countermeasures designed to increase [physiological responses to control questions] is effective in producing a substantial number of false negative outcomes...."

Specifically, "subjects in these studies were informed about the nature of the control question test and were trained to recognize control and relevant questions. Countermeasure subjects were then instructed to employ a countermeasure (e.g., bite their tongue, press their toes to the floor, or count backward by

---

25. Tracy Gordon Fox, *Doubt Cast on State Polygraph Tests: Lawsuit Testimony Questions Supervisor's Skill; Supervisor's Performance Focus of Investigation,* The Hartford Courant, August 1, 2004.

26. http://police-test.net; *Polygraph is Quackery,* http://antipolygraph.org.

seven) during the control question zones of a control question test. In one study, none of the guilty subjects who received this brief training was correctly detected.... Across all of the studies more than 50 % of the decisions on countermeasures subjects were incorrect."[27]

I asked Hammond to respond to this data. He says the issue is not whether countermeasures can influence the polygraph result. "The issue is that most subjects cannot successfully employ countermeasures or if they can, the experienced polygrapher will recognize them. The woman who came limping into my office, for example, pretty obviously had a tack in her shoe. The man who took a full minute before he answered each question was obviously trying to control his breathing." The polygraph measures breath rate directly, so if Hammond sees the breath rate slowing down, he will stop the polygraph and tell the subject what he sees. He says it is also pretty obvious when a person is trying to slow his breath from five breaths in 15 seconds—a normal rate—to one.[28]

Hammond uses a chair for the subject with a small black pad on the seat. This pad measures any change in the body below the waist, including tightening of sphincter muscles, wiggling feet, stepping on tacks, etc. Again, the action shows up on the screen. Beta blockers, says Hammond, will not create a false positive effect. The will simply dampen response rates altogether, but patterns will still emerge.

## Opponents to Polygraph

The belief in a high error rate has permeated general opinion about polygraph in society. For example, there is a website that supports Scott Peterson, the man convicted of killing his wife Laci and her unborn son and throwing her body in the San Francisco Bay. It quotes various authorities opposed to polygraph.[29] This includes the American Civil Liberties Union, the National Academy of Sciences National Research Council and the American Health Foundation. This website quotes the FBI as stating that polygraph should not be used unless there is other evidence of knowledge of guilt. It also quotes William G. Iacono, Ph.D, Professor of Psychology and Neuroscience at the University of Minnesota, as stating "The best studies of polygraph tests, using real-life cases and published in top scientific journals, find that innocent people fare little better than chance on these tests, with 40% or more failing on average."[30]

# Rejection of Polygraph in Court

The major reasons for the rejection of polygraph testimony are these:

1. Polygraph is not generally accepted as a reliable science.
2. Polygraph has too high an error rate.
3. The prejudicial effect of polygraph outweighs its probative value.

27. *Porter,* 241 Conn. 57 at 114.
28. Hammond, *supra.*
29. http://scottisinnocent.com/Research&Analysis/misconceptions/lie.htm.
30. *Id.*

4.   Polygraph takes away from the jury its right to find the defendant guilty or innocent.

According to the APA, twenty-seven states, including Connecticut, have adopted a ban on the use of polygraph in court, including testimony about whether the subject offered or refused to take a polygraph.[31] In some states, even the suggestion that a polygraph examination is involved is sufficient to cause a mistrial. Only two federal circuits have a *per se* rule banning polygraph—the Fourth circuit and the D.C. Circuit. However, most federal trial courts exclude polygraph under *Daubert*.

The *Porter* court summarized the status of polygraph in different jurisdictions this way:

### *State v. Porter,* continued

\* \* \*

The majority of the remaining states that have considered the issue admit polygraph evidence at trial only when its admission is stipulated to in advance by all parties. Even the jurisdictions that allow polygraph evidence by stipulation, however, generally do not assert that the evidence is probative, or that it gains validity by means of the stipulation. Instead, the allowance is simply based on the parties' right to waive evidentiary objections.

We are unpersuaded by this rationale. In our view, the limited reliability of polygraph evidence, taken together with its significant potential for prejudicial effect, compel the conclusion that such evidence should remain inadmissible even pursuant to a stipulation.

Of the states that do allow polygraph evidence without a stipulation, most allow it only in proceedings other than at trial.... These states have concluded that, at least under certain circumstances, polygraph evidence is sufficiently more probative than prejudicial to warrant admission.

\* \* \*

In this regard, it is particularly instructive to note that several courts, after experimenting with polygraph admissibility for several years, rejected its admissibility and reinstated the traditional rule of inadmissibility. In each case, the court realized that its earlier assessment, namely, that the probative value of polygraph evidence outweighed its prejudicial impact, was mistaken.

\* \* \*

In all, then, four states that at one time allowed polygraph evidence have subsequently, in light of their experiences, rethought and rejected this policy. Although not a decisive justification for our decision to retain our *per se* exclusionary rule, this pattern leads us to conclude that our concerns are, in fact, well founded.

Federal appellate courts generally grant trial judges more leeway to admit polygraph evidence than do their state counterparts, especially in the wake of *Daubert*. Indeed, the majority of federal courts of appeals do not have a *per se* rule that polygraph evidence is inadmissible at trial.

Nonetheless, most maintain that, although admission is within the discretion of the trial court, such evidence should, as a general policy, be excluded under Rule 403 of the Federal Rules of Evidence.

---

31. www.polygraph.org.

The Court of Appeals for the Eleventh Circuit has gone further than any other federal appellate court toward allowing polygraph evidence at trial in the absence of a stipulation. In *Piccinonna*, the court summarily concluded that, while polygraphy is still "a developing and inexact science," it is a sufficiently "useful and reliable scientific tool" to justify its admission to impeach or corroborate the testimony of a witness at trial, even without a stipulation. The court did emphasize, however, that "neither of these two modifications to the *per se* exclusionary rule should be construed to preempt or limit in any way the trial court's discretion to exclude polygraph expert testimony on other grounds under the Federal Rules of Evidence."[32]

## The New Mexico Approach

New Mexico adopted a rule that a party who wishes to introduce a polygraph must give his opponent notice, at which point the court may compel the person who took a voluntary polygraph to take another one with an examiner of his choice. If he refuses, no polygraph testimony maybe introduced.[33] This rule would permit a defendant to offer a polygraph, but only if he takes a second one. The New Mexico Supreme Court reported the results of a detailed *Daubert* hearing in 2004, in *Lee v. Martinez*,[34] on appeal by a defendant who had sought to have his polygraph results admitted at trial. The New Mexico Supreme Court found that polygraph met the *Daubert* standards. The court said that polygraph results are sufficiently reliable to be admitted under New Mexico Rule 11-702, provided the expert is qualified and the examination was conducted as required by the rule.

First, the court reviewed a report[35] of a study of the validity of polygraph testing published by the National Academy of Sciences ("NAS"), a private, non-profit group of scientists. The court addressed the control question technique only, as that was the test the defendant had taken. The court found the scientific hypothesis of polygraph to be that an innocent person will show a greater physiological response to the control questions; but, a guilty person will react more strongly to the relevant questions. The NAS concluded that there had been no systematic scientific study of which physiological indicators were the best to determine these reactions.

"The basic scientific knowledge of psychophysiology offers support for expecting polygraph testing to have some diagnostic value, at least among naïve examinees." *Lee v. Martinez*

However, it still concluded that "the basic scientific knowledge of psychophysiology offers support for expecting polygraph testing to have some diagnostic value, at least among naïve examinees."[36] In addition, the court said that the very fact that the state argued that some studies show polygraph does not work, concedes that the hypothesis is testable.

The court also held that polygraph had met peer review, citing the 102 studies that the NAS had included in its report. Those studies showed a median accuracy

---

32. *Porter,* 241 Conn. 57 at 125–127.
33. *Tafoya v. Baca,* 103 N.M. 56, 702 P.2d 1001 (1985).
34. 136 N.M. 166, 96 P.3d 291 (2004).
35. Found at http://www.nap.edu/openbook/030908369/html.
36. *Lee,* 136 N.M. at 174, 196 P.3d at 299.

rate of 85%, and the controlled question method had an 85% accuracy rate. The court quoted the NAS report as stating:

> [T]he NAS report concluded "the empirical data clearly indicate that for several populations of naïve examinees not trained in countermeasures, polygraph tests for event-specific investigation detect deception at rates well above those expected from random guessing."[37]

The court reviewed the standards and licensing for polygraphers in New Mexico, which included at least five years' experience as well as the requirement that the polygrapher must research the examinee's background, health, education and other relevant information. It concluded that the standards were in line with those proposed by the APA and concluded "sufficient standards are in place governing the control question polygraph technique, so as to allow expert testimony on the subject to be admissible."[38]

The NAS found no reliable studies of countermeasures and offered no opinion about them. The court said that any variations in error rate went to the weight of the evidence, rather than its admissibility. In other words, the jury should hear it, the opposing party could raise the error rates, and the jury could decide the issue of how much weight to give the polygraph. Polygraph licensing provided standards and controls in the court's view. The court then approved New Mexico Rule 11-707 (C) and (E), which contain the following safeguards, before a polygraph can be admitted:

- The examination was scored in a generally accepted manner.
- The examiner asked the subject about his background, health, education and other relevant information.
- At least two relevant questions were asked.
- The test was repeated at least three times.
- The pretest interview and actual test must be recorded on audio or video.

The court decided that the scientific community was undecided about the general acceptance of polygraph, but decided to give this factor little weight under the *Daubert* rule. Finally, the court said that it is unfair for law enforcement to use polygraph in their own decision-making in investigating crimes and then turn around and argue it should not be admissible at trial. Polygraph, for example, is often used to determine probable cause to arrest and whether to prosecute.

# Some Federal Courts Have Admitted Polygraph

Most federal courts have discretion to admit polygraph. In *United States v. Zeigler*,[39] the District Court for the District of Columbia held a hearing under the *Frye* test of general acceptance. It heard from experts, including John E. Reid, who wrote a major text on polygraph in 1966 called *Truth and Deception*. Reid stated that the accuracy of polygraph is greater than 91% among experienced examiners. Here is what the court concluded:

---

37. *Id.* at 176, 301.
38. *Id.* at 304.
39. *United Sates v. Zeigler,* 350 F. Supp. 685 (D.D.C. 1972).

Today, polygraphy has emerged from the twilight zone into an established field of science and technology. The polygraph has been and continues to be the subject of scientific study and investigation, and although the precise limitations of the device and the intricacies which affect its performance may not be understood to the complete satisfaction of the scientific community, enough is known about it to confirm that it is a useful tool for detecting deception.

Its extensive use by law enforcement agencies, governmental security organizations, and private industry throughout the country is testimony to the undeniable efficacy of the technique.

The practice has acquired the usually accepted indicia of a profession, such as a national professional organization, training schools, qualification standards, yearly seminars, and specialized publications.[40]

In 2001, a prosecutor tried to introduce a polygraph administered by the Kansas Bureau of Investigation against a defendant. The defendant argued the polygraph was inherently unreliable, but the court decided that the district court properly admitted the evidence after a gatekeeper hearing:

[Mr. Johnson] was able to articulate with sufficient precision the reasons supporting his opinion that the polygraph examination administered to Jay Dee Walters was reliable. The polygraph examiner was also able to explain in substantial detail the manner in which the polygraph worked, the manner in which the examination had been verified by Jay Dee Walters' post-examination interview, and the peer scrutiny to which that examination had been subjected and deemed reliable.[41]

Some federal circuits already have specific rules for admissibility, such as the 11th Circuit, which specifies what must be done for polygraph results to be admitted over objection, or under stipulation.[42] In 1995, an Eleventh Circuit appeals court in the federal court system opposed a *per se* rule that polygraph be inadmissible because it would take away the flexible inquiry that the trial judge was given in *Daubert*:

There is no question that in recent years polygraph testing has gained increasingly widespread acceptance as a useful and reliable scientific tool. Because of the advances that have been achieved in the field which have led to the greater use of polygraph examination, coupled with a lack of evidence that juries are unduly swayed by polygraph evidence, we agree with those courts which have found that a *per se* rule disallowing polygraph evidence is no longer warranted.

* * *

Thus, we believe the best approach in this area is one which balances the need to admit all relevant evidence against the danger that the admission of the evidence for a given purpose will be unfairly prejudicial.[43]

The Fifth Circuit decided that *Daubert* had effectively overruled a *per se* rule against the admissibility of polygraph because the admissibility was now an issue for the gate-

---

40. *Id*. at 688.
41. *United States v. Walters*, 28 Fed. Appx. 902, 2001 U.S. App. LEXIS 26284 (10th Cir., December 7, 2001), quoting the trial court opinion.
42. *United States v. Piccinonna, 885* F.2d 1529 (11 Cir. 1989).
43. *Id*. at 1535.

keeper.[44] Other circuits have left the decision to the discretion of the trial judge. The rules that states and federal circuits generally follow in stipulated admissibility were established in *State v. Valdez*,[45] to be used when polygraph results are admitted over objection of opposing counsel.[46]

# Would Admitting Polygraph Results Deprive the Jury of Its Role?

In *Porter*, the court decided that the prejudice of admitting a polygraph outweighed probative effect. In that case, the defendant wanted to introduce a polygraph that he passed in his defense. The issue is not whether the jury would be prejudiced *against* the defendant, but rather whether the jury would rely on the polygraph in order to determine the ultimate issue of guilt or innocence, instead of weighing all of the evidence. As the court said in *Porter:*

**State v. Porter, continued**

\* \* \*

The most significant, and fundamental, problem with allowing polygraph evidence in court is that it would invade the fact-finding province of the jury. The jury has traditionally been the sole arbiter of witness credibility. Indeed, an underlying premise of our legal system is that the jury is capable in this regard. Accordingly, we generally disallow expert testimony as to witness credibility when the subject matter of the testimony "is within the knowledge of jurors and expert testimony [therefore] would not assist them...."

\* \* \*

Very few studies have been done on the influence that polygraph evidence has over juries, and the cumulative results of those studies are inconclusive. In view of the importance of maintaining the role of the jury, this uncertainty alone justifies the continued exclusion of polygraph evidence. Moreover, polygraph evidence so directly abrogates the jury's function that its admission is offensive to our tradition of trial by jury. Indeed, the specter of polygraph evidence demonstrates why the traditional role of the jury in assessing credibility is so important and should be guarded so assiduously.

\* \* \*

Moreover, we afford criminal defendants the right to trial by a panel of several jurors partly out of the recognition that, although one person may be misled when a witness gives the "incorrect" physical signals, the cumulative impressions of the group are likely to lead to the truth. It violates the premise of this entire system to allow a single person—the polygrapher—to label a witness as honest or as dishonest based solely on the same type of indirect evidence that we generally maintain takes an entire jury to evaluate.

---

44. *United States v. Posado*, 57 F.3d 428, 431 (5th Cir. 1995).
45. *State v. Valdez*, 91 Ariz. 274, 371 P.2d 894 (1962).
46. *State v. Dorsey*, 88 N.M. 184, 539 P.2d 204 (1975).

In this regard, we do not dispute that polygraphers may often reach a correct conclusion regarding a subject's guilt or innocence. We conclude, however, that this fact, in and of itself, is irrelevant.... [T]he ability of the polygraph technique to tell whether a subject is lying or telling the truth is still highly questionable. Thus, one cannot say with any degree of certainty that a polygrapher's ultimate conclusion about a subject's veracity is in fact based upon the polygraph machine—that is, based upon science.

It is just as likely, if not more likely, that a polygrapher's conclusion will be based either on chance or on his or her general impressions of the subject's credibility. An assessment of witness credibility based simply on chance or on intuition is not, however, admissible at trial. Indeed, forming impressions and intuitions regarding witnesses is the quintessential jury function; moreover, to the extent possible, luck should be excluded from the assessment process altogether.[47]

Although critics of admitting polygraph assert that it should be inadmissible because it is evidence of guilt or innocence, and therefore would be highly prejudicial to a jury, Federal Rule of Evidence 704 states that opinion testimony that is otherwise admissible should not be banned simply because it "embraces an ultimate issue." The polygraph examiner could not be asked "does your study conclude that the defendant is guilty?" This would be taking away the right of a jury to determine guilt. However, a polygrapher examiner could be asked "does your study show that the defendant was deceptive in answering a particular question?" The jury could infer guilt from this testimony. But, as the judge instructs the jury, it is free to accept or reject the testimony of any witness, including that of an expert.

Therefore, polygraph could be used as one piece of evidence a jury could consider in determining guilt. The error rate, experience of the examiner, and other issues going to the reliability of the specific test could all be proper subjects for cross-examination.

The Connecticut Supreme Court in *State v. Porter*, upheld the state ban on using polygraph in court. Although it was asked to rule that polygraph met the *Daubert* test, it declined to do so because it found that the polygraph was unduly prejudicial under Rule 403.

### *State v. Porter*, continued

* * *

With the foregoing information in mind, we will assume, without deciding, that polygraph evidence satisfies *Daubert*. Although the subjective nature and highly questionable predictive value of the polygraph test weigh heavily against admission, we assume that polygraph evidence may have enough demonstrated validity to pass the *Daubert* threshold for admissibility.

We conclude, however, that admission of the polygraph test would be highly detrimental to the operation of Connecticut courts, both procedurally and substantively. Moreover, ... the probative value of polygraph evidence is very low, even if it satisfies *Daubert*.

Accordingly, we also conclude that any limited evidentiary value that polygraph evidence does have is substantially outweighed by its prejudicial effects.

We therefore reaffirm our *per se* rule against the use of polygraph evidence in Connecticut courts.[48]

---

47. *Porter*, 241 Conn. at 115–120, 698 A.2d at 769–771.
48. *Porter*, 241 Conn. at 115, 698 A.2d at 768–769.

# Sixth Amendment Rights and Polygraph As Exculpatory Evidence

Most of the cases involving polygraph are brought by a defendant who has passed a polygraph and wants to use it as a defense. He argues that this is part of the right to present a defense guaranteed by the Constitution. This claim was rejected in 1988 by the U.S. Supreme Court:

*United States v. Scheffer,* 523 U.S. 303 (1998)

This case presents the question whether Military Rule of Evidence 707, which makes polygraph evidence inadmissible in court-martial proceedings, unconstitutionally abridges the right of accused members of the military to present a defense. We hold that it does not.

\* \* \*

In March 1992, respondent Edward Scheffer, an airman stationed at March Air Force Base in California, volunteered to work as an informant on drug investigations for the Air Force Office of Special Investigations (OSI). His OSI supervisors advised him that, from time to time during the course of his undercover work, they would ask him to submit to drug testing and polygraph examinations. In early April, one of the OSI agents supervising respondent requested that he submit to a urine test. Shortly after providing the urine sample, but before the results of the test were known, respondent agreed to take a polygraph test administered by an OSI examiner. In the opinion of the examiner, the test "indicated no deception" when respondent denied using drugs since joining the Air Force. [footnote]

> [footnote] The OSI examiner asked three relevant questions: (1) "Since you've been in the [Air Force], have you used any illegal drugs?";
>
> (2) "Have you lied about any of the drug information you've given OSI?"; and
>
> (3) "Besides your parents, have you told anyone you're assisting OSI?"
>
> Respondent answered "no" to each question.

On April 30, respondent unaccountably failed to appear for work and could not be found on the base. He was absent without leave until May 13, when an Iowa state patrolman arrested him following a routine traffic stop and held him for return to the base. OSI agents later learned that respondent's urinalysis revealed the presence of methamphetamine.

Respondent was tried by general court-martial on charges of using methamphetamine, failing to go to his appointed place of duty, wrongfully absenting himself from the base for 13 days, and, with respect to an unrelated matter, uttering 17 insufficient funds checks. He testified at trial on his own behalf, relying upon an "innocent ingestion" theory and denying that he had knowingly used drugs while working for OSI. On cross-examination, the prosecution attempted to impeach respondent with inconsistencies between his trial testimony and earlier statements he had made to OSI.

Respondent sought to introduce the polygraph evidence in support of his testimony that he did not knowingly use drugs. The military judge denied the motion, relying on Military Rule of Evidence 707, which provides, in relevant part:

> "(a) Notwithstanding any other provision of law, the results of a polygraph examination, the opinion of a polygraph examiner, or any reference to an offer to take, failure to take, or taking of a polygraph examination, shall not be admitted into evidence."

The military judge determined that Rule 707 was constitutional because "the President may, through the Rules of Evidence, determine that credibility is not an area in which a fact finder needs help, and the polygraph is not a process that has sufficient scientific acceptability to be relevant." He further reasoned that the fact finder might give undue weight to the polygraph examiner's testimony, and that collateral arguments about such evidence could consume "an inordinate amount of time and expense."

Respondent was convicted on all counts and was sentenced to a bad-conduct discharge, confinement for 30 months, total forfeiture of all pay and allowances, and reduction to the lowest enlisted grade. The Air Force Court of Criminal Appeals affirmed in all material respects, explaining that Rule 707 "does not arbitrarily limit the accused's ability to present reliable evidence."

\* \* \*

A defendant's right to present relevant evidence is not unlimited, but rather is subject to reasonable restrictions. A defendant's interest in presenting such evidence may thus "bow to accommodate other legitimate interests in the criminal trial process." As a result, state and federal rulemakers have broad latitude under the Constitution to establish rules excluding evidence from criminal trials. Such rules do not abridge an accused's right to present a defense so long as they are not "arbitrary" or "disproportionate to the purposes they are designed to serve.

\* \* \*

The approach taken by the President in adopting Rule 707—excluding polygraph evidence in all military trials—is a rational and proportional means of advancing the legitimate interest in barring unreliable evidence. Although the degree of reliability of polygraph evidence may depend upon a variety of identifiable factors, there is simply no way to know in a particular case whether a polygraph examiner's conclusion is accurate, because certain doubts and uncertainties plague even the best polygraph exams. Individual jurisdictions therefore may reasonably reach differing conclusions as to whether polygraph evidence should be admitted.

We cannot say, then, that presented with such widespread uncertainty, the President acted arbitrarily or disproportionately in promulgating a *per se* rule excluding all polygraph evidence.

It is equally clear that Rule 707 serves a second legitimate governmental interest: Preserving the jury's core function of making credibility determinations in criminal trials. A fundamental premise of our criminal trial system is that "the jury is the lie detector." Determining the weight and credibility of witness testimony, therefore, has long been held to be the "part of every case [that] belongs to the jury, who are presumed to be fitted for it by their natural intelligence and their practical knowledge of men and the ways of men."

By its very nature, polygraph evidence may diminish the jury's role in making credibility determinations. The common form of polygraph test measures a variety of physiological responses to a set of questions asked by the examiner, who then interprets these physiological correlates of anxiety and offers an opinion to the jury about whether the witness—often, as in this case, the accused—was deceptive in answering questions about the very matters at issue in the trial.

> "A fundamental premise of our criminal trial system is that the jury is the lie detector."
> *United States v. Schaeffer*

Unlike other expert witnesses who testify about factual matters outside the jurors' knowledge, such as the analysis of fingerprints, ballistics, or DNA found at a crime scene, a polygraph expert can supply the jury only with another opinion, in addition to its own, about whether the witness was telling the truth. Jurisdictions, in promulgating rules of evidence, may legitimately be concerned about the risk that juries will give excessive weight to the opinions of a polygrapher, clothed as they are in scientific expertise and at times offering, as in respondent's case, a conclusion about the ultimate issue in the trial.

> "A polygraph expert can supply the jury only with another opinion, in addition to its own, about whether the witness was telling the truth."
> *United States v. Schaeffer*

Such jurisdictions may legitimately determine that the aura of infallibility attending polygraph evidence can lead jurors to abandon their duty to assess credibility and guilt. Those jurisdictions may also take into account the fact that a judge cannot determine, when ruling on a motion to admit polygraph evidence, whether a particular polygraph expert is likely to influence the jury unduly. For these reasons, the President is within his constitutional prerogative to promulgate a *per se* rule that simply excludes all such evidence.

## Admitting Polygraph As Character Evidence of Truthfulness in General

Should polygraph be admitted solely to prove the character of the witness? One defendant wanted to admit a favorable polygraph and argued that Federal Rule of Evidence 608 would permit it because it says "[t]he credibility of a witness may be ... supported by evidence in the form of opinion or reputation ..." The court was not convinced that the results of the polygraph could be restricted to support a conclusion that the defendant had a character for truthfulness. "As a practical matter, the result of the lie detector test is not a sufficient basis for an opinion that [the subject] is a truthful or honest person."[49]

Another court held that the issue of defendant's credibility is related to depriving the jury of its right as a fact-finder. It decided that a polygraph that indicated a defendant was truthful when he said he did not commit a murder was not a "fact" and therefore was inadmissible, even though it would boost the credibility of the defendant's denial of the crime:

---

49. David R. Strawbridge, *Daubert and the Polygraph*, 1–5 Mealey's *Daubert* Rep. 13 (May 1997).

*Idaho v. Perry,* 139 Idaho 520, 81 P.3d 1230 (2004)

\* \* \*

Perry asserts that the polygraph results will be offered at trial to prove only the truth of his statements by his body's involuntary physiological responses. Although jurors will need to determine whether they believe Perry's testimony as to the details of the death of his uncle, Perry's physiological responses to a polygraph test are not facts at issue. Further, the responses will not assist the trier of fact in understanding the evidence; rather, the evidence of the responses merely would re-present testimony presumably already testified to by Perry and attempt to bolster his credibility.

In general, expert testimony which does nothing but vouch for the credibility of another witness encroaches upon the jury's vital and exclusive function to make credibility determinations, and therefore does not 'assist the trier of fact' as required by Rule 702.

Idaho courts have routinely held that "an expert's opinion, in a proper case, is admissible up to the point where an expression of opinion would require the expert to pass upon the credibility of witnesses or the weight of disputed evidence. To venture beyond that point, however, is to usurp the jury's function."

It is the jury's function to assess the demeanor of the witnesses and make a determination of credibility.... This Court will not second guess the jury's determination on credibility or the weight to be given to witnesses' testimony. Statements by a witness as to whether another witness is telling the truth are prohibited.

In this case, the results of the polygraph are useful to bolster Perry's credibility but do not provide the trier of fact with any additional information that pertains to Perry's case. The fact of whether the alleged act occurred is for the jury to decide. Additionally, credibility questions are left to the trier of fact, in this case a jury.

The polygraph results in this case do not help the trier of fact to find facts or to understand the evidence as required by I.R.E. 702. To admit these results is an attempt to substitute the credibility determination appropriate for the jury, with Dr. Honts' interpretation of the alleged involuntary physiological results from the polygraph examination. Dr. Honts usurps the role of the jury as the ultimate finder of credibility.[50]

## Jury May Not Hear That Defendant Took a Polygraph

After O.J. Simpson was acquitted of murder charges, the families of Nicole Brown Simpson and Ron Goldman sued him for money damages for causing their deaths. A jury found Simpson liable and awarded damages of $8.5 million for wrongful death and $12.5 million for each death in punitive damages. In his opening statement, Simpson's attorney stated that Simpson had cooperated with investigators and had offered to take a polygraph but his offer was refused. Counsel for the Goldman family later asked Simpson "And you did take the test and you failed it, didn't you? Simpson said "No ... That's not correct." Counsel continued "You got a minus 22" Simpson's attorney ob-

---

50. 139 Idaho at 525, 81 P.3d at 1235.

jected.[51] Goldman's counsel argued that Simpson's attorney had "opened the door" to the topic of polygraph in his opening statement. Simpson's counsel moved for a mistrial on the ground that it is unlawful in California to admit the results of a polygraph as well as the fact of an offer to take, refuse to take, or the taking of a polygraph examination. The court refused to grant a mistrial and gave a strict instruction to the jury to disregard the testimony about the polygraph:

> I instruct you that his questions do not and cannot establish that Mr. Simpson took a … lie-detector test, a score and meaning thereof. Statements of counsel, that is, the statements or questions of Mr. Petrocelli, are not evidence and may not be considered by you for any purpose. The references or statements regarding a lie-detector test and Mr. Petrocelli's questions are not evidence unless they were adopted by Mr. Simpson in his answers. A question by itself is not evidence.
>
> You may consider questions only to the extent the content of the questions are adopted by the answer. Mr. Simpson's answer to the question of whether he took a lie-detector test was that he was given an explanation of how the test worked and that he did not take the test.
>
> There is no other evidence before you that Mr. Simpson took a lie-detector test, and the plaintiff is bound by Mr. Simpson's response. Likewise, when Mr. Petrocelli asked Mr. Simpson whether he knew what the score on the test was, whether it was a minus 22, or whether it indicated extreme deception, these were questions by an attorney and do not constitute evidence. Mr. Simpson denied any test score or any knowledge of what test scores meant, and there is no evidence before you of a test score or what a score means.
>
> There was only Mr. Petrocelli's questions which were not adopted by an answer. Plaintiff is bound by Mr. Simpson's response. Therefore, there is no evidence before you that Mr. Simpson took a lie-detector test, no evidence about any score on such a test, nor any evidence of what any score means. You must totally disregard the questions about taking lie-detector tests, test scores and their meanings, and treat the subject as though you had never heard of it.[52]

On appeal, the court ruled that the jury instruction was sufficient to cure any error in allowing the topic of polygraph to be raised before the jury.[53]

## Confessions Made Following a Polygraph Examination

If the polygraph is administered at the request of defendant's counsel by a private polygrapher, no Miranda warnings are required, as the defendant is not in custodial interrogation. If he confesses following the polygraph, the polygrapher may be called to testify against his client to the substance of the confession, although the jury may not hear that the defendant took a polygraph. Hammond has been called to testify about such confessions. Hammond acknowledges that it is sometimes difficult to state

---

51. *Rufo v. Simpson*, 86 Cal. App. 4th 573, 600–601 (Cal. App. 2001).
52. *Id.* at 602.
53. *Id.* at 603.

how and where he met the defendant when he is not permitted to testify that he is a polygrapher.

# Will fMRI Testing Meet the *Daubert* Tests?

"Brain mapping" or "brain fingerprinting" is a process that uses electronic measurement of brain waves to detect guilty knowledge. Brain mapping can supposedly detect whether a suspect recognizes elements about a crime scene that someone not involved in the crime would not know. The theory is that certain parts of the brain respond when someone sees something that the brain recognizes. There is apparently no way to circumvent this process, as it is involuntary. "Brain fingerprinting" as it is called by Dr. Lawrence A. Farwell, its inventor[54] is a process in which a suspect is shown a series of words or pictures relevant to a crime along with other irrelevant words or pictures. Electrical brain response [called MERMER] is measured through a headband equipped with sensors. The theory is that the brain will involuntarily "recognize" the words or pictures and the MERMER will show this recognition. The responses are coded by a computer, thereby theoretically removing human observational error.[55]

Although Farwell states on his website that brain fingerprinting was admitted by a court in the case of *Harrington v. State*,[56] a review of the opinions in that case show that this is not accurate. In 2001, Farwell testified that brain fingerprints exonerated Terry Harrington in a motion to overturn a 1978 murder conviction based on newly discovered evidence. However, the appellate court refused to review the adequacy/validity of that evidence:

> Because we conclude the due process claim is dispositive of the present appeal, we do not reach the question of whether the trial court erred in rejecting Harrington's request for a new trial on the basis of newly discovered evidence.... Because the scientific testing evidence is not necessary to a resolution of this appeal, we give it no further consideration.[57]

The defendant's motion had been granted based on other evidence. The appellate court did not authorize the admission of brain mapping evidence, nor did it even discuss this subject.

As to the science underlying brain fingerprinting, one commentator says:

> While the P300 phenomenon [measuring brain waves] has been discussed, dissected, and approved in countless peer reviewed journals to the point where it may well be considered to be beyond dispute, and is of such a nature that it is worth taking judicial notice of, the MERMER extension and methodology devised by Dr. Farwell has been published in only one professional journal. Thus if a multiplicity of technical exposure is required for the 'publication and peer review' factor of *Daubert*, MERMER fails to meet that requirement to date.[58]

---

54. http://forensic-evidence.com/site/Behv_Evid/Farwell.

55. *Id.*

56. *Harrington v. State*, 659 N.W.2d 509 (Sup. Iowa 2003).

57. *Id.* at 516.

58. Andre Moenssens, *Brain Fingerprinting—Can it be used to detect the innocence of persons charged with a crime?*, 70 UMKC L. Rev. 891, 918 (2002).

Farwell is not the only scientist involved in studying whether brain waves can un-cover guilty knowledge. Researchers at the University of Pennsylvania have published extensively on their research on the measurement of functional magnetic resource imaging,[59] or fMRI, and the topic was presented at a symposium of the American Academy of Science in Boston on February 2, 2007. In 2001, these researchers an-nounced work with volunteers in which they gave 18 people a playing card and $20. Each person was placed in an MRI machine, during which a computer presented the volunteers with different playing cards. When the computer showed the card the vol-unteer was holding, the volunteer was told to lie and say it was the wrong card. Vol-unteers were told they would get paid more if they could fool the machine into be-lieving them.

> Scans of the volunteers' brains during the deceptive periods revealed increased activity in multiple areas. The most significant was the anterior cingulate cor-tex—a small brain structure that looks like the two halves of an apple, some three inches behind the middle of the forehead. It is involved in such cognitive processes as paying attention, making judgments—and inhibiting a person's responses.[60]

Other researchers have formed companies to try to capitalize on this new technol-ogy.[61] As stated by Ronald Barndollar, a former FBI polygrapher who has reviewed some of this experimental work: "fMRI has the potential to do for lie detection what DNA did for forensic serology."[62]

What would happen if Brain Fingerprinting or fMRI becomes accepted science in the future and can conclusively show whether a person committed a crime? Could fMRI de-tect whether a subject was telling a lie without any risk of countermeasures? Could it be used as "newly discovered evidence," such as DNA, to exonerate the wrongly convicted? Is it possible that Ed Grant could be given an fMRI that would show he never had any-thing to do with the murder of Penney Serra? As far-fetched as this sounds, this tech-nology may possible. The one thing we know for sure is that science will continue to discover and uncover "truths" that so far, elude the courtroom.

# Summary

Polygraph has been one of the longest-running types of forensic evidence. It was rejected in 1923 in the *Frye* case because it was held not to be "generally accepted." This case set the standard for forensic expert testimony for many years and is still the test in some states, including New York. A number of states exclude polygraph *per se* from any criminal proceeding. As shown by the *Simpson* civil trial, even a statement to the jury that the defendant may have taken a polygraph is grounds to move for a mistrial.

---

59. Daniel D. Langleben, James W. Loughead, Warren B. Bilker, Kosha Ruparel, Anna Rose Childress, Samantha I. Busch, and Ruben C. Gur, *Telling Truth from Lie in Individual Subjects with Fast Event-Related fMRI, Wiley InterScience,* www.interscience.wiley.com, September 13, 2005.
60. Shankar Vedantam, *The Polygraph Test Meets its Match; Researchers Find brain Scans Can be Powerful Tool in Detecting Lies,* The Washington Post, November 12, 2001.
61. www.noliemri.com.
62. Interview with the author, March 20, 2007.

New Mexico is the only state that admits polygraph by statute, which includes controls over the qualifications of the examiner, the type of polygraph administered, and the use at trial. The federal courts consider the issue to be within the discretion of the trial judge. More courts are applying the *Daubert* tests of reliability to polygraph, and only a few have held that polygraph is reliable. Error rates and the effect of countermeasures are two areas of great concern with polygraph, particularly as the "control question" form of polygraph requires careful formulation of the control questions.

Additional concerns may still keep polygraph out of the courtroom. One issue is whether polygraph would substitute for the jury's role as a finder of fact, as polygraph is not "evidence" in a case, but merely corroboration of one party's version of the truth. Some defendants have argued that the Constitution gives them a right to present polygraph as part of the right to present a defense. So far, the U.S. Supreme court has rejected this idea, at least as it applies to military trials.

Newer technologies involving measuring brain wave response to questions similar to polygraph show real promise for identifying truth or deception, while removing concerns about "countermeasures," or conscious efforts to thwart the machine.

# Discussion Questions

1. What is the difference between the polygraph described in the *Frye* case and the *Porter* case? What did each of the courts rule about whether polygraph should be admissible and why?

2. What is the scientific hypothesis of polygraph? Do you believe this hypothesis has been proved?

3. If modern polygraph has a known error rate, even if it is 25%, why shouldn't it still meet the Daubert test and be admitted so that the jury can weigh its validity?

4. Why should polygraph be reliable enough to use for screening police and other applicants for jobs involving national security and not for criminal trials?

5. Do you see a difference between the prosecution introducing a polygraph that the defendant has failed and a defendant introducing a polygraph that the defendant has passed? Is one less prejudicial than the other? Why?

6. Do you believe that a defendant's confession to a polygraph examiner should be admissible in court? Is so, should the defendant receive a Miranda warning before taking a polygraph?

7. Explain the argument that a defendant has a Constitutional "right" to present exculpatory polygraph testimony. Do you agree with this?

8. Do you believe that the jury instruction in the civil trial of O.J. Simpson was sufficient to ensure that the jury would disregard any statements to the effect that Simpson took and failed a lie detector test?

# Chapter 13

# DNA and Its Role in Exonerations

## Overview

Over 300 prisoners have reportedly been exonerated and released from prison since 1989. Of these, about 30% were rape convictions that were reversed based on testing of DNA evidence that was not tested at the time of trial. The majority of DNA exonerations involve rapes, as DNA evidence was generally collected at the time of the rape.

A majority of the prisoners who request testing of DNA evidence prove not to be innocent after all. Therefore, groups like The Innocence Project, founded in 1994 at Cardozo Law School, must carefully review and choose those prisoners whom they will represent.

The phenomenon of DNA exonerations has captured the public interest and has led many states to adopt legislation to help with exoneration requests. These laws cover issues such as:

- A requirement that states preserve DNA evidence after conviction for some period of time.
- A process to request post-conviction DNA for testing.
- Costs to be paid by the state if the prisoner cannot pay.
- A process for petitioning the court for exoneration.
- Compensation statutes for exonerees.
- Laws to provide post-exoneration social services.

At least one state has proposed to take DNA samples upon arrest, just as fingerprints are taken. This has raised privacy issues.

## Chapter Objectives

Based on this chapter, students will:

1. Understand the role that testing of DNA evidence plays in exonerating prisoners.
2. Explain the efforts of groups such as The Innocence Project in representing potential exonerees.

3. Appreciate the evolution of state responses to post-conviction exonerations, including legislation to create a process for requesting DNA testing.

4. Distinguish between pardons, dismissal of charges, and findings of actual innocence.

5. Understand the importance of a finding of actual innocence as a prerequisite to suing for civil damages for wrongful incarceration.

6. Identify the role of *habeas corpus* petitions in the exoneration process.

7. Understand the effect of a prisoner's confession or plea to a lower offense on a claim for exoneration.

8. Explain the legal test for motions for a new trial based on newly discovered evidence.

9. Distinguish different state approaches to compensating exonerees for wrongful incarceration.

10. Appreciate the difficulty exonerees face in returning to society, the efforts of groups such as After Innocence, and proposed legislation to provide social services to exonerees.

# The Innocence Project

In 1989, Gary Dotson's conviction of a 1979 rape he did not commit was dismissed. Dotson had spent ten years in and out of prison as a result of this conviction. His was the first reported exoneration based on a testing of the DNA from the original rape kit. In 1994, Barry Scheck and John Newfeld founded The Innocence Project at Cordozo Law School in New York and began to review requests from prisoners for help in proving their innocence.[1]

The Innocence Project has resulted in 200 post-conviction exonerations through 2007 based on DNA forensic testing.[2] Theirs is not the only project. A study of all exonerations from 1989 through 2003 reports 340 exonerations—327 men and 13 women, of whom 144 were cleared by DNA.[3]

## Who Are the Exonerated?

The most well-known exonerations involve rape charges, simply because DNA can prove that semen from the rape kit did not belong to the prisoner. However, only 40% of those who request DNA testing are shown to be innocent. In other words, for 60% of prisoners who requested DNA testing, their DNA is actually present in the rape kit. And a number of prosecutors take the position that even if the semen did not belong to the defendant who was convicted, he could still be guilty of the rape.[4]

---

1. Barry C. Scheck, *Barry Scheck Lectures on Wrongful Convictions*, 54 Drake L. Rev. 597, 601 (Spring 2006).

2. http://innocenceproject.or.

3. Samuel R. Gross, Kristen Jacoby, Daniel J. Matheson, Nicholas Montgomery and Sujata Patil, *Innocence in Capital Sentencing*, 95 Crim. L. & Criminology 523, 524 (Winter 2005).

4. Gross et al., *supra* at 523.

Although rape exonerations are the best known, the total rape exonerations from 1989 to 2003 were 36%, compared with 60% for murder cases. In the vast majority of the rape cases, DNA testing was critical to the exoneration.

One reason that a majority of exonerations involve murder may be because attorneys are more likely to take on an exoneration claim for a high profile case, particularly one that may involve the death penalty. Wrongful murder convictions have been shown to result from coerced confessions, police pressure to close terrible crimes, and testimony by the real killer who had framed someone else for his crime. However, even in some of the murder cases, DNA has figured in the exoneration. DNA evidence collected at the crime scene can corroborate the exoneration and sometimes lead to the real culprit. Some argue that the absence of DNA evidence is irrelevant to proving innocence; however the presence of DNA evidence that excludes the prisoner generally creates reasonable doubt of his guilt.

In the study referred to above, 121 of the 340 exonerations were for rape (36%), and 88% of those involved an eyewitness misidentification.[5] Two-thirds of the exonerated were African American or Hispanic.

We do not know how many innocent defendants agree to plead to a lesser sentence to avoid serving long periods in prison before their case comes to trial, but there are doubtless a fair number of innocent prisoners who have pled guilty. This presents another problem in exonerations, as most people assume that a defendant who had pled guilty is guilty. As these prisoners might well be released by the time the DNA evidence is finally tested, and as their cases are not nearly as high-profile as death penalty cases, these prisoners stand little chance of being exonerated.

The top four states for exonerations are Illinois, New York, Texas and California, which account for 40% of the exonerations reported by the study.

## Laws to Preserve DNA Evidence

DNA is considered the gold standard of forensic evidence. A DNA profile of one person cannot wrongly implicate another. The statistics underlying DNA testing are such that the likelihood of a random person matching a defendant's DNA profile is generally greater than the entire U.S. population of 300 million. Although defense counsel can still argue to juries that poor testing procedures result in DNA profiles that are faulty, most scientists agree that a degraded or contaminated DNA sample will give no reading or a garbled reading, but it cannot give a false reading implicating another person. Of course, DNA from rape kits typically contains a mixture of DNA from the victim and the perpetrator, and in some cases, it may contain DNA from more than one sexual contact. However, DNA technicians can detect mixtures and determine the identity of the various contributors.

As DNA evidence from rape kits is frequently used in exonerations of rape convictions, most states have adopted laws requiring that DNA evidence be stored after trial. These laws include DNA not just from rape kits, but also hair, blood, or any other substances from which DNA may be extracted, including mitochondrial DNA.

---

5. Gross et al., *supra* at 530.

## What Is the Process Leading to Exoneration?

The process of exoneration would seem to be simple. All the prisoner would need to do is request the original DNA evidence, arrange to have it retested, show it to the prosecutor, and then the prosecutor would drop the charges. It is seldom so simple.

In the case of DNA exonerations, the defendant must first gain the attention of an attorney. This is often extremely difficult. The Innocence Project alone has file drawers of letters from prisoners asking for help. And in 60% of those cases,[6] retesting of DNA will not exonerate the defendant. Therefore, lawyers must choose carefully whom to represent in exoneration claims.

Next, the prisoner or his attorney must gain access to the DNA samples collected at trial and have them reexamined. There are three issues:

- Many samples have not been kept or are too degraded to test.
- The prisoner generally lacks funds to do the testing.
- He will have to convince the prosecutor who tried the case to release the evidence.

We will discuss below the various states that have enacted legislation providing for a right to DNA for post-conviction testing. But where such rights do not exist, the prisoner would typically bring an action alleging that the state, through the action of the prosecutor, has deprived him of his Fourteenth Amendment right to due process.[7]

This step is not a request for exoneration; it is simply a request to obtain DNA for testing. Before 2000, only New York and Illinois had statutes that authorized post-conviction DNA testing. Although some sympathetic judges were willing to order relief in the interests of justice, particularly when a prosecutor joined in the petitioner's request,[8] the only formal avenue was to move for a new trial based on newly-discovered evidence. If the time limit for moving for a new trial had run, the prisoner might have no recourse.

Even where a state has authorized applications for post-conviction DNA testing, the petition may not meet the requirements. The following case is an example of the legal hurdles a prisoner faces in attempting to obtain DNA test results.

### Reddick v. Florida, 929 So. 2d 34 (Fla. App. 2006)

The trial court denied the appellant's motion for postconviction DNA testing of evidence without a hearing, concluding that there was no reasonable probability that the movant would be acquitted or that he would have received a lesser sentence had the DNA testing occurred. We reverse, concluding that the appellant has alleged a facially sufficient claim.

The appellant, George Reddick, was convicted in 1985 of first degree murder and sexual battery of a seven-year-old girl who was staying in the same home as Reddick and several other people. No physical evidence was found linking Reddick to the crime. According to Reddick's motion, the sole testimony against him was the questionable identification of the victim's sister who testified that she saw Reddick take the victim out of a window.

---

6. Barry C. Scheck, et al., *supra* at 601.
7. Dylan Ruga, *Federal Court Adjudication of State Prisoner Claims for Post-Conviction DNA Testing: A Bifurcated Approach*, 2 Pierce L. Rev. 35 (March 2004).
8. Margaret A. Berger, *The Impact of DNA Exonerations on the Criminal Justice System*, 34 J.L. Med & Ethics 320 (Summer 2006).

However, this testimony was equivocal, as the witness apparently at first denied seeing anything, and at another time named another individual. Reddick maintained his innocence of the crime and asserted that another occupant of the home was the likely perpetrator.

In 2003, Reddick filed his motion for DNA testing pursuant to Florida Rule of Criminal Procedure 3.853. He recited the detailed facts and investigation of the case and listed the evidence for which he sought DNA testing. He also maintained his innocence and that the identity of the perpetrator was contested. He noted that in 1985 DNA testing was not available and none of the items had been tested other than for fingerprint analysis and semen analysis. Those tests failed to produce any results.

Reddick listed four categories of items to be tested for DNA:

(1) his clothing;

(2) items found near the victim's body, including beer cans, a plastic bottle, and a cup;

(3) sweepings of the victim's body, consisting of swabs of the vagina, rectum, and mouth; scalp hair, and fingernail clippings; and

(4) the victim's clothing, including her pajama bottoms, panties, etc.

As to his clothing, he stated that if DNA testing revealed no skin cells from the victim, it would exonerate him, as such cells would have to be on his clothing if he lifted her out of the house as the victim's sister testified. As to the items surrounding the victim's body, they might reveal that the victim was penetrated by a foreign object. DNA testing which did not reveal any of Reddick's DNA on such objects would create a reasonable probability that he was not in the area and did not use any of the objects to rape or murder the child.

With respect to the victim's clothing, he alleged that if they revealed no DNA from Reddick, this too would exonerate him of any rape, because skin cells would be present on the victim's pajamas if the perpetrator forcibly removed them, as was the testimony by experts. Finally, as to the victim's swabbings, these may reveal the DNA of the perpetrator, given the number of wounds and abrasions on the victim, particularly with respect to the fingernail clippings. Further, the rape of the victim would create DNA evidence, even if no semen was present.

The state responded, admitting the existence of the evidence sought to be tested. However, it claimed that Reddick's motion simply amounted to speculation that the clothing would have any DNA evidence on it or that the swabs would reveal any DNA. It suggested that the testing of Reddick's own clothing would not offer probative evidence in that the absence of the victim's DNA would be irrelevant. Finally, it also questioned the probative value of finding the victim's DNA on the bottles and cups around the victim's body.

Without conducting an evidentiary hearing, the court denied the motion. The court found that the items were available for testing and that the results would likely be admissible at trial. However, it concluded that there was no reasonable probability that Reddick would be acquitted or would receive a lesser sentence, adopting the state's response. It did not refer to the trial transcript or other portions of the record to support its conclusion.

In denying the motion without a hearing, the court must have assumed that it was legally insufficient for failing to show how the evidence would exonerate Reddick or lessen his sentence. However, as in *Schofield v. State,* we conclude that the motion was facially sufficient and alleged how he would be exonerated, at least as to some of the categories of evidence.

Identity was a disputed issue at trial, given the questionable eyewitness identification and the state's failure in its responses to refute that claim. With respect to the swabs of the victim's body and her clothes, the presence of the perpetrator's DNA is likely, as she was brutally beaten and sexually assaulted. If DNA testing confirms the presence of DNA of someone other than Reddick from the vagina, rectum, mouth or fingernail swabs, those results surely would create a reasonable probability that Reddick would be acquitted of the charges.

Although the state contends that there is no reason to suspect that testable skin cells or DNA would be found, that is not the criteria. What rule 3.853 requires the court to find is "whether it has been shown that physical evidence that may contain DNA still exists." Fla. R. Crim. P. 3.853(c)(5)(A) The court made that finding in its order.

As to DNA testing of Reddick's clothing, we agree that Reddick has failed to show how there would be a reasonable probability that he would be acquitted if the victim's DNA were not found on his clothing. Reddick has presented nothing to show that testable skin cells or other material would necessarily transfer to the clothing. Further, Reddick admits that his clothing was not delivered to the police until sometime significantly after the commencement of the investigation.

Even if there was no evidence of the victim's DNA on Reddick's clothing, given the passage of time and the possibility that the clothes were not in the same condition as they were on the night of the incident, it is apparent that this evidence would not reasonably result in an acquittal.

We also agree that Reddick did not adequately explain why the testing of the beer bottle, cup, and other material found around the body would exonerate him. The victim was found under a bush. No fingerprints were found on any of the surrounding items, nor were any of them tied to either the rape or the murder. In fact, there is nothing in the motion or the record before us which would indicate that these items were in any way connected to the crime, and instead were merely present under the bush when the body was found. We thus conclude that the motion was legally insufficient as to these items.

We therefore reverse and remand for further proceedings as the trial court erred in concluding that the motion was facially insufficient as to the testing of the victim's body sweepings and clothing.

# Getting the Conviction Reversed

In the 340 exonerations examined in the study mentioned above, 42 were pardoned by governors or other state executives, 263 had the charges dismissed by the courts, 31 were acquitted after a retrial, and 4 were posthumously acknowledged to have been innocent.[9]

---

9. Gross et al., *supra* at 530.

Assume that the prisoner does get access to DNA and the DNA is not his. Now the prisoner must convince a governor to pardon him, or a prosecutor to drop the charges, or a court to reverse his (most of the exonerated are men) conviction. Unless the DNA clearly implicates another known suspect, the prisoner may have a hard time convincing anyone that the DNA evidence should fully exonerate him.

Typically at this stage, the prisoner's state appeal rights have expired or all appeals have been denied. If he had brought a federal *habeas corpus* appeal, which is a collateral appeal to a federal court alleging a violation of a constitutional right, that right has also expired. A number of circuits have stated that the proper route to apply for exoneration is through a *habeas* petition.[10]

> *Habeas Corpus.* A petition made to a federal court alleging a U.S. Constitutional violation that justifies reversing a conviction.

A number of state legislatures are now adopting or considering laws that would give prisoners a right to post-conviction testing and would address how or when the prisoner might be released. We will discuss the legislation in Connecticut and at the federal level below.

In the absence of such legislation, the prisoner, assuming his appeals are exhausted, must bring a writ of *habeas corpus* claiming that he is actually innocent of the charges and should be released from prison.

## One State's Approach

Connecticut Legislation prescribes a process for convicts to request post-conviction DNA testing and request exoneration.

Connecticut enacted a statute that provides for a prisoner to obtain DNA for testing by petitioning the sentencing court if he states that the testing is related to his conviction and the evidence to be tested contains biological evidence.[11] After notice to the prosecutor's office and a hearing, the court **shall** order the DNA testing if it finds that:

1. A reasonable probability exists that the petitioner would not have been prosecuted or convicted if exculpatory results had been obtained through DNA testing;

2. The evidence is still in existence and is capable of being subjected to DNA testing;

3. The evidence ... was never previously ... [tested] or the testing ... [now] may resolve an issue that was never previously resolved by previous testing; and

4. The petition ... was filed to demonstrate the petitioner's innocence and not to delay the administration of justice.[12]

The Court **may** order DNA testing if there is a reasonable probability that the test results would have altered the verdict or reduced his sentence.

The cost of the testing shall be paid by the state or the petitioner as the court may order in the interests of justice. DNA testing may not be denied, however,

---

10. Ruga, 2 Pierce L. Rev. at 39.
11. Conn Gen. Stat. § 54-102kk (2006).
12. *Id.*

if the petitioner cannot pay for it. The petitioner may also be represented by court-appointed counsel if he cannot pay for counsel.[13]

The law also requires erasure of the petitioner's criminal record if the petitioner is found not guilty of the charge or the charge is dismissed.[14]

Connecticut law provides that a prisoner can petition for a new trial based on DNA evidence that was not discoverable or available at the trial any time after the discovery or availability of such evidence.[15]

## Federal Law

> Required for exoneration of federal crime: the petitioner must swear that he is innocent and the evidence led to conviction as a career offender or to the death penalty.

The Federal Government passed the Innocence Protection Act of 2003.[16] Under this act, an applicant who asserts that he is actually innocent of a federal offence for which he has been sentenced to prison or death may make a motion to the court that sentenced him if the petitioner swears that he is innocent and the evidence led to conviction as a career offender or the death penalty. The federal statute, therefore, is more restrictive than states such as Connecticut because it does not apply to all crimes.

The applicant must also have exhausted all other remedies, such as appeal to a state court, to request DNA testing, and the evidence must not have already been DNA tested, unless the applicant is requesting a new method of testing, the government still has the evidence, and the proposed testing is reasonable in scope.

Under the federal law, the identity of the perpetrator must have been an issue in the trial and the DNA testing would produce "material evidence" to support a defense and would "raise a reasonable probability that the applicant did not commit the offense."[17]

The FBI is to conduct the testing, with costs to be paid by the applicant or the government, if the applicant is indigent. The government may also submit the testing results to the Combined DNA Index System ("CODIS"), and may use any results to match the petitioner with another offense.

> The federal standard for granting the motion is if the DNA test results, when considered with all other evidence in the case, establish by a preponderance of the evidence that a new trial would result in an acquittal.

If the testing excludes the applicant as the source of the DNA, the applicant may file a motion for a new trial or re-sentencing. The standard for granting the motion is "if the DNA test results, when considered with all other evidence in the case (regardless of whether such evidence was introduced at trial), establish by a preponderance of the evidence that a new trial would result in an acquittal."[18] The law specifically states that it does not authorize a *habeas corpus* proceeding.

---

13. *Id.*
14. Conn. Gen. Stat. § 54-142a (2006).
15. Conn. Gen. Stat. § 52-582 (2006).
16. 18 U.S.C.S. Title 18, Chapter 228A § 3600.
17. *Id.*
18. *Id.* § 3600(g) Post-Testing Procedures; Motion for New Trial or Re-sentencing.

The Attorney General must file a report of all motions made under this Act within two years of its enactment.

# The Role of Eyewitness Misidentifications and Reform Efforts

By far the major explanation for the majority of wrongful rape convictions is false eyewitness identification. There have been many recent studies of error in eyewitness identifications and calls for changes in the line-up and identification process used by law enforcement About 71% of all rapes are committed by strangers, so the likelihood of a misidentification in those cases is great. In 85% of murder cases, the exonerated murder defendant knew the victim or at least one supposed eyewitness.[19] In these cases, there is often deliberate false evidence implicating the defendant, rather than a misidentification *per se*. As eyewitness misidentifications are often the cause of rape convictions from which prisoners are later exonerated, many commentators have called for reforms in the process of eyewitness identification. This topic is discussed in detail under the chapter "Eyewitness Identifications." The link between eyewitness identifications and wrongful convictions cannot be denied.

## Are the New Statutes Too Little, Too Late?

Barry Scheck, a co-founder of the Innocence Project, delivered a speech at Drake Law School on October 3, 2005,[20] in which he stated that his project of DNA exoneration was in a race against time. Although thirty-four states had adopted statutes to permit post-conviction DNA testing, he argued that less than ten percent of most serious felony cases have any biological evidence that would be susceptible to testing that could determine guilt or innocence. He added that the fact that there are innocent prisoners convicted of rapes or murders they did not commit means that the real perpetrator is still at large. "[I]n our cases where we have found the real assailant, in case after case it is a serial rapist. It is a serial murder. It is someone who has terrorized, pillaged, and hurt so many other people because of the wrongful conviction in the first place."[21]

Most DNA rape exonerations involve trials in which DNA evidence was not presented. As states now require DNA to be stored and kept, and as prosecutors routinely introduce DNA in trials, it is possible that fewer DNA exonerations will be brought in the future. Although this may reduce the number of wrongful convictions for rape, the issue of wrongful convictions for other crimes will likely persist, particularly in light of new studies demonstrating the fallibility of eyewitness identifications.

In 2007, a bill was introduced before the Connecticut legislature to require DNA testing of anyone arrested for a class A or B felony. Deputy Chief Public Defender Brian Carlow (who defended Grant) opposes the bill: "the presumed innocent would be providing their DNA before their guilt is proven."[22]

---

19. Gross et al., *supra* at 543.
20. 54 Drake L. Rev. at 603.
21. *Id.*
22. Christian Nolan, *Presumed Innocent?*, The Connecticut Law Tribune, April 30, 2007.

# Claims Based on Failure to Test DNA Evidence

Some defendants have appealed, claiming they were denied effective counsel if DNA testing is not requested and presented at trial. As the standard for reversal based on ineffective counsel is very high,[23] these appeals generally lose.

A recent Texas case dealt with an appeal based on the fact that no DNA testing had been done at trial and the evidence had subsequently been destroyed. The defendant had actually pled guilty at trial, which was why the DNA was destroyed. After conviction, he argued that he was entitled to have the DNA testing and that his conviction should be overturned because the DNA was no longer available. The court held that these claims did not justify relief under the Texas laws.

### Lewis v. Texas, 191 S.W.3d 225 (Tex. App. 2005)

Matthew Raymond Lewis appeals the denial of his request for a court appointed attorney to assist him in filing a post-conviction motion for forensic DNA testing, and the denial of his motion for DNA testing. Because Lewis is unable to demonstrate reasonable grounds for filing his motion for DNA testing, we overrule his issues and affirm the trial court's order.

In 2002, Lewis was indicted for the sexual assault of a minor under the age of 17, and, in a separate count, for aggravated sexual assault of a second minor under the age of 14. Lewis entered a plea of guilty to both counts and was sentenced by the trial court to incarceration in the Texas Department of Criminal Justice, Institutional Division, for a period of eleven years.

> *Pro se.* A court proceeding in which the defendant acts as his own attorney.

Nineteen months later, on September 13, 2004, Lewis, acting *pro se,* filed a motion for DNA testing of evidence secured in relation to his conviction of sexual assault, a sworn affidavit in support of the motion, a request for the appointment of an attorney, a declaration of inability to pay costs and an affidavit of indigence. Lewis requested that all the motions be set for a hearing.

The trial court asked for a response from the district attorney's office in Kerr County. Sergeant John Lavender, the evidence officer for the Kerr County Sheriff's office, and Ronald L. Sutton, the district attorney for Kerr County, filed sworn affidavits which stated, "The evidence in the above-mentioned case was destroyed after the Defendant's plea of guilty to one count of sexual abuse of a child and one count of aggravated sexual assault of a child with two different victims and the appeal time limit had expired."

Without holding a hearing, the trial court subsequently denied Lewis' motion for DNA testing, noting that Lewis entered a voluntary plea of guilty to the offenses and that there "was and is no issue of identity as required by Article 64 of the Texas Code of Criminal Procedure." The court further found, "based on the affidavit of John Lavender, evidence officer for the Kerr County Sheriff's Department, the evidence referenced in Defendant's motion no longer exists." Lewis filed a *pro se* appeal to this court.

---

23. *Gideon v. Wainwright,* 372 U.S. 335 (1963).

We review the trial court's ruling on a post-conviction motion for forensic DNA testing under a bifurcated standard of review. We afford almost total deference to the "trial court's determination of issues of historical fact and application-of-law-to-fact issues that turn on credibility and demeanor, while we review *de novo* other application-of-law-to-fact issues."

In his first three issues, Lewis contends the trial court erred in denying his request for a court appointed attorney. To determine whether Lewis was entitled to appointed counsel to assist him in filing a post-conviction motion for DNA testing, we must examine the applicable statute. See TEX. CODE CRIM. PROC. ANN. art. 64.01(c). As originally written in 2001, article 64.01(c) stated that a defendant was entitled to the appointment of counsel merely upon requesting counsel and establishing indigence.... The legislature, however, amended article 64.01(c) effective September 1, 2003 to read, in relevant part, as follows:

> The convicting court shall appoint counsel for the convicted person if the person informs the court that the person wishes to submit a motion under this chapter, the court finds reasonable grounds for a motion to be filed, and the court determines that the person is indigent.

Because Lewis filed his motion for DNA testing after the effective date of the amendment, he had the additional burden of establishing "reasonable grounds for a motion to be filed" in order to qualify for appointed counsel. "Reasonable grounds" are not defined within the statute. Generally, in interpreting a statute, we give words their plain meaning unless the language is ambiguous or its plain meaning leads to an absurd result. Words and phrases are read in context and construed according to the rules of grammar and common usage.

\* \* \*

In determining whether Lewis' motion sets forth reasonable grounds, we again examine the statute. Although anyone may request DNA testing, a court is required to order testing only if several statutory requirements are met. Two of those requirements are that the evidence "still exists" and that "identity was or is an issue in the case." TEX. CODE CRIM. PROC. ANN. art. 64.03(a)(1)(A)(i), (a)(1)(B). In its order denying Lewis' request for counsel, the trial court expressly found that Lewis failed to show both of these requirements.

As to the first of the requirements addressed by the trial court, the statute requires that the evidence still exists, and is in a condition to make DNA testing possible, before the court may order testing. TEX. CODE CRIM. PROC. ANN. art. 64.03(a)(1)(A)(i). Affidavit testimony from a relevant witness that no biological evidence from the case is maintained or possessed is sufficient, absent any contrary evidence, to support denial of a motion for forensic DNA testing. Such a determination may be made by the trial court without an evidentiary hearing.

Here, the trial court had before it the affidavits of the evidence officer and district attorney stating that "[t]he evidence in the above-mentioned case was destroyed after the Defendant's plea of guilty ... and the appeal time limit had expired." Therefore, on this record, the trial court could have reasonably concluded that the biological evidence referenced in Lewis' motion no longer exists.

> "[T]he presence of another person's DNA at the crime scene will not, without more, constitute affirmative evidence of appellant's innocence."
> *Lewis v. Texas*

As to the second requirement that identity "was or is" an issue, we note that Lewis' affidavit in support of his motion for DNA testing asserts that such testing is warranted because the minor was "sexually active" with other males, "lied about her age," and "did not want any sexual assault charges filed in this incident." Nowhere in his motion or affidavit does Lewis deny that he had sexual intercourse with the minor.

Instead, Lewis contends that no assault occurred because the minor was sexually promiscuous, lied about her age, and did not want to file sexual assault charges. Even if true, however, none of these claims exonerate Lewis. Assuming the minor was sexually promiscuous with other males, "[t]he presence of another person's DNA at the crime scene will not, without more, constitute affirmative evidence of appellant's innocence." ... Also, even assuming the minor lied about her age and did not want sexual assault charges filed in this incident, "[c]onsent is not an issue where the charged offense is sexual assault of a child because a victim under seventeen is legally incapable of consenting to the types of sexual relations described in the statute."

Moreover, Lewis confessed to the crime for which he was convicted; his identity was never an issue. Accordingly, the trial court could have reasonably concluded that there was and is no issue of identity in this case.

Because Lewis' motion for post conviction DNA testing fails to meet two of the preconditions to obtaining DNA testing under Chapter 64, specifically that the evidence still exists and that identity is or was an issue in the case, it also fails to demonstrate "reasonable grounds for a motion to be filed." We conclude that Lewis was not entitled to appointed counsel under article 64.01(c). We overrule Lewis' first three points of error.

In his fourth issue, Lewis claims the State violated the Texas Code of Criminal Procedure when it failed to preserve the biological evidence from his case, or notify him by mail before destroying the evidence. Lewis seeks reversal of his original conviction on the basis that such violations deprived him of his constitutional rights to due process and equal protection of the law.

In essence, Lewis seeks *habeas corpus* relief. The Code of Criminal Procedure does not authorize an appeal to a court of appeals for allegations that the State improperly destroyed DNA evidence; nor does a court of appeals have original jurisdiction to grant a writ of *habeas corpus* in criminal law matters. Accordingly, we have no jurisdiction to address Lewis' fourth issue.

In his fifth issue, Lewis complains that the trial court improperly denied his request for DNA testing based on his plea of guilty to the underlying charges. Lewis cites Chapter 64, which states in relevant part, "[a] convicted person who pleaded guilty or *nolo contendere* in the case may submit a motion under this chapter, and the convicting court is prohibited from finding that identity was not an issue in the case solely on the basis of that plea."

We disagree that the trial court improperly denied Lewis' motion. "Chapter 64 does not guarantee a person who pled guilty the right to DNA testing; it simply prohibits a convicting court from using a guilty plea to bar access to the filing of a motion for testing." Here, Lewis was not barred from filing his motion for

DNA testing. In addition, the trial court did not deny Lewis' motion solely on the basis of his plea.

As previously discussed, the trial court reasonably found that Lewis' motion failed to meet two of the preconditions to obtaining post-conviction DNA testing under Chapter 64, specifically, that the evidence still exists and that identity is or was an issue in the case. Lewis' fifth issue is overruled.

CONCLUSION

The trial court's order denying Lewis' motion for post-conviction forensic DNA testing pursuant to Chapter 64 is affirmed.


# *House v. Bell*—A Reversal Based on Improper Blood Testing

In *House v. Bell*,[24] pre-DNA blood serology was improperly performed at the trial and implicated the defendant House of murder of a woman on whom his alleged semen was found. Later DNA testing showed that the semen belonged to the victim's husband. Other evidence also showed that it was more likely the victim's husband, not House, who was the murderer.

The defendant had brought a *habeas* petition, which was denied by the Sixth Circuit on the ground that the prisoner failed to show actual innocence. The U.S. Supreme Court reversed, finding that the correct standard for granting a new trial was "whether it was more likely than not that no reasonable juror would not have reasonable doubt of the defendant's guilt after seeing the DNA evidence."

The case involved the murder of Carolyn Muncey in rural Tennessee in 1986. She was murdered outside her home in her nightgown and was found in some brush nearby. Although she was married to an abusive husband who had threatened her, the court convicted House based on a neighbor having seen House in the area on the night of the murder. House, when questioned, lied about spending the entire evening with his girlfriend. He had scratches on his arms and a bruise on his right ring finger. The girlfriend initially confirmed his alibi but recanted the next day, saying he left her trailer around 10 pm to go for a walk and returned some time later missing his shirt and shoes and hot and panting. House was not a particularly credible witness in light of his previous lies.

Investigators drove the evidence, consisting of Muncey's nightgown and House's pants, to the FBI for testing, a ten-hour drive. They packaged the pants, blood samples from the autopsy of Muncey and other evidence in one box. The FBI stated that the semen was consistent with House's and that small bloodstains consistent with Muncey's blood but not House's appeared on his jeans. This conclusion, formed in 1986, was not based on DNA testing, but rather testing based on "serology," a study of the blood types of the blood and the blood type and "secretors" in the semen.

House, Mrs. Muncey and Mr. Muncey all had type A blood. The FBI found that the semen was from a contributor with type A blood who was a "secretor," one who secretes ABO blood group substances in semen—a characteristic shared by 80 percent of the

---

24. 126 S. Ct. 2064 (June 12, 2006).

population, including House. The expert, Bigbee, testified he was unable to determine the secretor status of either Muncy.

> Agent Bigbee found only the H blood-group substance, which A and B blood-type secretors secrete along with substances A and B and which O-type secretors secrete exclusively. Agent Bigbee explained, however—using science an *amicus* sharply disputes ... that House's A antigens could have "degraded" into H.... Agent Bigbee thus concluded that both semen deposits could have come from House, though he acknowledged that the H antigen could have come from Mrs. Muncey herself if she was a secretor—something he "was not able to determine."[25]

Bigbee acknowledged that a saliva test would have answered the question, but the state did not provide a saliva sample. Bigbee testified that the blood spots on House's pants were type A but had slight chemical traces consistent only with Mrs. Muncey's blood. Based on this, he concluded the blood could have come only from Mrs. Muncey. Muncey's shoes, found several months after the crime, had no blood on them.

The Supreme Court agreed with House's contention that the blood on the pants may well have come from a leak in the sample of Mrs. Muncey's blood that occurred during the 10-hour drive to the FBI lab. Four vials of Mrs. Muncey's blood were packed with the pants, but a vial and a half of the four vials were missing when it arrived for testing. There was also seepage of her blood in one corner of the packing box, and there was a forked streak of blood on a plastic bag with a label listing the pants.[26]

Later DNA testing confirmed that the semen had come from the victim's husband and not the defendant. The blood on the pants was too degraded to be tested, but the state's blood spatter expert testified that the majority of the stains were "transfer stains" resulting from "wiping across the surface of the pants" rather than seeping or spilling. The Supreme Court found that "the record before us contains credible testimony suggesting that the missing enzyme markers are generally better preserved on cloth than in poorly kept test tubes, and that principle could support House's spillage theory for the blood's origin."[27]

Additional witness testimony supported the view that Mr. Muncey had beaten his wife and threatened to kill her. The jury had not heard this evidence. The Court concluded:

> This is not a case of conclusive exoneration ... Yet the central forensic proof connecting House to the crime—the blood and the semen—has been called into question, and House has put forward substantial evidence pointing to a different suspect. Accordingly ... had the jury heard all the conflicting testimony—it is more likely than not that no reasonable juror viewing the record as a whole would lack reasonable doubt.[28]

The Court remanded the case for a new trial. Justice Roberts, joined by two other Supreme Court justices, wrote a dissenting opinion questioning the standard in the majority opinion for remand based on DNA testing.

> House must show more than just a "reasonable probability that ... the fact finder would have had a reasonable doubt respecting guilt ... House must pre-

---

25. *Id.* at 2072.
26. *Id.* at 2080.
27. *Id.* at 2082.
28. *Id.* at 2086.

sent such compelling evidence of innocence that it becomes more likely than not that no single juror, acting reasonably, would vote to convict him.[29]

None of the Justices concluded that the DNA evidence exonerated House. The only question was whether enough new evidence had been presented, including DNA testing of the semen and evidence about the source of blood on House's pants, to require a new trial in which the jury would hear all the evidence. Thus, we see the Supreme Court divided on what legal standard should be used where DNA retesting is not conclusive, but where it *may* affect the outcome of the case.

Here is part of the opinion in *House v. Bell:*

**_House v. Bell,_ 126 S. Ct. 2064 (June 12, 2006)**

\* \* \*

First, in direct contradiction of evidence presented at trial, DNA testing has established that the semen on Mrs. Muncey's nightgown and panties came from her husband, Mr. Muncey, not from House. The State, though conceding this point, insists this new evidence is immaterial. At the guilt phase at least, neither sexual contact nor motive were elements of the offense, so in the State's view the evidence, or lack of evidence, of sexual assault or sexual advance is of no consequence. We disagree. In fact we consider the new disclosure of central importance.

From beginning to end the case is about who committed the crime. When identity is in question, motive is key. The point, indeed, was not lost on the prosecution, for it introduced the evidence and relied on it in the final guilt-phase closing argument. Referring to "evidence at the scene," the prosecutor suggested that House committed, or attempted to commit, some "indignity" on Mrs. Muncey that neither she "nor any mother on that road would want to do with Mr. House."

Particularly in a case like this where the proof was, as the State Supreme Court observed, circumstantial, we think a jury would have given this evidence great weight. Quite apart from providing proof of motive, it was the only forensic evidence at the scene that would link House to the murder.

Law and society, as they ought to do, demand accountability when a sexual offense has been committed, so not only did this evidence link House to the crime; it likely was a factor in persuading the jury not to let him go free. At sentencing, moreover, the jury came to the unanimous conclusion, beyond a reasonable doubt, that the murder was committed in the course of a rape or kidnapping. The alleged sexual motivation relates to both those determinations. This is particularly so given that, at the sentencing phase, the jury was advised that House had a previous conviction for sexual assault.

A jury informed that fluids on Mrs. Muncey's garments could have come from House might have found that House trekked the nearly two miles to the victim's home and lured her away in order to commit a sexual offense. By contrast a jury acting without the assumption that the semen could have come from House would have found it necessary to establish some different motive, or, if the same motive, an intent far more speculative. When the only direct evidence of sexual assault drops out of the case, so, too, does a central theme in the

---

29. *Id* at 2096.

State's narrative linking House to the crime. In that light, furthermore, House's odd evening walk and his false statements to authorities, while still potentially incriminating, might appear less suspicious.

Bloodstains

The other relevant forensic evidence is the blood on House's pants, which appears in small, even minute, stains in scattered places. As the prosecutor told the jury, they were stains that, due to their small size, "you or I might not detect[,] might not see, but which the FBI lab was able to find on [House's] jeans." The stains appear inside the right pocket, outside that pocket, near the inside button, on the left thigh and outside leg, on the seat of the pants, and on the right bottom cuff, including inside the pants. Due to testing by the FBI, cuttings now appear on the pants in several places where stains evidently were found. (The cuttings were destroyed in the testing process, and defense experts were unable to replicate the tests.)

At trial, the government argued "nothing that the defense has introduced in this case explains what blood is doing on his jeans, all over [House's] jeans, that is scientifically, completely different from his blood." House, though not disputing at this point that the blood is Mrs. Muncey's, now presents an alternative explanation that, if credited, would undermine the probative value of the blood evidence.

During House's *habeas* proceedings, Dr. Cleland Blake, an Assistant Chief Medical Examiner for the State of Tennessee and a consultant in forensic pathology to the TBI for 22 years, testified that the blood on House's pants was chemically too degraded, and too similar to blood collected during the autopsy, to have come from Mrs. Muncey's body on the night of the crime. The blood samples collected during the autopsy were placed in test tubes without preservative.

Under such conditions, according to Dr. Blake, "you will have enzyme degradation. You will have different blood group degradation, blood marker degradation." The problem of decay, moreover, would have been compounded by the body's long exposure to the elements, sitting outside for the better part of a summer day. In contrast, if blood is preserved on cloth, "it will stay there for years,"; indeed, Dr. Blake said he deliberately places blood drops on gauze during autopsies to preserve it for later testing.

The blood on House's pants, judging by Agent Bigbee's tests, showed "similar deterioration, breakdown of certain of the named numbered enzymes" as in the autopsy samples. "If the victim's blood had spilled on the jeans while the victim was alive and this blood had dried," Dr. Blake stated, "the deterioration would not have occurred," ... and "you would expect [the blood on the jeans] to be different than what was in the tube." Dr. Blake thus concluded the blood on the jeans came from the autopsy samples, not from Mrs. Muncey's live (or recently killed) body.

Other evidence confirms that blood did in fact spill from the vials. It appears the vials passed from Dr. Carabia, who performed the autopsy, into the hands of two local law enforcement officers, who transported it to the FBI, where Agent Bigbee performed the enzyme tests. The blood was contained in four vials, evidently with neither preservative nor a proper seal. The vials, in turn, were stored in a styrofoam box, but nothing indicates the box was kept cool. Rather, in what an evidence protocol expert at the *habeas* hearing described as a violation of proper procedure, the styrofoam box was packed in the same cardboard box as other evidence including House's pants (apparently in a paper bag) and other clothing (in separate bags).

The cardboard box was then carried in the officers' car while they made the 10-hour journey from Tennessee to the FBI lab. Dr. Blake stated that blood vials in hot conditions (such as a car trunk in the summer) could blow open; and in fact, by the time the blood reached the FBI it had hemolyzed, or spoiled, due to heat exposure. By the time the blood passed from the FBI to a defense expert, roughly a vial and a half were empty, though Agent Bigbee testified he used at most a quarter of one vial. Blood, moreover, had seeped onto one corner of the styrofoam box and onto packing gauze inside the box below the vials.

In addition, although the pants apparently were packaged initially in a paper bag and FBI records suggest they arrived at the FBI in one, the record does not contain the paper bag but does contain a plastic bag with a label listing the pants and Agent Scott's name—and the plastic bag has blood on it. The blood appears in a forked streak roughly five inches long and two inches wide running down the bag's outside front. Though testing by House's expert confirmed the stain was blood, the expert could not determine the blood's source. Speculations about when and how the blood got there add to the confusion regarding the origins of the stains on House's pants.

Faced with these indications of, at best, poor evidence control, the State attempted to establish at the *habeas* hearing that all blood spillage occurred after Agent Bigbee examined the pants. Were that the case, of course, then blood would have been detected on the pants before any spill—which would tend to undermine Dr. Blake's analysis and support using the bloodstains to infer House's guilt. In support of this theory the State put on testimony by a blood spatter expert who believed the "majority" of the stains were "transfer stains," that is, stains resulting from "wiping across the surface of the pants" rather than seeping or spillage.

* * *

In this Court, as a further attack on House's showing, the State suggests that, given the spatter expert's testimony, House's theory would require a jury to surmise that Tennessee officials donned the pants and deliberately spread blood over them. We disagree. This should be a matter for the trier of fact to consider in the first instance, but we can note a line of argument that could refute the State's position. It is correct that the State's spatter expert opined that the stains resulted from wiping or smearing rather than direct spillage; and she further stated that the distribution of stains in some spots suggests the pants were "folded in some manner or creased in some manner" when the transfers occurred.

While the expert described this pattern, at least with respect to stains on the lap of the pants, as "consistent" with the pants being worn at the time of the staining, ... her testimony, as we understand it, does not refute the hypothesis that the packaging of the pants for transport was what caused them to be folded or creased.

It seems permissible, moreover, to conclude that the small size and wide distribution of stains—inside the right pocket, outside that pocket, near the inside button, on the left thigh and outside leg, on the seat of the pants, and on the right bottom cuff, including inside the pants—fits as well with spillage in transport as with wiping and smearing from bloody objects at the crime scene, as the State proposes. (As has been noted, no blood was found on House's shoes.)

* * *

In sum, considering "all the evidence," on this issue, we think the evidentiary disarray surrounding the blood, taken together with Dr. Blake's testimony and the limited rebuttal of it in the present record, would prevent reasonable jurors from placing significant reliance on the blood evidence. We now know, though the trial jury did not, that an Assistant Chief Medical Examiner believes the blood on House's jeans must have come from autopsy samples; that a vial and a quarter of autopsy blood is unaccounted for; that the blood was transported to the FBI together with the pants in conditions that could have caused vials to spill; that the blood did indeed spill at least once during its journey from Tennessee authorities through FBI hands to a defense expert; that the pants were stored in a plastic bag bearing both a large blood stain and a label with TBI Agent Scott's name; and that the styrofoam box containing the blood samples may well have been opened before it arrived at the FBI lab. Thus, whereas the bloodstains, emphasized by the prosecution, seemed strong evidence of House's guilt at trial, the record now raises substantial questions about the blood's origin.

### A Different Suspect

Were House's challenge to the State's case limited to the questions he has raised about the blood and semen, the other evidence favoring the prosecution might well suffice to bar relief. There is, however, more; for in the post-trial proceedings House presented troubling evidence that Mr. Muncey, the victim's husband, himself could have been the murderer.

* * *

### Other Evidence

Certain other details were presented at the *habeas* hearing. First, Dr. Blake, in addition to testifying about the blood evidence and the victim's head injury, examined photographs of House's bruises and scratches and concluded, based on 35 years' experience monitoring the development and healing of bruises, that they were too old to have resulted from the crime. In addition Dr. Blake claimed that the injury on House's right knuckle was indicative of "getting mashed"; it was not consistent with striking someone. (That of course would also eliminate the explanation that the injury came from the blow House supposedly told Turner he gave to his unidentified assailant.)

### Conclusion

This is not a case of conclusive exoneration. Some aspects of the State's evidence—Lora Muncey's memory of a deep voice, House's bizarre evening walk, his lie to law enforcement, his appearance near the body, and the blood on his pants—still support an inference of guilt. Yet the central forensic proof connecting House to the crime—the blood and the semen—has been called into question, and House has put forward substantial evidence pointing to a different suspect.

Accordingly, and although the issue is close, we conclude that this is the rare case where—had the jury heard all the conflicting testimony—it is more likely than not that no reasonable juror viewing the record as a whole would lack reasonable doubt.

…

The judgment of the Court of Appeals is reversed, and the case is remanded for further proceedings consistent with this opinion.

It is so ordered.

> "We conclude that this is the rare case where—had the jury heard all the conflicting testimony—it is more likely than not that no reasonable juror viewing the record as a whole would lack reasonable doubt." *House v. Bell*

# Exoneration and Post-Conviction Mitochondrial DNA Testing

The case of Mark Reid combines issues of expert testimony about hair analysis and subsequent mitochondrial testing of the hairs. Reid was convicted in 1997 of sexual assault and kidnapping. At trial, Kiti Settachatgul, a lead criminologist at the Connecticut state police forensic laboratory, testified that three pubic hairs taken from the victim's clothing were similar to the characteristics of hairs provided by the defendant. At Reid's appeal, he argued that the court improperly admitted the expert testimony without a *Daubert* hearing. The appeals court concluded that a *Daubert* hearing was unnecessary, as hair analysis, like shoe print analysis, is a matter than is within the jury's common knowledge:

> Settachatgul's testimony is akin to that of the podiatrist in *Hasan*. Although Settachatgul's training is based in science, he testified about a subject that simply required the jurors to use their own powers of observation and comparison. During his testimony, Settachatgul displayed an enlarged photograph of one of the defendant's hairs and one of the hairs recovered from the victim's clothing as they appeared side-by-side under the comparison microscope. Settachatgul explained to the jurors how the hairs were similar and what particular features of the hairs were visible.

> He also drew a diagram of a hair on a courtroom blackboard for the jurors. The jurors were free to make their own determinations as to the weight they would accord the expert's testimony in the light of the photograph and their own powers of observation and comparison. The jurors were not subject to confusing or obscure scientific evidence, but were able to use the testimony to guide them in their own determination of the similarity of the two hairs.

\* \* \*

We conclude that microscopic hair analysis is not the type of evidence that we contemplated in *Porter* to be subject to the *Daubert* test. Accordingly, a hearing as to the admissibility of the evidence was not required by *Porter*, and the trial court properly admitted the evidence.[30]

---

30. *State v. Reid*, 254 Conn. 540, 547–559, 757 A.2d 482, 487–488 (2000).

Reid also challenged the admissibility of the hair comparison on the ground that the expert did not take measurements of the diameter or length of the hair, or quantify the density of pigment, the degree of curliness or the color. The court held that these issues went to the weight of the evidence, but not its admissibility.

> As a result of mtDNA testing, the trial testimony and visual comparison of the hairs which appeared to be identical was shown to be absolutely wrong.

Two years later, Reid petitioned for a new trial, alleging that mitochondrial DNA had excluded him as the source of the hair specimens. The Connecticut trial court granted the petition,[31] and charges against Reid were subsequently dropped. The discussion of the mitochondrial DNA analysis appears under the DNA chapter.

The result in the Reid case is particularly troubling because it shows that the trial testimony and visual comparison of the hairs was absolutely wrong, yet it appeared to be correct. The mitochondrial evidence showed that any "similarity" between the hairs was prejudicial and highly misleading, as the hair was absolutely not the defendant's. Does this mean that no hair comparisons should be submitted to a jury without DNA or mtDNA testing? This is certainly one conclusion to be drawn from *Reid*.

# Can Exonerees Sue for Money for Wrongful Imprisonment?

As states generally have statutory immunity from civil suits, exonerees generally cannot sue for civil damages unless they have been declared actually innocent (as opposed to being pardoned or a verdict of not guilty after a retrial) or the state adopts legislation permitting a suit or a statutory damage award.

Although an exoneree can potentially demonstrate the loss of income from employment during imprisonment, damages for the "pain and suffering" resulting from unjust imprisonment could total millions. In 1995, the family of Sam Sheppard, convicted of the 1954 murder of his wife, and held not guilty after a second trial, showed flawed analysis both of blood spatter and DNA evidence proving a third party was at the crime scene, attempted to have a trial court declare Sheppard actually innocent in order to sue the state of Illinois for civil damages. Even though there was substantial evidence that Sheppard had not committed the crime, the suit was denied and the Sheppard heirs have never collected for the many years that Sheppard spent behind bars.[32]

On the other hand, Larry David Holdren, who spent fourteen years in prison for a crime he did not commit, received a substantial court award. In 1999, when Holden was 44, the court reversed his conviction and dismissed the indictment. He sued, and received $1,650,000, approximately $110,000 for each year in prison.[33]

---

31. *State v. Reid*, CV 020818851, 2003 Conn. Super. LEXIS 1496, May 14, 2003.

32. Cyril Wecht and Greg Saitz with Mark Curriden, *Mortal Evidence*, Prometheus Books, 2003 at 129.

33. Adele Bernhard, *Justice Still Fails: A Review of Recent Efforts to Compensate Individuals Who Have been Unjustly Convicted and Later Exonerated*, 52 Drake L. Rev. 703, 709–710 (Summer 2004).

In 1999, only fourteen states, the District of Columbia and the federal government had laws to compensate individuals who had been unjustly convicted.[34] "Most offered compensation so skimpy as to be insulting. Many statutes were virtually inaccessible because they required a gubernational pardon."[35] Since 1999, more states have enacted compensation statutes, but some provide very low compensation. For example Montana pays for tuition only. Ohio limits compensation to $40,333 per year, plus lost wages. Missouri proposed legislation that would limit economic loss to the amount the federal government regards as poverty level plus twenty percent.[36]

To receive such benefits, the exoneree must generally release the right to sue the state. However, a number of exonerees have refused the benefits and sued lawyers, police, prosecutors and police departments under theories such a deprivation of civil rights under § 1983 of the federal code. Prosecutors generally have the defense of absolute immunity. Although police officers may be sued for reckless or intentional failure to investigate a crime, they are not liable if their failure was based on an objectively reasonable basis for believing their conduct was reasonable.

# How Does the Exoneree Return to Society?

We Americans like a happy ending—we picture an exonerated prisoner, the iron prison doors clanging shut behind him, as he clutches a satchel containing his belongings and squints like a mole suddenly confronted with the sun. But what really happens after the exonerated returns to society? Does he receive job training, social services, medical treatment, therapy? Does he even get a formal apology? The answer is frequently "no." Unlike parolees, who generally receive these benefits, the exonerated do not qualify.

A project called Life After Exoneration[37] has been formed to highlight this injustice and call for reform. The project produced a film called After Innocence, tracking the lives of exonerees after release. Some are still viewed as pariahs in their community. Some are so angry about their treatment that they cannot move forward with their lives. Many cannot obtain a job because their primary years for learning a skill have been spent behind bars,

The film interviews Wilton Dedge, who spent twenty-two years in a Florida jail, serving two concurrent life sentences, until mitochondrial DNA tests proved that a hair found on the victim's bed and "matched" to him could not be his. Dedge fought for eight years to get the DNA testing that would eventually exonerate him. At the end of the film, he is shown returning to his childhood bedroom, decorated in boyish blue by his white-haired parents, the scene oddly sad for the homecoming of a man in his 40's.

Dennis Maher served nineteen years of a life sentence. The film shows him working fixing trucks and awaiting the birth of his first child. He's one of the lucky ones, willing to go out drinking in a local bar and listen to his buddies rail at what they would do if they'd been wrongfully imprisoned.

---

34. *Id.*
35. *Id.* at 703.
36. *Id.* at 706–712.
37. www.exonerated.org.

*Attorney Karen Goodrow, of the Connecticut Innocence Project, James C. Tillman, exonerated after 18 years for a crime he did not commit, and the author*

Some are not so lucky. Scott Hornoff, a former police officer, whose only crime was a casual sexual affair with a woman who was later raped and murdered by someone else, was eventually exonerated. The film interviews his father, also a police officer, who believed his son was guilty and did not visit him once in prison. Hornoff tried to get his license as a cop reinstated. But the force was in no hurry to give him back his old life.

Others complained that they cannot get a job or housing with a criminal record. Their conviction is not automatically expunged. One exoneree discovered it would cost $6,000 to get the conviction removed from his record.

## James Tillman

The state of Connecticut established an Innocence Project in 2004, when two public defenders—Brian Carlow (who defended Edward Grant) and Karen Goodrow—agreed to lead the project. They were instrumental in the release of Mark Reid, when mtDNA excluded him from the hairs introduced as a match at his trial for rape. By June of 2006, they had secured the release of James Tillman, who had been convicted in 1989 of rape and sentenced to forty-five years.[38] Their first challenge was simply finding the evidence that had been used to secure Tillman's conviction. Fortunately, they were able to obtain the evidence used in the trial from a box stored in the back room of a local legal aid office that contained a dress and a pair of panty hose—both had been exhibits in Tillman's trial.

*Nolle Prosequi* is latin for "we shall no longer prosecute." When the prosecution "nolles" a charge, it drops the charge.

Carlow and Goodrow then obtained a court order for new testing of the semen stains. The genetic profile categorically eliminated Tillman as the source. Tillman was granted a new trial and released from prison on June 6, 2006. The judge found that had the jury known of the DNA results that showed Tillman was not the secretor of

38. Lisa Siegel, *A Criminal Justice 'Nightmare,'* The Connecticut Law Tribune, week of June 12, 2006.

the six semen stains, it would have found him not guilty of the charges against him—the standard of law required for the granting of a new trial. At a pretrial conference on July 11, 2006 prosecutors "nolled"[39] the charges against Tillman and the judge then granted his motion for dismissal.

On May 16, 2007, the Connecticut legislature voted to award $5 million to Tillman as compensation,[40] and the governor publicly apologized to Tillman.

Although his attorneys acknowledged that prosecutors had not done anything underhanded at Tillman's trial, as DNA testing was not available at the time, the Tillman case illustrates the extent to which rape convictions of the innocent have depended upon false eyewitness identifications.

> The white victim testified that she was beaten, abducted and raped by an unknown black assailant, near Columbus Boulevard in Hartford. She testified that she focused during the attack on memorizing identifying details about the perpetrator. A few days after the attack, she was given photo books to look through by the Hartford police, who did not have a suspect at the time. After turning a few pages, she became emotionally distressed when she saw Tillman's photo. She identified him as the perpetrator, but said he looked younger than at the time of the attack.[41]

Tillman now works for a private non-profit educational entity. Says one of his attorneys, Karen Goodrow: "Mr. Tillman is a gracious and dignified man whose genuine faith has helped him through the extreme burden of being wrongfully convicted and incarcerated for over 18 years. Since his release, he has been contributing to society through his work, his faith and his desire to mentor young men and those less fortunate than he."[42]

Legislation providing for job training, medical and psychological services and other re-entry services was introduced in the Connecticut legislature in January of 2007.

# Summary

Over 300 prisoners have reportedly been exonerated and released from prison since 1989. Of these, about 36% were rape convictions that were reversed based on testing of DNA evidence that was not tested at the time of trial. The majority of DNA exonerations involve rapes, as DNA evidence was frequently collected at the time of the rape.

The phenomenon of DNA exonerations has captured the public interest and has led many states to adopt legislation to help with exoneration requests. These laws cover issues such as:

- A requirement that states preserve DNA evidence after conviction for some period of time.
- A process to request post-conviction DNA for testing.

---

39. The state chose not to re-try Tillman; it could have chosen to dismiss the indictment and acknowledge that Tillman was wrongfully charged, but it did not.
40. Mark Pazniokas and Colin Poitras, *Payment for the Pain,* The Hartford Courant, May 17, 2007.
41. Siegel, *supra.*
42. Interview with author, February 13, 2007.

- Costs to be paid by the state if the prisoner cannot pay.
- A process for petitioning the court for exoneration.
- Compensation statutes for exonerees.
- Laws to provide post-exoneration social services.

The legal standard for relief based on post-conviction testing remains high. The prisoner must show that no reasonable juror would have voted to convict, if the results of the DNA test were presented at trial.

We can expect DNA exonerations to decrease as trials today that involve DNA evidence usually present the DNA test results in evidence. However, defendants will continue to be wrongfully convicted, particularly because of the problems with the reliability of eyewitness identification. These defendants may have a much more difficult time in proving their innocence, particularly if the public no longer perceives a major miscarriage in justice.

# Discussion Questions

1. What does your state provide about whether DNA evidence must be kept?

2. Does your state have a process for requesting DNA for testing? For exoneration? For post-exoneration compensation?

3. With limited money and time, do you think it is better to open old cases and try to exonerate the wrongly convicted or to require that a defendant could not be convicted if DNA samples were available and had not been tested?

4. What is the legal standard required to petition for post-conviction testing in Connecticut? Give an example of what a prisoner would have to prove.

5. How does the federal law applicable to post-conviction testing differ from Connecticut's? Which do you think is the better law and why?

6. What is a *habeas corpus* petition and why is it often used in post-conviction exoneration cases?

7. What are some of the actions the court can take based on a petition for post-conviction exoneration? Under what type of condition might the court order a new trial?

8. Why was a finding of "actual innocence" important to exonerees in some states? Review the chapter on blood spatter and explain the result of the civil trial in which the family of Sam Sheppard attempted to have a court declare Sheppard actually innocent.

# Chapter 14

# Closing Statements, Jury Instructions, Verdict and Appeal

## Overview

Trial lawyers on both sides regard closing statements as a vital component of their respective cases. These statements occur after all of the evidence has been presented to the jury, and just before the judge gives instructions to the jury. Closing statements provide each side with the opportunity to summarize all of the testimony which it believes is important in persuading the jury of the strength of its case. The attorneys may not refer to any evidence that was not presented at trial in their closing arguments.

In *Grant*, the prosecution closing statement listed all of the inferences which the jury was entitled to draw based on the circumstantial evidence presented in the case. The defense listed all of the issues that would give the jury reason to find reasonable doubt.

The court's Jury Instructions told the jury the legal elements of the crime of murder and how to apply the law to the evidence. The instructions also told the jury that they were free to accept or reject the testimony of any witness, including the expert witnesses. The court also gave standard instructions on the meaning of circumstantial evidence and reasonable doubt.

Grant's attorneys moved for a new trial after the verdict because of speculation by the prosecution about a possible motive for Grant to kill Serra—the idea that he may have wanted to steal her car. The court denied the motion.

Grant filed a notice of appeal after his conviction. His appellate brief was filed in August of 2006, and the State of Connecticut reply brief was filed in March of 2007. Grant's primary argument on appeal is that the presence of his fingerprint on the tissue box did not establish probable cause to justify the search warrant for his blood. He argues that the affidavit supporting the warrant was misleading because it failed to disclose certain facts about other suspects investigated for the crime. He also argues that his statement about a suspect in another murder being apprehended based on "a fingerprint, too" was improperly admitted.

After Grant has an opportunity to file a rebuttal to the State's brief, the case will be set for oral argument before the Appellate Court. Attorneys for the state do not expect a ruling on the appeal before 2008.

# Chapter Objectives

Based on this chapter, students will be able to:

1. Explain the role of the Closing Argument and the limitations on what counsel can say.

2. Evaluate the Closing Arguments for both the prosecution and Grant and point to the strategies of each party in the closing.

3. Understand the legal basis for Grant's objections during the Closing.

4. Distinguish between Grant's motion for a directed verdict, his issues on appeal, and the legal standards for each.

5. Relate the Jury Instructions to the elements of murder, to the jury's role in evaluating the testimony of expert witnesses, and to its consideration of circumstantial evidence.

6. Explain the issue of motive and what effect it might have on jury deliberations.

7. Evaluate the meaning of *reasonable doubt* as it applies in general and in the *Grant* case.

8. Relate the issues on appeal to objections made at trial or before trial and preserved for appeal.

9. Understand the consequences if the court were to rule in Grant's favor in his appeal.

10. Explain the legal standard for a ruling of prejudice based on the admission of certain statements Grant made to investigators.

11. Describe the legal standard used for appeals based on insufficiency of the evidence and for *habeas corpus* petitions based on insufficiency of the evidence.

# The Closing Arguments in the *Grant* Case

There are actually three closing arguments in a criminal trial. The prosecution goes first and presents its side of the case. Its goal is to summarize the evidence from trial and fit the evidence into the legal elements of the crime that it must prove beyond a reasonable doubt. Then the defense makes its closing argument, also referring to the evidence and the issues where the defense argues there is reasonable doubt of guilt. Finally, the prosecution has the opportunity to respond to (or rebut) the points made in the defense's presentation.

By the end of the *Grant* case, both prosecution and defense offered detailed closing arguments. You have already read much of the prosecution argument earlier, in the chapter on the Theory of the Case. The prosecution summarized all of the testimony to support its theory of how the crime occurred and to convince the jury—beyond a reasonable doubt—that Grant was the murderer. The prosecution's closing was simply a story of what happened, with abundant references to the forensic evidence (presented by the prosecution's expert witnesses) and the eyewitnesses who supported its theory of the case.

In contrast, the defense had one job: to convince the jury that there were enough holes in the prosecution's evidence to create a reasonable doubt as to Grant's guilt. If the defense could accomplish that, then Grant must be acquitted. Certainly, there was a lot of confusion about the eyewitness testimony. Among other points, the defense was able to raise questions based on the fact that two different suspects were investigated before Grant was charged. The lack of motive was also helpful to the defense. But motive is not an element of the crime of murder and, therefore, the prosecution did not have to prove Grant's motive.

In summary, the defense conceded that the two pieces of incriminating forensic evidence were accurate. That is, the fingerprint was Grant's and the DNA found at the crime scene matched Grant's DNA. The defense argued the fingerprint was put on the box before the crime. It also strongly suggested that the DNA evidence was planted by the police at the crime scene, or was altered thereafter, in an effort to implicate Grant and solve a high-profile, cold case. However, the defense did not say this directly. Rather, counsel simply said "something is not right with the handkerchief."[1] He pointed out that the bloody parking ticket had needed two days for the blood to dry, but the handkerchief was "bone dry" when it was picked up from the garage floor on the day of the murder.

Before we begin with the closing arguments, let's review again the three elements of first degree murder. They are:

- Grant was the perpetrator.
- Grant intended to cause Serra's death.
- Grant did, in accordance with that intent, kill Serra.

## The Prosecution's Initial Closing Argument

Here is what the prosecution told the jury at the end of the case. His job was to summarize the evidence and convince the jury that it has proved guilt beyond a reasonable doubt. The prosecution must simply refer to the evidence and not offer its own opinions. It must not offer any facts that do not appear in the record:

> The elements of murder. This is what the State has to prove…. [The] first one [is] the intent to cause the death of another person. Intent is necessary pretty much in any crime and certainly all the serious ones. Intent can be proven in a number of ways. Normally, we can't crawl into somebody's head and understand what that person was actually thinking to determine their intent. So the Judge is going to tell you, common sense, that normally we infer intent from the actions that we see somebody take. Common sense tells you that we usually mean to do what we do.

> And what did this killer do? Chase the barefoot Penney Serra from her car or at least the direction of her car, caught her in the stairwell … and **stabbed her to death directly in her heart. Does common sense tell you that's intent to kill?** Of course it does. In fact, the medical examiner told you that his thrust was so efficient into her heart that even if she had been stabbed on the steps of St. Raphael's Hospital, [to which Serra was taken], she would not have survived.

> Second element. There will be a lot of discussion about this one. The defendant has to be shown beyond a reasonable doubt to be the person who committed this crime.

---

1. Transcript, May 22, 2002 at 53.

And the third element is that he caused the death of Penney Serra, and there is clearly no doubt that that is what happened.

Three elements, that's it. Those are the elements of murder. That's what has been charged. That's what you have to find.

Did we prove those three things beyond a reasonable doubt? And I submit that there is going to be very little, if any, challenge to the ones on top and bottom because the question here is who was the killer.

And to know the answer to that question, you have to look at what happened between 12:37, when the killer entered the garage, and 1:01, when he handed the bloody ticket across his body to Christopher Fagan and drove out. And some of that, what happened in that period of time, you're never going to know. Some things only Penney Serra knew and the killer knows.

**So, while it would be extremely interesting to know everything that happened in that garage on July 16, 1973, it's unlikely that you will.** But if it's not part of those three elements, we don't have to prove it.

And I submit that the evidence you have is sufficient for you to make your decision without knowing everything that happened in that garage. And any suggestions that you do know what happened, for instance, between the time that the parking ticket was checked in at the entrance, where you all stood the other day, and the car was seen in approximately that location by Mr. Petzold and Mr. Woodstock, is pure speculation.

\* \* \*

We don't know exactly how it happened and we don't know exactly what the **murder weapon** is, and we don't have to prove that. But you do know that there was a knife in her car from a week earlier, that that knife was never returned to the Hurleys. In fact, you have an exhibit which is an exact copy from the same set of that same knife. Is that the weapon she was killed with? You will probably never know, but we don't have to prove that. And certainly it's an inference that you could draw, that that is not only the knife that killed her, but the knife that injured him.

\* \* \*

Now, one thing you don't have any direct evidence of in this case is **the motive for this crime**. And one of the things that the Judge is going to tell you is that is not an element. You know, you might not like it. You might even find that the lack of motive is something that is really important to you. You might find that it raised reasonable doubt. But you've got to look at the issue of motive, was there a lack of motive completely in this case? Was there a motive that you could infer? And even if there isn't, the Judge will tell you that if you find the case proved otherwise beyond a reasonable doubt, then that's okay because it isn't an element of the crime.

But you know this about motive; you know that that killer had some reason to kill Penney Serra. You may not ever know what the motive was. But he stabbed her in the heart, most likely after she cut him, and you know that or you could conclude that from the evidence because you got blood on the left-hand side coming down here, and you have those two blood spots on the back of her dress completely consistent with a lunge to grab her, the location of where her fall would have been because there are two O blood spots, that's the only non-A blood on her dress.

And the cuttings are there, they are the only holes in the back of that dress and they are right there where your hand would be if you grabbed for that wig and contacted the dress. Whether it was at the car or as he stabbed her, it's not an element of the crime. You could make your own decisions. Like many of the other things that you can't know the details, that you can't know, motive may be one of them.

But you know this, that every important piece of evidence in this case points to Edward Grant as being at the scene and it points to no one else.

* * *

So, what points to Ed Grant as the person who murdered Penney Serra? There are some things you know for sure and these may not be seriously challenged. **You know that the killer stabbed Penney Serra with a knife. You know that the killer drove Penney Serra's Buick and, therefore, was in the car.** You know that the killer had to have the keys to that car because he drove the car. **You know that the killer had O type blood.** You know that the killer left O type blood that had this DQ Alpha, this one in 20 at 1.2, 3. **You know the killer touched the tissue box** because there are all these bloody fingerprints on it — fingermarks, not fingerprints. **You know the killer left a blood trail** from the car to the keys that he had to be carrying because he drove the car to that location. Those things you know about this killer, whoever he is.

And then you've got to ask yourself, whose fingerprints are on the bloody tissue box? Edward Grant.

Who has O type blood? Edward Grant. Who has DQ Alpha 1.2, 3? Edward Grant. Who carries a handkerchief, according to his own sister, just like his father did? Edward Grant.

**Whose DNA is on the bloody handkerchief** which has type O blood on it next to the blood trail which is type O in every place it was tested six to eight feet from the keys to the car that the killer had to have? Edward Grant.

**And whose DNA is on it in the level of certainty of one in six trillion? Edward Grant.**

**And who looked stunningly like the drawings taken,** done in 1973 by the only two people who got a clear view of this killer?
Edward Grant.

You know this evidence is overwhelming that the killer could only be Edward Grant. And that's a lot more than proof beyond a reasonable doubt because of the power of this evidence. There may be lots of stuff that happened around that time, but none of it can contradict this evidence at any level.

In a moment you are going to hear the defense argue to you and you may hear suggestions that you should look at one piece of evidence and say, well, that doesn't prove guilt beyond a reasonable doubt, and then some other piece of evidence, and that doesn't prove guilt beyond a reasonable doubt or some relatively innocuous fact that for some reason you are going to be told you should conclude that raises a reasonable doubt.

> "You know this evidence is overwhelming that the killer could only be Edward Grant. And that's a lot more than proof beyond a reasonable doubt because of the power of this evidence." *Prosecution Closing*

Judge Blue, though, is going to tell you that it's not one at a time, that the determination, and you have heard this instruction in *voir dire*, it was awhile ago, the determination of guilt in any case has to do with every piece of evidence, and to use your common sense and your knowledge of the way things work and your understanding of how this crime scene developed to say those things can't all happen by coincidence in the real world that we have lived in all our lives that developed our common sense. The patterns of Edward Grant's guilt are clear in all this evidence.

> "There is not one shred of evidence in this case offering an innocent explanation for Edward Grant's fingerprint being on that tissue box." *Prosecution Closing*

And there are two other things that are also clear. There is not one shred of evidence in this case offering an innocent explanation for Edward Grant's fingerprint being on that tissue box. And there is not one shred of evidence offering an innocent explanation for his DNA being on that bloody handkerchief.[2]

[The prosecution closing argument also contained a point by point list of all of the logical inferences that the jury could make from the evidence before it. This material is reprinted in the chapter on circumstantial evidence.]

* * *

## The Defense's Closing Argument

What follows are portions of the closing statement made by the defense. After the defense closing argument, the prosecution has the right to "rebut" the argument, which it did. The prosecution has the last word. Here is part of what Grant's attorneys said:

* * *

Your job is to assess the evidence and decide whether or not you are convinced beyond any reasonable doubt that Edward Grant, not anybody else, but Edward Grant is the one on July 16th who caused Penney Sera's death.

That "beyond a reasonable doubt," the term, we talked about that with you during jury selection. And I think we told you that if you were selected you would hear more about that concept and you would have that explained to you at the end of the trial.

I just want to point out a couple of different pieces of what I think the Court's instruction is going to be. You are going to be able to hear what he has to say and you will also have it in the jury room with you so you could take a look at it as well, but I have been listening to similar instructions for probably now about 16 years.

One of the parts that I think helps understand exactly what that concept means is this idea, and his Honor will tell you that **a reasonable doubt is a doubt which has its foundation, it's basic in either the evidence you hear or the lack of evidence.** The lack of evidence in a case is just as important in terms of that concept as the evidence itself. You are allowed to focus on both.

---

2. Transcript, May 22, 2202 at 16–34.

You are required to focus on both. And if the evidence causes you to have a reasonable doubt or the lack of evidence, including such things as motive, causes you to have a reasonable doubt, that is sufficient and requires a verdict of not guilty.

We talked in jury selection about this concept beyond a reasonable doubt and how certain you need to be and it's more certain than a possibility. We even talked it's more certain than even probabilities. That in a criminal case, when someone is on trial facing a criminal charge, in this case or any criminal case, you have to be more certain than that.

Is there evidence which points towards Edward Grant? Of course there is. But the evidence has to be such that you are convinced beyond any reasonable doubt that it was Edward Grant that caused Penney Serra's death. You will hear part of the instruction when His Honor talks about reasonable doubt; that beyond a reasonable doubt is proof that precludes any reasonable hypothesis consistent with innocence.

> "A reasonable doubt is a doubt which has its foundation, it's basic in either the evidence you hear or the lack of evidence. The lack of evidence in a case is just as important in terms of that concept as the evidence itself ... beyond a reasonable doubt is proof that precludes any reasonable hypothesis consistent with innocence." *Defense Closing*

So, if you have several, based upon these facts, several different hypotheses that you think might have happened, if any of those are not consistent with Ed Grant having done this crime, if they are consistent with Phil DeLieto having done this crime, consistent with Selman Topciu having done this crime or someone we don't know about having done this crime, if any of those are reasonable, based upon this evidence, the law requires you to come back and say not guilty. It's not kind of balancing, here is Phil DeLieto, here is Selamn Topciu, here is Ed Grant, which one do we think fits best.

**You have to be convinced beyond any reasonable doubt that it was Ed Grant to the exclusion or every other person on this planet. That is the level of certainty that is required, that is mandated in a criminal case.**

I am going to talk with you about some of the evidence. I'm going to talk with you, as probably most of you could guess, about the science in the course of this case because I was talking with witnesses about science. When Dr. Nelson was on the stand the other day, at the end of his questions, Mr. Clark asked her a question, and basically the bottom line of the question was, look, your conclusion is that these hairs are inconclusive? She said, yes.

And then he said, so that any other conclusion or if people try to kind of draw more out of it—I suppose he was suggesting either us or me—draw more out of it, that would be inappropriate? And she said, yes, because the science can tell us this and it can't tell us more.

The physical evidence in the case, one of the issues that I think is important to understand is the storage of the physical evidence. And I think that it's probably fair to say—and understand we're not blaming folks from 1973 or four or five, they didn't know that these advances in technology were coming. But I think it's fair to say that **the manner in which this evidence was stored during the course of almost three decades really until it got into Carl Ladd's hand or maybe the advent of the new building at the State Police**

**Forensic Crime Lab in 1994 was awful.** Bill Paetzold, who used to work in the lab, and Elaine Pagliaro told you that he was the one, one of the two people assigned to be the custodian of this evidence, he told you how that was stored. And we heard from every expert witness, you got to keep it cool, you got to keep it dry.

The evidence in the case, the tissue box, the tissue box has blood on it. The tissue box has a fingerprint on it. The fingerprint is a latent print, Mr. Grant's print is a latent print; that means it is not visible, it has to be processed to be observed and compared. There is some blood on top of that print.

> "There is absolutely no way to date that finger-print, whether it was on a particular day, a particular month or a particular year." *Defense Closing*

The evidence from Chris Grice is as clear as it could conceivably be. **There is absolutely no way to date that fingerprint, whether it was on a particular day, a particular month or a particular year.** There is a stipulation the court read into the record in terms of that too, that science does not allow one to date a latent fingerprint, it simply cannot be done.

The handkerchief, it was tested by Dr. Maxwell and she came up with some paint-like substances, I think tested in about the last year or so. I think you have the report, maybe you could check on that in terms of the dates. Paint-like substances used for cars, repainting, respraying, also used for household applications, exterior trim for any areas in the house that have a lot of—a lot of business is not the right word. But a lot of activity, bathrooms, kitchens, that's what she could tell you about that.

Five stains were tested on that handkerchief by Dr. Ladd. Let me start right off, there is no contest here to either Dr. Ladd's qualifications, the work that he did and how he did it. He told you how meticulously they handled this evidence to make sure that it's not contaminated. So, I think that we could all feel comfortable from December, 2000, when Dr. Ladd was requested to do work on the handkerchief, until his work was done, that that handkerchief was handled in precisely the way we would all hope it would have been handled for the 30 years, but we know it wasn't handled that way before that. It is not an issue of Dr. Ladd's work and Dr. Ladd's conclusions.

He does five stains; from those 5 stains Selman Topciu and Phillip DeLieto are excluded. Ed Grant is included. The State talks a lot about G4, one of the four—five stains because G1, G3 and G5 have some other DNA in there, they are mixtures, some of it requires some interpretation, Dr. Ladd said. He gave his best interpretations. But the State focuses on G4, the clean stain. How do we know they focus on G4 when they are having people like Dr. Kidd come in and talk about numbers or having people like Ed Blake look at the numbers? They are talking about G4, that one stain, so we could talk about G4.

**Dr. Ladd in his work on G4 says that the probability of that DNA profile in the random population is one in 300 million. He also said that science cannot tell you how it was deposited, under what circumstances it was deposited, and most critically when it was deposited. The science can't tell you that.**

The State's theory is July 16, 1973, but the science can't answer the question.

Mr. Clark indicated there is blood all over the seat. There is O blood in a variety of locations and I jotted them down because I didn't want to miss them, but the tissue box has blood, the tissue next to the tissue box has blood, the steering column and floor pedal have blood, the outside door handle has blood, small white envelope has blood, pink rag on the floor has blood, metal trim of the left door, metal trim of the left seat, metal door handle, debris from the floor has blood, blood from the blood trail in three different locations, and the back of the dress had blood, all those locations have type O blood.

Mr. Clark talked about the fact that the blood on the back of the dress was consistent with whoever was reaching their hand dripping blood onto the back of the dress.

**So, we have all that type O blood all over the seat, all of it would include Phillip DeLieto, Edward Grant and Selman Topciu, no way to distinguish between them.**

The items I talked about, I'll talk about them further. **The storage of those items and the manner in which they were stored and the handling of those items and the manner in which they were handled destroy the ability of present science to tell us who was the source** or who was a potential source of all that evidence. And we're talking about blood on the tissue box, blood in the car, blood on the tissue next to the tissue box, blood on the back of Penney Serra's dress, that the storage, and just the awful way in which this evidence was handled, will not change one to another, but will destroy your ability to have information that will tell us about the source of that DNA.

There is something just not right about the handkerchief. That's the center piece of the State's DNA case. And there is something that is just not right about it. **We heard that although the parking ticket needed to dry for two days, the handkerchief in the parking lot was bone dry.** And we know that former detective or former Lieutenant Perricone told you that. And the reason he could even remember that now because it was immediately put in a plastic bag, and he said he would never do that with even something that was remotely damp. The handkerchief was bone dry.

> "There is something just not right about the handkerchief. That's the center piece of the State's DNA case. And there is something that is just not right about it." *Defense Closing*

According to the State, the DNA on that handkerchief has been there for 28 plus years, about 28 years from what Dr. Ladd testified. The DNA on that handkerchief was then subjected to the age factor in degradation, just as every other piece of evidence was. All the other old blood I talked about, the blood in the car, the same degradation factors in terms of age. So, as those other items would degrade, so would the DNA on the handkerchief. The same environmental insult is what they call it, but the heat, the humidity, the dampness, the handkerchief was exposed to all those variables just like every other piece of evidence in this case, no difference. The handkerchief yields us results in 2001 of one in 6.9 trillion.

All other evidence was available, in terms of the blood on the dress, the tissue box, all of that that I mentioned so far was subjected to the same technology, that PCR technology that they talked about which takes minute amounts of DNA and makes copies, copies, and millions of copies so you could test it. All this blood is so degraded that technology, as advanced as it is, can't give them anything, not even a partial profile, it can't even give them a profile. **But this handkerchief somehow maintains its integrity for 29 years and is able to give us numbers of one in 6.9 trillion. Something is just not right about that handkerchief.**

What motive does Ed Grant have to kill Penney Serra? There is not a shred of evidence that gives you any indication regarding that. The State tries to downplay motive in the case, it is not an element of the crime, but motive drives what happens in criminal cases. And **the lack of a motive, as you will hear in an instruction from the Court, can create on its own a reasonable doubt.** And that makes some sense because crimes aren't committed out of the blue, there are reasons for things happening; not a shred of evidence in this case.

> "The State tries to downplay motive in the case, it is not an element of the crime, but motive drives what happens in criminal cases. And the lack of a motive, as you will hear in an instruction from the Court, can create on its own a reasonable doubt."
> *Defense Closing*

**What's the relationship or association that Ed Grant has with Penney Serra?** None. There isn't a shred of evidence regarding such an association or a relationship. Why? Because Ed Grant is not the killer of Penney Sera, that's why.

Everything in this case points towards the direction that the person who killed Penney Serra knew her. I'm going to start going through some of that for you....

The suspect is—there is a range of times here that the suspect could have entered the building. It says here that the range of time between the suspect's entry and the victim's entry is between three and five minutes. In fact, I think if you compute this, it's **two to six minutes. It's an extremely short window of time for two strangers to get in touch with each other and meet somewhere** above, extremely short. It almost seems like it was a planned meeting.

The suspect comes into the garage. You were there, George Street passes underneath the garage. And as you are looking one way on George Street, Macy's is on the left and Malley's is on the right. The suspect's vehicle enters the George Street entrance north going towards Crown Street, the northern end of the building, that's the way that ramp takes you at that point in time, that's why it says George Street.

Miss Serra is coming in from the connector, from the East Haven area, Morris Cove area, and comes in the Frontage Street entrance, the southern end of the building. You were there at both the southern entrance, Frontage Street, and also the exit where the perpetrator left. They are in two completely different ends of the building, about anywhere from two to six minutes apart.

The suspect's car ends up on 7B, assuming the keys and the handkerchief lead you to the car. Miss Serra's car ends up on 9C, 9D, up on the top of the garage where Mr. Petzold and Woodstock see them. How did these two get together in that short window of time? How does that happen without some planned meeting? Was the planned meeting on 7B where both cars parked and then the vehicle went upstairs? It doesn't make any sense in terms of the time, the time that they have to get together. Clearly, it's not a situation where some guy is sitting there for hours watching who is coming, watching who is parking, watching who is coming back from shopping, none of that is taking place. There is not enough time for that to happen. But they end up in completely different places from where they actually entered the building.

**Why is she up on the ninth floor?** July 16th, we heard the testimony; it's a summer, sunny, beautiful day. Normally she parks anywhere from the third to fifth level, I think the testimony was. This is not a packed building that day. **Why is she going up there? To meet somebody.**

> "How did these two get together in that short window of time? How does that happen without some planned meeting?" *Defense Closing*

Now, Mr. Petzold and Mr. Woodstock are sitting in the vehicle, here is what their description is when they see the guy chasing the woman, among other things, male, early twenties, 5'10" tall, dark-skinned, Hispanic male, Mr. Petzold says under oath at a proceeding, and also in this statement and in a pre-hypnotic session that he had later on. I mean, we talk about these witnesses, they were all very young, but every one of them spent hours with the police attempting to help the police in this case. Really, if you think about it, they are all 17, 18 year old kids, happened to be in the wrong place at the wrong time. They went to the police department, they gave statements, they did their best. And this is what they come out with: Mr. Woodstock, he has the male chasing the woman in a Polo shirt, described as the same kind of shirt that he was wearing, a golf-type shirt or Polo shirt; we all know what they are. He has him dressed in black dress shoes, I don't know how he could see that, that's what he said, black dress shoes.

Now, Mr. Clark will lead you back, as he already has, to the composites in this case, and how much they look like Ed Grant back in '73. So, what I want you to do is every time you think or he flashes that composite or you take a look at that composite, think about a dark-skinned Hispanic male, think about what it doesn't show you of all the other features, 5'10", these are the descriptions, think about that.

Composites.

Now, Jane Merold and Gary Hyrb, they are smoking pot up there, and that vehicle, as they are about to go back to Malley's and work, that vehicle comes by. We heard Jane Merold's testimony; Hyrb is either in front of her or immediately to the right when that car comes by.

> "If you want to convict Ed Grant, you could look at the composite and find the features that match. And if you don't, you could look at the composite and figure out the features that don't." *Defense Closing*

What we do know about what Gary Hyrb observed? Well, Don Beausejour from the police department, Beausejour told us Mr. Beausejour after the homicide is looking for evidence in the case. Maybe two hours after the body had been found, no one has discovered the car, the police are scouring the garage, but they haven't found this vehicle yet. They do not know the identity of the victim. And Mr. Hyrb approaches Mr. Beausejour and tells him that he thinks he saw something. And Mr. Beausejour testifies that Gary Hyrb said that he saw the driver of the vehicle on two separate occasions, one upstairs and one downstairs when the vehicle was parked. And who is the person who leads the police to the Buick? Gary Hyrb. Up until the point that Gary Hyrb shows up, I'm sure they would have found it at some point, but up until Gary Hyrb gets there, they have not found the car. And when Don Beausejour is led to that car by Gary

Hyrb, he sees the blood all over the place and he knows immediately that this car is involved. And that's when the dispatches go out to everybody. And that's when they open the car and find the pocketbook in the back on the floor.

Gary Hyrb. When Don Beausejour testified here, he told you what Gary Hyrb's description of the drive of the vehicle was and the person who got out of the vehicle. What was that description? White male, 21 to 27 years of age, 5'10", 180 to 185 pounds, medium build, dark complexion, again, and heavy, well-trimmed mustache, well-groomed.

\* \* \*

Now, Henry Lee comes in and testifies in the case.... Let me go over for a moment his theory about the tissue box and the print. Mr. Clark referred to that. The killer gets into this vehicle. He is obviously getting out of the area quick. The car is described by Jane Merold as speeding by. He is sitting in that front seat, the tissue—he is bleeding from the left hand, he is driving with his one hand. He has got to lean back. First of all, he has to know that the tissue box is upside down. I guess he scanned the whole car when getting in because his theory has to be that the tissue box is upside down in order for those three smudge prints to get on there.

Now, the person has to put their hand behind, you saw the demonstration, has to flip—he is driving, he has to flip the box over, flipping a box going in the other direction. This is not a car with bucket seats where you could lean around, that seat goes all the way across. Look at the photographs. He flips it over and now he has to pick it up and bring it around. Look at the photographs in terms of the space that is between that seat and the door closed while you are driving, it doesn't make any sense. It makes assumptions about where that box was prior to sitting in that position.

Who knows where the box was? It could have been in front. It could have been in the back, we just don't know that answer. But those assumptions would cause you, if you grab it the way he has suggested; it would make you find some blood underneath where you have to grab it with your other fingers. Picture that in your mind as you walk through that. I don't think it sits well, and I think there is all kinds of different explanations. And it's really disturbing that that theory was expounded here on the stand for the first time.

**There are remaining fingerprints in the car that have never been identified**, and I'll just briefly mention it. There is LP2, this was testified to by Christopher Grice, one on the right passenger window in the interior, not the defendant's. One on—LP3, one on the right passenger window, interior. LP4, right window exterior, AFIS quality print. To this day they are running that print to see if they could identify it. Is it the killer or is it just some other person? I don't know.

\* \* \*

Of course, we do not have, as you remember, we do not have close-up photographs of this handkerchief, none were taken at the garage, none were taken at the police department. Does this look like the handkerchief to you? That's the blow-up of that. **Even looking at that picture, it does not look like the handkerchief. It does not come close.** It looks like a shirt; it looks like it has sleeves. It looks like it could be a towel. Look at the bulk on this picture of this object. And remember the handkerchief that was — the picture of the handkerchief that was introduced when Ken Zercie was on the stand, it was a photograph that they said the range of the photograph could have been anywhere from late '73 to 1980.

Remember the nature of the stains that were on that photograph, they were dark. Whether they were blood or paint or whatever it was, where is that? You don't even see a trace of that in these photographs. Please look at those photographs. That is not a handkerchief.

* * *

How do all these details differ from Ed Grant? Ed Grant is 30 years old at the time, born in 1942. He works at Midway, a family business in Waterbury. He is fair-skinned. When you look at that picture from '73, he is fair-skinned. He is not a dark-skinned individual. He has no scars, they specifically looked for it. He doesn't speak in broken English or a foreign accent.

**Here are the distinctions that are relevant:**

- White male, Hispanic male, that's reasonable doubt.
- Dark-skinned versus light-skinned or fair-skinned, that's reasonable doubt. 5'10" versus 5'6", according to Mr. Hanahan, that's reasonable doubt.
- Foreign language or broken English versus English, that's reasonable doubt. Substantial injury occurred during the incident, no scars or cuts, that's reasonable doubt.
- Polo shirt versus work uniform, completely different description, that's reasonable doubt.
- Dark blue pants versus light green dressier pants, that's reasonable doubt. Short sleeved shirt described by several people at the scene, whereas the work shirt is a long sleeved shirt with a logo.
- And look at the shirt that he is wearing in the 1973 photo. Even on July 16th of '73, they are rolling up the sleeves; there is no short sleeved shirts, reasonable doubt.
- Description of the perpetrator, early twenties, Edward Grant, 30 years old on July 16th of 1973, reasonable doubt.

* * *

**Here is what we don't know:** Where did Penney Serra and the killer meet? Was it a planned meeting? Are they both in the car? What happens in the car? Is there any sexual activity or attempted sexual activity? If so, is it consensual or coerced? How did the male DNA get on the underpants and the slip? Is it connected to this killing in some way or not? Whose type O blood is all over the items inside the car, backside of the — outside of the car, inside of the car, the blood trail, backside of the dress? Ninth floor, tenth floor, whose blood is that? Where does the weapon come from? How does it come into play to begin with? How did the dental bills get into the car? Was it that morning? By whom?

Whose fingerprint is on L4? Whose fingerprint is on the chrome strip on the side of the seat? Whose are the other fingerprints where they are — where they are identifiable characteristics? Some are not, but there are some that are. Are they the killer's or someone else's? We know that they are not Ed Grant's. Whose palm print was it on the Jeep upstairs? Whose palm print was it on the railing upstairs? When did the biological material get on the handkerchief?

What connection does Ed Grant have to New Haven? What connection does Ed Grant have to Penney Serra? Where is the accent or broken English who is the person that has it? Where is the scar from this substantial injury that was inflicted by Penney Serra? Who owns the vehicle with the MR license plate? Why did DeLieto not attend the funeral or pay any respects? Why doesn't DeLieto acknowledge the Liberos when he sees them at the police department when the Liberos are there and they see Phil DeLieto? What does the father say at the time? Why is she getting dressed up to buy some patio furniture? What is she doing on the ninth floor on the day where you would expect her to park far below? What is Ed Grant's motive to kill? Why is he in New Haven?

There are more holes in this, the State's case, than there are holes in the handkerchief.

**In order for you to believe that Ed Grant did this, here is what you have to believe:** That Ed Grant, a married man with two children three years old and 18 months old, living in the city of Waterbury, goes to work in the City of Waterbury at a family business, that he has to drive, he drives his vehicle to work every day, an orange or gold colored Jeep Wagoneer, goes to work in his work clothes every day, dark blue pants, light blue shirt with the logo on it.

You have to believe that at some point in time he drives to a city that he usually doesn't work in and he drives in a vehicle that he doesn't drive, a blue car with an MR license plate on it. And at some point he has to change his clothes and then get into some kind of a Polo shirt and dress shoes, and at some point he has to pick out the Temple Street garage for some unknown reason to arrive there, and then he has to meet a complete stranger virtually.

And then at some point Ed Grant has to chase her for some unknown reason and kill her for some unknown reason. And then he has to get back into her car and he has to put on his Phil DeLieto mask because that's how he is described after that. And then he has to park that car, get back into this foreign car, assume a foreign accent, real remarkable for someone who has received this substantial wound on his left arm, side, hand or wrist and drive off. And in the meantime, look like he is a dark-skinned Hispanic male. That's what has to happen.

And he has to go back to Waterbury. After 26 years, nothing comes up. He raises his kids. You heard he was at the Christening for his grandchildren in December of 2000 or 1999. Every time he is approached by the police, he is at work. The last time when he was arrested, he is working on a car in the driveway of his house. That's the set of facts that have to happen for him to be the killer in this case. It's totally preposterous.[3]

* * *

---

3. Transcript, May 22, 2002 at 34–87.

# The Prosecution's Rebuttal to the Defense's Closing Argument

Here are excerpts of the Prosecution's Rebuttal argument:

You know the killer had a motive. You know that he got in Penney Serra's Buick and he drove it from the scene of the crime and then he abandoned it. Did he abandon it because he was driving the wrong way and was going to have to go back up to another level or did he plan to abandon it on the eighth level? Was he taking the car from the ninth level because he wanted the car? There is not a clear answer to that question, but there is an inference that you could draw if you choose to, that that could be the motive.

\* \* \*

You are supposed to look at pictures that witnesses have come in and sworn under oath were taken of the handkerchief that you have in evidence that has the DNA on it, and because those photographs look weird, because of the way the handkerchief was dried, you are supposed to say it's not the handkerchief, given all of that evidence.

It is absolutely correct the only testimony in this case is that you cannot scientifically date a fingerprint. And nobody suggests that you can. But common sense and logic and reason can cause you to draw a conclusion about when the fingerprint was put on that tissue box and that's different, and you know what? That all it takes is common sense and logic to do that.

\* \* \*

There are no prints from anybody except Edward Grant. There are no prints from the stock boys at Pathmark There is only one print that was identifiable on that whole box, and it's Edward Grant's, the same guy whose DNA matched.

**You also know that his access to the box innocently was essentially eliminated in this case,** that's why they've got to talk about Pathmark, I guess because on June 29th that box went into Penney Serra's father's car when Mrs. Hurley gave it to them to go to Florida, it then went to Florida. It came back on the 8th of July, there were three days when Mr. Serra was driving the car before it then goes to Rhode Island. Mr. Serra went, according to Rosemary Serra, to work and back, to work and back, to work and back because Penney was home after being away for awhile and he wanted to get home quickly to spend time with her.

> "There are no prints from anybody except Edward Grant. There are no prints from the stock boys at Pathmark. There is only one print that was identifiable on that whole box, and it's Edward Grant's, the same guy whose DNA matched."
> *Prosecution Rebuttal*

\* \* \*

Sure, Phil DeLieto was drawn and he sure doesn't meet any of those criteria, except the O blood. But that's not all the evidence you have … You also have the blood trail. And so far all of it matches Mr. Grant, doesn't it? And you have the keys to the car next to the handkerchief. And you've got the handkerchief and you have … spray paint … [a]nd the only evidence that you have of Mr.

Grant that was spraying any paint was in the shop. And that paint is consistent with shop paint.

* * *

And you have this … You have just been arrested on a murder and your mind goes to the other murder that you have just read about and you say this word, **they got him on a fingerprint "too."** That's not a nothing. That's not a nothing. That's not what you would have said if you brought up Raphael Ramirez. You would say, well, they picked him up because they found his fingerprint, not that they picked him up because they found his fingerprint "too."

Mr. Grant had been waiting 26 years, he thought he had gotten away with it, and here they are knocking on his door saying that he was under the arrest for the murder of Penney Serra.

* * *

> "Mr. Grant had been waiting 26 years, he thought he had gotten away with it. …" *Prosecution Rebuttal*

When you look at all this evidence, Mr. Ullmann asked you to be sure that justice was done, that is your job. And your job isn't an easy one in the sense that you have to make a decision which is a very weighty decision, but I submit to you that this evidence is overwhelming of the defendant's guilt and in that sense your decision is easier thanit might have been.

When you finish, you, like Dr. Kidd, will be virtually certain that the killer is up there on the board with his victim [referring to the trial exhibits] and that you will come back and find this defendant, Edward Grant, guilty of the murder of Penny Serra.[4]

# Objections Made in Closing Arguments

During the prosecution closing statements, defense attorneys objected to a number of statements, thus preserving those issues as possible prejudice on appeal. First, they objected to the state suggesting that Grant may have had a motive to steal Serra's car, as there was no evidence at trial on this issue. Second, the defense objected to a statement that the jurors would have to disbelieve the crime scene investigators to believe the defendant's arguments about the evidence. Connecticut courts have held that it is error for a party to suggest that a witness may have lied.[5]

The defense also renewed its request for the court to give the jury an instruction that the fact that Serra's keys were lost should be held against the state—that the jury should draw an "adverse inference on the missing property, particularly because of the manner in which the State highlighted the keys during its final argument."[6]

---

4. Transcript, May 22, 2002 at 88–122.
5. *State v. Singh*, 259 Conn. 693, 793 A.2d 226 (2002).
6. Transcript, May 22, 2002 at 128.

# Jury Instructions

Here is a portion of the judge's instructions jury in *State v. Grant:*

\* \* \*

Ladies and gentlemen, you heard the evidence presented in this case and it's now my duty to charge you on the law that you are to apply to the facts that you find from the evidence.

You, as the jury, and I, as the Judge, have separate functions. It's your function to find what the facts are in this case. With respect to the facts, you and you alone are charged with that responsibility.

My function is to charge you on the law to be applied to the facts that you find in order to decide this case.

With respect to the law, what I say to you is binding on you and you must follow all of my instructions. The parties are entitled to have this case decided pursuant to established legal standards that are the same for everybody. Those are the standards that I will give you and that you must follow.

\* \* \*

### [Elements of the Crime of Murder]

The statute cited in the information, Connecticut General Statute Section 53a-54a defines the crime of murder. The statute provides that, and again I'll quote, "A person is guilty of murder when, with intent to cause the death of another person, he cause the death of such person," end of quote.

For you to find the defendant guilty of this charge, the State must prove each of three elements beyond a reasonable doubt:

> One, that it was the defendant and not some other person who was the perpetrator.

> Two, that the defendant intended to cause the death of another person.

> And three, that in accordance with that intent, the defendant caused the death of that person.

The State must prove beyond a reasonable doubt that it was the defendant and not some other perpetrator who committed the crime alleged in the Information.

You must be satisfied beyond a reasonable doubt that the defendant was the perpetrator of the crime in question before you may convict him.

### [Was Grant the Perpetrator?]

The element of identity or, more simply put, who committed the crime, is obviously a disputed issue in the case. The identity of the perpetrator is a question of fact for you to decide after a full consideration of all the evidence including the testimony of witnesses, the full exhibits and your observations during the view.

The State has the burden of proving beyond a reasonable doubt that it was the defendant, Edward Grant, who committee this crime.

\* \* \*

[Intent]

[W]hat a person's purpose or intent has been is ordinarily a matter of inference. The nature of the wound inflicted and the instrument used may be considered as evidence of the perpetrator's intent and from such evidence an inference may be drawn that the perpetrator had an intent to kill or to cause death. This is an inference of fact that you are permitted to draw after a consideration of all the evidence in accordance with my instructions.

You may draw reasonable and logical inferences from the conduct that you find in light of all the surrounding circumstances, and from this determine whether the State has proven the element of intent beyond a reasonable doubt. This inference is permissive rather than required. You are not required to infer a specific intent from the conduct that you find, but it's an inference that you may draw if you find that it's reasonable and logical and in accordance with the instructions on circumstantial evidence.

The State has the burden of proving the specific intent to cause death. If you find that the State has proven beyond a reasonable doubt each of the elements of the crime of murder, you must find the defendant guilty.

[Lack of Motive]

Motive is not an element of either the crime of murder or the crime of manslaughter in the first degree. And the State is not required to prove or show motive.

Evidence of a motive may strengthen the State's case. An absence of evidence of motive may tend to raise a reasonable doubt of the guilt of the defendant, but **even a total lack of evidence of motive would not necessarily raise a reasonable doubt as to the guilt** of the defendant as long as there is other evidence produced that is sufficient to prove guilt beyond a reasonable doubt.

If the absence of an apparent motive does not raise a reasonable doubt that the defendant is guilty, then the mere fact that the State has been unable to prove what the motive of the defendant actually was does not prevent you from returning a verdict of guilty.

[Circumstantial Evidence]

You may consider both direct and circumstantial evidence. Direct evidence is testimony by a witness about what that witness personally saw or heard or did. Circumstantial evidence is evidence involving inferences reasonably and logically drawn from proven facts.

Let me give you an example of what I mean by direct and circumstantial evidence. If you wake up in the morning and see water on the sidewalk, that is direct evidence that there is water on the sidewalk. It is also circumstantial evidence that it rained during the night. Of course, other evidence such as a turned on garden hose may explain the water on the sidewalk.[7]

\* \* \*

[Meaning of Reasonable Doubt]

The defendant does not have to prove his innocence in any way or present any evidence to disprove the charge against him. The state must prove each

---

7. Transcript, May 22, 2002 at 134.

and every element necessary to constitute the crime charged beyond a reasonable doubt.

The meaning of reasonable doubt can be arrived at by emphasizing the word "reasonable." It is not a surmise, a guess or a mere conjecture. It is not hesitation springing from any feelings of pity or sympathy for the accused or any other persons who might be affected by your decision.

It is a real doubt, an honest doubt, a doubt that has its foundation in the evidence or lack of evidence. **It is doubt that is honestly entertained and is reasonable in light of the evidence after a fair comparison and careful examination of the entire evidence.**

Proof beyond a reasonable doubt does not mean proof beyond all doubt. The law does not require absolute certainty on the part of a jury before it returns a verdict of guilty. The law requires that after hearing all of the evidence, if there is something in the evidence or lack of evidence that leaves in the minds of the jurors as reasonable men and women a reasonable doubt as to the guilt of the accused, then the accused must be given the benefit of that doubt and acquitted.

**Proof beyond a reasonable doubt is proof that precludes every reasonable hypothesis except guilt and is inconsistent with any other rational conclusion.** If you can in reason reconcile all of the facts proved with any reasonable theory consistent with the innocence of the accused, then you cannot find him guilty.

\* \* \*

### [Credibility of Witnesses]

Now, the credibility of witnesses and the weight to be given their testimony are matters for you to determine; however, there are some principles that you should keep in mind. You may believe all, none or any part of any witness's testimony....

You must consider all of the evidence in the case. You may decide that the testimony of a smaller number of witnesses on one side has greater weight than that of a larger number of the other side. It's the quality and not the quantity of evidence that controls. All of these are factors that you may consider in finding the facts ...

Police officers and other officials have testified in this case. You must determine the credibility of these witnesses in the same way and by the same standards that you would use to evaluate the testimony of ordinary witnesses.

**The testimony of a police officer or other official is entitled to no special or exclusive weight merely because it is from an official.** You should recall the witness's demeanor on the stand and manner of testifying and weigh and balance the testimony just as carefully as the testimony of any other witness. You should neither believe nor disbelieve the testimony of a police officer or any other official just because the witness is an official.

\* \* \*

### [Expert Opinions]

You have heard some testimony of witnesses who have testified as expert witnesses. **Expert witnesses are witnesses who, because of their training, skill, education and experience, are permitted not only to testify about facts that they have personally observed, but to state their opinions.** However, the fact that a witness has qualified as an expert does not mean that you have to accept that witness's opinion. You could accept an expert witness's opinion or reject it in whole or in part.

In making your decision whether to believe an expert's opinion, you should consider the expert's education, training and experience in the particular field, the information available to the expert, including the facts the expert had and the documents or other physical evidence available to the expert, the expert's opportunity and ability to examine those things, the completeness or incompleteness of the expert's report, the expert's ability to recollect the facts that form the basis for the opinion, and the expert's ability to tell you accurately about the basis for the opinion.

You should ask yourselves about the methods employed by the expert and the reliability of the result. You should further consider whether the opinions stated by the expert have a rational and reasonable basis in the evidence.

Based on all of these things together with your general observation and assessment of the witness, it's up to you to decide whether or not to accept the opinion. **You may believe all, some or none of the testimony of an expert witness.** An expert's testimony is subject to your review like that of any other witness.[8]

\* \* \*

# The Verdict

The jury returned a verdict of guilty on May 28, 2002. On September 27, 2002, Grant was sentenced to 20 years to life. At his sentencing, Grant spoke in court for the first time, saying:

I'm sorry for the pain, sorrow and loss of the Serra family. I can't begin to imagine it. I had no part in this tragic event. However, the jury has convicted me, and I ask for leniency. I lived my entire life trying to make life better for my family. I'm devastated by the jury's decision.[9]

Judge Blue made the following statement in sentencing Grant:

No one can deny that someone killed Penney Serra and thrust a knife in her heart. Someone left that beautiful young woman dead or dying in a dirty stairwell in a parking garage. No one can deny what the evidence shows beyond any doubt—that someone was you.[10]

The judge took Grant's lack of a criminal record into account, but refused leniency because Grant did not come forward when another suspect was arrested and because of Grant's "refusal to accept responsibility and apologize" for the murder.

\* \* \*

---

8. Transcript, May 22, 2002 at 129–161.
9. Michelle Tuccitto, *Grant gets '20-to-life' in Serra murder,* New Haven Register, September 28, 2002.
10. *Id.*

# Post-Trial Motions

Following the verdict, Grant's attorneys moved for a new trial, citing such errors as the prosecution's offering a possible motive in their closing statement that Grant was trying to steal Serra's car, although no evidence to that effect had been introduced. The motion also argued that the prosecution had impermissibly stated that the jury would have to believe two investigators had lied in order to acquit Grant. Finally, it asserted error because of the judge's failure to sanction the state for losing significant pieces of evidence.[11] The motion was denied.

As you will see below, the standard to overturn a jury verdict is exceptionally difficult to meet. Although Grant did not ask for a new trial on the ground that there was insufficient evidence to convict him, the case of *State v. Payne*,[12] discussed earlier, is a good example of how difficult it is to win an appeal on this ground. In *Payne*, the defendant was convicted of kidnapping and rape based primarily on one fingerprint on the outside of a car. He moved for judgment of acquittal after his conviction, and the Connecticut Supreme court reversed his conviction because it decided that evidence of one fingerprint on the outside of a car and the inability of the victim to identify the defendant was insufficient evidence to justify the verdict.

### *State v. Payne,* 186 Conn. 179 (1982)

\* \* \*

The defendant, Arnold Payne, was convicted by a jury of robbery in the second degree and of unlawful restraint in the first degree. He has appealed, claiming various errors in the trial court's rulings and instructions to the jury. His principal claim, however, is that the evidence against him was insufficient to sustain a verdict of guilty and that the trial court, therefore, erred in denying his motion for acquittal after the verdict of guilty. We agree. Because of our resolution of the defendant's claim of insufficient evidence, we do not consider the defendant's other claims of error.

In determining whether the evidence is sufficient to sustain a verdict, we employ the test of "whether the jury could have reasonably concluded, upon the facts established and the reasonable inferences drawn there from, that the cumulative effect of the evidence was sufficient to justify the verdict of guilty beyond a reasonable doubt." The defendant claims that the evidence against him was insufficient as a matter of law because of the well-established rule that a conviction may not stand on fingerprint evidence alone unless the prints were found under such circumstances that they could only have been impressed at the time the crime was perpetrated.

---

11. Christa Lee Rock, *Citing misconduct, Grant's lawyers seek new trial*, New Haven Register, June 4, 2002.

12. 186 Conn. 179, 440 A.2d 280 (1982).

> "We employ the test of 'whether the jury could have reasonably concluded, upon the facts established and the reasonable inferences drawn therefrom, that the cumulative effect of the evidence was sufficient to justify the verdict of guilty beyond a reasonable doubt.'"
> *State v. Payne*

The state has not contested the validity of the rule relied upon by the defendant, nor has the state attempted to argue that this is a case where the fingerprints could only have been impressed during the commission of the crime. The state was unable to present any evidence dating the defendant's fingerprints or otherwise limiting their impression to the circumstances of the crime. The state, however, has attempted to distinguish this case from those in which the rule has been applied on the ground that there was other evidence upon which the jury could have relied in reaching their verdict against the defendant. The evidence on which the state relies is the victim's description of one of the perpetrators as a short, black male no more than sixteen or seventeen years old.

\* \* \*

# *Habeas Corpus* Petitions Based on Insufficient Evidence

The United States Supreme Court has stated the test to win a *habeas corpus* petition based on a claim of insufficient evidence to be even higher. A *habeas corpus* petition is a claim brought by a convict after all normal appeals have been made and lost. It is based on a claim that for the state or federal government to hold the convict violates his Constitutional rights. In such a case, the U.S. Supreme Court has ruled that the standard is whether the reviewing court finds that upon the record of the evidence at the trial, no rational trier of fact could have found proof of guilt beyond a reasonable doubt.

**Jackson v. Virginia, 443 U.S. 307 (1979)**

\* \* \*

[T]he Due Process Clause of the Fourteenth Amendment protects a defendant in a criminal case against conviction "except upon proof beyond a reasonable doubt of every fact necessary to constitute the crime with which he is charged."

\* \* \*

The standard of proof beyond a reasonable doubt, said the Court, "plays a vital role in the American scheme of criminal procedure," because it operates to give "concrete substance" to the presumption of innocence, to ensure against unjust convictions, and to reduce the risk of factual error in a criminal proceeding. At the same time, by impressing upon the fact finder the need to reach a subjective state of near certitude of the guilt of the accused, the standard symbolizes the significance that our society attaches to the criminal sanction and thus to liberty itself.

The constitutional standard recognized in the *Winship* case was expressly phrased as one that protects an accused against a conviction except on "proof beyond a reasonable doubt...." In subsequent cases discussing the reasonable-doubt standard, we have never departed from this definition of the rule or from the *Winship* understanding of the central purposes it serves.

A "reasonable doubt," at a minimum, is one based upon "reason." Yet a properly instructed jury may occasionally convict even when it can be said that no rational trier of fact could find guilt beyond a reasonable doubt, and the same may be said of a trial judge sitting as a jury. In a federal trial, such an occurrence has traditionally been deemed to require reversal of the conviction.

After *Winship* the critical inquiry on review of the sufficiency of the evidence to support a criminal conviction must be not simply to determine whether the jury was properly instructed, but to determine whether the record evidence could reasonably support a finding of guilt beyond a reasonable doubt.

But this inquiry does not require a court to "ask itself whether it believes that the evidence at the trial established guilt beyond a reasonable doubt." Instead, the relevant question is whether, after viewing the evidence in the light most favorable to the prosecution, any rational trier of fact could have found the essential elements of the crime beyond a reasonable doubt.

This familiar standard gives full play to the responsibility of the trier of fact fairly to resolve conflicts in the testimony, to weigh the evidence, and to draw reasonable inferences from basic facts to ultimate facts. Once a defendant has been found guilty of the crime charged, the fact finder's role as weigher of the evidence is preserved through a legal conclusion that upon judicial review, all of the evidence is to be considered in the light most favorable to the prosecution.

Under 28 U. S. C. § 2254, a federal court must entertain a claim by a state prisoner that he or she is being held in "custody in violation of the Constitution or laws or treaties of the United States." Under the *Winship* decision, it is clear that a state prisoner who alleges that the evidence in support of his state conviction cannot be fairly characterized as sufficient to have led a rational trier of fact to find guilt beyond a reasonable doubt has stated a federal constitutional claim. Thus, assuming that state remedies have been exhausted, see 28 U. S. C. § 2254 (b), and that no independent and adequate state ground stands as a bar, it follows that such a claim is cognizable in a federal *habeas corpus* proceeding.

We hold that in a challenge to a state criminal conviction brought under 28 U. S. C. § 2254—if the settled procedural prerequisites for such a claim have otherwise been satisfied—the applicant is entitled to *habeas corpus* relief if it is found that, upon the record evidence adduced at the trial no rational trier of fact could have found proof of guilt beyond a reasonable doubt.

*  *  *

Under the standard established in this opinion as necessary to preserve the due process protection recognized in *Winship*, a federal *habeas corpus* court faced with a record of historical facts that supports conflicting inferences must presume— even if it does not affirmatively appear in the record—that the trier of fact resolved any such conflicts in favor of the prosecution, and must defer to that resolution. Applying these criteria, we

> "The applicant is entitled to habeas corpus relief if it is found that, upon the record evidence adduced at the trial, no rational trier of fact could have found proof of guilt beyond a reasonable doubt."
> *Jackson v. Virginia*

hold that a rational trier of fact could reasonably have found that the petitioner committed murder in the first degree under Virginia law.

\* \* \*

# Grant's Appeal

Grant's attorneys announced at his sentencing that they intended to file an appeal. Although a notice of appeal must generally be filed within 20 days of sentencing,[13] the appeal brief need not be filed until after the final pages of the trial transcript have been typed and released. Grant's appeal brief was filed in August of 2006—four years after his conviction, sentencing, and imprisonment.

## The Grounds for Grant's Appeal

### No Probable Cause for Warrant to Take His Blood

Grant asserts a number of reasons why the trial was so tainted that he deserves a new trial. One argument is that the police did not have probable cause based on the fingerprint identification alone to issue the warrant for his blood sample. If the warrant lacked probable cause, then the state would have only the fingerprint to present as evidence. Grant points out in his brief that Dr. Henry Lee testified at trial that the fingerprint was underneath the bloodstain—in other words the fingerprint was not made by a bloody finger, but covered by blood. Dr. Lee also testified that there is no way to date a fingerprint—the fingerprint could have been placed on the tissue box from a moment to months before the blood was added.

On this point, the brief concedes that the location of Grant's fingerprint under the blood stain does not necessarily exonerate the defendant. Grant's lawyers argue that relative location of the print made it impossible to conclude that there was probable cause to believe that Grant's print was impressed on the box at the time of the crime. For that reason, the defense contends, there was insufficient evidence to allow the police to secure a court order ("warrant") requiring Grant to submit to a blood test. Thus, the defense argues that the blood drawn from Grant pursuant to the warrant was impermissibly secured and was, therefore, inadmissible.

Grant also argues that his attorneys were wrongly denied a hearing on the issue of whether certain material facts had been improperly omitted from the affidavit used by the police to secure the warrant. Specifically, he asserts the affidavit failed to connect either Grant or his blood to the crime scene or to the perpetrator of the crime. It stated that the lab "determined that [the victim's] blood type is 'A' and that blood scrapings taken from the scene and believed to be that of the perpetrator is Type 'O.'[14]

The brief argues that as 45% of the population has Type O blood, that fact, by itself, does not show probable cause to connect Grant with the crime. As to whether the fingerprint, by itself, is sufficient to show probable cause, the brief states that, given the

---

13. Connecticut Rules of Appellate Procedure, Chapter 63, §63-1.
14. Appellant Brief at 2.

fact that no one can state when the fingerprint was placed on the tissue box and given also that a tissue box is highly moveable, the fingerprint does not establish probable cause. In other words, even if the defense admits that the fingerprint is Grant's and therefore Grant touched the box at some point, there is no evidence that he touched the box *at the time of the crime* because the box is an easily moveable item. Grant's appellate brief says:

> This proves that the person whose fingerprint it is touched the outside of the box, but given the *portability* of the box, it does not even prove the tissue box was touched while [in the car] as opposed to at some other time prior to the tissue box being put [in the car.] Does the print on the tissue box provide probable cause that the person who made it is the [murderer]? Not if the fingerprint belongs to anyone who touched the box before the [murder] at any of its many prior locations before it ended up on the [car.][15]

Grant's attorneys also argue that, as there was no fingerprint of Grant's anywhere on the car itself, including on the bloody steering wheel or any of the car handles, there is no way to place him in the car as a result of a fingerprint match on the tissue box.

## Wrongful Admission of Statement by Grant to Police

Another ground for appeal is the admission as evidence of the following statement made by Grant to Officer Rouella after he was booked and after Grant said that he was not waiving his rights [under Miranda] and would wait for his attorney. According to Rouella, he and Grant were sitting in silence at the table where the booking was done, when Grant said to him, "Did you read about the guy in Texas that killed all those people? They got him on a fingerprint too." The statement was admitted to the jury over a defense objection. Grant's appeal argues that once a defendant is in custody, no questioning can take place unless the requirements of Miranda are met. Therefore, the statement made without counsel was inadmissible.

## Prosecutorial Misconduct

Grant also contends that the Prosecutor committed misconduct in statements made during the Closing Argument, including his statement about a possible motive for Serra's death being that Grant may have wanted to steal her car. There was no evidence of motive at trial, so counsel was not permitted to speculate about it in his closing.

* * *

## The State's Response

Grant's first claim on appeal is that the warrant for his blood was issued in error because the affidavit upon which it was based omitted material facts. The State's Reply Brief summarizes the omissions Grant claims were made from the warrant as follows:[16]

1. "several identifiable fingerprints were located in or on the Serra vehicle and were identified *not* to be the defendant's";

---

15. Appellant Brief at 26–27.
16. Appellee Brief at 22.

2. that the affiants omitted a statement from a 1992 affidavit directed against another suspect, Selman Topciu, that "it has never been substantiated that the latent prints lifted from the Serra vehicle belong to the perpetrator";

3. that "a microscopic examination of the fingerprint lifted from the tissue box showed that it was placed there prior to the time the blood was deposited";

4. information regarding how long the tissue box had been in the Serra vehicle;

5. certain eyewitness descriptions of the perpetrator that "do not match that of the defendant";

6. the opinion of certain investigators that "the perpetrator had suffered a serious injury to his left hand and that the perpetrator would thus be likely to have a significant scar in that area and that "there was no evidence of any scar" on Grant;

7. that another suspect, Philip DeLieto, had been confidently identified by an eyewitness and that he had "some domestic disputes" with the victim shortly before her death;

8. that the reference in ¶ 14 of the affidavit to the "suspect under investigation whose blood has genetic markings that are consistent with those of the perpetrator's blood" was to Selman Topciu, not Grant.

The State argues that none of these statements were required and that even if they were, the result was harmless error. Grant's attorneys had moved before trial for a *Franks* hearing to ask the court to hear these issues; the motion was denied on January 7, 2002. Here is the standard for a *Franks* hearing, according to the State:

> Before a defendant is entitled to a *Franks* hearing, he "must make a substantial preliminary showing that the information was (1) omitted with the intent to make, or in reckless disregard of whether it made, the affidavit misleading to the judge, and (2) material to the determination of probable cause."

> *Frank's* Hearing. Defendant has a right to challenge the veracity of allegations in an affidavit supporting a search warrant provided defendant shows a false statement was knowingly made. *Franks v. Delaware*, 438 U.S. 154 (1978).

The case contends that not all omissions, even if intentional, will invalidate an affidavit. An affiant may 'pick[]and choose[]' "the information that he includes in the affidavit and he may omit facts that he believes to be either immaterial or unsubstantiated. Cases like this one, which involve allegedly material omissions, are "less likely to present a question of impermissible official conduct" than those which involve allegedly material false inclusions."[17]

The State specifically rejects Grant's claims about omissions of information as follows: As to the issue of the fingerprint on the tissue box being under the blood and therefore possibly placed there days before the commission of the crime, the state responds that even had "Dr. Lee's statement ... been included in the affidavit, it would not have defeated a finding of probable cause because it was entirely consistent with the inference implicitly drawn by the issuing judge, based on the totality of the other information in the affidavit, that the defendant's [bloody] and admittedly inexplicable fin-

___
17. *Id.* at 20.

gerprint could have been deposited on the tissue box during the commission of the crime or its immediate aftermath."[18]

The failure to describe in detail conflicting eyewitness descriptions of the perpetrator was not material because all the eyewitnesses described a white man between 5 feet 8 inches and 5 feet 10 inches in height. As to the likelihood that the perpetrator would have a significant scar on his left wrist, the state responds "[c]ommon experience, moreover, dictates that not all injuries, even substantial ones that result in bleeding, leave a permanent visible scar."[19]

The failure to disclose that Phil DeLieto had been identified earlier by an eyewitness and that Selman Topciu had been investigated and arrest warrants sought against him are irrelevant, argues the State, because by the time of the *Grant* warrant, both had been eliminated as suspects.

The state contends it was not error to admit Grant's statement: "did you read about the guy in Texas that killed all those people? They got him on a fingerprint too." The State repeats its position that Grant's statement was voluntary, not in response to a question from authorities, but that "Grant wanted to talk and that the police allowed him to do so."[20] The State also claims that, even if the statement had violated Grant's Constitutional rights, it was "harmless error" because the "properly admitted evidence showed beyond a reasonable doubt that Grant was guilty."

The state then summarized its view of the evidence that "overwhelmingly established guilt:"

1.  the defendant's admittedly unexplained bloody fingerprint on the tissue box.

2.  the defendant's unique DNA profile on the handkerchief found near the terminus of the type O human blood trail;

3.  type O human blood bearing the defendant's DQ Alpha genotype on a trim piece inside the Buick;

4.  composite drawings of the killer that both bear remarkable similarities to the 1973 photo of the defendant; and

5.  the traces of aftermarket automotive paint on the handkerchief.[21]

Grant also appealed that certain testimony should have been excluded at trial, specifically any reference to "blood" unless there had been independent evidence that the substance had in fact been tested and found to be blood. The State's Brief sets out the legal standard for claims that evidence has been improperly admitted:

> The trial court has broad discretion in ruling on the admissibility of evidence. A reviewing court must make every reasonable presumption in favor of upholding a trial court's evidentiary ruling and will overturn it only upon a clear and manifest abuse of discretion. "Relevant evidence is evidence that has a logical tendency to aid the trier in the determination of an issue.
>
> \* \* \*
>
> [E]vidence need not exclude all other possibilities [to be relevant]; it is sufficient if it tends to support the conclusion [for which it is offered], even to a

---

18. *Id.* at 24.
19. *Id* at 28.
20. *Id.* at 37.
21. *Id.* at 44.

slight degree.... [T]he fact that evidence is susceptible of different explanations or would support various inferences does not affect its admissibility, although it obviously bears upon its weight. So long as the evidence may reasonably be construed in such a manner that it would be relevant, it is admissible.[22]

Finally, as to Grant's argument that certain statements made by the prosecution were misconduct, the state contends:

The standard to be followed in analyzing claims that allege prosecutorial misconduct is the fairness of the trial rather than the culpability of the prosecutor. This Court does not scrutinize each comment in a vacuum, but rather examines the comments both in the context of the entire trial and in the context in which they were made.... A prosecutor may argue the state's case forcefully, provided the argument is fair and based upon the facts in evidence and the reasonable inferences to be drawn therefrom.[23]

The State filed its brief in March of 2007. Grant will have an opportunity to file another rebuttal Brief. Then oral argument will be scheduled. It is unlikely, in the opinion of attorneys for the state, that the appeal will be heard and decided by the Connecticut appellate court before the year 2008.

# Summary

Trial lawyers on both sides regard closing arguments as a vital component of their respective cases. These arguments occur after all of the evidence has been presented to the jury, and just before the judge gives his or her instructions to the jury before its deliberations. Closing arguments provide each side with the opportunity to summarize all of the testimony which it which is important in persuading the jury of the strength of its case. The attorneys may not refer to any evidence that was not presented at trial in their closing arguments.

In *Grant*, the prosecution closing argument listed all of the inferences which the jury was entitled to draw based on the circumstantial evidence presented in the case. The defense listed all of the issues that would give the jury reason to find reasonable doubt.

The trial judge gave the jury instructions on how to apply the facts to the law. These instructions included:

The elements of murder

Intent to commit murder

Reasonable Doubt

Circumstantial Evidence

Credibility of witnesses

Weight to give to expert witnesses

Grant made a number of objections during the Closing Argument, some of which are in his appeal. He also moved for a directed verdict based on insufficiency of the evi-

---

22. *Id.* at 46.
23. *Id.* at 51.

dence, which was denied. The legal standard for this motion in Connecticut is whether the jury could have reasonably concluded, upon the facts established and the reasonable inferences drawn therefrom, that the cumulative effect of the evidence was sufficient to justify the verdict of guilty beyond a reasonable doubt.

Grant filed a notice of appeal after his conviction. His appellate brief was filed in August of 2006, and the State of Connecticut reply brief was filed in March of 2007. Grant's primary argument on appeal is that the presence of his fingerprint on the tissue box did not establish probable cause to justify the search warrant for his blood. He also argues that the affidavit supporting the warrant was misleading because it failed to disclose certain facts about other suspects investigated for the crime.

After Grant has an opportunity to file a rebuttal to the State's brief, the case will be set for oral argument before the Appellate Court. Attorneys for the state do not expect a ruling on the appeal before 2008.

# Discussion Questions

1. Who made the more effective closing argument — the state or the defense? Why?

2. Find the various inferences the state told the jury it was entitled to make. Do you have a different view of circumstantial evidence than you did at the beginning of this course? Why?

3. What did the judge tell the jury it should decide based on the expert opinions? How did he tell the jury they should evaluate experts?

4. What is your opinion about the lack of motive in the case/ If you were a juror, could you ignore the issue of motive in deciding the case?

5. What facts does Grant contend were omitted from the affidavit supporting the warrant to take his blood?

6. Do you believe these facts were material?

7. Do you believe that the officers intended to make any false or misleading statements?

8. Why did the Connecticut Supreme court reverse the conviction in the *Payne* case? Do you think this was rightly decided? How would you compare the case in *Payne* to *Grant*?

# Chapter 15

# The Judge, the Jury, and Forensic Evidence

## Overview

Following the U.S. Supreme Court decision in *Daubert* in 1993, federal trial judges were required to conduct hearings to determine whether expert testimony in the forensic sciences was reliable and could be admitted under Federal Rule of Evidence 702. This assumes that a party objected to the expert and requested a *Daubert* hearing. No court has held that a judge has any independent duty to hold such a hearing, and a party who fails to request a gatekeeper hearing may be barred from raising the issue on appeal.

Many states decided to adopt rules for the admission of expert testimony similar to *Daubert*. For example, the state of Connecticut adopted the same test in a case called *State v. Porter*, so the test in Connecticut is called the *Porter* test. Other states, such as New York, continued to use the *Frye* test of general acceptance. Even in states using *Frye*, gatekeeper hearings are held to determine if expert testimony is generally accepted.

Many predicted that judges would need to learn a lot about science to act as effective gatekeepers. Others expected a flood of new science in the courtroom. As you have seen in this text, courts all over the country have considered whether to admit experts testifying about DNA, fingerprints, blood spatter, eyewitness identification, polygraph and handwriting. And even in areas where the courts have decided that the science is not reliable, such as polygraph and handwriting, researchers are busy trying to develop and test methods that will meet the tests of scientific reliability.

It has been over ten years since *Daubert* was decided, and many of the predicted results have not materialized. Courts appear to have coped with issues of expert reliability. Appellate courts defer to the trial judge's decision whether to admit or exclude expert testimony unless the judge has "abused his discretion." This is a very high standard to meet. Even if the appellate court concludes the trial court was wrong, the appeal will lose if there was sufficient other evidence supporting guilt.

Although the popularity of shows such as Crime Scene Investigation has led some to speculate that jurors will acquit unless the prosecution shows them flashy forensic evidence, there does not seem to be much change in juror conviction rates over the past few years. Experts who present complex and rambling forensics may confuse and frustrate jurors. This was true in the trial of Reverend Herbert Hayden in 1878 and of O.J.

Simpson in 1996. But individual juror comments tend to show that jurors take their responsibilities very seriously.

Should the jurors hear all forensic experts rather than letting the judge filter out those that are based on junk science or where the expert lacks qualifications? There are good arguments for retaining the judge as a gatekeeper, including the fact that judges can hold hearings to learn about the area. They will also hear the same areas of forensic testimony again and again. The value of having the judge exert control in the courtroom, particularly in this age of junk science, probably outweighs the jury's right to "hear all the facts."

# Chapter Objectives

Based on this chapter, students will be able to:

1. Evaluate research based on post-*Daubert* gatekeeper hearings.

2. Distinguish between the abilities of the judge and jury in evaluating forensic testimony.

3. Explain the standard for reversal based on abuse of discretion.

4. Discuss the possible effect of the popularity of forensics in today's culture, the effect it might have on jury behavior, and how to assess that result scientifically.

5. Evaluate the cases of Herbert Hayden, O.J. Simpson, and Ed Grant and the jurors' reaction to forensic evidence in those cases.

# How Well Do Trial Judges Evaluate Science?

The Supreme Court in the *Daubert* decision changed the admissibility of expert testimony about forensic evidence in two important ways: first, it set out a number of objective tests to ensure reliability when the science was not yet "generally accepted." Second, it identified the judge as the "gatekeeper," who would decide this issue outside the hearing of the jury. Based on this change, we would expect to see:

1. An increase in trial court hearings that applied the new tests for reliability.

2. More expert testimony admitted as "reliable" cutting-edge science that had not yet been generally accepted.

3. An increase in appeals based on whether the trial court properly applied the *Daubert* factors.

As mentioned earlier, the Federal Judicial Center commissioned a Reference Manual on Scientific Evidence to help guide judges in making decisions in *Daubert* hearings. The chapters on different areas of science are difficult to read, particularly for a non-scientist. And at hundreds of pages, it is a formidable reference book. It also prompted a strong reaction from trial lawyers, many of whom considered the manual to be biased in favor of defendants. The Association of Trial Lawyers of American and Trial Lawyers for Public Justice both protested the manual as more "a road map on how to exclude evidence than a neutral guide through the rough terrain of science and technology."[1]

Yet others have concluded that, even if judges are ill-equipped to make scientific judgments, they are still more objective than jurors:

> While meticulous *Daubert* inquiries may bring judges under criticism for donning white coats and making determinations that are outside their field of expertise, the Supreme Court has obviously deemed this less objectionable than dumping a barrage of questionable scientific evidence on a jury, who would be even less equipped than the judge to make reliability and relevance determinations and more likely than the judge to be awestruck by the expert's mystique.[2]

The trial judge already has much of the expertise needed to evaluate whether an expert's testimony will be reliable. As one commentator has said, judges are experienced in deconstructing arguments, testing them for logic, assessing the magnitude of the inference a witness may draw in forming an opinion, and determining if there are sufficient facts to support the inference.[3]

# Studies of *Daubert* Hearings

Studies show less of a change toward admission of novel expert testimony than might be expected. In a report of two surveys of federal judges and one of attorneys about expert testimony in federal civil trials, researchers found that during the five years after *Daubert*, judges were holding many more *in limine* hearings regarding expert testimony, but:

> The bases for limiting or excluding testimony do not appear to have been greatly affected by *Daubert*, at least not with respect to the cases we sampled. Judges who excluded testimony in the recent [1999] survey did so most often because it was not relevant, the witness was not qualified, or the testimony would not have assisted the trier of fact.[4]

And when judges did exclude testimony based on reliability, they tended to use the general acceptance test rather than the *Daubert* factors. Nonetheless, the survey found that judges have become more discerning about admitting expert testimony. A third of the judges surveyed in 1998 said they admitted expert evidence less often than they did before *Daubert*.[5] But as these were civil cases, over 40% of the testimony involved

> "The bases for limiting or excluding testimony do not appear to have been greatly affected by *Daubert*, at least not with respect to the cases we sampled." *Krafka, et al.*

---

1. Evam Rodriguez, *Plaintiffs Bar Slams Judges' Evidence Guide: Junk Science or Junk Study?* American Lawyer Newspapers Group, Inc., July 25, 1994.

2. Neil Vidmar and Shari Seidman Diamond, *Juries and Expert Evidence*, 66 Brooklyn L. Rev. 1121, 1126 (Summer, 2001), citing *Allison v. McGhan Med. Corp.*, 184 F.3d 1300,1310 (11th Cir. 1999).

3. *Note: Reliable Evaluation of Expert Testimony*, 116 Harv. L. Rev. 2142, 2150 (May 2003).

4. Carol Krafka, Meghan A. Dunn, Molly Treadway Johnson, Joe S. Cecil and Dean Miletick, *Judge and Attorney Experiences, Practices, and Concerns Regarding Expert Testimony in Federal Civil Trials*, vol 8, no. 3 Psychology, Public Policy, and Law 2002, American Psychological Association, Inc.

5. *Id.*

medical issues, with 25% relating to business and financial issues and 22% relating to engineering issues.

Another researcher compared the results of expert testimony challenges in criminal versus civil cases.[6] The number of challenges to expert testimony rose significantly, as expected. Risinger examined nearly 1,600 cases that cited the *Daubert* decision as of August 2, 1999—six years after the decision. First, he found that in the five years before *Daubert*, there were 21 federal appeals cases that cited the *Frye* case. Yet in the five years after *Daubert*, he found 416 cases that cited *Daubert*. Of these 416 cases, 31% were criminal cases. In the state courts, of the 528 cases that cited *Daubert*, 55% were criminal cases.

Risinger also found that plaintiffs in civil cases frequently lost in pretrial hearings to admit their experts, but that state prosecutors generally won. And if a criminal defendant offered an expert, he generally lost.

> So, just looking at the federal numbers, it seems that civil defendants win their *Daubert* dependability challenges most of the time, and that criminal defendants virtually always lose their dependability challenges. And when civil defendants' proffers are challenged by plaintiffs, those defendants usually win, but when criminal defendants' proffers are challenged by the prosecution, the criminal defendants usually lose.[7]

There may be many explanations for the phenomena Risinger reports. As discussed earlier, civil cases often involve causation issues, where a plaintiff may not be able to exclude causation by any other factor. On its face, it is not surprising that civil plaintiffs might lose more expert challenges. One might also conclude that criminal defendants lose more often than the civil defendants. The typical criminal defendant lacks the resources to hire expensive forensic experts.

The cases presented in this book support the argument that criminal defendants frequently lose their appeals based on improperly admitted experts for the state or improperly excluded experts offered by the defense. This is due, in part, to the tendency of appeals courts to find such errors to be "harmless," meaning that there was sufficient evidence to convict that the expert testimony would not have affected the outcome. In addition, the standard on appeal based on a trial court's evidentiary hearing is whether the trial court "abused its discretion." This is a difficult standard to meet, even in cases where the trial court failed to hold a hearing at all.

> An abuse of discretion can occur where the district court applies the wrong law, follows the wrong procedure, bases its decision on clearly erroneous facts, or commits a clear error in judgment. When the standards are not clearly defined, as in the admissibility of expert testimony, it is difficult—if not impossible— to demonstrate that the wrong law or procedure was used. This makes it particularly challenging for an appellate court to overrule a district court's ruling.[8]

One example of a trial court that was held to have abused its discretion was in a civil case for sexual harassment in which the plaintiff offered an expert opinion by a social

---

6. D. Michael Risinger, *Navigating Expert Reliability: Are Criminal Standards of Certainty being left on the Dock?*, 64 Alb. L. Rev. 99 (2000).

7. *Id.* at 108.

8. Note: *Flexible Standards, Deferential Review: Daubert's Legacy of Confusion*, 29 Harv. J. L & Pub. Pol'y 1085, 1093 (Summer 2006), quoting *United States v. Brown*, 415 F.3d 1257 (11th Cir. 2005).

worker that the cause of her relapse into substance abuse and depression was sexual harassment. The appellate court reversed a $21 million verdict for the plaintiff and said the
trial court was wrong to admit a social worker to give a medical conclusion. It said the
court should have precluded such speculative and unreliable evidence or that it should
have held a hearing regarding the expert's theories before allowing the testimony.[9]

## Is General Acceptance Good Enough?

We have examined a number of cases after *Daubert* in which a court has admitted expert testimony because it is generally accepted, but under circumstances where it would
probably not pass the remaining *Daubert* tests. This appears to stand *Daubert* on its
head. For example, the trial court in New York applied the *Daubert* tests to handwriting
analysis and came to the clear conclusion that handwriting analysis is not reliable.[10]
However, as the decision was after *Daubert* but before *Kuhmo*, the court admitted the
testimony as a "technique." Then *Kuhmo* held that the tests apply to techniques as well
as science. The logical next step would be for New York to exclude handwriting analysis.
The court had already made the factual analysis that it lacked reliability under the tests.
However, later opinions in New York have continued to accept handwriting expert testimony because it is generally accepted:

> Defendant insists that the conclusions and opinions of the Government's
> handwriting expert should not be admitted. Defendant refers to several cases
> where other district courts have limited handwriting expert testimony, citing
> the unavailability of testing of this type of expertise, as well as the lack of gen-
> eral standards in this field ...

> The Second Circuit has demonstrated an adherence to the reasoning in
> *Daubert v. Merrell Dow*, where the Supreme Court held that the common law
> "general acceptance" requirement for the admission of expert testimony is in-
> consistent with the "liberal thrust" of the Federal Rules of Evidence.

> Vigorous cross-examination, presentation of contrary evidence, and careful in-
> struction on the burden of proof are the traditional and appropriate means of
> attacking shaky but permissible evidence. Blanket exclusion is not favored, as
> any questions concerning reliability should be directed to weight given to testi-
> mony, not its admissibility. If there is some question regarding the handwriting
> expert's conclusions, Defendant will have ample opportunity to attack these
> findings during cross-examination or with contrary evidence.[11]

Notwithstanding the emphasis on science in gatekeeper hearings, a national study of
400 trial judges that asked about how they applied the *Daubert* factors[12] found that
about half who weighed the *Daubert* factors gave the most weight to general acceptance.
The answers also indicated that many judges did not understand the scientific meaning
of the terms "falsifiability" or "error rate."[13]

---

9. *Gilbert v. DaimlerChrysler,* 470 Mich. 749, 685 N.W.2d 391 (2004).

10. 880 F. Supp. 1027.

11. *United States v. Jabali,* No. 01 CR 801, 2003 U.S. Dist. LEXIS 26022, *7 (E.D.N.Y, September
12, 2003).

12. Sophia I. Gatowski et al., *Asking the Gatekeepers: A National Survey of Judges on Judging Expert Evidence in a Post-Daubert World,* 25 Law. & Hum. Behav. 433 (2001).

13. *Id.*

# Should Jurors Hear All Forensic Testimony?

Some commentators have argued that the gatekeeping process under *Daubert* deprives the jury of the right to hear all evidence and therefore may unconstitutionally violate the accused's right to a jury trial under the Seventh Amendment. Others have argued that much scientific testimony is beyond the ability of judges to evaluate and may be beyond jurors' ability as well.

One researcher found that jurors had a difficult time distinguishing between evidence that proved general causation and evidence that proved specific causation. For example, in the Bendectin cases, jurors over-estimated the percentage of scientists who believed that Bendectin was a teratogen—a drug that caused birth defects. They also did not understand that Bendectin could be a teratogen in some cases but not necessarily in the case before them.[14] Another set of studies showed that jurors tended to discount the testimony of experts who were both highly credentialed and highly paid as being professional witnesses.[15]

## How Well Do Jurors Understand Complex Forensic Testimony?

The average juror will hear forensic testimony on a scientific issue in one case. Judges, by contrast, hear challenges to experts frequently and have the advantage of hearing arguments by opposing attorneys as to the reliability of the testimony. In general, therefore, the judge is better equipped to make a decision about the reliability of expert testimony than is the jury.

# Can Experts Confuse a Jury into Ignoring Forensic Evidence?

Many people believe that the jury in the *Simpson* trial ignored the forensic evidence to "send a message" to the Los Angeles police about some of their racist practices. Others believe that the DNA expert testimony was just too complicated to understand, so the jury simply ignored it. As you will see below, jurors from that trial state that they listened carefully, understood the evidence, but found it conflicting. Nevertheless, the idea that juries may be too uneducated or patient to understand forensic evidence prevails.

This was the view following the acquittal in 1878 of a Reverend for the murder of his former mistress in Connecticut. The case relied on some cutting edge testimony about the effect of arsenic poisoning on the body and the microscopic characteristics of arsenic mined from different areas. The jury was bombarded with defense questions and strategies that apparently made them lose sight of the scientific testimony.

---

14. Vidmar and Diamond, 66 Brooklyn L. Rev. at 1147.
15. *Id.* at 1155.

This case shows that expert testimony about complex forensic issues is not new. The jury was both confused by the experts and influenced by factors that were not relevant in this case too. The crime details were pieced together from the trial transcripts by Virginia A. McConnell.[16]

In 1878, in Madison, Connecticut, a town not far from New Haven, where Penney Serra died, a 22-year old unmarried woman named Mary Stannard, who had worked as a domestic, was found bludgeoned in a wooded area called Fox Ledge. The man arrested for her murder was Reverend Herbert Hayden, for whose family Stannard had previously worked. Mary, believing that she was pregnant, confronted Hayden, who promised to help her get an abortion. He met Mary at Fox Ledge, handed her a package filled with arsenic for her "abortion," and stood by as the arsenic caused Mary to scream in agony. When she attempted to run, Hayden hit her twice with a piece of wood, knocking her to the ground and creating a scalp wound. Hayden then knelt behind Mary, took out his jackknife, and slit her throat. By that point, Mary's heart had slowed so much that even severing her carotid artery did not result in much blood loss.

Stannard was found on autopsy to have been poisoned by arsenic. Hayden was identified after a short investigation, as he had been seen going into his barn alone with Mary shortly before her death, and had raised suspicions with a number of nosey neighbors. Hayden also had a receipt for arsenic that he had recently bought, in his words, "to kill some rats." Neighbors testified to having heard Mary's screams. Mary's sister Susan testified that Mary had told her she was pregnant by Hayden and had written to him about her predicament.

Hayden staged a charade in which he attempted to show neighbors that his wife had used his knife the day of the murders for cutting pears.

At the inquest, Hayden was questioned about his whereabouts on the day of the murder. He said he had been out chopping wood. Hayden's wife Rosa had heard the rumors about her husband and Mary. Shortly after the inquest, he told his wife that Mary had come to him for advice as a minister of God because she thought she was pregnant. He said he had agreed to meet her out of sight of the neighbors at Fox Ledge, but by the time he got there, she was dead, he believed, a suicide. Rosa agreed to support his alibi.

Hayden's first trial took place in the basement of a local church, as the local press printed verbatim from the testimony for the news the next morning. The proceeding was like a preliminary hearing. No jury was present. Mary's body was exhumed for a second autopsy, this time looking for arsenic. Hayden's wife took the stand and testified about her loving marriage and seeing Hayden go to the wood lot, not the big rock, on the day of the murder. Although the prosecution asked for a recess to finish its testing of Mary's organs, the judge denied their request and dismissed the charges against Hayden.

Shortly thereafter, Professor Samuel Johnson of Yale Medical College discovered 90 grains of arsenic in Mary's organs. Based on this evidence the state procured a new arrest warrant. Dr. Moses White of Yale Medical College testified about the arsenic in Mary's body. The defense tried to show that a kidney laced with arsenic could have been planted in Mary's body or that the medical examiner could have put arsenic on his hands and transferred it into the body that way. White testified that it would have

---

16. Virginia A. McConnell, *Arsenic under the Elms, Murder in Victorian New Haven,* Praeger Publishers, 1999.

taken fifteen minutes for the arsenic to travel to Mary's kidney, based on an experiment he conducted on himself, by ingesting a tiny amount of arsenic and detecting it in his urine fifteen minutes later.

> White testified that it would have taken fifteen minutes for the arsenic to travel to Mary's kidney, based on an experiment he conducted on himself.

The defense also tried to get White to admit that Susan, Mary's sister, could have rinsed the jar in which Mary's organs would be stored, in water laced with arsenic. White defended his chain of control. He had locked the jar containing Mary's stomach and liver in his strongbox, put it in a closet in his office, and kept the keys with him constantly. The testimony about the comparison of the arsenic in Mary's stomach and that found in Hayden's barn "was the most forensically sophisticated that had ever been presented in a courtroom. The problem was whether the jury would be able to understand it."[17]

Arsenic at that time was an all-purpose remedy. It was used to kill insects and rodents, but also to improve appetite and digestion (in much smaller amounts, of course). It was also consumed, in ever increasing quantities, by young women hoping to achieve a pale and delicate complexion. Druggists bought arsenic in packages of five to ten pounds, at eight cents a pound, and resold it at ten cents an ounce. They would dispense the powder with a jar or bottle into a paper, wrap it in another paper, and typically label it as arsenic and poison. A fatal dose is two to four grains. Mary had 90 grains in her system, about a teaspoonful. There were sixty grains in the stomach and twenty-three grains in the liver. There were also grains in the brain, kidney and lungs. As the arsenic had permeated the body, it had entered the victim while she was still alive. The arsenic testimony took three weeks in a three-and-a-half month trial.

> Dr. Johnson conducted an experiment in which he placed arsenic in two freshly dead human stomachs, 74 grains in one and 90 in the other. Neither stomach showed inflammation.

Dr. Johnson, also working for the defense, had conducted an experiment in which he placed arsenic in two freshly dead human stomachs, 74 grains in one and 90 in the other. Neither stomach showed inflammation or engorged blood vessels, as had Mary's, adding to the conclusion that the arsenic in Mary's stomach was ingested before death. The defense demanded the names of the dead people, the cause of death, and other details. Rather than invade the privacy of the donors, the state withdrew the evidence.[18]

The arsenic testimony also included a comparison of different samples of arsenic by another expert at Yale. Hayden admitted to having bought arsenic prior to the murder, but stated he had put it in a tin on a rafter in his barn. This tin was eventually turned over by Hayden's attorney. As the tin contained almost a full ounce, the defense argued that Hayden could not have poisoned Mary, as none of the arsenic was gone. The expert showed that the arsenic in the tin contained brilliant crystals shaped like hexagons and was not consistent with either the arsenic in Mary's body nor that sold at the store

17. *Id.* at 75.
18. *Id.* at 89.

where Hayden said he bought it. The expert explained how a microscope worked and showed diagrams that represented the microscopic qualities of the samples.

The defense strategy was to ask so many questions on cross examination, including many far-fetched hypotheticals, that the jury became totally lost. Notwithstanding a wealth of forensic testing and evidence, the jury acquitted Hayden. In the author's view "the bottom line was that no one wanted to believe that a family man, a preacher of God's holy word, could have done what he was accused of doing. And, in the absence of concrete proof, proof they could see for themselves and understand, no one *would* believe it."[19] The jury deliberated for days and finally admitted they could not agree. It was a hung jury—11 for acquittal and 1 for conviction of second degree murder. The defense viewed the result as a victory. No one could imagine that the state would go through such a trial again. And it did not.

This case illustrates the value of selecting expert witnesses with care, and the strong effect of their credibility upon the jury. It also shows that sophisticated forensic testimony based on the scientific method was presented as far back as 1878. Finally, it shows how the "planting" argument can succeed with a jury.

## Was Evidence Ignored in the *Simpson* Trial?

If the trial of Hauptmann for the kidnapping of the Lindbergh baby was the "trial of the century" in the 1930s, surely the *Simpson* trial won that title in the 1990s.

After the acquittal of O.J. Simpson, a number of commentators argued that the jurors must have ignored the forensic evidence in order to acquit. In their view, the jury engaged in a renegade action of acquitting Simpson in protest over the racist practices of the L.A. Police Department. As presented below, you can read the views of some of the *Simpson* jurors, who defend their verdict based on reasonable conclusions they could have drawn from the blood evidence. Many of the jurors themselves have written that they carefully considered all the evidence and the instructions and simply concluded that the state had not proved guilt beyond a reasonable doubt.

Most accounts of jury deliberations show that juries take their role very seriously and genuinely try to apply the court's instructions to the evidence.

> … [C]laims about jury incompetence and irresponsibility in assessing and considering the testimony of scientific experts are not supported by research findings. There is a consistent convergence in juror interview studies and experimental studies involving both civil and criminal juries. Jurors appear motivated to critically assess the content of the expert's testimony and weight it in the context of the other trial evidence, as they are instructed to do. They appear to understand the nature of the adversary process, at least in the context of their specific trial. Even though many jurors may not have had prior exposure to the trial process, it appears that they develop an understanding from the give and take of examination and cross-examination and exposure to opposing experts. Indeed, rather than simply deferring automatically to experts, as critics have claimed, the trial process appears to make them aware of the fallibility of expert testimony.[20]

---

19. *Id.* at 114.
20. Vidmar and Diamond, 66 Brooklyn L. Rev. at 1174.

# Do Juries Have Unrealistic Expectations about Forensics Evidence?

## The CSI Effect

When the first Crime Scene Investigation television show called "CSI" premiered, the American public had little idea that it would become one of the most popular television shows in history and spawn a virtual industry of shows about crime scenes and the search for perpetrators of crime by evaluating evidence in a laboratory.

Of course, CSI does not accurately reflect what actually happens in criminal investigations. Real crime scene investigators in the field are mostly experienced police officers. Processing a crime scene is meticulous and time-consuming. The evidence is processed in a laboratory by technicians who generally do not interview witnesses or wear cleavage-revealing tank tops. Fingerprint reports do not appear as a photograph of a fingerprint with a flashing sign that says "match" accompanied by a photograph of the owner of the print.

Most crimes are solved by a combination of footwork, interviews, leads from witnesses, and review and evaluation of the crime scene and evidence. Forensic evidence is but a part of a puzzle. "In reality, the kind of 'smoking gun' evidence found on CSI is rarely available. Typically, the state attempts to bear its burden by piecing together many types of evidence, each having some probative value but also carrying a degree of uncertainty and, potentially, error."[21]

> "In reality, the kind of 'smoking gun' evidence found on CSI is rarely available." *Tom Tyler*

The mass media has written extensively about the so-called "CSI effect" on juries, speculating that jurors expect to see forensic evidence in every criminal trial and will be more likely to acquit a defendant if there is no forensic evidence that links him to the crime. "For example, after the recent, well-publicized acquittal of Robert Blake, jurors complained about the lack of fingerprints, DNA, and gunshot residue —evidence not often available in criminal trials but frequently used on television."[22]

So far, there are no research studies to back up the claim that juries are less likely to convict unless their appetite for fancy forensics is met. The psychology of juries and what influences their verdicts has been studied extensively.

One outgrowth has been the mock juries hired by teams of attorneys to simulate their trial strategy and judge its strengths and weaknesses. Marcia Clark, the lead prosecutor of O.J. Simpson, used a mock jury and concluded that she would be likely to convict Simpson.[23] Unfortunately, she failed to predict some of the problems the state would have with its forensic evidence. She also failed to account for the fact that the real jury was less influenced by evidence of Simpson's domestic violence and whether that proved Simpson was likely to have killed his wife than the mock jury had been.

---

21. Tom R. Tyler, *Viewing CSI and the Threshold of Guilt: Managing Truth and Justice in Reality and Fiction,* 115 Yale L.J. 1050, 1053 (March 2006).

22. *Id.* at 1053.

23. Carl E. Enomoto, *Public Sympathy for O.J. Simpson: the roles of race, age, gender, income, and education,* The American Journal of Economics and Sociology, January 1, 1999.

In fact, it may be just as likely that jurors are more likely to convict based on more familiarity with CSI-type shows, as they focus on the victim and solving the crime. The shows reinforce the natural inclination of juries to do "justice" and right a wrong. This was emphasized by Grant's attorney in his closing argument, when he cautioned jurors against the natural desire to solve a "cold case." In short, it is far too soon to know what effect, if any, shows like CSI have on juries.

There is some evidence, however, that juries more frequently are unable to reach a verdict today than in the past. "For decades, a 5 percent hung jury rate was considered the norm.... In recent years, however, that figure has doubled and quadrupled, depending on location. Some local courts in California, for example, have reported more than 20 percent of trials ending in hung juries. Federal criminal cases in Washington, D.C., averaged 15 percent hung juries in 1996 ..."[24]

> **Hung Jury.** If a jury cannot reach a unanimous decision, it is considered a hung jury, and the case is declared a mistrial. The state may elect to try it again.

# What Do Jurors Say about Forensic Evidence?

The nation was shocked when the jury in the *Simpson* criminal trial did not convict based on the mass of forensic evidence linking the defendant with the crime. In their book, *Madam Foreman: A Rush to Judgment?*[25] jurors Amanda Cooley, Carrie Bess, and Marsha Rubin-Jackson tell their side of the story. Here is what Carrie Bess said:

> I had ups and downs quite a few times because, when they first started on the case, they had O.J.'s cut finger on the left side, with the Bruno Magli shoe, with the blood drops falling right next to it, and I believed that Mr. Simpson was guilty. But then here comes the defense saying the blood was degraded, they never found any Bruno Magli shoes, and there was EDTA [a blood preservative used in labs] in some of the drops. That posed a problem for me.
>
> Second, I could not figure out who could leave a scene that was so bloody, get rid of clothes, leave some evidence, and never track anything—not even a blade of grass—in the house. Even though he left blood in the Bronco, I couldn't see how you could manage not to leave some blood somewhere, up the stairs or somewhere as you changed clothes. Even on the tiles in the bathroom. I could never understand that.[26]

Amanda Codey added:

> One of the crucial moments where I changed my thinking was when I heard evidence about the glove. The testimony about the drying time of blood on leather was that it would take anywhere from three to four hours, and the glove was not picked up until seven or seven and a half hours later. Another issue was about the blood drops on the socks and the location of the drops.

---

24. Joan Biskupic, *In Jury Rooms, a Form of Civil Protest Grows,* Washington Post, February 8, 1999.

25. Amanda Cooley, Carrie Bess, and Marsha Rubin-Jackson, as told to Tom Byrnes, *Madam Foreman, A Rush to Judgment?,* Dove Books, 1995.

26. *Id.* at 196.

Another episode that changed my mind was basically the picking up of the evidence weeks later and when they tested it, the results were so much different—the DNA content being so much different than the original drops were.[27]

Contrary to public belief, the jury statements show that they struggled to make sense of the forensic evidence. In the end, perhaps there was too much evidence, some of it contradictory. There was definitely some evidence pointing toward tampering. There was also lots of potentially damning evidence that the jury never heard: such as the fact that O.J. fled with $10,000 and a fake beard, Nicole's diary stating examples of physical abuse, etc. A subsequent civil jury held Simpson liable in damages for both killings.

In the trial of Herbert Hayden for the murder by arsenic of Mary Stannard in 1878, the jury hung, 11 to 1 for acquittal. Notwithstanding substantial forensic testimony about the arsenic found in Mary Stannard's body, the various witnesses who testified to a relationship between the married Hayden and Stannard, and the fact that Hayden had purchased arsenic shortly before the murders, the jury members who voted to acquit did so mostly because they were impressed by Mrs. Hayden's alibi testimony and concerned about her fate were Hayden to be convicted. She was referred to daily in the press as demure and gentle. Mary was a lower class domestic. Mrs. Hayden, although economically not much higher on the rung, was a lady.

> In the end, then, the case came down, not to sophisticated forensic evidence, but to two women: Susan Hawley as the representative of her dead sister, and Rosa Hayden as the representative of her accused husband. Susan was defensive and uncooperative on the stand, a member of a family of poor illiterates whose sister, the victim, had already proved herself to be immoral. Rosa Hayden, on the other hand, was beautiful, vulnerable, loyal, educated, articulate, and highly moral.

> As would happen in the O.J. Simpson trial almost 120 years later, the prosecution fumbled a winnable case. The jurors had completely disregarded the expert testimony on arsenic and blood. They probably didn't even understand it.[28]

# Comments from the *Grant* Jury

The jury found Edward Grant guilty. They were not required to state the reasons for their decision and they did not. However, one of my students[29] tracked down one of the jurors and asked her a series of questions. What she answered says a lot about the jury system:

**What was your opinion of the DNA evidence that was collected? Since the evidence was so old, were there times that you felt that the evidence would not prevail?**

I felt the DNA evidence was certainly adequate. I'm sure we all would have loved to have had the bloody parking ticket in evidence, as well, but there was

---

27. *Id.*
28. McConnell, at 120.
29. With thanks to Kimberly Berry.

plenty of genetic material on hand for identification. Once we'd heard expert testimony regarding the DNA evidence, I had no worries about its age or quantity.

**Whose expert testimony did you rely on the most? Why?**

I relied heavily on the prosecution's DNA expert and the prosecution's fingerprint expert in making my decision. In the end I think that's what convinced all of the jurors in their decisions. You can't argue with facts, and the prosecution's expert witnesses left no doubt in my mind that both the DNA and the fingerprint combined matched with no one other than Ed Grant.

**What is your most memorable moment?**

It would have to be the time I held Penney's bloody blue dress in my hands.... The dress was so small, she'd been a petite little girl. There was so much blood—Penney's blood—and the fabric was slashed right where her heart had been. There were several smaller holes in the dress where samples had been taken for blood analysis. And that tiny blue dress had been examined by the hands and the eyes of so many strangers, and put on display so many times,—it seemed a horrible invasion of an innocent girl's privacy, and disrespectful somehow. It was the last thing she picked out to wear on the last day of her too-short life. It was all too human.

One juror, Linda Linsky, said that she became convinced that Grant had murdered Serra as she watched the fingerprint testimony. Joe Braychak, another juror who was an engineer said:

We just started with the evidence ... I'm an engineer, or was an engineer, and everything I do has to have a logical basis. So I went to the crime scene, and [Grant's] blood type was there, but that's not enough to convince me. Then I went through the blood trail, his blood was there, too. I went into the car and his fingerprint was there. And once I looked at the handkerchief and it has his DNA on it, I said "You know, there's nobody else on the planet that has that."[30]

The New Haven Register published a poll of 14 citizens following the trial, asking "Do you agree with the verdict in the Penney Serra murder case?" Nine of the fourteen felt the state had not proved Grant guilty. Two disagreed. The other three did not express an opinion. Given the substantial coverage of the trial in the New Haven papers, it is interesting to realize that if these 14 people had been jurors, Grant would not have been convicted.

In a subsequent letter to the editor, William Doriss of New Haven said:

There is no way a murder case with as many unanswered questions as this can be solved on the basis of one and only one 29-year-old fingerprint, which in and of itself is debatable. His thumbprint looks exactly like mine, and I didn't do it. This is a sad day for criminal justice in Connecticut.[31]

*State v. Grant* came down essentially to a case of forensic evidence—at least that is the way the juror quoted above saw it. Although she appeared to be emotionally swayed by Penney's dress and a desire to find her killer, she made it clear that her decision was based on expert testimony about one fingerprint and one drop of blood. The eyewitness

---

30. Christa Lee Rock, *Serra jurors talk evidence pointed only to Grant*, New Haven Register, May 30, 2002.

31. *Serra Trial raised reasonable doubts*, letter to the editor, New Haven Register, June 1, 2002.

testimony was confused and contradictory. There was no evidence of motive. The time-line of the crime, eight minutes from entry into the garage to exit, seems almost unbe-lievable. But as one New Haven reporter put it, "blood doesn't lie."

# Summary

This text has examined six common types of forensic evidence, four of which figured prominently in the trial of Ed Grant: fingerprint, DNA, eyewitness identification, and blood spatter. The remaining two areas—handwriting and polygraph—have shown the many reasons courts give for admitting evidence that may not be reliable, as in handwriting, or in refusing to admit evidence even though it has been tested and has a known error rate—polygraph.

The *Daubert* case and related state cases have ushered in a new responsibility on the part of trial courts to apply tests of reliability before a trial begins and exclude testimony that is not reliable. Although there has been an enormous increase in requests for such hearings since 1993, it is less clear that more scientific testimony is being admitted, which was the goal of the U.S. Supreme Court in making an "easier path" to admission than general acceptance.

Because the standard for reversing a trial court's decision is "abuse of discretion," it is likely that courts will continue to make inconsistent rulings that will stand up on appeal.

Studies of the behavior of judges and juries are ongoing. Judges are doubtless becoming more comfortable with gatekeeper hearings. Whether juries are being influenced by the media to require forensic evidence before they will convict is a matter of speculation.

Juries can be confused by poor experts. They can also react poorly to experts who are condescending or otherwise lack credibility. However, looking at three case stud-ies—Reverend Hayden in 1878, the O.J. Simpson case in 1994 and the Ed Grant case in 2002—we can draw some interesting conclusions. First, complex forensic testi-mony was being presented to juries in 1878. Second, juries are impressed with foren-sic evidence if it is clear and well-presented. And finally, juries respond to the story of the case and the credibility of the witnesses. Herbert Hayden was a pillar of the community. Mary Stannard was a house maid. O.J. Simpson began the case as a fa-mous former football player and was overshadowed by a racist policeman with a mo-tive to frame him. Ed Grant never took the stand. He had no story to tell. That left the prosecution with a tragic death of a young vibrant woman whose family had searched for her killer for more than twenty years. That story, coupled with 2 pieces of uncontested forensic evidence linking Grant to the crime scene, led to the solution of a twenty-nine-year old cold case.

# Discussion Questions

1.  Do you think judges are better equipped than juries to evaluate the reliability of forensic experts? Why or why not?